RAMESSES II

T.G.H. JAMES

WHITE STAR PUBLISHERS

PREFACE

"Who is your favorite ancient Egyptian?" I have been asked this question from time to time by curious friends and strangers. There must be, they think, someone, king, queen, commoner, with whom I must have a special sympathy. Some people fall in love with Akhenaten, or Nefertiti, or Hatshepsut; they believe they know enough about them to allow judgments to be made and affections engaged. The difficulty for the professional Egyptologist is that sentiment alone cannot be a good basis for judgment. The paucity of written evidence of a human or personal kind from ancient Egypt makes it very difficult to get close to any ancient Egyptian, and for a king it is virtually impossible. Consequently, I have never been able to say "X is my favorite ancient Egyptian." But I can say quite unequivocally that it is not Ramesses II. His reported pronouncements are many, but almost without exception they are boastful and vainglorious, and many of the physical remains of his reign are equally grand and pompous. The picture that Ramesses would have us accept as being a true representation of himself is probably that contained in the florid texts on the so-called rhetorical stelae, the long inscriptions that proclaim his greatness and achievements in the most general terms. The Ramesses of these inscriptions is not therefore particularly attractive.

Nevertheless, it cannot be denied that there is a singular engaging impressiveness to Ramesses, much of which, no doubt, he – through the agency of his high officials – set out to promote through buildings, statues, and inscriptions. And we must not forget his mummy, with a head so well preserved (for a man nearing his century) that a convincing match can be made between it and those sculptures that seem to offer the best portraits. As a result, Ramesses has been much written about over the years, and particularly so during the last half century. In a sense, people believe that they know him, and are able to deduce something about his personality. There was all the publicity surrounding the moving of the Abu Simbel temples, the conservation of the wonderful tomb of his wife Nefertari, the excavation of Piramesse, the Delta Residence, and the regal journey of the king's mummy to Paris for scientific examination. Scholarly monographs have been published on the great monuments; a spectacular exhibition of objects from his reign toured North America in the 1980s; there have been popular biographies, and even a many-volumed novel on his life and times.

As far as this Egyptologist is concerned, the greatest boost to studies of the reign of Ramesses II has been the publication of the texts of the Nineteenth and Twentieth Dynasties, under the unassuming title *Ramesside Inscriptions*. The diligence and energy of the author, Professor Kenneth Kitchen, is almost unequaled in the history of Egyptological scholarship. Two large volumes contain all the known significant texts of Ramesses II's reign, one for the king himself and his family, and one for his contemporaries, from the highest officials to humble workmen. And there are supplementary volumes of translations and commentaries. Kitchen's own *Pharaoh Triumphant* offers in popular form the results of his scholarly compilation. The present book owes so much to Kitchen's pioneering efforts in Ramesside studies; to him I am hugely grateful.

In this general survey of Ramesses and his reign I have attempted to treat my subject without bias. I may occasionally be dismissive, but I hope never disrespectful. Ramesses may not be my favorite ancient Egyptian, but he certainly commands much of my interest and a great deal of admiration.

1
Detail of the statue of Ramesses II in front of the Cairo railway station, showing an arm with an armlet made up of royal cartouches with protective cobras, the fist holding a formalized baton carrying the king's prenomen.

2
Figure of Ramesses II from one of the Hathor pillars in the hall of the Hathor temple at Abu Simbel.

3
Emile Prisse d'Avennes' drawing (1847) of Ramesses II at the battle of Qadesh.

4-5
The heads of the two northern colossi at the great temple at Abu Simbel.

6-7
Two colossi inscribed for Ramesses II flanking the entrance to the colonnade of Horemheb at the Luxor temple.

8
Royal head with nemes-headdress from a granite colossus ascribed to Ramesses II in the forecourt of the temple of Luxor. It was possibly made at first for King Amenophis III.

© 2002 White Star S.r.l.
Via C. Sassone, 22/24
13100 Vercelli, Italy
www.whitestar.it

All rights reserved. No part of this publication may
be reproduced, stored in a retrieval system or trans-
mitted in any form or by any means, electronic,
mechanical, photocopying, recording or otherwise,
without written permission from the publisher.

ISBN 88-8095-826-7

Reprints:
1 2 3 4 5 6   06 05 04 03 02

Printed in Italy by Grafedit, Bergamo
Color separation by Fotomec, Turin

TEXT
T.G.H. James

PROJECT EDITORS
Valeria Manferto De Fabianis
Laura Accomazzo

GRAPHIC DESIGNERS
Patrizia Balocco Lovisetti
Paola Piacco

C O N T E N T S

10
*Relief figure of Ramesses II as a child,
seated on a cushion in the form of the
horizon sign. He has the lock of youth
and holds his finger to his mouth, in
the characteristic attitude of a child
(Louvre, N522).*

11-14
*South wall of the great hall at Abu
Simbel. At the top: Ramesses II makes
offerings to various deities and has the
years of his reign confirmed by Thoth
and Sefkhet-abu in the presence of Re-
Herakhty. In the middle: scenes of
triumph in the Syrian, Libyan, and
Nubian wars.*

16-17
*A scene from the Ramesseum in which
Ramesses kneels before Amon-Re,
receiving the elaborate atef-crown and
a plurality of jubilee (sed) festivals, which
are suspended from a palm rib notched
with the expected years of a long reign.*

18-19
*The façade of the great temple of Abu
Simbel at night, the floodlighting
dramatically revealing the subordinate
figures of queens, princes, and
princesses accompanying the four
colossal figures.*

RAMESSES
THE GREAT

20 and 21
Granite colossus of Ramesses II from the temple precinct of Ptah at Memphis, a statue later usurped by Ramesses IV of the Twentieth Dynasty. It now stands in Cairo, near the main railway station.

The modern traveler, arriving in Cairo probably after dark, is introduced to ancient Egypt as the tourist coach drives into town and passes the main railway station. Here a great granite colossus of a king tries to dominate the chaotic environment of the tangle of roads at high and low level, which confuse the visitor. Here is the first view of Ramesses II, not seen as he would have wished to be seen, but seriously diminished by urban disorder. A tour guide may try to excite interest in the statue; most travelers, however, will continue to doze gently, or to mop up without commentary the strange and colorful scenes of modern Cairo life as they pass by. This great figure achieved for only a short time the attention that town planners had expected it to provide in front of the railway station; as the system of elevated throughways has developed in this busy part of Cairo, so has poor Ramesses languished in a pool of pollution, little

regarded, and seriously worrying not only lovers of the pharaonic heritage of Egypt, but also the national and civic authorities. Ramesses no longer performs a function, and, what is worse, he stands as an admonitory reminder of the dangers of unconcerned planning. He will be moved, perhaps to the relative calm of the garden in front of the Egyptian Museum, perhaps back to Memphis, perhaps to some other public position in the city, less environmentally dangerous than Ramesses Square. It will not happen too soon.

When the monumental memorial of the great king was brought into Cairo in 1955, its transfer from Memphis, not many miles to the south of Cairo on the west side of the Nile, formed part of a plan to improve and modernize the city following the revolution of 1952. Ramesses II was an outstanding symbol of native Egyptian greatness, hailing from the distant past.

He was, furthermore, in statue form being moved to a part of the city where

visitors arriving and leaving by train would encounter him, in greeting or in farewell, where he would stand dominantly and appropriately in what was already Place Ramsès, Midan Ramsis, Ramesses Square. He was, in a sense, at that time coming home in triumph, a proper object for national pride.

It might never have been so, however, for that colossus was at one time destined to travel to London. Long ago, in the early nineteenth century, it had been offered to Great Britain by Muhammad Ali Pasha (1769–1849), virtual ruler of Egypt and founder of the modern Egyptian state. It was one of many extravagant gifts offered to helpful governments by that great leader, who might have seen himself as a reincarnation of Ramesses, if the reading of ancient Egyptian names and the identification of the great historical figures of antiquity had been sufficiently advanced in the formative years of his power.

22 top
The French boat Louxor moored at Luxor in preparation for the removal of the western obelisk from the temple of Luxor, under the direction of Jean Baptiste Apollinaire Lebas.

23 right
The obelisk of Ramesses II in the Place de la Concorde, Paris. One of the pair erected in front of the great pylon of the Temple of Luxor, it was presented to France by Muhammad Ali in 1830.

22-23
Painting by François Dubois of the Place de la Concorde on 25 October 1833 at the moment when the Luxor obelisk was finally raised into an upright position.

23 top left
Inlays on the northern face of the base of the Paris obelisk illustrating the skillful methods devised by J.-B. Lebas to lower the stone shaft for transfer to the boat Louxor.

23 bottom left
Metal inlays in the southern face of the granite base of the Paris obelisk showing the processes by which the monument was raised to its present position.

Another product of mighty Ramesses' reign, the great obelisk now in the Place de la Concorde in Paris, was another presentation by Muhammad Ali, readily accepted by the French nation, which has nursed a deep and abiding interest in ancient Egypt dating back to Napoleon's Egyptian adventure in 1798. The obelisk was erected in Paris in 1836, some years after the death of Jean-François Champollion, who by then knew how to read the royal names and much of the rest of the texts which embellished the monument. Would Ramesses have approved of the recent gilding of the pyramidion at the top of the obelisk? I suspect he would have nodded assent. He would certainly have arranged for his entourage to raise a cheer, even if it had been inappropriate for the divine ruler to display such emotion himself.

In his early years of working on the decipherment of hieroglyphs, Champollion had deduced the name of Ramesses in ancient cartouches, the ovals which were used to enclose royal names in ancient Egypt. His supposition was soon confirmed by his reading – again with a degree of guesswork – of the name of the king Thothmes, or Tuthmosis, or as many now prefer, Thutmose. It is said that Champollion was so excited by his discovery that he rushed to his brother Jacques Joseph, crying out his success and collapsing in a faint for several days. And so the 'father' of Egyptology knew how to recognize the name Ramesses; and by 1836, when the Luxor obelisk was set up in Paris, there were many who could read the name, and who even knew something about the creator of that great monument.

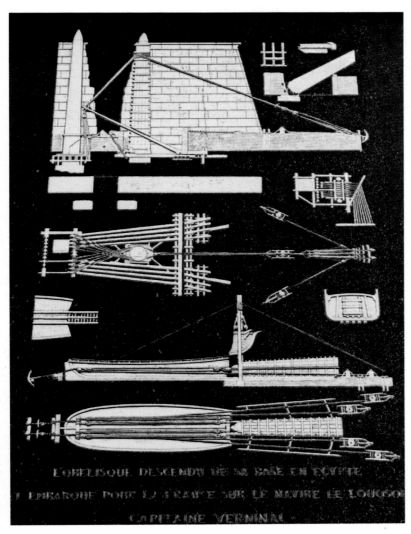

L'OBELISQUE DESCENDU DE SA BASE EN ÉGYPTE
EMBARQUE POUR LA FRANCE SUR LE NAVIRE LE LOUQSOR
CAPITAINE VERNINAC

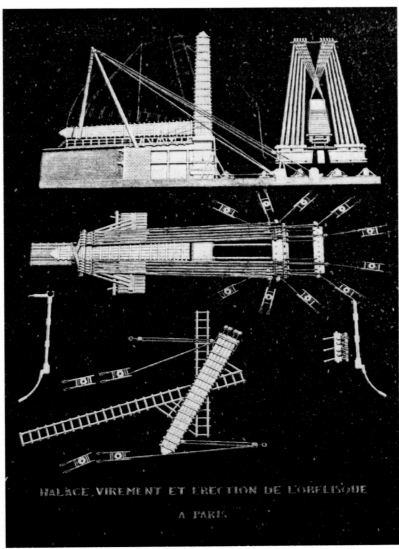

HALAGE, VIREMENT ET ERECTION DE L'OBELISQUE
A PARIS

Ramesses II

24 top left
The Egyptian Sculpture Gallery in the British Museum in about 1860, with the bust of Ramesses II on the left, and in the distance, a cast of one of the Abu Simbel colossal heads.

24 top right
A squad of Royal Artillerymen moving the bust of Ramesses II from the Townley Galleries to the new Egyptian Sculpture Gallery in the British Museum in 1834.

24-25
Giovanni-Battista Belzoni's illustration of the removal of the Younger Memnon from the Ramesseum. It took place during the heat of the summer, to utilize the waters of the flooded Nile.

25 top
The 'Young' or 'Younger' Memnon, the upper part of a granite colossus of Ramesses II from the Ramesseum, the mortuary temple of the king in Western Thebes; now in the British Museum (EA 19).

Paris then had a visible presence of Ramesses II. London was denied its own magnificent colossus of the king because, it was said, the problems of moving the great sculpture from the mounds of Memphis were at that time insurmountable for local resources on the grounds of engineering, and, probably more crucially, of expense. But London in fact already had its image of Ramesses II, one very much finer artistically than the Memphite colossus. It was not known to be a representation of the great king when it first reached London in 1817. It had been identified as "certainly the most beautiful and perfect piece of Egyptian sculpture that can be seen throughout the whole country [i.e., Egypt]" by William Hamilton, an envoy of Lord Elgin who had traveled through Egypt in 1803 and published his *Aegyptiaca* in 1809. The statue's reputation attracted the attention of Jean-Louis Burckhardt, a Swiss scholar living in Cairo who in 1816 persuaded the new British Consul-General in Egypt to join him in the enterprise of removing the royal bust from the Ramesseum in Western Thebes, and presenting it to the British Museum. With all the proper official permissions of the time in order, the work was accomplished by Giovanni-Battista Belzoni, Italian strongman turned incipient archaeologist.

It was the first great piece of Egyptian art to enter the British Museum, and its arrival was much appreciated by visitors to the museum and by the museum's trustees. The latter were not at that time fully convinced that Egyptian art could ever be compared in level terms with Greek and Roman art. Nobody was sure about the identity of the sculpture's subject. It was royal – surely; it came from a temple – certainly. But whose temple? The French scholars who accompanied Napoleon's expedition to Egypt had called the Ramesseum – now known to be the king's mortuary temple – the Memnonium, the temple of Memnon, erroneously associating it with the two massive quartzite statues known since antiquity as the Colossi of Memnon. Memnon in classical literature was an Ethiopian king; his identification with the subject of the so-called Colossi of Memnon [Greek crap] in Western Thebes (in fact the Eighteenth Dynasty Pharaoh ~~Amenophis~~ [Amenhotep] III) demonstrates the ingenious desperation of classical and post-classical scholars to explain Egyptian buildings and sculptures by reference to information provided by the only ancient texts they could read.

It need hardly be stated that the Ramesseum and the colossi of Amenophis III had nothing to do with the mythical Memnon; but names persist, and even today in the British Museum the great bust of Ramesses II is affectionately known as the Young or Younger Memnon.

It would be some years after its arrival in London before the Younger Memnon would be recognized to be part of a great figure of Ramesses II, but by then that king, seemingly incognito, had already made his mark on the consciousness of the British public.

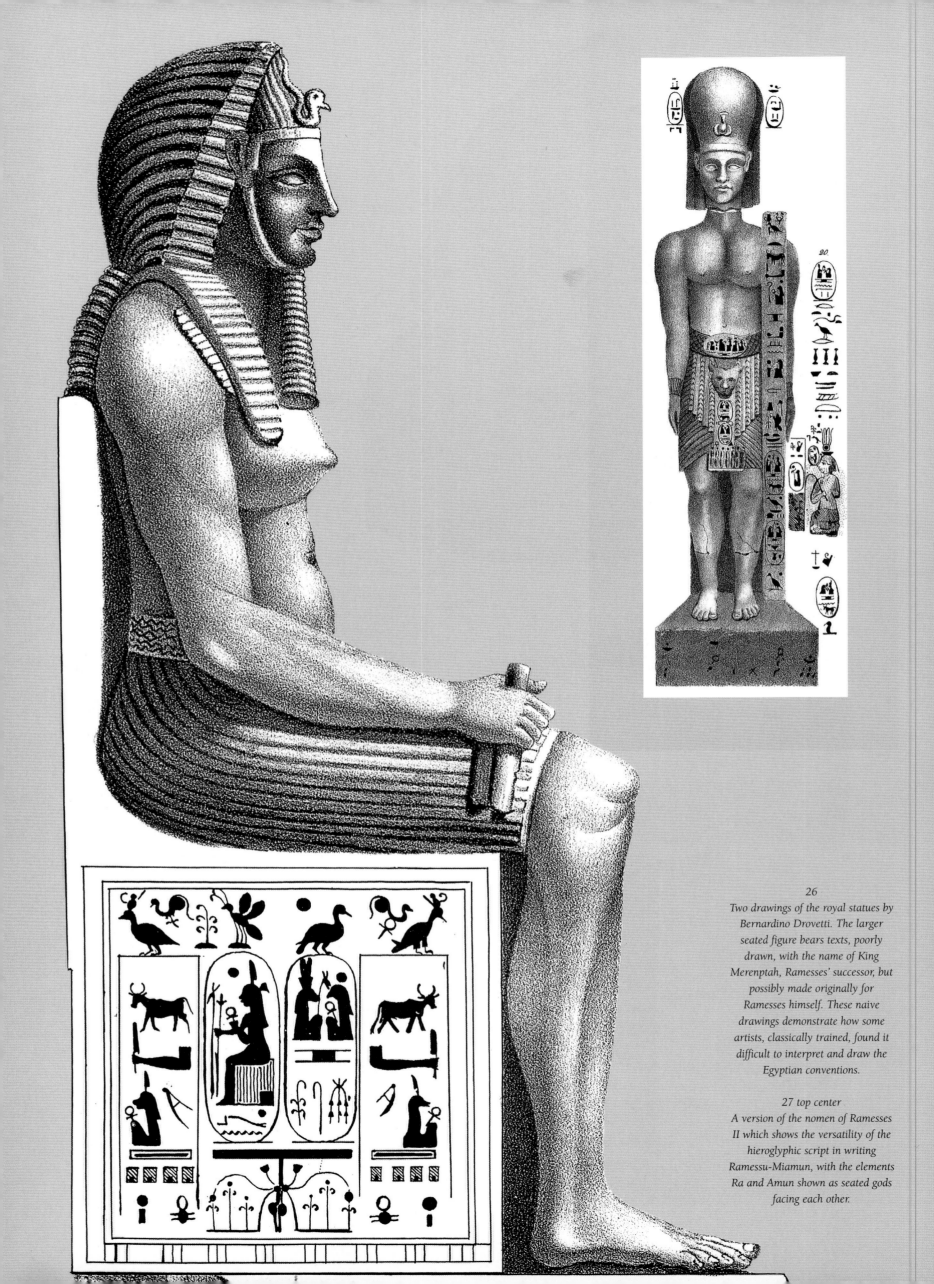

26
Two drawings of the royal statues by Bernardino Drovetti. The larger seated figure bears texts, poorly drawn, with the name of King Merenptah, Ramesses' successor, but possibly made originally for Ramesses himself. These naive drawings demonstrate how some artists, classically trained, found it difficult to interpret and draw the Egyptian conventions.

27 top center
A version of the nomen of Ramesses II which shows the versatility of the hieroglyphic script in writing Ramessu-Miamun, with the elements Ra and Amun shown as seated gods facing each other.

So too he had, in a less powerful but equally artistic manner, in the third important collection of Egyptian antiquities in Europe, in the Egyptian Museum in Turin. The Paris obelisk was a towering memorial to the fame of the great king. The London Memnon was wholly impressive, and distinguished further by possibly being the inspiration for the poet Shelley's sonnet "Ozymandias." The Turin black-granite, life-size seated figure was human in scale and in its sympathetic treatment; it is Ramesses as a young man, its style harking back to the refined post-Amarna artistic standard of his father Sethos I. It was found in the temple of Karnak by Jean Jacques Rifaud, a French artist who worked for Bernardino Drovetti, French Consul-General in Egypt from 1811 to 1814 and from 1821 to 1829. Drovetti was a native of Piedmont, a highly intelligent, somewhat devious diplomat and politician who engaged in serious rivalry concerning the collection of antiquities with Belzoni, the agent of Henry Salt. It was a sad conflict between men whose aims were similar but who were unable to divide between themselves the rich collecting fields of the Theban area. Part of Drovetti's fine collection found its way to Turin in the 1820s, including the most distinguished statue of Ramesses II.

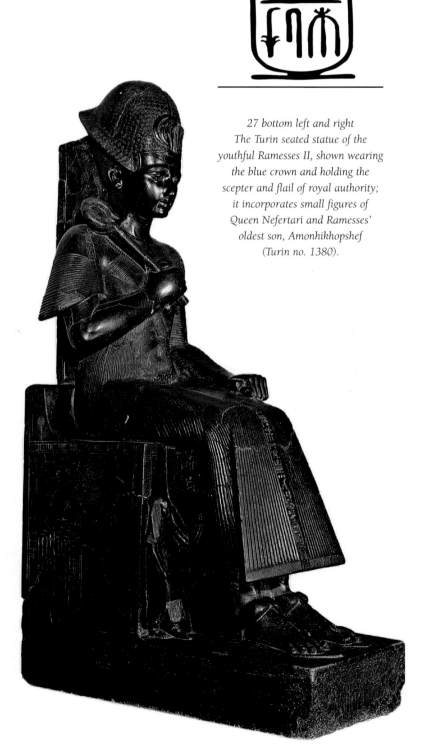

27 bottom left and right
The Turin seated statue of the
youthful Ramesses II, shown wearing
the blue crown and holding the
scepter and flail of royal authority;
it incorporates small figures of
Queen Nefertari and Ramesses'
oldest son, Amonhikhopshef
(Turin no. 1380).

28 and 29
Cartouche containing the prenomen of Ramesses II, 'Usimare Setpenre,' surmounted by the sun-disk and two ostrich feathers, and flanked by uraei, *wearing the white (left) and red (right) crowns, symbolic of Upper and Lower Egypt.*

So, at a very early stage in the history of Egyptology, Ramesses was well placed in the centers of budding Egyptological scholarship to provide his own image as the exemplar of pharaonic power. But what was known of Ramesses at this early time, before the hieroglyphs were deciphered and the texts read? The name at least was known from the Bible, though not always clearly as the designation of a royal person: "Joseph placed his father and his brethren, and gave them a possession in the land of Egypt, in the best of the land, in the land of Rameses, as Pharaoh had commanded" (Genesis 47:11). Under a new king, unspecified, the oppression of the Children of Israel is said to have begun: "Therefore they did set over them taskmasters to afflict them with their burdens. And they built for Pharaoh treasure cities, Pithom and Raamses" (Exodus 1:11). From this place began the actual Exodus of the Israelites: "And they departed from Rameses in the first month, on the fifteenth day of the first month; on the morrow after the passover the children of Israel went out with a high hand in the sight of all the Egyptians... And the children of Israel removed from Rameses, and pitched at Succoth" (Numbers 33:3-5). Here in the biblical record Rameses and Raamses refer to places and not directly to a person, or more

specifically to a king or Pharaoh. Yet a tradition had grown up that the oppression and even perhaps the Exodus of the Children of Israel had taken place in the reign of a king called Ramesses. So any king so named was threatened with a poor reputation by those who found truth in the very words of the Bible. CRAP

We shall see toward the end of this book how the myth of Ramesses lasted in Egyptian history and in the secondary literary tradition. Some of this tradition persisted into classical times, with Ramesses appearing in various forms and under a variety of names in the classical record in-so-far as it touched on Egypt. Herodotus, that most entertaining of Greek writers, whose history was written in the fifth century B.C. and included sections on Egypt based partly on a personal visit to that land, had the closest contact with the living tradition among the late pharaonic Egyptians. Yet he talks of Rhampsinitus. The much later historian, Diodorus Siculus, writing in the first century B.C., talks of Remphis, and quite separately provides at secondhand an account of a building which he calls the tomb of Osymandyas. Other classical writers speak of Rhamsesis and of Rhamses, and there was some confusion between the king of these names and the great

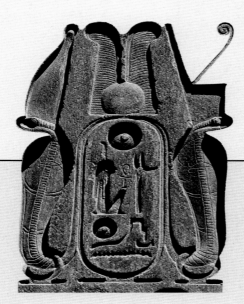

Greek crap

conqueror Sesostris, or Sesothis, who should be identified with Senwosret III of the Twelfth Dynasty. The priest Manetho, a native Egyptian historian from Sebennytos who composed in the third century B.C. an account of Egyptian history in the form of annals and based on surviving Egyptian records, was apparently the first to divide the kings of Egypt into the dynastic structure still used today. His history is preserved in minimal form in a number of later classical writers, and in his listing of the kings of the Nineteenth Dynasty there occurs a Rapsaces or Rampses, who reigned for sixty-six years – clearly Ramesses II.

In terms of reliable historical information, the classical writers, like those of the Bible, provided little useful evidence from which European scholars in the early nineteenth century could form a coherent idea of the reign and achievements of the king who was to be known as Ramesses, Rameses, or Ramses II. Egyptian names are not easily converted into modern forms. To be more precise, they can easily be converted, but different scholarly systems and traditions prefer certain forms of conversion over others. The name we give here as Ramesses, consisted in Egyptian of three parts: Ra-mes-su, 'Ra (or Re) created him.' This was the king's principal name,

usually written in the second of the two cartouches in the royal titulary. It was usually given the added epithet 'beloved of Amun.' The first cartouche contained what may be called the throne name; in the case of Ramesses II, it was User-Ma'at-Re, usually abbreviated to Usimare and meaning 'one strong in *ma'at* (truth or order) is Re,' with the added epithet Setpenre, 'one chosen of Re.' The first cartouche name, now usually called the prenomen, was for the Egyptians the principal royal name. The second cartouche contained the 'family' name by which the king was known before his accession. For Ramesses II, the various forms, like Rampses, are easily explained by textual confusion or even imperfect memory. Usimare is thought with good reason to be the origin of the Osymandyas of Diodorus, or the Ozymandias of Shelley. Shelley never saw the Ramesseum, the funerary temple of Ramesses II and almost certainly the tomb of Osymandyas of Diodorus. Shelley may never have seen the great bust from the Ramesseum in the British Museum, the Younger Memnon, thought by some to be the inspiration for Shelley's sonnet. It is certain, however, that Burckhardt and Henry Salt, who removed the bust from the Ramesseum, were quite in the dark as to its identity.

It is piquant to consider the extent to which Salt became obsessed with the opening up and subsequent copying of the scenes of the great rock-cut temple of Ramesses II at Abu Simbel. In 1813 Burckhardt had been the first European to report the existence of the Abu Simbel temples, and he stimulated the interest not only of Salt but also of William John Bankes, a wealthy British traveler who first journeyed into Nubia in 1815. Salt sent Belzoni to open the great temple in 1816, but success came only at a second attempt in 1817. It is difficult now to comprehend how little was known of ancient Egypt and its history at this early time. When Salt and Bankes came to Abu Simbel in the autumn of 1818 they had no way of judging whether the temples there were contemporary with Karnak or with the great late temples of Edfu and Dendera and Philae. By the examination of a Greek text scratched on the leg of one of the great seated colossi of the main temple, Bankes deduced that this temple predated the reign of the king Psammetichus mentioned in the text. From his classical knowledge Bankes remembered that there were kings named Psammetichus in the Twenty-sixth Dynasty (Saite), which was understood to have flourished in the seventh and sixth centuries B.C. Bankes rightly concluded that Abu Simbel was much earlier than the Ptolemaic and Roman temples, and predated the Saite period by a fair number of years. In 1818, however, the hieroglyphic decipherment debate continued unresolved, conducted principally between Jean-François Champollion in France and Thomas Young in Britain. The crucial steps were still to be taken, and Champollion had not yet recognized the cartouche of Ramesses II, which would have given the workers at Abu Simbel the chance of dating the temples there to the reign of that king.

William John Bankes for a short time took a lively interest in decipherment, and even made a few small contributions of value to it. He also discovered the king-list in the Abydos temple of Ramesses II, and recognized its importance without in fact being able to read any of the royal names. Henry Salt, on the other hand, believed he could do much more. He had built up a library of the earliest Egyptological publications and entered into correspondence with the leading scholars working on decipherment. His results were not always accepted, and he resented the gentle derision that was often shown toward his writings. Nevertheless, he provided at least one excellent service to Egyptology by taking under his wing the young John Gardner Wilkinson, who arrived in Egypt from Naples in 1821. Wilkinson had been diverted from a career in the army to one of Egyptological scholarship by Sir William Gell, who maintained an intellectual salon in Naples, acting, among other things, as an intermediary between desk-scholars in Europe and field-workers in Egypt. At the start of his long sojourn in Egypt, Wilkinson devoted his attention especially to collecting and identifying royal names in cartouches. In his travels throughout the country he noted new examples, subsequently analyzing them and developing great skill in identifying the kings so named. Salt wrote to Gell about Wilkinson's abilities: "I have not indeed seen any person here who has entered with so much spirit into the study of hieroglyphics... he works *like a horse at it.*" Champollion may have first recognized the name of Ramesses in hieroglyphs, but Wilkinson preceded him in noting that royal names could be written in more than one way. His own collections of cartouches from the monuments provided him with

ample evidence of variant writings, and he became utterly familiar with what might be termed the vagaries of the hieroglyphic script in the writing of royal names. When he traveled for the first time into Nubia in 1823, accompanied by an old college friend, James Samuel Wiggett, on the occasion of their crossing the Nile at Semna in a flimsy improvised ferry boat, down to the gunwales in the water, he commented in his journal that he and Wiggett sat facing each other "like the 2 gods in the name of Ramesses." Here he is referring not to the simple writing of Ramesses' cartouche, but to one in which the gods Re and Amun confront each other in the writing of Ramesses-Meryamun.

30 top
Portrait of Giovanni-Battista Belzoni
in Turkish dress. European travelers
in Egypt commonly dressed à la
turque, as they called it, for reasons
of comfort, convenience, and even
safety.

30-31
Belzoni's version of a scene in the
first hall of the great temple at Abu
Simbel showing Ramesses II smiting
a Libyan captive. To the left
stands Queen Nefertari.
It is not a careful copy.

31 bottom left
Belzoni's illustration of the
first hall of the great temple.
He was disappointed by the
meager harvest of objects found
within the temple.

31 bottom right
Belzoni's illustration of the temple of
Abu Simbel viewed from the east
bank of the Nile. He first attempted
to enter the great temple in 1816,
but only succeeded on his second
visit in 1817.

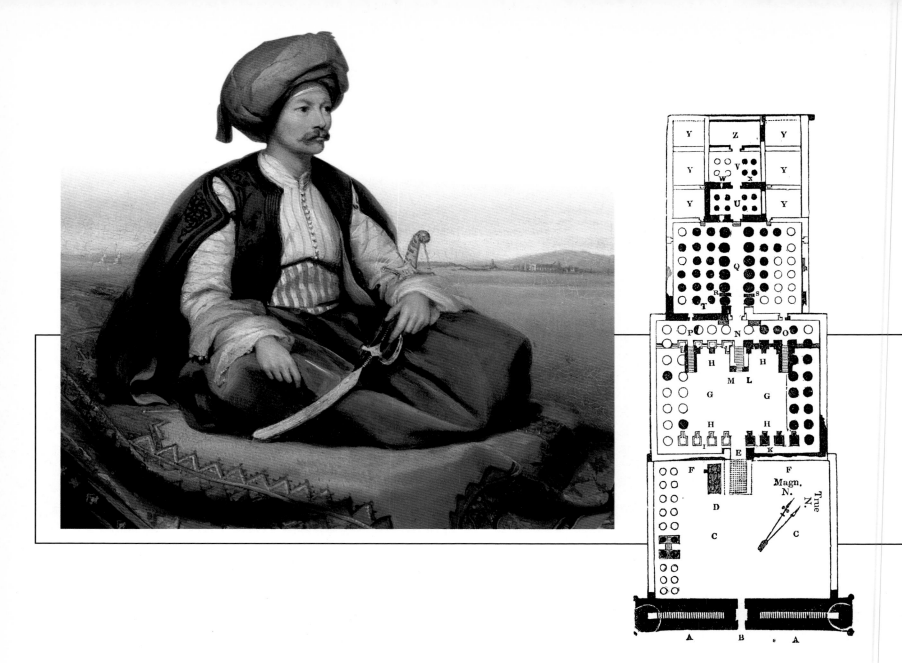

Wilkinson spent twelve years continuously in Egypt collecting inscriptional and graphic material from the monuments, acquiring in the process not only a competent grasp of the hieroglyphic script and the Egyptian language, but also an unparalleled knowledge of the culture of ancient Egypt. In 1837, after his return to Britain, he published the three-volume work for which he is best known, *The Manners and Customs of the Ancient Egyptians*. His second chapter is devoted to the history of Egypt, and it is instructive to see to what extent he was able to provide an account of the reign of Ramesses II, bearing in mind that he was writing within fifteen years of Champollion's crucial announcement of the decipherment principles in 1822. Active field-workers and serious desk-scholars were still few; many were limited in their interests, and some were not prepared to accept Champollion's system. The whole Egyptian field was open to wild theorizing and guesswork, much of which was based on slender or shaky evidence. Scholars of integrity, competent in understanding the

solid advances of the respected few and acquainted firsthand with the monuments, were needed to distinguish between what was true and what was false. Such a scholar was Wilkinson.

What then did he have to say about Ramesses II? Not a great deal, although he devoted ten pages to his reign. Misled by some classical sources, he placed the king, whom he called Remeses, toward the end of a long Eighteenth Dynasty. He felt able to accept the Manethonian sixty-six years for the length of his reign, supporting this opinion by his own recording of dates on the surviving monuments up to the king's sixty-second year, and by reckoning that the vast number of monuments left by the king at places as far apart as Tanis in the Delta and Abu Simbel in Nubia "bear ample testimony to the length of time required for their execution." This last argument was somewhat fallacious, but Wilkinson may be excused for marveling at the multiplicity and magnitude of Ramesses' structures, all of which he had visited and studied himself. From his observations, particularly in the temples of Luxor, Karnak, Abu Simbel, and the

Ramesseum (which he continued to call the Memnonium, because of its established usage), he drew wide and detailed conclusions on the state of the army in Remeses' reign, on its range of weaponry, and on the elaboration of its practical procedures in open battle and in sieges. He accepted the identification of Remeses with Sesostris, and in consequence, again following classical sources, attributed to Remeses the digging of the canal from the Nile to the Red Sea. Time and more abundant evidence would in due course correct these mistaken claims. Yet in spite of his understandably inadequate knowledge, Wilkinson captured something of the flavor of the reign, although his general opinion was touched with hyperbole: "The reign of Remeses was conspicuous as the Augustine era of Egypt, when the arts attained a degree of perfection which no after age succeeded in imitating, and the armies of Egypt were extended by this prince considerably farther into the heart of Asia than during the most successful invasions of his predecessors." Already for Wilkinson he was "Remeses the Great."

The pre-eminent position Wilkinson allotted Ramesses II was based primarily on the evidence provided by the standing monuments of Egypt. As we have noted, he had himself visited and studied the great structures and the remains of great structures from Tanis to Abu Simbel, all liberally stamped with Ramesses' name. He believed that there must be many more still to be revealed "at Memphis, and other principal cities, whose sites are now unknown or concealed by mounds." To judge a king's reputation by the abundance of his monuments is, unfortunately, a risky business. It does not allow for the quality or the morality of his rule, the state of the administration, the prosperity of his country, or the conditions under which his people lived. For ancient Egypt it is rarely possible to present a rounded picture of an individual ruler, or to provide an adequate factual account of his reign. For Ramesses II much information, unknown to Wilkinson, has been gained in the subsequent period from inscriptions, written documents, the contents of tombs, and the careful investigation of towns and settlements.

Much of this information will be used in later chapters of this book, and a better position should be reached from which better judgments can be made than Wilkinson was able to achieve. And yet even today the view that Wilkinson expressed on Ramesses and his reign is one which would be recognized and endorsed by a very large part of the armies of tourists who tramp the sites of Egypt at the present time. In so many places on the usual course followed by visitors in their short holidays in Egypt, the guide will declaim: "And here we see the king, Ramesses II, offering to the gods"; or "This colossal statue is of Egypt's greatest ruler, Ramesses II"; or "This part of the temple was added by Ramesses II to the structure begun by his predecessors"; or "This building (or that statue) was usurped by Ramesses II, who carved his name over those of King... who built the temple (or had the statue carved)."

The guide, when he has reached the point of understanding his group, may say: "And who built this temple?" or "Whose cartouche is this?" The chorus will answer: "Ramesses II."

32 left
Sir John Gardner Wilkinson in Turkish dress, seated on a cushion with a fanciful Theban background. He spent 12 years continuously in Egypt, mostly in Thebes, and wrote the first useful books on the monuments and culture of Egypt.

32 right
Plan of the Ramesseum by Sir John Gardner Wilkinson. During his years in Egypt he drew, and subsequently published, the plans of many of the great temples, tombs, and ancient sites.

33 left
Jean-François Champollion, the "Father of Egyptology," who was the first to understand and explain the principles of hieroglyphic script. This portrait was posthumously painted by Léon Cogniet.

33 right
Henry Salt, British Consul-General in Egypt from 1816 until his death in 1827. He was a keen student of hieroglyphs, and an excellent artist, making careful copies of Egyptian inscriptions.

The quintessential traveler in Egypt of the nineteenth century was Amelia Blandford Edwards, a successful novelist who with a companion abandoned a trip to Italy in 1873 because of bad weather and fled eastward to Egypt and the sun. At once she was fascinated by the country, wrote up her travels in *A Thousand Miles up the Nile* (published in 1877 and revised in 1889), and helped to found the Egypt Exploration Fund (later Society). The account of her travels makes most entertaining reading, and she took much trouble to get her facts right. But for our story here the point of interest is that she included a whole chapter on "Rameses the Great." By the time of her visit, much more was known than when Wilkinson wrote in the 1830s. The 'greatness of Ramesses' idea had been nurtured and matured. She starts the chapter in positive manner – she did not like to show hesitation, or to be contradicted – and sets out the case for her hero without equivocation: "The central figure of Egyptian history has always been, probably always will be, Rameses the Second. He holds this place partly by right, partly by accident. He was born to greatness; he achieved greatness; and he had borrowed greatness thrust upon him." She then outlines the known events of Ramesses' reign, from time to time eulogizing him, criticizing him, reflecting dogmatically on his character, but ultimately admiring him. She is not afraid of attributing intentions and emotions as a confident novelist may, but a trained historian would not: "The evening of his life was long and splendid.

It became his passion and his pride to found new cities, to raise dykes, to dig canals, to build fortresses, to multiply statues, obelisks and inscriptions, and to erect the most gorgeous and costly temples in which man ever worshipped." Then: "To estimate the cost at which these things were done is now impossible. Every temple, every palace, represented a hecatomb of human lives... We know how the Hebrews suffered... . Yet even the Hebrews were less cruelly used than some who were kidnapped beyond the frontiers." Having expressed herself freely on many of his achievements, Amelia Edwards admits that it would be in vain to try to state what manner of man Ramesses was. Yet she tries: "That he was personally valiant may be gathered, with due reservation, from the poem of Pentaur [the account of the battle of Qadesh]; and that he was not unmerciful is shown in the extradition clause of the Khetan [Hittite] treaty. His pride was evidently boundless." Finally she can conclude "that he was neither better nor worse than the general run of Oriental despots – that he was ruthless in war, prodigal in peace, rapacious of booty, and unsparing in the exercise of almost boundless power." She ends with a neat dig at what might today be thought of as Ramesses' male chauvinism: "His princes and ministers habitually addressed him in the language of worship. Even his wives, who ought to have known better, are represented in the performance of acts of religious adoration before him. What wonder then, if the man so deified believed himself a god?"

34
Amelia Blandford Edwards, a Victorian novelist and travel writer who visited Egypt in 1873-74, wrote the best-selling account A Thousand Miles up the Nile *in 1877. She helped found the Egypt Exploration Fund in 1882.*

Seduced by the image of Ramesses II proclaimed by means of the great buildings and by the grandiose scenes and texts with which they were embellished, Amelia Edwards in a sense accepted the estimation of the king's achievements as they were presented by his administrative and priestly high officials. She should not be blamed too severely for this. In dealing with remote antiquity, the scholar – and, by extension, the interested member of the public – has to form judgments on the basis of the evidence available. In the case of Ramesses II the evidence is considerable, but it is dominated by the great works of his reign; it is difficult to avoid the use of words loaded with secondary, but critical, meanings. Ramesses II was from the time of Wilkinson 'the Great'; his works are mighty, magnificent, grandiose, ostentatious, even pompous; he himself is characterized as self-centered, self-glorious, bombastic, full of pride, a prime promoter of his own greatness. Even good historians have fallen into the trap of judging him by the external manifestations of his reign. James Henry Breasted, a scholar of impeccable training, wrote in the early twentieth century a *History of Egypt*, which became a standard work, retaining its authority for many decades, but never revised after 1909. It is still available, and still worth reading, but more for the flow of his narrative than for his frequent moralistic reflections, mostly no longer sustainable in the face of new evidence and more recent interpretations.

Breasted was more restrained than Amelia Edwards in his estimation of Ramesses II, but even he could not resist the attempt to humanize him on doubtful premises and criticize him in consequence. Breasted considered the Rifaud/Drovetti statue in Turin as an outstanding sculpture: "Nothing better was ever produced by the Egyptian sculptor." It was for Breasted "a faithful portrait," judging on the basis of the features of the king in his strikingly well-preserved mummy. So: "In person he was tall and handsome, with features of dreamy and almost effeminate beauty, in no wise suggestive of the manly traits which he certainly possessed. For the incident at Kadesh [Qadesh] showed him unquestionably a man of fine courage with ability to rise to a supreme crisis." The "indomitable spirit" he showed in his subsequent Asiatic campaigns "more than redeemed the almost fatal blunder at Kadesh." Subsequently "he was quite ready to enjoy the well-earned peace," which would last for the rest of his long reign. Then comes the Protestant censure: "He was inordinately vain and made far more ostentatious display of his wars on his monuments than was ever done by Thutmose [~~Tuthmosis~~] III. He loved ease and pleasure and gave himself up without restraint to voluptuous enjoyments." To exemplify this last statement Breasted adds, "He had an enormous harem, and as the years passed his children multiplied rapidly." In later years "Ramses lived on in magnificence even surpassing that of Amenhotep III... He had lost the vitality for aggressive rule." His realm became threatened by foreign infiltrators, but "senile decay rendered him deaf to alarms and complaints which would have brought instant retribution upon the invaders in the days of his vigorous youth." The threats "never roused him from the lethargy into which he had fallen." In the end "he passed away... none too soon for the redemption of his empire. We are able to look into the withered face of the hoary nonagenarian, evidently little changed from what he was in those last days of splendour in the city of Ramses, and the resemblance to the face of the youth in the noble Turin statue is still very marked."

In judging the man and his achievements in these terms, Breasted offered more than one hostage to fortune. The discovery in subsequent years of new and significant inscriptions and other written evidence from Egypt itself and from other sources, in particular Hittite records, requires substantial reassessments of what happened during the sixty-seven years of Ramesses II's reign. Breasted might now be obliged to modify some of his judgments on the king himself, but it would still be unwise of him to prepare a new character reference on the basis of changed, but woefully inadequate, evidence. Those who work close to a period or a person who lived many millennia ago often believe that they achieve insights which allow them to leap beyond the available material to form assumptions, to draw conclusions on tenuous evidence supported by 'deep understanding.' Egyptologists are often so closely involved in scholarly investigations that they come to believe that they are almost tuned in to the same wavelength as their own particular fragment of antiquity. In the course of this book we shall be examining many different aspects of the reign of Ramesses II 'the Great,' but the whole story will not be told. Egyptian history is constructed from a diverse mixture of sources: many are public and official, and therefore of uncertain validity; many are private inscriptions, but couched in terms favorable to the existing regime; many are wholly private, personal, and generally more trustworthy. In the case of Ramesses II it is evident that the surviving evidence of all kinds is very unevenly spread over the whole reign, and that there are many gaps in the record. Some evidence which one feels ought to exist just has not survived.

A significant case is that of the biblical oppression of the Israelites in Egypt, which many scholars have believed should be dated to the reign of Ramesses II, with the Exodus following in the reign of Merenptah. From Egyptian evidence alone the whole sequence of oppression and exodus could be considered as something that never happened. People who accept the biblical account find it hard to believe that such a significant episode (from the Jews' point of view) could have left no trace in Egyptian records. Egyptologists who understand the patchiness of surviving records, the nature of the Delta environment in which the Israelite sojourn is thought to have taken place, and the probable insignificance (in Egyptian eyes) of the existence of a relatively small alien group in the northeast of the country are mostly not surprised that nothing has so far been found to support the biblical account. It is not necessary to deny the general truth of the biblical account, but it is possible, and right, for scholars to question much of the detail. Wilkinson accepted the biblical account and placed it in the reign of Thutmes III. Amelia Edwards considered it to be generally accepted that

the oppression took place under Ramesses II, and the Exodus under Merenptah. Breasted, like the good historian he truly was, expressed caution and reasonably suggested: "There is probably little question of the correctness of the Hebrew Jew tradition in attributing the oppression of some tribe of their ancestors to the builder of Pithom [in the eastern Delta] and Ramses; that a tribe of their forefathers should have fled the country to escape such labour is quite in accord with what we know of the time." More cannot reasonably be said. In the near century that has elapsed since Breasted wrote, no material evidence has emerged which seriously changes Breasted's opinion. Much more is known of the city Ramses, which Egyptologists identify as Piramesse; excavations in the eastern Delta have clarified the circumstances of life in Ramesside and earlier times. But a clinching text remains to be found. The Children of Israel, therefore, will not play a significant part in the chapters that follow. Ramesses will occupy the center of the stage, as he would have expected. But first we must see how it all came about that Egypt became his stage.

38-39
The face of one of the granite standing colossi in the forecourt of the Luxor temple. The serene nature of the features belies the strength of the personality represented. The eyes are angled to look down at the viewer.

POST-AMARNA EGYPT: HOREMHEB TO ~~SETHOS~~ I
Seti I

CHAPTER 1

40
A realistic portrait of Akhenaten from one of the sandstone colossi placed in the Aten temple at Karnak in the early years of the king's reign. The royal features are shown almost in caricature (Luxor Museum, J53).

41 top
A talatat block retrieved from the Ninth Pylon of the Karnak Temple, showing Akhenaten worshiping the Aten with his hands raised to receive its life-giving rays. Between the royal figures is a small Nefertiti (Luxor Museum, J223)

41 bottom
A scene in relief found in the royal tomb at Amarna showing Akhenaten, Nefertiti, and their two oldest daughters presenting flowers in offering to the Aten (Cairo, RT 10.11.26.4).

42-43
Karl Richard Lepsius's drawing of the royal family in the tomb of Ay at Amarna, with Akhenaten, Nefertiti holding one of their daughters, and two other daughters behind her. This scene is now badly damaged.

If Ramesses II and his father ~~Sethos~~ *Seti* I (Sety) were to return to this twenty-first-century world, or were able to view from their vantage point in the day-boat of the sun-god Re, they would surely be very vexed to observe the matters that most interest the Egyptologists who write so prolifically about the history and civilization of the "Beloved Land" of Kemet. They would be horrified to see the amount of paper devoted to the reign of Akhenaten, the great attraction generated by the heretical religious views of that king, and the attention devoted to the artistic peculiarities of the so-called Amarna period. How could it have happened that, in spite of the best efforts of royal agents following the deaths of Tutankhamun and Ay, the reputation of 'the criminal of Akhetaten' (as Akhenaten was sometimes called) stands so high, not only in the close world of the scholar, but even in the consciousness of the literate public! Not that ~~Sethos~~ *Seti* or Ramesses would know much about scholarship or the literate public.

The dazzling city of Akhetaten, the spiritual center of Akhenaten's regime which the king declared he would never leave, had been razed to the ground. Much of its stone was reused in the construction of buildings in Khmunu (Hermopolis) across the river in the reign of Ramesses II. The unusual temples erected at Karnak by Akhenaten and Nefertiti before the move of the court to Akhetaten had been dismantled and used to fill the pylons constructed by Horemheb. For an Egyptian visiting the centers of Akhenaten's power in the early years of the Nineteenth Dynasty, not much in the way of great buildings would have remained visible. There was then good reason to believe that the land of Egypt had been purged of the sickness that had afflicted it during the reigns of Akhenaten and of his immediate successors who could be considered in some way contaminated by the Amarna infection. What precisely was the reason for the deep hatred of the Amarna regime? It may not

just have been the Atenist cult, which had subverted the established religion of the land, incurring the deep hostility of the ancient priesthood. It may have been the disastrous effect of an inadequate foreign policy which had seriously threatened the integrity of the kingdom. It may have been a general malaise resulting from the neglect of the established social system of the country, with the bulk of the population alienated from the strange new culture of the court. It may just have been because the reign of Akhenaten, with its strange, exclusive practices affecting all aspects of life in Egypt, rendered the country almost unrecognizable for what it had been. The period was simply one to be forgotten, and the removal from the recorded national memory of Akhenaten's reign took with it also the reigns of Neferneferuaten, Tutankhamun, and Ay. These last reigns were of little consequence, but they were contaminated by their blood links with Akhenaten.

Consequently, when the list of the ancestors was drawn up to be recorded in the great temple of Sethos I at Abydos, the names of the Amarna Pharaohs were omitted. After Amenophis III, the dazzling monarch of the late Eighteenth Dynasty, the next recorded name was that of Horemheb. The young prince Ramesses is shown presenting to his father the papyrus roll bearing the names of the ancestor kings who were to participate in the offerings for the Kings of Upper and Lower Egypt. So the Amarna kings were not to be included in the distribution of offerings. But it must be noted that they were not the only ones to suffer this exclusion. Hatshepsut, the female Pharaoh of the mid-Eighteenth Dynasty, was not listed, presumably because her reign was thought to have been a usurpation of part of the rightful reign of Tuthmosis III. And no room was found for any of the kings who reigned between the Twelfth and the Eighteenth Dynasties, some of whom were monarchs of substantial achievement and worthy of memorial, particularly those who had initiated and largely carried through the expulsion of the Hyksos, the contaminators of the integrity of Egypt during the so-called Second Intermediate Period. Nevertheless, the deliberate omission of the Amarna Pharaohs, who had reigned in the relatively recent past, can only be accounted for on the grounds that they were not thought worthy of association with the names in the noble roll-call of acceptable ancestors. To

say the least, they had rocked the boat of state; they had upset the balance of the land; they had seemingly ignored Ma'at, the goddess of order, on whose influence Akhenaten had laid such stress.

Horemheb, however, was one of the chosen, in spite of his link with the rejected regime through his holding of important offices of state during the reigns of Tutankhamun and Ay. He had himself possibly no blood relationship with the Amarna royal family, although a qualification in this respect needs to be made. His second wife, Mutnodjmet, may have been a sister of Nefertiti and daughter of Ay, who was probably the senior non-royal person in Egyptian life even in the later years of Akhenaten. This identification is by no means certain, but if it is true, it would provide a slender basis for the legitimacy of Horemheb's claim to the throne after the death of Ay. On the other hand, such a link with the Amarna regime, and particularly a family relationship with Nefertiti, should not have commended him to those who were determined to eradicate the memory of 'the criminal of Akhetaten.'

44 left
Seated figure of the god Amun,
protecting King Horemheb, shown
standing and holding the heqa-scepter of
royal authority. This remarkable group
was found buried in the main court of
the Luxor temple (Luxor Museum).

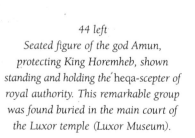

44 right
Massive gold ring with rectangular
bezel. On one side is the prenomen
cartouche of King Horemheb,
Djesekheperure Setpenre; on the
other, the king shown as a lion and
described as "lord of power"
(Louvre, N747).

45
Head of the schist statue of
Tuthmosis III from the cache of
sculpture found in the Karnak temple
in 1904; a perfect representation
of New Kingdom royalty carved
with consummate skill and artistry
(Luxor Museum, J2).

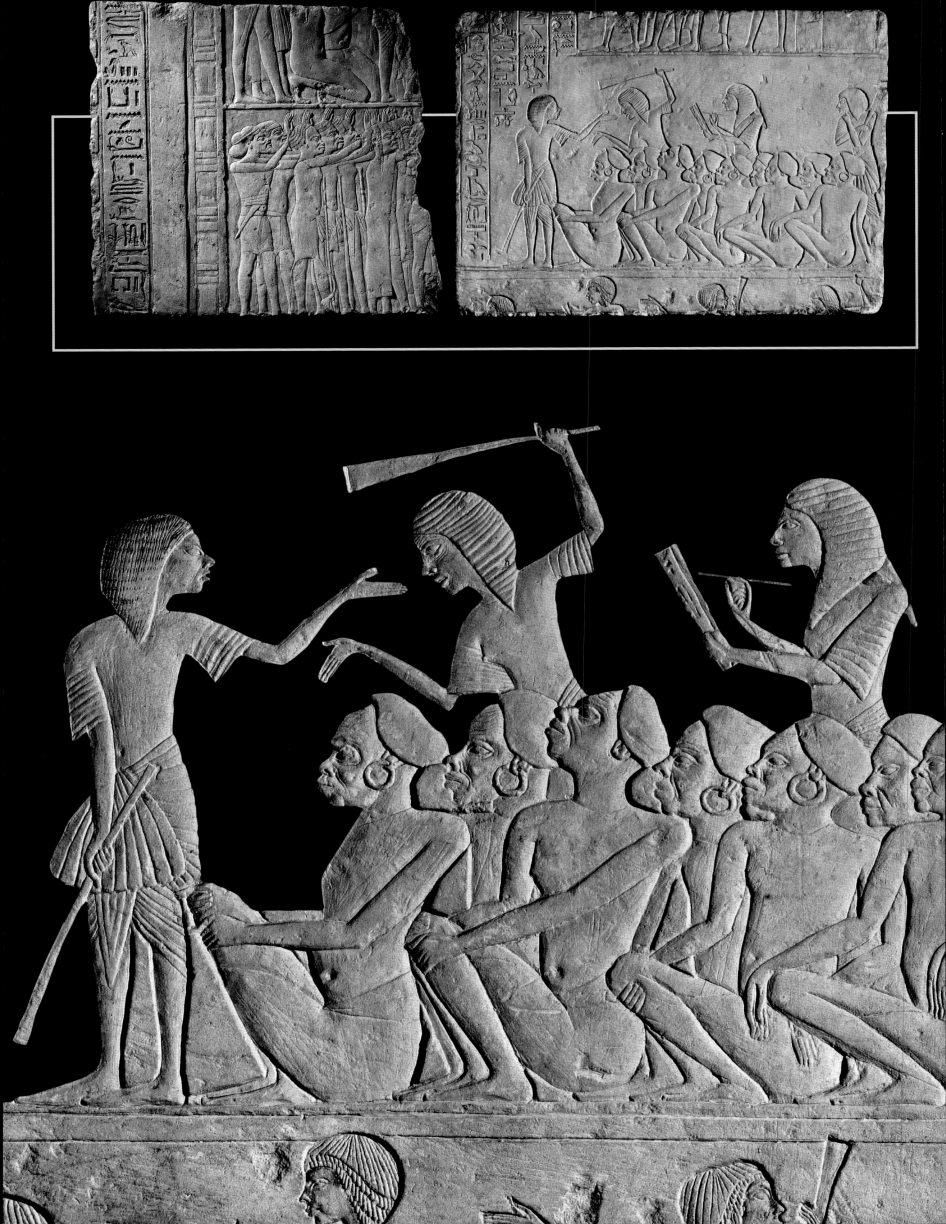

We may never know how it came about that Horemheb became king, but what is clear is that his reign was seen as meritorious by his successors of the Nineteenth Dynasty, who even set up, or allowed to be set up a personal cult in his memory. It was centered on the spectacular tomb he had prepared at Saqqara, built probably during the reign of Tutankhamun. Some scholars even believe that it was begun during the reign of Akhenaten, when Horemheb's rise in the ranks of the army and administration in Memphis commenced. The great Saqqara tomb, rediscovered in 1975 and fully excavated for the first time in the subsequent years, reveals in its size, quality of decoration, and the tone of its inscriptions, the standing of Horemheb in the period following the abandonment of Akhetaten. It is not clear to what extent the return to Thebes on the religious front, and the rehabilitation of Memphis as the administrative center of the north, or even the whole country, were due to the activities of Horemheb. It must be presumed that he worked closely with Ay, perhaps already viewing the possibility of his own accession to the throne of Egypt in due course. He may also have organized, if not led, the few small expeditions of a punitive, but not necessarily acquisitive, nature in Asia Minor and Nubia.

In about 1323 B.C., King Ay died, and he was buried in a substantial tomb in what is known as the Western Valley of the Kings. It is situated near the tomb of King Amenophis III, father of Akhenaten, and it may well have been started in the reign of Tutankhamun, intended for that monarch. Ay had reigned for less than four years, scarcely time to prepare a decent traditional Eighteenth Dynasty tomb. The tomb in which Tutankhamun was interred was in all probability intended for Ay. In switching the sepulchres and supervising the burial of the young Tutankhamun, Ay by tradition established his right to the throne. And it may be supposed that in performing a similar duty for Ay, Horemheb established his own right to succeed, although no explicit scene or text in Ay's tomb establishes the fact. There is nothing in the surviving record to suggest that Horemheb usurped the royal power against any opposition, and it seems clear from his own surviving record in the form of buildings and texts of achievement that he ruled without any uncertainty. With his record of many years of service in the army and the civil administration, he knew the problems of Egypt and understood the methods to be used to solve them. In the text on the back of a double statue in Turin, showing himself as king with his wife, Queen Mutnodjmet, the account of the royal coronation includes a reference to his having spent many years as deputy or vice-regent of the Two Lands (of Egypt). He clearly stepped into the royal role as if he had been waiting in the wings for the expected cue for his entry.

46 top left
Relief from Horemheb's Saqqara tomb showing a group of foreigners – Syrians, Nubians, and Libyans – raising their hands in greeting, possibly to Horemheb; not captives, but possibly envoys (Louvre, E11273).

46 top right and 46-47
Relief from Horemheb's Saqqara tomb showing a group of African captives squatting on the ground, being supervised by attendants with batons, and having their details noted by a scribe (Bologna, 1887).

47 center
Relief, probably from Horemheb's tomb at Saqqara. The middle register shows female mourners, the other registers, male mourners, all attending the funeral of the tomb-owner (Louvre, E11247).

47 right
Gold earring with small blue glass inlays, from the tomb of General Horemheb at Saqqara. The standing sphinx in the center, wearing the blue crown has the profile of a king of the Amarna Period (Cairo JE97864).

48 top left
Part of a scene of the Opet festival reliefs in the Luxor temple in which sacrificial animals are led in procession. The prize bull shown here, suitably fattened, wears a feathered garland between its horns.

48 bottom left
Priestly attendants bear the great weight of one of the divine barks in which the images of the gods Amun, Mut, and Khonsu travel from Karnak to Luxor for the Opet festival.

48 top right
Attendants with papyrus flowers bring geese for the Opet festivities, followed by others who lead prize bulls decked with garlands, so heavy that their hooves turn up under the weight.

48 bottom right
Music and dancing were important elements in Egyptian festivals, and groups of musicians are shown in the Opet reliefs. Here three lutenists with long-necked instruments are followed by four percussionists with hand-clappers.

Some serious consideration needs to be given to Horemheb because he was undoubtedly the progenitor of the kings of the Nineteenth Dynasty – if not physically, then politically and inspirationally. A long but, sadly, damaged inscription in Karnak sets out the extensive steps he took to wipe out corruption and the exploitation of the helpless lower ranks of society. No doubt there had been a serious deterioration in the administration of justice and the practices of day-to-day government during the Amarna and post-Amarna periods. An even less well-preserved stela set up in Memphis included much of what is found on the Turin double statue. Horemheb is declared to be the son of Amun, thereby reinforcing his royal origin by divine connection. The text also states that he rehabilitated the temples and the old cults of the land. The evidence of his work in the Theban area shows that he revivified the cults at Luxor and Karnak, and in so doing not only built afresh, but also usurped work that had been started in the reign of Amenophis III, and then taken up again during the reign of Tutankhamun. The prime example of Horemheb's conscious elimination of Tutankhamun can be seen in that part of the Luxor temple which is still

usually called the colonnade of Horemheb, with the scenes and inscriptions carved on the walls of the court in which the colonnade stands. Here the work representing the celebration of the Festival of Opet, ostensibly under Horemheb, was mostly carried out in the reign of Tutankhamun, and wherever his names appeared in the texts, they have been altered to those of Horemheb. The scenes themselves, wonderfully designed and carved, have much in common stylistically with those found in the Saqqara tomb of Horemheb, which were also designed and carried out in the reign of Tutankhamun. Many sculptures in the temples of Karnak and Luxor show the unmistakable features of the young king, but were usurped and inscribed for Horemheb. Quite clearly the decision to eliminate Tutankhamun, along with his Amarna predecessors and Ay, from the memory of the Egyptians was a deliberate act of policy, the precise reasons for which are now not easy to determine. And yet, the royal tombs of Tutankhamun and Ay were not officially desecrated in the reign of Horemheb. These kings were dead, and their tombs inaccessible; they were out of the way; their tombs were not public monuments that might serve as reminders of the past.

The case was very different with the unusual temples built by Akhenaten and Nefertiti at Karnak. They had to be dismantled, just like the temples and palaces at Akhetaten. In Karnak it is certain that the destroyer was Horemheb because the neatly shaped blocks used for their construction were reused to form the fillings of the pylons built in the great temple of Amun under Horemheb. These blocks, approximately three handspans long and known as *talatat* (from the Arabic for

three), were laid neatly in layers within the outer skin-walls of the pylons. The blocks have been removed and, since World War II, studied and partially reassembled. In a sense, therefore, the elimination of the temples of Akhenaten and Nefertiti has turned out to be somewhat temporary.

Although Horemheb had a distinguished military career behind him, if one may judge from his titles, there is not much evidence of his having conducted any substantial campaigns either during the reign of Tutankhamun, or when he was king. He had been in every respect commander in chief: his titles, as presented in his Saqqara tomb, rather overemphasize his position: "Overseer of Generals of the Lord of the Two Lands, General, General of the Lord of the Two Lands, Greatest General, Greatest General of the King, Greatest General of the Lord of the Two Lands." In presenting his position with such hyperbole he was simply emphasizing the evident fact that he was number one in the military hierarchy; he undoubtedly saw himself primarily as a military man.

49 left
Relief representation of a king in the Luxor temple, named by the cartouche as Horemheb. The royal features, however, show indubitably the young Tutankhamun; the cartouche has clearly been carved over.

49 right
Painted quartzite colossal statue. Stylistically it may be dated to the reign of Tutankhamun, but it was usurped by both of his successors, Ay and Horemheb, in whose funerary temple it was found (Cairo, JE59869).

In making promotions he unsurprisingly favored other military men, the most notable of whom was Pramesse. Scribal statues of this distinguished officer of state, set up by the tenth pylon at Karnak, bear texts that trace the rise to power of Pramesse. He was the son of Sety, an army officer of fairly modest rank, who hailed from the Delta. The texts may not chart with precision the steady course of Pramesse through the ranks of the military hierarchy. He had been overseer of horse, charioteer of His Majesty, king's messenger in all foreign lands, general of the lord of the Two Lands, and royal scribe of troop commanders. He also held important civil and religious positions: overseer of the treasury, overseer of the river mouths, overseer of the priests of all the gods. He eventually was made deputy of His Majesty in the South and the North and vizier. By fortune or by sheer talent, Pramesse gained Horemheb's favor and was promoted from rank to rank until he occupied the highest positions in the civil, religious, and military sections of Egyptian life.

It was a remarkable advancement, and it has been concluded, probably rightly, that at a relatively early point in his reign Horemheb decided that Pramesse was the man to succeed him on the throne of Egypt. Much emphasis has been placed by historians of the New Kingdom on the

military element in this rise to great offices of state, of someone from an apparently simple Delta family. But Pramesse presumably demonstrated in his career more than a military efficiency and a capability to command. Like Horemheb himself, his abilities became apparent through the success with which he exercised his successive offices; in the end, no doubt, his handling of administrative matters at a high level, combined probably with a loyal trust in his monarch, commended him as the possible successor to the throne of Egypt.

The question of succession and the legitimacy of the claim to royalty by Egyptian kings were always matters of concern for the ruling Pharaoh. For a king

with a family including sons, the question of succession was on the whole determined by the principle of primogeniture in the first instance; there might be difficulties, however, in following this principle in some cases, especially where the claim to the throne might be complicated by marriage – the status of the wife of the prospective heir having herself the possibility of affecting the succession through her own royal parentage. The background to succession is rarely clear, but the need for a king to ensure the 'right' succession might require the use of some constitutional device like co-regency, or simple regency. We shall see shortly what arrangement King Sethos I used to establish the smooth succession for his son Ramesses to the kingship. For Horemheb, growing old and still childless, and furthermore suffering from a constitutional impediment of his own uncertain claim to divine kingship, the matter of succession was of great, if not paramount importance.

Horemheb had but the slightest blood relationship with the Eighteenth Dynasty royal line. With no children, he could not expect to be the founder by blood of the line which would follow him. He himself had, however, acted as "Deputy of the Two Lands," according to the text on his Turin double statue; this title has usually been taken to mean that he acted as co-regent

---

50
Head of King Horemheb from a scene in his tomb in the Valley of the Kings; he offers wine to Hathor, goddess of the West. The bright colors contrast strongly with the blue-gray background.

51 top
The prenomen and nomen of Horemheb, finely carved and painted in his Theban tomb. The prenomen (right cartouche) reads Djeserkheperure Setpenre; the nomen (left cartouche) Horemheb Meryamun.

51 bottom
Horemheb honors Isis four times; a scene from the king's Theban tomb. The goddess is "mother of the god, lady of heaven, mistress of all the gods." On the right stands jackal-headed Anubis.

52-53
In the antechamber of Horemheb's royal tomb the king makes offerings and greeting to a series of deities; jackal-headed Anubis, Isis the Great, Horus-son-of-Isis, Hathor, "Lady of Heaven," and Osiris.

53 bottom
Upper part of a figure of the goddess Hathor, from Horemheb's tomb. She receives wine from the king, and is here described as "chief of the West, lady of heaven, mistress of all the gods."

Ramesses II

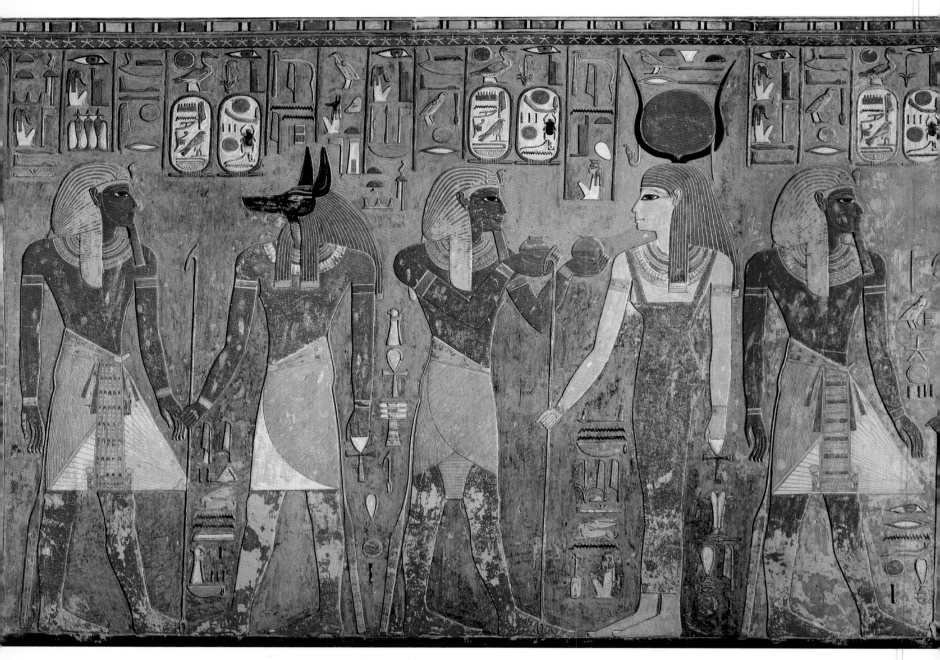

with King Ay, who himself was childless. In Horemheb's case the device worked well, and he became king in due course on the death of Ay. And so, to secure the succession for Pramesse, he appointed him "Deputy of His Majesty in the South and the North," a title perhaps more explicit than "Deputy of the Two Lands." Again the device worked, and when Horemheb died in about 1295 B.C., Pramesse succeeded him, dropping the *p* or *pa* (the definite article) at the start of his name, becoming Ramesse, or Ramesses as he is now usually called, using the Greek form. He is seen to be the founder of the Nineteenth Dynasty, but some historians with very good reason prefer to consider Horemheb himself as the founder. His reign was a kind of transitional period between the final 'eliminated' rulers of the Eighteenth Dynasty and the new Delta line of the Nineteenth Dynasty. We should remember, however, that the

dynastic divisions were not established as such at this period of Egyptian history, although changes in family lines were recognized. In this respect Horemheb was undoubtedly seen to belong to the succeeding kings of the line of Ramesses, and, as we noted earlier, his first tomb at Saqqara became an honored cult-center especially during the reign of Ramesses, when his sister Tia had her tomb built adjacent to that of Horemheb, the illustrious progenitor of the Ramesside Dynasty.

Pramesse, now for us Ramesses I, officiated at the burial of Horemheb in the main Valley of the Kings, thereby reinforcing his legitimacy. The tomb is large and finely decorated with texts and representations from the compositions used for royal burials in the New Kingdom; they are set against a very distinctive blue-gray background. The whole scheme and its

execution are very different from what was placed in his non-royal Saqqara tomb. There is no evidence of a cult attached to the Theban tomb, apart from the common royal funerary cult. The latter, however, was usually practiced in the royal mortuary temple built on the edge of the cultivated plain in Western Thebes. Horemheb's mortuary temple was built at the south end of the line of temples, adjacent to the site of what was to become the mortuary temple of Ramesses III at Medinet Habu. Its remote position was determined by the existence of a temple foundation for Ay, and possibly even one for Tutankhamun. Nothing of consequence can now be seen on the ground; it has disappeared along with other Eighteenth Dynasty mortuary temples, dismantled during the Ramesside Period.

Very little has survived to suggest that Horemheb developed an aggressive foreign

policy during his reign to counteract the weaknesses of the Amarna Pharaohs. He was undoubtedly fortunate that, for other reasons, the most threatening forces in the Near East were preoccupied and unable to exploit the weakened state of Egyptian imperial power, particularly during the reign of Akhenaten. A moment of real danger had occurred when the Hittite king, Suppiluliumas, sent one of his sons as a prospective husband for a widowed Egyptian queen, probably to be identified as Ankhesenamun, wife of Tutankhamun. From Hittite records it emerges that things went badly wrong, and the young prince was killed in Egypt. This tragedy happened when Ay was king; there was then a real danger of an explosive situation developing into conflict between Egypt and Hatti, the Hittite kingdom. Nothing, however, was done to avenge the death. Suppiluliumas died in about 1323 B.C., and his successor,

Arunwandas II, shortly afterward. His brother and successor, Mursilis II, young and inexperienced, was more immediately concerned with troubles brewing in Arzawa to the west, in the lands bordering the Black Sea to the north, and in the kingdom of Azzi-Hayasa to the east. The re-establishment of Hittite influence in these regions engrossed the attention of the Hittites for many years. In the lands formerly closely associated with Egypt, further trouble arose in Syria involving Carchemish, and it seems probable that Horemheb took advantage of the Hittite involvement elsewhere to launch a raid on the coast of Lebanon, his forces possibly pushing as far east as Carchemish. Details are uncertain, but it does not appear that this small campaign represented more than a testing of local weaknesses. A rebellion in Nubia was also dealt with promptly and firmly.

By concentrating on rebuilding the economy of Egypt, rehabilitating the cults and shrines of the gods, and restoring a degree of national confidence and pride, Horemheb prepared the way for his chosen successor. It was presumably evident that there could be trouble in Asia Minor, and in choosing Pramesse to succeed him, Horemheb based his judgment on Pramesse's military background and his tested administrative abilities. So we may conclude on the evidence of inscriptions which would hardly have been composed in contrary terms. But the evidence is positive, and in the absence of any different indications, we should accept that Horemheb chose wisely. The one possible drawback was Pramesse's age. At the time

of his accession he may already have been in his mid-sixties, an advanced age for ancient Egypt, and scarcely the age at which to assume so awesome a role. But a man in his sixties with a distinguished record would be more acceptable as king and founder of a new line than someone of less tried achievement. Pramesse also had a son, Sety, who was in his forties when Horemheb died. The succession looked promising, and Horemheb's expectations were not to be disappointed.

On assuming the throne, Pramesse, now Ramesses, took as his distinctive name (after called the throne-name) Menpehtyre, which means 'one enduring of strength is Re.' It suggested positive action, and by intention or by chance it recalled the throne-name of

Amosis, first king of the Eighteenth Dynasty, Nebpehtyre, 'one who is possessor of strength is Re.' Sadly, he had little chance to prove himself as a ruler of strength. His reign lasted less than a year and a half, and his son Sety found himself, far sooner than he might have expected, turned from Ramesses' deputy into his successor, King of Upper and Lower Egypt. The change might have been disastrous for the new dynasty and for Egypt, but no evidence has survived to suggest that the careful foundations of stability laid by Horemheb, and presumably consolidated by Ramesses in his short reign, were disturbed by internal discord. Egyptian official records, however, do not usually mention matters which might reflect badly on the established regime.

54-55
*Scenes in the burial chamber of
Ramesses I. Left: beetle-headed
Khepri, the sun-god at dawn,
receives offerings from the king.
Right: he is led to Osiris by Horus-
son-of-Isis, Atum, and Neith.*

55 top
*Ramesses is greeted by falcon-
headed Horus-son-of-Isis, wearing
the double crown, and jackal-
headed Anubis, god of embalming.
A blue-gray wash is used for
the background color, as in
Horemheb's tomb.*

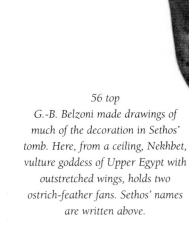

Sety became king – he is often given the Greek form Sethos – and took as his throne-name Menmare, 'one enduring in *ma'at* (truth or order) is Re.' He took over the running of the country and the prosecution of a lively foreign policy, following no doubt the plans his father had drawn up with him.

Sethos honored the memory of his father and promoted a cult in his honor by dedicating a chapel close to his own remarkable temple at Abydos, and later by including a further chapel for him in his mortuary temple in Western Thebes. Most of the very fine reliefs from the Abydos chapel are now in the Metropolitan Museum of Art, New York – but not the surviving part of the great stela of dedication, the text on which sets out what Sethos regarded as his debt to his father, and the extent to which he had put into practice the policies they had surely discussed together in his father's lifetime. Sethos reorganized the army, led a campaign against the Fenkhu (Phoenicians) in the Levant, and generally cleaned up rebellious peoples – possibly infiltrating tribesmen – in the desert. Much of this activity took place while Ramesses was still alive, and Sety, the crown prince, more than suggests in retrospect that whatever good happened in Ramesses' short reign was the result of his own skills and initiative. As King Sethos, he set out to take most of the credit without actually rubbishing his father and his achievement. He was also prepared to view the beginning of his reign as the start of a new era. In the Karnak scenes depicting his triumphs in the early part of the reign, he designates his first year as *wehem mesut*, 'repeating of births.'

56 top
G.-B. Belzoni made drawings of much of the decoration in Sethos' tomb. Here, from a ceiling, Nekhbet, vulture goddess of Upper Egypt with outstretched wings, holds two ostrich-feather fans. Sethos' names are written above.

56 bottom
Belzoni's illustration showing Sethos being led into the presence of Osiris "first in the West and Great God," by Horus. Behind Osiris stands Hathor with the emblem of the West on her head.

57
Head of Sethos from a composite statue made in a number of pieces. The head and upper part of the body are made of alabaster (calcite), originally with eyes and eyebrows of other materials (Cairo, JE36692).

58 left
*Ramesses II embraced by Ptah-Tatenen, a
form of the creator god Ptah, associated
with Tatenen, an underworld god; from a
pillar of the colonnade before the first
hypostyle hall at Abydos, completed by
Ramesses for his father Sethos.*

58 top right
*A ritual scene in fine low relief from
Karnak temple showing Sethos wearing
the crown of Lower Egypt, kneeling and
offering burning incense to Amon-Re.*

58 center right
*Sethos kneels before Amun, offering the
god two bouquets of papyrus flowers.*

*The god in return offers long life, among
other gifts. This is one of the ritual scenes
inside the hypostyle hall.*

58-59
*The vizier Paser in his tomb is invested with
the gold of honor in the presence of King
Sethos I, here shown mummiform in a kiosk,
with the goddess Ma'at. Wilkinson drawing.*

59 right
*A temporal equivalent of the funerary
scene of Paser's presentation:
King Sethos I leans from a window
of appearances, supervising the
granting of the gold of honor
to Hormin, a senior harem official.
From Hormin's tomb at Saqqara
(Louvre, C213).*

These words were used from time to time in Egypt to indicate the start of a new era – renaissance is the word often used to translate them – but nearly always as seen at the time or shortly afterward. By regarding the start of his reign as a *wehem mesut*, Sethos endowed himself with an importance which had perhaps been intended by Horemheb for Ramesses I.

Sethos in fact had some justification in making this claim, because it was he who put into effect the prospective policies of Horemheb, and in most ways prepared the ground for his son Ramesses II. Sethos achieved so much in his moderately long reign of eleven to fifteen years that had he survived a little longer, he might have confronted the Hittite challenge at Qadesh and secured a reputation which would now stand higher than that of his great successor. But that is idle speculation. Sethos had enough to do from the outset of his reign in continuing the rehabilitation of the internal condition of Egypt, and in re-establishing a strong Egyptian presence in Asia Minor. His campaigns are graphically and finely recorded on the outside of the northern wall of the great Hypostyle Hall of the Karnak temple. The foray made while he was still crown prince had introduced him to the kind of campaigning to be expected in Asia Minor. He did not delay in delivering a sharp reminder to the unruly tribes of Palestine that the Egyptian lion was once more awake and ready to pounce. In his very first year (c.1294 B.C.), an attack was launched from the border post of Sile at the northeastern edge of the Delta. His first target was the Shasu tribe, or collection of tribes, noted for their independent spirit, the ancestors of the modern Bedouin. Sethos' forces were already organized into three divisions named after the great gods Amun, Re, and Sutekh, or Seth, the last of whom had risen to prominence through the patronage of the kings of the Nineteenth Dynasty who came from the region of Seth's cult center in the Delta. These divisions would figure in the great Qadesh adventure of Ramesses II, joined with a fourth named after Ptah, the great Memphite god.

Ippolito Rosellini's drawing of the scene shown in the photograph on its right. A comparison illustrates the damage suffered by the temple wall since the 1820s, much of it caused by the women of Luxor scraping off sandstone dust for magical purposes.

From Gaza Sethos moved north into Palestine, the land then known to the Egyptians as Canaan, and here a number of towns were captured. In the same campaign in Year 1, or a little later, Egyptian power was extended into Lebanon, and in what was probably a campaign of later years, his forces moved against Amurru, in northern Lebanon, and went east to take the town of Qadesh. By that time the Hittites were not involved in any confrontation, although in another campaign, unfortunately undated, and only partly visible on the outer wall of the Hypostyle Hall, Sethos claimed to have attacked and seriously defeated the land of 'vile Kheta,' a designation commonly applied to the Hittites. It is not always possible to confirm the details of campaigns and conquests set out in the triumphant scenes placed by Egyptian kings on temple walls. The tradition of overemphasizing the extent and success of campaigns was well established by the time of the Nineteenth Dynasty, and it was not the practice to underestimate the outcome of foreign adventures. Scenes and inscriptions in temples within Egypt were composed as statements of intent as much as of achievement. They contained a religio-magical element designed always to vaunt the power of the reigning monarch. They were prompted not by simple braggadocio, but by the need to proclaim the greatness of the king. It should not, however, be understood from this that nothing in these temple scenes should be believed. But their claims need always to be treated with caution, and checked when possible against

60-61
Scene from the outer wall of the Karnak Hypostyle Hall, showing King Sethos smitting the collected foreign rulers from north and south, to the glory of Amon-Re, who receives the presentation with upraised scimitar.

61 top
In another Karnak relief, Sethos I smites a foreign notable with his mace, in front of an approving (but noticeably smaller) Amon-Re. The prisoners are all Asiatics.

62-63
*A scene reproduced in the
Description de l'Égypte showing
Sethos I in his war chariot hunting
down and shooting at his Syrian
enemies, some of whom have been
struck by his arrows and have fallen
in the water to die.*

other evidence. In the case of Sethos' campaigns a number of inscriptions set up in the regions penetrated by his armies confirm an Egyptian presence. Two inscriptions found at Beth-Shan in northern Canaan, one dated to Year 1, the other with its date lost, record Egyptian military activities in the region. The remains of a stela of Sethos found at Tell al-Shihab, some miles to the east of the Sea of Galilee, although lacking its main text, further confirms the presence of Egyptians there during his reign. In addition, there is a suggestion from Hittite records that some form of treaty may have been concluded between Mursilis II and Sethos. No date is offered, but we should probably be right to conclude that it was in Sethos' early years; as a result the Asiatic situation was stabilized for the rest of his reign. And so Egyptian influence in Asia Minor was partially restored, with a limited Egyptian presence in the region.

The other places from which trouble might have been expected, especially at times when Egypt appeared to be vulnerable, were Libya to the west and Nubia to the south. One part of the series of scenes on the outer wall of the Hypostyle Hall does in fact deal with a Libyan campaign, unfortunately without a date and singularly unspecific in detail. There need be no doubt that such a campaign occurred. Although the northwestern boundary of Egypt had apparently been untroubled for a

62 bottom
*Sethos steps down from his chariot
to accept the submission of the chiefs
of the Lebanon, some of whom are
organizing the felling of trees for the
royal bark and flag staves. From the
Description de l'Égypte.*

63 bottom
*Sethos in his war chariot, raising his
scimitar, charges headlong into his
Syrian enemies. A scene on the outer
north wall of the Hypostyle Hall at
Karnak. From the Description de
l'Égypte.*

very long time, the absence of evidence for military activity in the region may disguise the brewing of potential trouble. Ramesses II would in due course be obliged to set up fortresses in the area, and any aggressive inroads by Libyans would take place later in the Nineteenth Dynasty. Again, in this vaguely recorded campaign Sethos may have been pre-empting an attack, or simply suggesting to the Libyans that it would not be profitable to mount hostile activity now that Egyptian power had been revivified.

In the south, in Nubia, things remained peaceful for most of Sethos' reign. A local skirmish, prompted by good intelligence information, nipped in the bud a possible revolt in Kush. It was probably a very modest campaign, not thought worthy to appear among those commemorated on the walls of the Hypostyle Hall at Karnak; it was, however, the subject of two inscriptions found on Sai Island and at Amara, both administrative centers between the second and third cataracts of the Nile. In general, Nubia was well settled, and Sethos even chose the very distant site of Nauri, near the third cataract, to carve a huge inscription dealing with the legal arrangements concerning his great Abydos temple about six hundred miles to the north in Middle Egypt. Its position there seems beyond explanation; the local inhabitants would not have been able to read it, and if they had asked its meaning from some passing Egyptian scribe, they would have been very puzzled by the detailed instructions concerning the temple's lands and the immunities of those who worked on them. Other indications suggest that Sethos may have been considering the development of Nubia beyond its simple imperial function; he may have begun the work on the great temple at Gebel Barkal (Napata), downstream from the fourth cataract, one of his son's foundations.

Sethos returns to Karnak from his campaign against the Hittites (undated), driving before his chariot two files of prisoners for presentation to Amun. The king, looking backwards, is about to mount his chariot. From Karnak.

65 right
A detail from a scene in the Karnak temple in which Sethos is shown attacking a Hittite force. Beneath the king's horses, a tangle of confused and slain enemy is ridden over by the supporting Egyptian chariots.

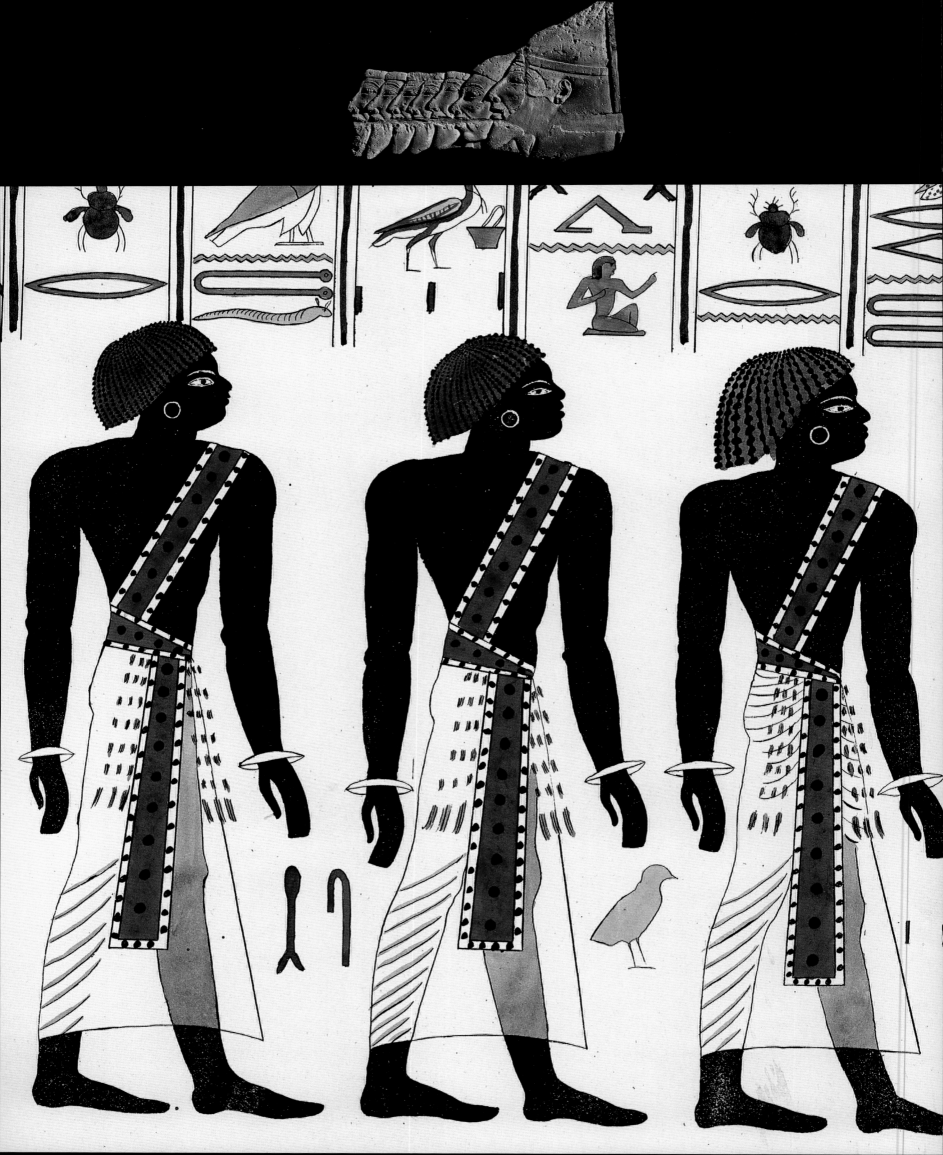

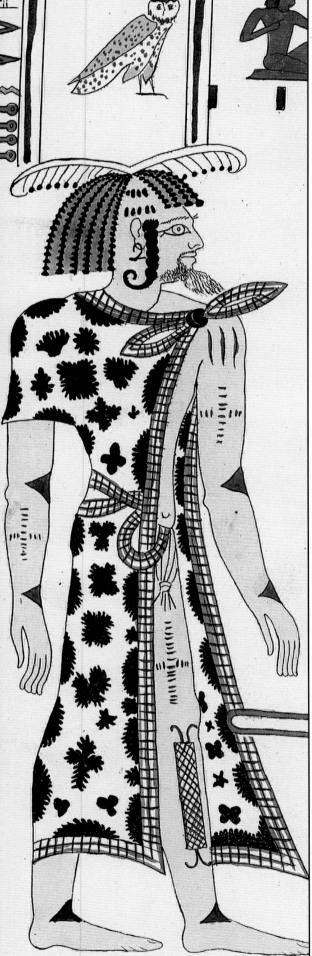

His hand may also be detected at other sites where Ramesses II left major memorials. In so many ways, the great works of the son seem to have taken up, expanded, and then surpassed what the father may have intended or even begun.

Among the most memorable structures surviving from ancient Egypt, few make such a stupendous impression as the Hypostyle Hall in the great temple of Amun at Karnak. Here is a forest of massive columns, 12 with open papyrus capitals forming the center aisle, with 122 smaller columns with closed capitals, 61 on either side of the central colonnade. Here, as in so many places in Egypt, the visitor is reminded of Ramesses II, under whom much of the decoration of the hall was carried out. But the history of the planning of the hall goes back at least to the reign of Horemheb, who put in hand the building of

66 top
The heads of Asiatic princes about to be struck by the royal mace. From Karnak.

66-67
Belzoni's copy of the representatives of the four races of mankind, shown in the fifth hour of the Book of Gates in Sethos I's tomb. On the right are Libyans, and on the left, Nubians.

67 right
Karnak scene of uncertain date, copied by Wilkinson, of the attack on the Hittites by Sethos I. The king drives his chariot into the Hittite forces, firing arrows as he goes. For its time, this copy is remarkably accurate.

the Second Pylon of the temple, thereby creating a great court to the west of the Third Pylon, built by Amenophis III. Some work at the entrance to this great court may be dated to the reign of Ramesses I, and much of the subsequent inner construction of the columns and the decoration of the internal and external walls was carried out in Sethos' reign. Who can now tell what the original plan entailed: an open court with a colonnade, as at Luxor, or the majestic columned hall we know today? The work of a successor can so easily conceal the work and the intentions of his predecessor.

*A scene from the north wall of the
second hypostyle hall in the Abydos
temple, Sethos I, holding a long
incense burner, makes offering to the
many forms of Osiris. He wears a
tight cap crown.*

*68 bottom left
Sethos offers ma'at (truth or divine
order) in the form of a small
kneeling figure, to the divine triad
Osiris, Isis, and Horus-son-of Isis
(Harsiese), set in a kiosk.
From Abydos.*

*68 bottom right
In the chapel of Ptah-Sokar at
Abydos, a scene showing the
resuscitation of the dead king, here
described and identified with the god
of the dead Sokar-Osiris. Isis and
Horus attend the ceremony.*

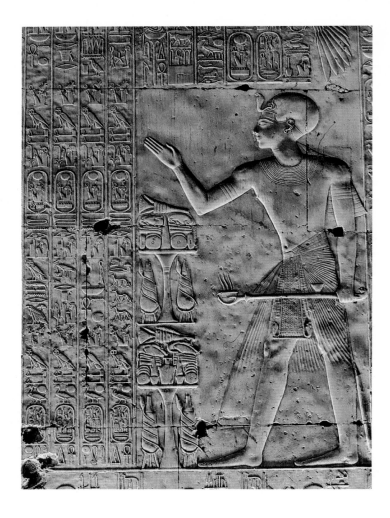

*69
Sethos in youthful appearance
makes an offering of incense to Isis,
who in turn extends to Sethos' nose
the symbols of endurance and life;
the short text says, "entering into the
sacred precinct." From the Abydos
temple.*

Greater certainty attends the foundation and building of Sethos' most splendid construction, the unusual but stupendous temple of Osiris at Abydos. Although much of the work on the building was carried out in the reign of Ramesses II, the textual record makes it clear that Sethos instigated the project. Abydos was one of the most sacred sites in Egypt; the center of the cult of the dead king, the divine Osiris. It was almost exclusively a place of pilgrimage and never was, or ever became, an important administrative center. Earlier kings had built cenotaphs or similar structures at Abydos, but no great cult temple had been built, possibly because of the remoteness and lack of political importance of the site. Sethos' family came from the Delta, from the heartland of Seth, the brother, rival, and murderer of Osiris; Sethos' very name meant 'the one of (or belonging to) Seth,' and he may well have been advised that the still uncertain legitimacy of the new dynasty needed further strengthening by an important act of devotion to Osiris, with whom he would in due course be identified in death.

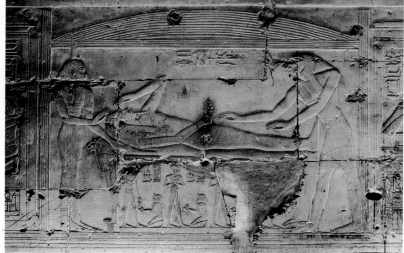

Whether the primary purpose of the foundation was religious or political, the result was exceptional, both in its originality and its decoration. Here, sadly, is not the place to examine this temple in detail, but at least it may be said that the exquisite limestone reliefs in the second hypostyle hall and in the chapels dedicated to the principal gods of Egypt, in the main Osiris chapel, and in the chapel dedicated to the king himself, represent the most perfect expression of ancient Egyptian relief carving. They have an exceptional purity where color has been lost, and stunning splendor where color has survived. The style and execution hark back to the best work produced in the reign of Amenophis III, but with a relaxing of formality, which can be ascribed to the lasting influence of the revolutionary art of the Amarna Period.

The same artistic quality can be found in the work in Sethos' mortuary temple at Thebes, but there the medium – sandstone – was less receptive of the sensitivity of line and the precision of carving which the limestone of Abydos allowed. Similarly, his tomb in the Valley of the Kings is generally recognized as containing the artistically finest versions of the standard New Kingdom royal tomb compositions, whether in painted carved relief or just in painted

outline. The tomb sadly has suffered dreadfully at the hands of man and at the depredation of Nature since it was first rediscovered by Belzoni in 1817. The standard of work set by the royal craftsmen in Sethos' reign was not to be maintained in subsequent reigns, in the case of Ramesses II presumably because the scale and quantity of what was built in his time far exceeded the capability of skilled craftsmen to decorate to the level of Sethos' reign. The works carried out under Sethos in the great northern capital of Memphis can now scarcely be determined, and little remains from the buildings set up in the new Delta Residence.

From a relatively early point in his reign, Sethos associated his young son Ramesses with his activities in the field of war and in peaceful events at home. In the Karnak scene dealing with the Libyan foray, the figure of the young Prince Ramesses was inserted into the composition, in one place just simply added, in another replacing an original figure of an official. The insertions were presumably made during Sethos' reign; if later, then more emphasis would surely have been placed on them.

Some years before his death, Sethos decided to clinch the succession by associating Ramesses with him as co-regent.

The circumstances are set out in the course of a great inscription in Sethos' Abydos temple, and dated in Ramesses Year 1. It is, as might be expected, an account full of hyperbole and quite unspecific in detail. Ramesses states that his father in principle made over Egypt to him before he was born, "while I was in the egg"; in due course "while I was a child in his arms" Sethos in the presence of the people said, "Crown him as king that I may see his beauty while I am still living."

The words make up a kind of myth: Ramesses was scarcely a child when he became co-regent. In fact he was probably in his teens, even approaching twenty. But the reality of his promotion cannot be doubted. Yet he was still not given royal titles; in the corridor of the king list in Sethos' Abydos temple, Ramesses is shown as a youth, wearing the side-lock, and described as "hereditary prince and senior king's son." His co-regency was not a full co-regency, such as was not uncommon in ancient Egypt; he did not share regnal years with his father. But he was poised to take over the kingship, as Sethos had planned. On Sethos' death in about 1279 B.C., the transition was apparently seamless. And so Year 1 of Usimare, Ramesses-mery-Amun began.

70 top
The Gallery of the Lists at Abydos.
Right: Sethos and his son Prince
Ramesses make presentation of
offerings to various deities. Left: They
present the names of the kings of
Egypt to be included in the
presentation.

70 center
The young Prince Ramesses stands in
front of his father Sethos, holding
open a papyrus roll from which he
reads out the names of the ancestor
kings who are to be included in the
offerings.

70 bottom
Part of the king list from Ramesses II's
temple at Abydos, close to his father's
temple. The middle row contains the
cartouches of the kings of the
Eighteenth Dynasty, omitting
Hatshepsut and the Amarna rulers
(British Museum, EA117).

71
From the chapels in the Abydos temple:
Sethos is embraced by the jackal-headed
Wepwawet, the local necropolis deity;
above Sethos, Nekhbet, the vulture deity,
offers the king life and dominion.

RAMESSES II AND THE EXTERNAL WORLD

CHAPTER 2

72

Ramesses II grasps the hair of three representative enemies: Asiatic, Nubian and Libyan. From Memphis, on a block reused by Merenptah. This small scene recalls the grander representations of domination found on temple pylons (Cairo, JE 46189).

73

A painting by Prisse d'Avennes of the young Ramesses shown as the iunmutef-priest, with side-lock and leopard garment, offering to the deity: he holds a pellet of incense between his fingers.

Self-confidence, backed by some years of near-royal authority and experience, is thought to have characterized the reign of Ramesses II from its outset in about 1279 B.C. The great text which was set up in the temple of Sethos in Abydos, dated in Year 1 of Ramesses, dwells chiefly on the extraordinary works which the son would accomplish in the memory and honor of the father. There is no mention of what was to be done in Asia Minor, Libya, and Nubia. The tone and content are domestic, and little doubt could be left in the mind of the reader of the text that young Ramesses knew what was to be done and how it was to be done. How long would he have to complete his program? His grandfather had become king in his sixties, and reigned for less than two years; his father was probably in his mid-thirties when he succeeded, and he reigned for possibly sixteen years. Old age was not expected in ancient Egypt even for kings, and Ramesses on accession in his early twenties could not have expected a reign of more than thirty years. Was he then starting a sprint or a middle-distance race? How could he have expected that it was to be a marathon? Bombastic inscriptions, not unexpectedly, always predicted long life for the king, and in the Abydos inscription toward its end, the deceased Sethos thanks his son for his devotion to his memory, and states that Re, the great sun god, has granted him an eternity of years: "Pass eternity for your lifetime as King of Upper and Lower Egypt." He, Sethos, had suggested to Osiris that he should double Ramesses' lifespan while again Re granted him eternity and everlastingness, and millions of jubilees. Rarely was such a prediction to be so amply fulfilled. In his exceptional reign of sixty-six years plus a few months, Ramesses would celebrate more jubilees than were ever recorded for an Egyptian king.

In about 1279 B.C., however, Ramesses had no idea that he would have plenty of time to carry through any programs that he may have considered suitable for his reign. He may have had no program, but just a wish to make his mark at home and abroad, in building, in improving the lot of his people, in establishing good administration, in reimposing Egyptian power in lands that once were under the control of the Pharaoh. These were traditional purposes for a new Egyptian king, and in Ramesses' case, he had no serious pieces of unfinished business left over from the reign of his father. In the Abydos inscription, references are made to the structures left incomplete but completed by Ramesses, and to all the commercial and administrative arrangements made for the running of the temple of Abydos, and in the land of Egypt generally. But every Egyptian king left great works uncompleted, to be finished by his successor, and no living king would pretend in a formal text that he was simply carrying out what his predecessor had started. And we know from the provisions made in the great inscription set up by Sethos at Nauri, far to the south in Nubia, that very adequate arrangements had been made in his lifetime for the running of the temple and the temple estates.

Numerous building works and other domestic activities engrossed Ramesses' attention in the early years of his reign, and it was not until Year 4 that he turned his gaze to the east and began to consider military activities in a region which had been mostly dominated by Egyptian power up to the reign of Amenophis III – the last of the 'recognized' kings of the Eighteenth Dynasty before the disintegration of influence under that 'criminal of Akhetaten.' It will be recalled that a short campaign under Sethos into Canaan had begun the process of imperial rehabilitation. The lurking presence of Hittite power to the north was now an important factor in the balance of power in Western Asia, and some kind of treaty between Sethos and Mursilis II, the Hittite king, appears to have temporarily settled relations between Egypt and Hatti. But the endemic instability of the region could only in time lead to further confrontations. In about 1295 B.C. Mursilis II died, and was succeeded by his son Muwatallis, who apparently recognized that the threat of attack by Egypt was increased after the accession of Ramesses II. In this he was not mistaken.

The first campaign into Asia took place in Year 4 (c.1276–1275 B.C.). Details are rather sketchy: the remains of two inscriptions set up by Ramesses at Byblos and at Nahr al-Kalb (Dog River) near modern Beirut, both dated to Year 4, provide the reliable confirmatory evidence of the campaign. No specific record can be identified among the many war scenes found in the Theban temples or elsewhere in Egypt. The Egyptian forces apparently moved quickly through Canaan, up into Phoenicia, and even convinced the king of Amurru to switch allegiance from the Hittite king to the Egyptians. It may have been a trial campaign for what would follow in Year 5. Still, numerous small towns and districts were reoccupied after about fifty years of submission to other masters; their names are not recorded in the dated records of the campaign, but they may well be included in the lists of foreign dependencies carved on the walls of the Theban temples.

74

A group of New Kingdom bronze weapons including a khepesh-sword inscribed for Ramesses II. In the scene opposite, such a weapon is being offered to the king by Amon-Re as a pledge of victory.

74-75

Reproduction by Rosellini of a scene of the King Ramesses holding the topknots of Asiatics, Nubians, and Libyans, ready to be smitten by his bladed mace. The king is in the presence of Amon-Re, who is presenting him with the khepesh-sword.

76-77
Part of a scene showing prisoners bunched together, presumably waiting for the king's mace or sword to descend on their heads. The faces are finely carved with the features of Nubians clearly distinguishable (Cairo, JE69306).

77 top
Detail of a drawing by Lepsius of part of a scene in the temple at Abu Simbel of submissive prisoners about to be destroyed by the royal mace. The three usual racial types are shown: Asiatic, Nubian, and Libyan.

77 bottom
Drawing by Rosellini of a kneeling captive, certainly of Asiatic origin as indicated by his beard and the meager strapping on his body. The royal arm is shown wearing a guard to protect it from the snapping bowstring.

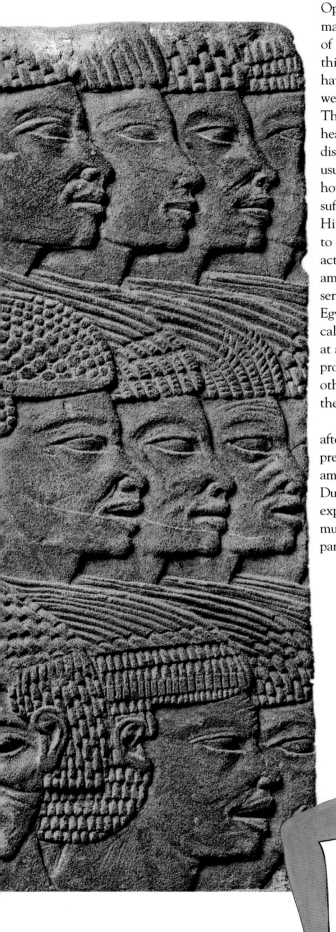

Ramesses was presumably pleased with the outcome of his first punitive strike into Asia. Opposition was slight, and one major result was the defection of the king of Amurru. While this switch of allegiance may have delighted the Egyptian king, it was not well received by the Hittite king Muwatallis. The Hittite empire, strategically strong in its heartland, was surrounded by potentially dissident vassals to whom a firm hand was usually applied when necessary. Egypt, however, was another matter. It was sufficiently far away to be safe from a direct Hittite strike, but something could be done to counteract the results of Egyptian activities in areas now seen to be within the ambit of Hittite power. If there were to be a serious settlement of the rivalry between Egypt and Hatti (or Kheta, as the Egyptians called it), it would have to take place in Asia at a point where the rival powers would most probably seek naturally to confront each other. Such a place was Qadesh in Syria, to the east of Amurru.

The contest which took place soon afterward, in Ramesses' Year 5, was wholly predictable, and the kings on both sides made ample provision for a major confrontation. During the winter following Ramesses' 'first expedition of victory,' Muwatallis began to muster his forces, calling up support from all parts of his imperial domain. Ramesses,

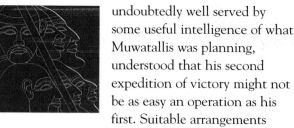

undoubtedly well served by some useful intelligence of what Muwatallis was planning, understood that his second expedition of victory might not be as easy an operation as his first. Suitable arrangements were made to prepare and equip a very substantial Egyptian force; allies might have been forewarned of what might be expected of them. It was to be a classic encounter. In the spring of about 1274 B.C. the operation was launched. The army set out on the ninth day of the second month of summer (according to the Egyptian calendar, out of step with the natural year) in Year 5. What followed was to be so important for the rest of Ramesses' reign that a full treatment of the campaign will be postponed for the next chapter. For the present let us record just that after a difficult and seemingly inconclusive, battle, the forces of Egypt and Hatti disengaged; Ramesses returned to his Delta capital, to pursue activities elsewhere, and, no doubt, ponder his options. As for Muwatallis, his forces did not retire immediately to his capital, Hattusas, in the Anatolian uplands, to lick their wounds, metaphorically speaking. Muwatallis took advantage of the Egyptian withdrawal to move south, recover Amurru, and take over the part of Syria in the neighborhood of Damascus known as Upe. Threats from the east, from Assyria, diverted the Hittites and prevented progress south.

For some years Ramesses apparently considered it prudent not to renew operations in Asia Minor. He had many other things on his mind, and he would undoubtedly have wished to delay any further 'expeditions of victory' in Asia until he could be sure of some success. Egyptian power remained recognized by many vassal rulers in Canaan and adjacent lands, and it may be assumed that good information was sent regularly to the Egyptian court at Piramesse in the Delta by agents operating in these parts. An Egyptian king with pretensions to restore the power and influence of his country in regions formerly well within the sphere of Egyptian dominion could hardly remain idle for long. In the case of Ramesses II there exists much pictorial and some inscriptional evidence to show that he did campaign in the east. Unfortunately, many of the great tableaux of war carved on the walls of Luxor, Karnak, and the Ramesseum and elsewhere are undated, or have lost their dated epigraphs. Some of the expeditions can

be assigned probable dates from inference and by means of other dated monuments. In Ramesses' Year 8 (c.1272–1271 B.C.), a sharp campaign was conducted in Canaan, extending eastward into Moab, where there were strong indications of a slackening of allegiance to Egypt. Ramesses was accompanied by his oldest son, Amonhikhopshef, who was allowed to conduct a foray on his own. Apparently the opposition put up little fight, and it was not long before Egyptian forces could move north as far as Damascus, recovering parts of the territory that had defected to the Hittites after Qadesh. A list of the places retaken or captured anew was carved on the front pylon of the Ramesseum, although many of the names have been lost.

Encouraged by his relatively easy success in the south of the Levantine lands, Ramesses directed his forces north into Syria, into lands that were more directly affected by Hittite suzerainty. After reasserting his control over the seaports of Lebanon, he turned east,

driving north to Qadesh along the Orontes valley, subduing the small principalities of Dapur and Tunip. He set his mark on Dapur characteristically by having a statue of himself erected there. No trace has survived. The Egyptians were playing a dangerous game in campaigning so openly in regions which were nominally under Hittite control; but it is very probable that Ramesses engaged in such provocative action because he knew through good intelligence that Hatti was troubled not only by threats from the east, but also by internal dynastic squabbling. At about the time of the campaign of Years 8–9, the Hittite king Muwatallis died and was formally succeeded by Urhi-Teshub, his young son by a concubine, whose position was challenged by his active uncle Hattusilis. Ruling as Mursilis II, Urhi-Teshub had a short and uneasy reign, and he was eventually supplanted by Hattusilis in abour 1264–1263 B.C., Year 16 of Ramesses.

In the meanwhile not much seems to have passed between Egypt and Hatti. The

78 left
Detail of a Syrian fortress attacked by Ramesses II, as shown by Rosellini. The defenders are slaughtered by the king's arrows, while, below, cattle are driven away to escape from the Egyptians.

78 right
Scene from the north wall of the great hall at Abu Simbel as drawn by Franz Chrétien Gau in the early nineteenth century. Ramesses II attacks a Syrian fortress, supported by his sons in chariots.

79
Rosellini's depiction of the three princes in chariots, supporting their father Ramesses in his attack on a Syrian fortress: Amonhikhopshef, Ramesses, and Prehiwonemef, the three oldest, but scarcely old enough to engage seriously in battle.

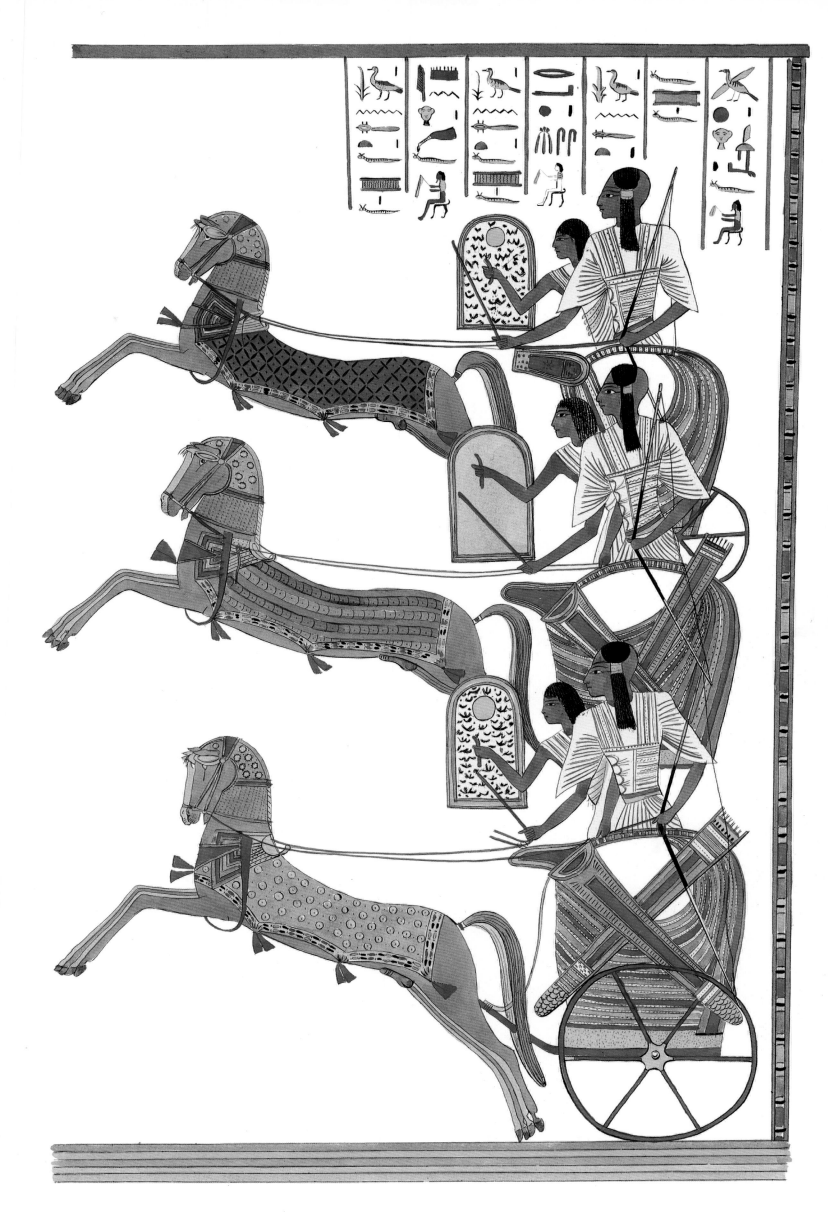

Detail of the relief in the Ramesseum depicting the assault on Dapur in the Orontes Valley, a Hittite stronghold. This kind of action-filled scene, not in horizontal registers, was developed in the Nineteenth Dynasty.

The Assault on Dapur; a drawing by Rosellini. Ramesses directs from his chariot, and his troops engage with the enemy on foot and in chariots, while others use ladders to scale the walls of the citadel.

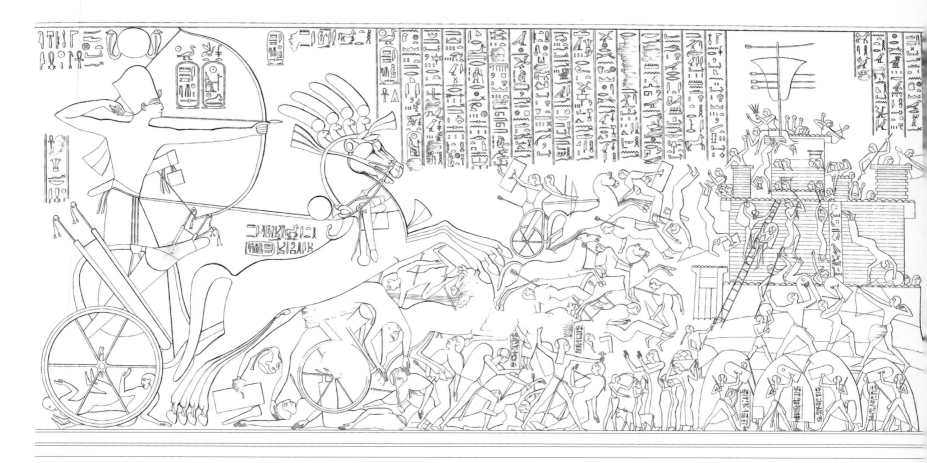

last dated campaign into Asia took place in Ramesses' Year 10, commemorated by a very damaged stela at the Nahr al-Kalb in Lebanon. It may have recorded yet another small foray into Syria, perhaps to recover Dapur and Tunip. These towns may have reverted to the Hittites, and an assault to recover them seems to be depicted in reliefs in the Luxor temple and the Ramesseum. In the accompanying text Ramesses boasted that he took part in the battle without troubling to put on his body armor, and only bothering to collect it after spending two hours in the field. No further dated texts have been found referring to Asiatic activities until Year 18. In the intervening time it is quite probable that further expeditions were sent into Asia, whether led by Ramesses or by one of his sons. It seems unlikely that Ramesses would have failed to test the political temperature of the region, especially as there was much movement from Assyria to the east, and internal trouble in Hatti. Peace, on the other hand may have seemed a favorable alternative to war; campaigning was expensive, especially in Asia Minor and the Levant, if no tribute was being received from vassal peoples. Revenues from the region were undoubtedly much reduced

from what they had been in the heyday of the Egyptian Empire one hundred years earlier. But the necessity to show the flag weighed heavily on Egyptian monarchs of the New Kingdom. Minor irritations such as local defections, as well as probings into the imperial domain by peripheral states owing ultimate allegiance to Hatti (or, increasingly, to the Assyrians), could develop into serious confrontations. An unusual source of irritation between Egypt and Hattusilis, the Hittite king, developed when the usurped Urhi-Teshub, at first exiled to central Syria, fled as a political refugee to Egypt. From Hittite sources it emerges that this unexpected development contained the seeds of possible conflict. It happened in about 1262–1261 B.C. Hattusilis demanded the handing over of Urhi-Teshub, but Ramesses refused. Hittite annoyance was extreme, and a serious confrontation, that might have led to a repeat of the Qadesh campaign, was threatened. It was not, however, a good time for Hattusilis to march south. As for Ramesses, he seems to have felt that some steps should be taken to indicate his readiness to fight, even if he had no particular desire to do so in the cause of Urhi-Teshub. A large formal inscription

dated in Year 18 was set up at Beth-Shan in the north of Canaan. Its text is of the kind sometimes called 'rhetorical'; it praises the king and vaunts his achievements without stating any specific actions. Historically, therefore, it tells us very little, except that it was set up in Asiatic lands in Year 18. Whether or not Ramesses himself accompanied any army that may have moved into Canaan in that year is not stated. The text is full of eulogy and bombast. It could serve as a marker of what might happen if a new and serious war started. Nothing seems to have followed. The saber-rattling had presumably been effective. Things had at last settled down in Asia as far as Egypt was concerned. There seemed little prospect of advantage in renewing large-scale military activities. Hattusilis on the Hittite side had much to engross his attention without engaging unnecessarily in conflict with Egypt. Assyria had now become a distinct and serious threat from the east. Why, then, continue the tense relationship with Egypt when a treaty of mutual support might be negotiated? Consequently, long, drawn-out negotiations with Egypt began, which ended in about 1259–1258 B.C., Year 21 of Ramesses II.

Generally speaking, formal treaties were not commonly entered into by Egypt. The kinds of foreign policies followed by Egyptian kings scarcely ever involved adversaries who would have been considered on equal footing with Egypt. For the Hittites, however, the case was very different, and so too for other major players on the diplomatic stage of Western Asia. Formal treaties were regularly used to establish peaceful relations both with important foreign powers and also with less important, but significant, vassal states. It may be assumed, therefore, that the impetus for a treaty came from the Hittite side, and that the negotiations leading to the preparation of an acceptable text were conducted mostly in Hatti and not in Egypt. There seem to have been perhaps two treaties of earlier dates between the two countries, so that the idea of such a diplomatic agreement was not entirely novel to the Egyptians. Nevertheless the ending of hostilities could not have come as an unwelcome development to Egypt.

By exceptional but fortunate chance, the text of the treaty has survived in Egyptian and Hittite versions. Two monumental inscriptions, one in Karnak and one in the Ramesseum, give the Egyptian version. The Hittite version has survived on a clay tablet found at Hattusas,

the capital of Hatti; it is written not in Hittite but in Babylonian cuneiform, which was much used for international diplomatic exchanges at that time. It may represent the agreed text, drawn up in Hattusas and sent to Piramesse, where presumably it was translated into Egyptian. The hieroglyphic version represents a further stage of textual transmission from a hieratic rendering on papyrus. From the reading of the hieroglyphic text it is made clear that the original text was the one sent by Hattusilis, inscribed on a silver plate or tablet. It arrived in Piramesse on the twenty-first day of the first month of winter, Year 21 of Ramesses II, that is, late in about 1259 B.C. The text given in hieroglyphs follows precisely the text on the cuneiform tablet, with some changes in the order of the sections resulting probably from a misunderstanding by the Egyptian secretaries who prepared the translation. An Egyptian version was presumably sent back to Hatti to clinch the agreement.

The treaty clearly represented a very important diplomatic event. Nothing in the text suggests that either side played politics in claiming credit for the agreement. Important envoys from Hattusas brought the silver tablet with the text of the treaty, made by Hattusilis, the great ruler of Hatti, son of Mursilis II and grandson of

Suppululiumas, for Usimare-Setpenre (Ramesses II), great ruler of Egypt, son of Menmare (Sethos I) and grandson of Menpehtyre (Ramesses I) to establish peace and brotherhood between them forever. The main text begins with a short historical preamble. Then the clauses of the agreement establish that peace should remain between the two countries forever. Neither party will encroach on the lands of the other. If an enemy attacks Egypt, Hatti will come to help, or send suitable help; and the same should happen if an enemy attack Hatti. If fugitives flee from Egypt to Hatti, they will be extradited back to Egypt; and so too for fugitives from Hatti to Egypt; in neither case should severe action be taken against the returned fugitives. The gods of Hatti and of Egypt are then called upon to witness the treaty. The Egyptian version of the agreement ends with a detailed description of the two circular seals stamped on the reverse of the silver tablet – a positive indication that the Hittite text was the basis for the Egyptian version.

Although Egyptian sources are silent about reactions to the Hittite treaty, this is not unusual. In the absence of appropriate documents nothing can be known. But from Hittite sources it becomes evident that there was relief and pleasure on both sides. Hattusilis wrote a congratulatory

letter to Ramesses, and the two principal queens, Puduhepa and Nefertari, similarly exchanged enthusiastic greetings and gifts. Letters of approval were received in Hattusas from the queen mother Tuy (widow of Sethos I); from Sethhikhopshef, at that point the oldest surviving king's son, and therefore crown prince; and even from the distinguished vizier Paser. The richness of surviving documents on the Hittite side considerably enlarge our knowledge of the extent to which exchanges could be made between Near Eastern countries both on the diplomatic level and the personal. Clay tablets, the common medium for international correspondence at this time, do not easily deteriorate, and if burned become terra cotta, which is even more durable. Papyrus documents, on the other hand, unless preserved in very dry conditions, are destroyed by damp or by insects, and would never survive fire. The Delta, unlike Thebes, was damp and not kind to organic remains. At least major documents might be set up in temples, carved in stone.

It would take some years before the Hittites and the Egyptians would achieve a reasonable *modus vivendi*. Mutual distrust could hardly be dispelled by the signing of a treaty. Again from Hittite records, it appears that Hattusilis had reason to object

to a tendency on Ramesses' part to treat him as less than an equal. Similarly, there was some tension over the continued exile in Egypt of Urhi-Teshub. His flight from Hatti had taken place before the treaty was concluded, and its terms over fugitives were not to be applied retroactively. Ramesses seems to have done nothing about the ex-king's presence in Egypt, and there is no evidence to suggest that the Hittite refugee plotted against his uncle. Indeed, he probably enjoyed the small niche he had been granted in the Egyptian court, and ceased to be considered a threat at Hattusas. When negotiations began toward arranging a marriage between Ramesses and the daughter of Hattusilis and Puduhepa, the Hittite queen even suggested to Ramesses that he should consult Urhi-Teshub about the parlous state of the Hittite treasury.

In the matter of this marriage, which was concluded in Ramesses' Year 34 (c.1246–1245 B.C.), while the event itself was celebrated by monumental texts set up in Egypt and Nubia (the best preserved in the great temple at Abu Simbel), again the accounts of preliminary negotiations have been found, in part at least, in the Hittite archives. From the formal Egyptian inscriptions the impression is gained that the event resulted ultimately from Ramesses' own

victorious activities in Asia and against the Hittites. He claimed outrageously that he had conquered Hatti entirely on his own, and that the Hittites were obliged thereafter to pay annual tribute to Egypt, so draining the treasury in Hattusas. The inscription further describes attempts made by the Hittites on an annual basis to appease Ramesses, but such efforts were met with no favorable response. In the end the Hittite king consulted his army and high officials, suggesting that he should offer his eldest daughter as a wife to Ramesses, together with what treasure remained in their coffers. The Egyptian text continues with an account of the dispatch of the daughter with quantities of precious metals, slaves, and livestock, and of Ramesses' delight when he heard of her approach. It is reported as if he had no idea of what was happening, as if it were all a great surprise. So an escort was sent to accompany the bridal procession through the last stages of the journey. It arrived in Piramesse in the third month of winter, Year 34. Ramesses was very pleased with his new wife, and she was given the Egyptian name Mahor-neferure, which means something like 'she is one who sees Horus, the beauty of Re,' Horus presumably being Ramesses himself. Sometimes the name was abbreviated to Maneferure. The reality behind the marriage may have been significantly different. Hittite

82 top left
Cuneiform tablet with the text of a letter from Ramesses II to the Hittite Queen Puduhepa. It is written in Akkadian, and concerns the sending of envoys to pour rich oil on the head of the future Queen Mahor-neferure (Istanbul, Bo.1231).

82 top right
Cuneiform tablet with a letter from Ramesses II to Queen Puduhepa concerning the marriage of her daughter. He calls Puduhepa "sister," and assures her that his new wife will be well treated as a queen in Egypt (Ankara Museum, 24265).

83 top
Cuneiform tablet with a prayer in Hittite addressed to the sun-goddess Arinna by Queen Puduhepa, seeking the goddess's intervention for the health of the ailing king: "Grant life to Hattusilis, your servant" (Istanbul, Bo.2125+2370+8159).

84 top
Cuneiform tablet with a text in Hittite recording a legal protocol brought by Queen Puduhepa against certain people accused of diverting property entrusted to them. It demonstrates the authority of the queen (Istanbul, Bo.2131).

84 center
Seal impression with a design including a winged sun-disk and the names and titles of King Hattusilis and Queen Puduhepa, written in Hittite hieroglyphs on the face, and in Hittite cuneiform in the margin (Çorum Museum, 1.229.90).

records in the form of letters and other documents, rather less formal than the Egyptian grand inscriptions, suggest that the course of events began with the offer by Hattusilis of his oldest daughter as a bride, together with a bigger dowry than anything similar in recent times. Some kind of haggling followed, including the intervention by Queen Puduhepa, who pointed out that resources were not too great on the Hittite side, a fact that Ramesses could confirm by reference to Urhi-Teshub, as mentioned earlier. She chided Ramesses for claiming that he also was impoverished, and she was worried that after the marriage her daughter would be kept in isolation, and not allowed to receive visits from Hittite envoys. The exchanges between Ramesses and the Hittite royal couple probably lasted for several months or longer; in the end all difficulties were resolved, and Puduhepa announced that it was time for envoys to come from Egypt to pour rich oil over her daughter's head, no doubt an important element in the betrothal ceremonies. So, ritually committed, or sanctified, she could travel to Egypt. There were no more difficulties, the envoys came, the oil was poured, and Puduhepa, who took a leading part in the negotiations, announced that "on that day, the two mighty countries had become one country, and you, the two mighty kings, had found true brotherhood."

The marriage seems to have been a success, both in political terms and in respect to Ramesses' regard for Mahor-neferure. No serious differences between Egypt and Hatti apparently occurred during the rest of Ramesses' reign. Also for the Hittites new, tempting opportunities were available. From the Hittite archives evidence emerges to suggest that Egypt became a fancied place for important visits by influential Hittites. Egypt, it seems, had been discovered as a desirable tourist venue.

The life and the climate of Piramesse were very different from what was experienced in the Anatolian heartland of the Hittite empire. One important visitor was the Hittite crown prince Hishmi-Sharruma, who would succeed Hattusilis in about 1237 B.C., taking the name of Tudhaliyas. Ramesses also attempted to bring Hattusilis himself to Egypt. The Hittite, possibly suspecting a plot, showed no eagerness to accept the invitation, giving as an excuse his wondering what he would do in Egypt. The reason may have been more fundamental. Hittite kings were much occupied with ritual activities, and it may have been the case that Hattusilis saw nothing but danger in a long absence from Hattusas. Unfortunately Hittite records do not tell of the outcome of this exchange of courtesies, and it seems possible that the visit was finally cancelled because Hattusilis developed problems with his feet. It is

tantalizing to speculate whether a meeting between the two great kings did ever take place, if not in Egypt, then in Canaan or Syria. Further, did Egyptian doctors help to heal Hattusilis' feet? The possibility is suggested in Hittite sources, and it is known that Egyptian medicine was highly thought of in the Near East at this time. An echo of such medical help may be found in the story of the princess of Bakhtan, ostensibly dated to Ramesses' reign, but inscribed a thousand years later. We shall return to this story toward the end of this book. The mentioning of Mahor-neferure on a colossal statue found at Tanis, and on a number of small objects, indicates her ready acceptance into the court of Ramesses II, and there is no reason to doubt that Ramesses was happy with this testimony to the Hittite alliance. Nothing, sadly, is known of her later life, and it is not impossible that she died prematurely. It is known, however, that a

second Hittite princess joined Ramesses as a wife some time before the death of Hattusilis in about 1237 B.C. (Year 44). The event is commemorated on two stelae, one found at Coptos, cult-center of the god Min about forty miles north of Thebes, and the other, much damaged, at Abydos. Not so much fuss was made on this occasion, although a large dowry accompanied the princess in her progress to Egypt; no great greeting party was sent to accompany her on the last stages of her journey. It was not such a significant diplomatic occasion as the earlier marriage: peace was well established between Hatti and Egypt; it was almost a routine event. Not even the name of the princess is included in the inscriptions. In a few years Hattusilis would be dead, but the change of ruler seems to have made little difference to the good relations between the two powerful kingdoms. And so it remained for the rest of Ramesses' reign.

84-85
A relief from Fraktin, in central Turkey, showing the remarkable status of Queen Puduhepa in relation to her husband Hattusilis. She offers a libation to the great Hittite goddess Arinna, while the king separately performs a similar ceremony for the weather god.

A papyrus in the Berlin Museum contains a literary composition of the kind called a 'model letter.' It is not a real letter, but one composed as an exercise, probably for student scribes. Such letters usually contain lists of places, commodities, and equipment, and they presumably were intended to test the abilities of young scribes to deal with rare vocabulary and unusual names. The Berlin letter, written in a good Nineteenth Dynasty hand, purports to having been sent by a senior Egyptian official in Nubia, called by the common name Paser. He requests the unnamed recipient to prepare the tribute to be sent. Then comes the list of commodities to be included; some are strictly Nubian, others come from tropical Africa to the South, brought to Nubia along ancient trade routes. There are domestic cattle and wild creatures like gazelles, oryx, ostriches, monkeys, and baboons; animal products like ivory, panther skins, and ostrich feathers; plant products like ebony and special fan-shaped palm fronds; and much gold and semi-precious stones – hematite, jasper, amethyst, crystal. In addition there was human tribute, people from Irem, tall Terek people, and Nehesyu (a general name for Nubians). Paser advises his correspondent to increase the contributions every year. This list demonstrates the value of Nubia as a source of unusual and precious materials, above all gold, the greater part of the Egyptian supply of which came from Nubian mines.

In the Nubian temple of Bayt al-Wali, now re-erected just south of the new High Dam, there are exceptionally well-designed and carved low-relief scenes of warfare, with one series devoted to a campaign against Nubians in which sons of Ramesses, Amonhiwonemef, and Khaemwese took part. If this campaign took place very early in his reign, or even when Ramesses was still co-regent, as has been suggested, then these sons would have been almost infants. After the rout of the Nubians, the presentation of tribute is shown, here supervised by the Nubian viceroy Amenemope, whose father was a Paser. The splendid procession of tribute could be seen as a complete illustration of the list of products itemized in the model letter in Berlin. There are additions: a giraffe, ostrich eggs, ostrich-feather fans, and bows. No doubt the list of Nubian products was to a great extent traditional, even standardized; but there may be no doubt about the actuality of the campaign depicted. It may, however, have been quite a modest skirmish in Lower Nubia, scarcely warranting more than a mention, but used in this temple as a vehicle for a heroic scene of battle, and a highly imaginative scene of tribute. No small campaign in Lower Nubia would have yielded the tribute from tropical Africa shown at Bayt al-Wali.

86-87

Ramesses presents two files of Nubian prisoners to Amon-Re of Thebes and the goddess Mut, between whom sits the deified Ramesses himself, with a sun-disk on his head and ram's horns. Abu Simbel; by Rosellini.

Ramesses II

88-89
*A scene of triumph in Abu Simbel: after
an unspecified campaign against Nubia,
Ramesses returns with files of Nubian
captives. The text describes him as "the
Good God, strong of horns, who strikes
the South and tramples on the North."*

Ramesses II and the External World

Ramesses II

90-91
*Nubian captives on their knees with
arms bound tight, and all roped
together. From the base of the
colossal figure of Ramesses II on the
south side of the entrance to the
great Abu Simbel temple.*

90 center
*Rosellini's illustration of a scene in
the Nubian temple of Bayt al-Wali, in
which Ramesses II srikes a Nubian
chief. The king is "the Good God who
subdues the nine bows and tramples
on the leaders of vile Kush."*

90 bottom
*Rosellini's outline drawing of a
Nubian and an Asiatic prisoner,
arms tied and roped together,
kneeling before the king. From their
dress, both captives are shown to be
men of importance.*

91 right
*Cartouche containing the nomen of
Ramesses II, Ramessu-Meryamun
(Ramesses-beloved-of-Amun). The
sign representing Ra is here not a
simple sun, but a divine figure with
falcon-head wearing the sun disk.*

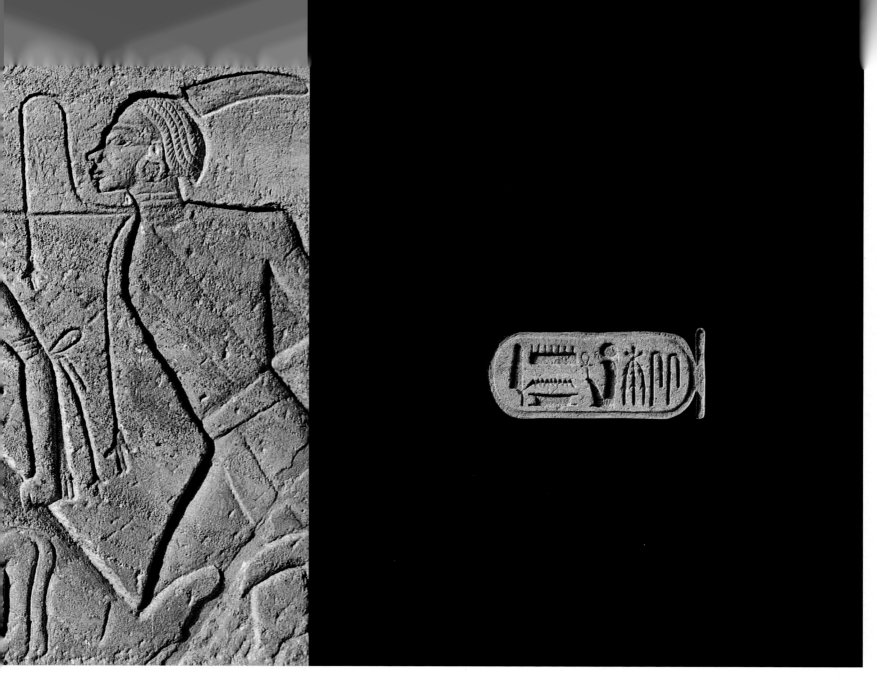

For most of Ramesses' reign, Nubia remained a peaceful land, well settled by Egyptians, but not on a permanent basis. Nubia was very different from the Asiatic territories so regularly troublesome to Egypt. Nubia was in a sense a continuation of Egypt to the south, linked to Egypt by the Nile. It was valued as a source of raw materials, and as the conduit for goods from tropical Africa. But it was never considered as part of Egypt proper. Egypt began in the south at Elephantine (Aswan); what lay beyond was territory that could be dominated, but not integrated into Egypt. It was a kind of external province to be administered by the Nubian viceroy, known formally as the 'King's Son of Kush.' The hinterland of the Nile valley in Nubia was vast, home to tribes ever ready to exploit Egyptian weaknesses, with a tradition of strong local princes, and in earlier times a powerful principality based on Kerma, south of the third cataract. During the Middle Kingdom, when Nubia was first seriously occupied by Egyptians, a series of commanding forts was constructed in the region of the second cataract. These forts were lost to Egypt in the Second Intermediate Period but reoccupied and rehabilitated in the Eighteenth Dynasty. To a great extent they had lost their

strategic value by the reign of Ramesses II; they were superseded by settlements and towns constructed more for reasons of trade and administration than security. Strangely, following the establishing of temples and towns under King Amenophis III at places like Soleb, Sesebi, and Sedeinga, great interest was shown in these rather remote reaches of the Nile by Akhenaten, at least in the early years of his reign; traces of structures built at that time have even been found recently at Kerma, once the center of Nubian native power. Towns were founded in Nubia under Ramesses II, and a new administrative center was developed at Amara, between the second and third cataracts; it was given the resounding name Piramesse-Miamun, 'the house (or town) of Ramesses, beloved of Amun.' It became the principal Nubian base of the viceroy of Kush, which had formerly been at the fortress of Buhen at the second cataract, and at Miam (Aniba) farther north, opposite the rocky bluff of Qasr Ibrim. The impression is certainly gained that Nubia was no longer troublesome, an impression reinforced by the statements of achievement found in inscriptions of high officials who served in these southern lands. In particular,

the viceroy of Kush Setau, who held office in the latter part of Ramesses' reign, concentrates on non-warlike activities. We shall examine his personal record later in this book. Here, however, it is worth mentioning that in his great stela set up in the temple of Wadi al-Sabua, Setau mentions a campaign against Irem, a part of Nubia that has not been located with certainty. It may lie to the west of the Nile, to the south of the third cataract, in the region once dominated by the kingdom of Kerma. A tradition of independence perhaps still persisted there, well removed as the region was from the centers of Egyptian power in Nubia. Seti I had been obliged to deal with an uprising in Irem, in a small campaign in which the young Ramesses had taken part. Then, in Year 38 of Ramesses (c.1242 B.C.) or possibly a little later, trouble in Irem led to another punitive campaign, which yielded over seven thousand captives; it was graphically recorded on the town walls of Amara. On this occasion several sons of Ramesses had their small experience of active service, of whom the names of only two have survived: Merenptah, ultimate successor of his father, and Setemuia, his eighth son, who did not outlive Ramesses.

92 top
Asiatic prisoner from one of
the lines of foreign captives
shown at Abu Simbel.
Although the theme of
captives is much repeated, the
individual carving of their
heads is noticeably distinctive,
not repetitive.

Perhaps the most remarkable part of Ramesses' activities in Nubia was the construction of temples. He did not inaugurate the practice of temple-building in the country – it had a history extending back in a modest manner to the Twelfth Dynasty, and more substantially to the beginning of the Eighteenth Dynasty – but he developed it to an extraordinary degree, for reasons which passed far beyond simple devotion to the great gods of Egypt. We shall return to this matter in a later chapter. One of the temples constructed late in the reign, under the supervision of the viceroy Setau at Wadi al-Sabua, was built partly with the help of captive labor. A smaller inscription also erected in that temple by Setau and dated to Year 44 (c.1236 B.C.) records the sending of a punitive expedition led by an officer named Ramose into the Tjemeh-land to acquire labor for the building of the temple. There has been much debate about the precise location of Tjemeh-land. It certainly lay to the west of the Nile valley, and contained peoples who from time to time sought to infiltrate the fertile land of Egypt. It may not be a precise geographical designation, but a vague name for 'those out there to the west.' In the later Nineteenth Dynasty, Tjemehu seems to be used more precisely for tribal groups threatening Egypt from further north, on the west side of the Delta. Other words occur for these western infiltrators, like Tjehenu and Meshwesh, who also seem mostly to inhabit the northern and coastal regions of modern Libya. The word Libya, or Libu in ancient Egyptian, occurs for the first time in a papyrus of the Nineteenth Dynasty in the British Museum containing so-called scribal exercises like the mock letter describing the products of Nubia. In a passage containing an encomium of Ramesses II, after some general account of his triumphs over foreign lands, the scribe writes: "Libu is fallen to his slaughtering, fallen to his knife."

It would appear that no great organized power existed out to the west, comparable with Hatti or the Assyrian empire in the east. But, as in Nubia, there were 'peoples,' tribes, some probably settled in or near the oases in the Western Desert, others in the more fertile coastal plains. Their movements could be checked by occasional punitive expeditions, which could also be used for the 'recruitment' of workmen for temple-building, or even for the Egyptian army. However, the attraction of the fertile Egyptian lands exercised a strong pull on the western peoples, and later in the Nineteenth Dynasty serious campaigns had to be mounted to defeat their inroads into the Delta. It is likely that the threat of such inroads already existed in the reign of Ramesses II, but could for the time being be settled by occasional forays. The threat for the future remained, and steps were taken by Ramesses to secure the western approaches to the Delta by the construction of desert forts.

Traces of possible forts, not yet properly investigated, suggest that they were built at intervals of about two days' march, and the largest, and perhaps the last in the chain, is at Zawiyat Umm al-Rakham, over two hundred miles to the west of Alexandria, in the neighborhood of Marsa Matruh. Recent excavations have shown that it was much more than a simple fortress. The main enclosure measures about 15,000 square meters (16,500 square yards) with massive mud-brick walls more than 4 meters thick, and one great gateway flanked by towers clad in limestone. There are the remains of a small temple and a number of storage magazines containing pottery vessels from Canaan and the eastern Mediterranean lands. The fort seems to have doubled as a trading center, or at least a place for landfall for trading vessels arriving in Egyptian territory in an area where they might be attacked and plundered by Libyan tribes. At that time there were no recognized ports on the western side of the Delta – Alexandria would not be founded for nearly one thousand years. The commandant of the fort at the time when the inscribed doorframes of the magazines were installed was called Nebre. Excavation has not yet revealed whether Nebre was ever called upon to engage in punitive forays against the Tjemehu, the Tjehenu, the Meshwesh, or the Libu, or to defend the fort against direct attack. At such a distant outpost of Egyptian power, many days away from the nearest places that could be considered to be in Egypt, the garrison may well have felt isolated, but ready to kill time by engaging in modest trade well away from the sharp-eyed government officials who supervised imports and the collection of duty at the more regular ports of entry into the Delta from the Mediterranean.

Ramesses II

94 and 95
Two details of the scene of Ramesses II slaying Libyans. Left: he treads firmly on the head of the fallen foe. Right: he grasps the upraised arm of the standing Libyan before spearing him.

96-97
Photograph of the scene depicted by Rosellini. It demonstrates vividly the energy and stark realism of the actual wall carving, unencumbered by coloring and detail.

Mention was made in the first chapter of this book of the oppression in Egypt and the Exodus of the Children of Israel. Further consideration needs to be made at this point. The Israelites were a foreign people in Egypt who made their escape with disastrous consequences for the forces of Egypt – so goes the biblical account. There is no evidence from Egypt to confirm the presence of Israelites in the country at any time, and none to confirm the biblical account of the Exodus. This lack of evidence has not deterred scholars from postulating what may lie behind the biblical account, and from assigning dates to the various events and stages of 'enslavement' mentioned in the Bible. Views differ widely. Some believe that the mentions of Ramesses in the Bible should not be taken at face value. For the Israelites at the time when the texts of the biblical books were established, the name Ramesses could have been invoked as the very embodiment of Egyptian power and tyranny. So the name was included anachronistically; its use was almost an irrelevance, a red herring. The oppression and Exodus should then be taken back to the beginning of the Eighteenth Dynasty, to the time when Egypt was being purged of the Hyksos (Asiatic) rulers and their peoples, who had dominated parts of Egypt for many years. Other scholars take a more literal view of the biblical narrative, maintaining that the construction of Piramesse took place near the beginning of Ramesses II's reign. Then the Exodus could be dated to the middle of his reign. A more generally accepted view is that the oppression continued during Ramesses' reign, but that the Exodus occurred under Merenptah, his successor. In the absence of better evidence than is at present available, I cannot see how the question can be resolved. The idea that foreigners might be impressed to work on royal buildings is, however, well established; the case of the carrying off by Ramose of Libyans to work on the temple at Wadi al-Sabua demonstrates conclusively that such exploitation did take place. It was surely not exceptional, and Israelites may indeed have been used to work on Piramesse and Pithom. So it is not difficult to believe that the oppression did take place during the reign of Ramesses II. The date of the Exodus is another matter; it must remain undecided until the unlikely discovery of new and clinching evidence. The last twenty or more years of Ramesses' reign passed with scarcely any recorded troubles with external powers. For more than twenty years – longer than the reigns of most Egyptian kings – peace prevailed between Egypt and those lands from which trouble traditionally came. There was peace, but trouble was brewing in the east and in the west. No surviving records from the time suggest that Egypt regretted the absence of conflict, or Ramesses the opportunity to display once again his military prowess. When he died in about 1213 B.C. it was already his Year 67. He was a very old man, a survivor from heroic times. In this way he would surely have wanted us to remember him, even if the reality at times had not been so heroic.

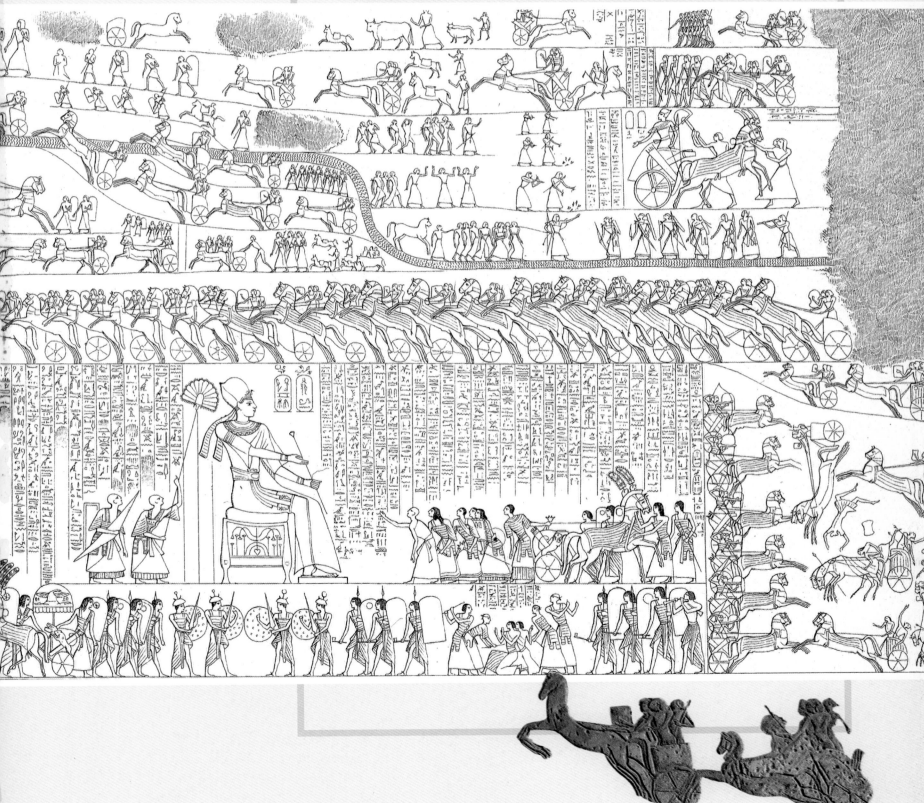

106
Some of the large party of reinforcements, the Nearin, who had marched from the coast of Amurru, arriving at a crucial moment in the battle. The force consisted of infantry and chariotry; a phalanx of the infantry is shown here. At Abu Simbel.

107
At Abu Simbel the two main scenes of the Egyptian camp and of the battle of Qadesh are separated by a register of chariotry, both Egyptian and Hittite, riding in all directions. Rosellini's depiction.

It will be recalled that interest in western Asia was actively revived in the reign of Sethos I, and one campaign succeeded in re-establishing Egyptian influence in parts of Canaan and Lebanon. Ramesses II conducted his first campaign into Asia in his Year 4 (c.1276–1275 B.C.), achieving some limited gains but at the same time alerting the Hittite king Muwatallis to the threat offered to his southern client states which had acknowledged Hittite suzerainty. The way in which events could develop to the disadvantage of Hatti was signaled by the defection of the land of Amurru, occupying roughly the seaboard of Lebanon. This change of allegiance may have provided the crucial factor which determined the future course of action for Muwatallis. Power politics in the Near East were always complicated, and the Hittites could not risk ignoring the additional threat from distant Egypt. There was surely a fair degree of understanding between Hatti and Egypt about how things were turning. Diplomatic contacts between the two powers were well established, and it must be supposed that both sides realized that the issue could only be resolved by a passage of arms, a full-scale encounter between the armies of both sides. Skirmishing would not settle the matter.

To this end, therefore, both sides set about preparing for the expected clash. It would occur, if not by mutual arrangement, almost certainly by tacit understanding, on 'neutral' territory, that is, neither in Egypt proper nor in the heartland of Hatti in the Anatolian uplands. Lebanon and the lands to the east represented the region for a classic encounter; it may be doubted, however, that this 'away' fixture for both sides had a venue fixed in advance. Much depended for the timing and the place on the intelligence collected by both sides, with the knowledge that the campaign season usually began in the late spring when some months of good weather could reasonably be expected.

And so, following Ramesses' campaign of Year 4, during the autumn and winter months, both sides made ready for the next campaign season. On the Egyptian side, apart from his native infantry and chariotry, Ramesses had at his disposal troops called Sherden, who are described as having been captured by the king in battle. The Sherden were a people from the sea who from time to time launched piratical raids on the Delta coast, with or without the encouragement of the Libyans. They are generally thought to be the people who ultimately gave their name to the island of Sardinia, and who might have come in

earlier times from the region of the Caucasus. They were good professional fighters, distinctively armed with long swords and helmets fitted with horns and spikes ending in circular knobs. By the time of Ramesses II many may have been settled in fortresses in the Delta, prepared to fight as mercenaries in Pharaoh's army. They formed a distinct contingent in the army that Ramesses led out from the frontier fortress of Tjel (Sile) on the sixth day of the second summer month of his Year 5.

What was the opposition to be? Rather formidable! Muwatallis had not wasted his time, or spared his clients and allies in collecting a force made up of contingents from "all the foreign lands as far as the sea." So said the Egyptian account, which then lists the places which provided these contingents: Hatti itself in force; then Naharin, the most important of the Hittite allies, often in confrontation, but for the moment in alliance; it lay to the east and south. From the west support came from Arzawa, Luka, Pidasa, Masa, and Dardany, the last being undoubtedly the Homeric Dardanoi, here first mentioned in surviving records. Beyond the Hittite heartland to the north, the land of Keshkesh on the Black Sea sent a contingent, and from the east of Asia Minor, Kizzuwadna joined forces.

108-109
*Among the Egyptian forces was
a detachment of Sherden, ancestors
of the Sardinians who were
distinguished by their horned
helmets and round shields.
Here they are shown with Egyptian
infantry in Rosellini's illustration.*

There were contingents listed from principalities closer to Qadesh, including that city itself, along with Carchemish, and Ugarit on the Levantine coast. Other places less easily located also joined in. It was a formidable grouping – 'coalition' is probably not the right description; Muwatallis had called in all his favors, and most places had obliged and responded to the Hittite demand. According to figures attached to scenes in the Pictorial Record, two groups of forces on the Hittite side are given as 18,000 and 19,000, and a force of 2,500 chariots is specified. There is nothing to indicate whether these figures represent the totality of the fighting troops

facing the Egyptians, but it should be remembered that warfare in those distant times was not conducted on a vast scale. There is, furthermore, little reason to accept the Egyptian figures.

On the Egyptian side, Ramesses' forces were organized into four divisions, named after the major gods, Amun, Re (or Pre, as he is called in these texts), Ptah, and Sutekh (or Seth), the tutelary deity of the Nineteenth Dynasty. Apart from the Sherden, impressed troops who marched with the main army, Ramesses also expected to be helped in due course by a force of Nearin, being mustered on the coast in Amurru. They would prove their

worth at a most crucial point in the coming battle. In considering the arrangements to be made in preparation for a substantial campaign in antiquity, we must appreciate the difficulties of communication over long distances and rough terrain, and the need to prepare well in advance orders for the movement of troops which would actually work out fairly precisely when a planned engagement took place. So many campaigns in medieval and modern times have failed to develop in accordance with initial plans, and the ability of a commander to improvise on the ground has often determined whether or not the

outcome was successful. How difficult it must have been both for Ramesses and for Muwatallis in the thirteenth century B.C. to ensure that all the contingents turned up on time and in the right place, according to plan! In the case of the Qadesh campaign, success and failure on both sides were to be determined by prompt action or improvisation, bad timing, and poor communications. The unusual amount of tactical and strategic detail contained in the various compositions and scenes has enabled students of warfare to reconstruct the battle and its preliminaries with a high degree of probability.

110 top
First aid in Ramesses' camp before
reaching Qadesh. After the long march
from Egypt, the feet and legs of the
infantry needed much attention. This
intimate scene shows a soldier receiving
some sort of treatment from a comrade.

And now to the campaign. Armed no doubt with the best intelligence his agents could provide, Ramesses would have known that the forces of Hatti were on the move from the various countries of the Hittite alliance, ordered to muster at some convenient place in Syria, possibly Aleppo. Timing was crucial. From previous campaigns it would have been known how long a force of a certain size would need to travel from the eastern Delta to Qadesh or thereabouts. On this occasion, however, the forces were larger than previously employed, and the support and supply arrangements correspondingly more complex. Some day-to-day supplies would certainly be expected to be provided by the friendly (or vassal) peoples through which the army would pass; but much would have to be brought along from Egypt, notably the paraphernalia required for the Pharaoh, his sons, and his senior staff, including apparently the vizier of Lower Egypt. The distance from the eastern Delta to Qadesh was about 460 miles (643 kilometers) by a very direct route. Aleppo, on the other hand, was in relatively easy reach of the main Hittite force and contingents from countries like Naharin and Kizzuwadna; troops from the Black Sea coast and central and western Asia Minor had much farther to travel, but should have timed their arrival in northern Syria accordingly. At this point we may note with what a degree of disdain the writer of the Egyptian monumental texts regarded the Hittite forces, and in particular the Hittite king. He is never mentioned by name, but usually called "the Fallen One of Hatti," or even more dismissively, "the vile Fallen

One of Hatti." In public pronouncements in the ancient world, there was no room for politeness and magnanimity.

Leaving Egypt in the spring, the Egyptian army took precisely one month to travel to Djahy, a general name for Palestine/Canaan in its northern part. The journey had been without trouble, the army moving through the "narrow passes" as if it were traveling "on the roads of Egypt," and all along the route it was made welcome by the local peoples. Moving forward to the north, the army came to Shabtuna, a place seven or eight miles south of Qadesh. At this point Ramesses decided to press forward without delay, and closed up to Qadesh, where he received news that the "vile Fallen One of Qadesh" (a variant form of the insulting appellation of Muwatallis) was on the move with his mustered allies; and he was brought news of possible disaffection in the Hittite horde. Two

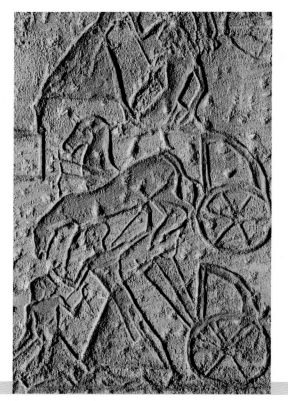

Shosu Bedouin came to Ramesses to report that their fellow tribesmen who were serving with the Hittites were prepared to defect and come over to the Egyptian side. They also informed the Egyptians that the enemy forces were massed in the region of Aleppo. This news – false as it turned out – was much better than Ramesses could have expected, and he decided without further checking to ford the Orontes river and set up camp to the northwest of Qadesh. He had in support his own immediate entourage and the division of Amun.

Without independent intelligence this was a rash move. Most of the Egyptian army lay far back to the rear, led by the division of Pre, followed by the divisions of Ptah and Seth, some miles further back in the woodlands to the south of Shabtuna. The country was such that it would not be easy to call up the successive divisions in support if a general battle developed. But a major engagement was not expected at that time, and Ramesses no doubt felt confident to prepare his camp within sight of Qadesh. That city itself was well protected from sudden attack.

The Orontes and a tributary flowing into it from the southwest, north of Qadesh, formed a natural moat all around the city except on the south side, and here the water protection had been completed by the cutting of a canal between the main river and the tributary. While his camp was being prepared, Ramesses had his traveling throne brought out and positioned in a kiosk, so that he could sit and observe Qadesh, the countryside around, and the activity of his troops.

111 top
Ramesses' tent within the compound of the Egyptian camp. It is marked by the king's prenomen flanked by two falcons with outstretched wings and sun disks – the god Re-Herakhty. Attendants pay their respects.

110 bottom
In scenes of Qadesh in Theban temples, one vignette shows a tussle between Egyptian and Hittite charioteers in a corner of the Egyptian camp – a preliminary skirmish, less clearly shown at Abu Simbel.

111 bottom
Time for running repairs on equipment before the battle commences. In this relief at Abu Simbel, craftsmen work on chariots, badly rattled by the rough roads of Syria; the one on the left uses an adze.

112-113 and 113 bottom
The hieroglyphs are explicit: "Coming of
Pharaoh's scout with two scouts of the
Fallen One of Hatti, into the presence of
Pharaoh. They beat them to say where
the vile Fallen One of Hatti is."
At Abu Simbel and in Rosellini's depiction.

113 top
Rosellini's illustration of Ramesses'
horses being made ready for the king.
A groom stands by waiting for his lord.
The horse, as is common in such scenes,
is splendidly caparisoned.

Then came an intelligence bombshell. His marauding scouts picked up two Hittite spies and brought them to the royal presence after their resolution had been softened by a severe beating; a vignette shows the wretched men being beaten with staves. They then readily told Ramesses that they were from the Hittite king, sent to discover the Egyptian positions. When Ramesses said that he had heard that his adversary was in the neighborhood of Aleppo, they told him that Muwatallis with all his forces was waiting in hiding to the east of Qadesh: "See," they said, "they stand armed and ready for combat behind Old Qadesh."

In fury, no doubt, and certainly in anxious anticipation of imminent trouble, Ramesses called a council of war to inform his advisers and commanders of what the

Hittite spies had told him. How could this have happened when he had been assured that the Hittites were many miles away at Aleppo? His commanders threw the blame chiefly on the rulers of the vassal lands through which the Egyptians had traveled, but also on Pharaoh's advisers. Daily situation reports should have kept him fully informed of the Hittite movements. And now the positions were reversed, with Muwatallis being fully informed of the movements of the Egyptian army, while his own army was ready and waiting in concealment behind Old Qadesh. The advantage lay with Muwatallis, and he did not delay in exploiting it, sending a force of chariots and infantry across the Orontes to cut through the division of Pre, and to swing round to attack directly the unfinished camp of the Egyptians.

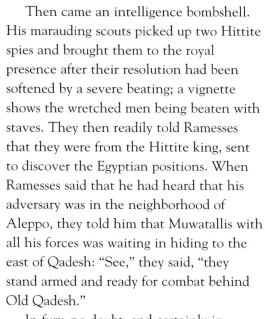

The Battle of Qadesh

There was near-panic in the Egyptian lines; hasty arrangements were made to evacuate the royal sons who had come on campaign, while Ramesses scrambled into his armor, ready for the fight. He had his chariot with his trusty horses, Victory-in-Thebes and Mut-is-contented, and somewhere about the camp was his pet lion Killer-of-his-enemies. It may not be doubted that at this critical juncture Ramesses, who was still a young man in his twenties, showed real courage and royal leadership. The official accounts of course make out that he alone was left to meet the enemy assault and bring about their defeat. The forces on the Hittite side at this moment included 2,500 chariots, by the Egyptian estimate. The battle was intense, and one may imagine that a very confused situation developed in which the troops of the division of Amun were unable to be deployed satisfactorily. In fact, Ramesses in his desperation felt that he had been deserted not just by the division of Amun but also by the great god Amun himself. He had to remind Amun of the extent of his devotion to him, and of the vast quantities of booty which had been lavished on him. Why was he deserting him? Naturally Ramesses' prayer of complaint was answered, and Amun came to his aid with unparalleled effect: he was "more efficient than millions of foot-soldiers and ten thousand of chariots." As a result Ramesses was fully reinvigorated; in his many charges he overcame the host of Hittite chariotry, securing a total victory.

114-115
Prisse d'Avennes' representation of Ramesses II in his chariot driving headlong into the Hittite enemy, which is scattered and trampled down. The lion on the arrow quiver holds a human head in its mouth. From the Ramesseum.

The Battle of Qadesh

116 bottom

*A bare-backed horseman rides off: "The
arrival of the scout to hasten the army."
In other Qadesh scenes he is said to be
hurrying the army of Ptah, as Pharaoh was
in the battle unsupported.*

117

*Rosellini's illustration of the encounter between
Egyptian and Hittite chariots, in which the
former are shown drawn up with arrows being
discharged in unison, while the latter are partly
disorganized and in disarray.*

The reality was rather different. Among the scenes in the Pictorial Record is one showing the arrival of a large force of reinforcements, advancing in perfect order. The accompanying text announces "the arrival of the Nearin of Pharaoh from the land of Amurru." These were the troops whom Ramesses had apparently mustered in Amurru to march to the east to join the Egyptians in the neighborhood of Qadesh. The name Nearin is a puzzle; it does not seem to refer to any particular place or tribe; it may mean 'young men,' and in military terms, perhaps 'newly raised troops.' Whatever the meaning, the Nearin arrived and, again according to the accompanying text, found the Egyptian camp surrounded and pressed by the Hittite attackers. In the camp "His Majesty sat alone without his army," hemmed in by hostile chariots. The text notes that the division of Amun had not completed the establishment of the camp, while the other divisions were still on the march, some being in the woods of Rabwy or Labwy. Then "the Nearin smashed into the host of the vile Fallen One of Hatti, just as it was on the point of entering Pharaoh's camp, and the entourage of His Majesty killed them, not allowing any to escape, for their hearts were sure in the great strength of Pharaoh, their good Lord; for he was behind them like a mountain of copper and a wall of iron for ever and ever."

So was the course of the battle turned. The intervention of the force from Amurru had come just in time, like the Prussian Blücher to the support of Wellington at Waterloo. How chancy are military matters: the Nearin are not mentioned in the Literary Record, nor in the main text accompanying the Pictorial Record. Their contribution, however, was so crucial for success that they could not reasonably be omitted from the scenes which illuminate so strikingly the course of the battle – not only animating the conflict but also providing dashes of realism. As for what happened in the Egyptian camp, the official narrative is a highly unsatisfactory source. It was composed with the intention of placing all the glory on the king: "I was like Monthu [the Theban war god], I discharged arrows to the right and took captives to my left. In their eyes I was like Seth in his time. I found the 2,500 chariots, in the middle of which I was, tumbling before my horse. None found his hand to fight, their hearts disconcerted in their bodies because of fear of me; their arms were all weak and they were unable to shoot." And there is much more in similar vein to demonstrate the power of Ramesses, so that at the end of the day "my army came to praise me, turning their faces to one side at what I had done, my senior officers coming to extol my strong arm, while my chariotry similarly boasted by my name, saying: 'What a fine warrior, who steadies the heart; you save your infantry and your chariots. You are the son of Amun, who achieves success with his two arms... . You are great in victory in the presence of your army, in the sight of the whole land.'" And then, without a tongue in the cheek, the soldiers declare that Ramesses is not speaking boastfully, that he protects Egypt and curbs the foreign lands; and that he has broken the back of Hatti forever. What more could Ramesses have said if he had spoken boastfully?

In an attempt to inject a little reality into the events of that first fateful day, we need to discount the extravagant claims made by Ramesses, without necessarily impugning his bravery in action. The brilliant attack by the Hittites had caught the Egyptians off guard; the division of Pre was scattered, and confusion descended on the division of Amun at the camp. In the mêlée that ensued, Ramesses led what might have appeared to be a last stand in the Egyptian camp. But he was never quite alone; he had his own bodyguard and enough supporting units to prevent the Hittite chariotry from overrunning the camp entirely. Then came the Nearin from Amurru, hoped for, no doubt, but scarcely expected to arrive with such good timing. In respect of this counterattack, it appears that the Hittite intelligence system, up to that point shown to be much superior to the Egyptian, slipped up. The advance of a large military force from the west, moving up the valley of the Eleutheros river toward Qadesh, could scarcely have been overlooked if spies had been operating in that direction. In fact, the relief was the one successful strategic move made by the Egyptians in the campaign, and credit must be given to them, if not to Ramesses himself, for the forethought that planned the intervention from Amurru.

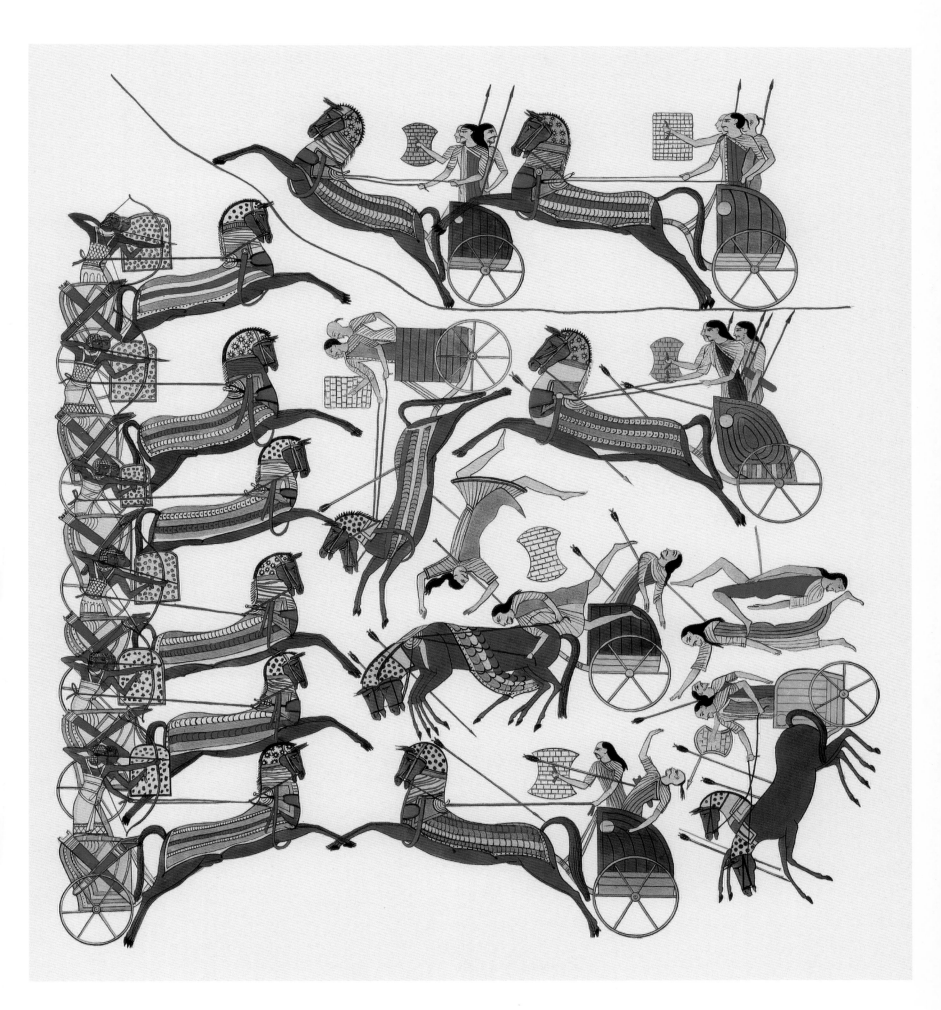

The Battle of Qadesh

From the main Literary Record supplemented by vignettes in the relief representations, it seems that after the happy arrival of the Nearin, the advantage passed to the Egyptians. Ramesses talks of having made six charges into the Hittite ranks, and slowly the enemy was forced back toward the Orontes, and obliged to retreat across the river to where the main body of Hittite troops remained waiting to be engaged. Many were drowned in the river, and some important Hittites and their allies were killed in this stage of the conflict. Lively scenes illustrate some of the calamities that

befell them. For the moment, as dusk fell, danger had been averted, and the Egyptians were able to regroup and pull themselves together. What was the situation? The division of Amun had panicked, and was presumably badly mauled by the Hittite chariotry. The division of Pre was taken by surprise while still on the march, thrown into confusion, and also badly mauled. The division of Ptah, which the vizier had been sent to bring forward, had probably arrived just in time to see the final stages of the battle; it was intact. The division of Seth had so far played no part in the battle, but

had by evening come up to join the rest of the Egyptian army camped northwest of Qadesh.

Ramesses was not at all satisfied with the showing of his troops; and with very good reason: "What's the matter with you, my senior officers, my foot-soldiers, and my chariotry, who don't know how to fight?" There was he, in the middle of the turmoil with his shield-bearer and household staff, setting about the enemy while his troops were abandoning him. They should be ashamed of themselves. Perhaps they could do better on the next day. And indeed,

they would need to do better, because the bulk of the Hittite army remained unbeaten. On the other hand, from details contained in the vignettes, it becomes clear that a number of important leaders on the Hittite side, including members of Muwatallis' family, had been killed on the first day of fighting; and much of the chariotry, which was used for speed and surprise in attack, had been lost.

When the next day dawned, Ramesses marshaled his divisions for immediate action. He himself was eager to repeat his noble deeds of the previous day, while his troops, at least in outward show, were prepared to support him with a better will than before. The details of this second stage of the battle of Qadesh, as recorded in the Literary Record, are very sketchy.

On this occasion the Egyptians made the first strike, crossing the Orontes by ford, and driving into the massed Hittite army.

Now the advantage in chariots lay with the Egyptians, and seemingly it was fully exploited. The Hittites were not only surprised, but terrified, according to the Official Report: "Get ready, don't go near him; the great goddess Sakhmet [a fierce lioness deity of Memphis] is with him. She rides with him on his horse, and her hand is with him. Whoever approaches him, a breath of fire will come to burn his body." So one of the enemy called out.

It may be inferred from the lack of

further description of the battle that the result of the first great charge by the Egyptians was significant, but not decisive. Much more effort would be needed to secure outright victory. And Ramesses may not have had confidence in the determination of his officers to seek victory with enthusiasm. For the Hittites also there seems to have been a realization that any victory would be a bloody victory, and such an outcome might not be acceptable to the leaders of the allied contingents. In fact a stalemate had been reached, and the Hittite king – the Vile Fallen One of Hatti – made overtures to Ramesses. The Literary Record suggests that Muwatallis groveled before Pharaoh before sending him a letter in which he accepted Ramesses' superiority and his claims over all territories, including Hatti. Too many had been killed: "Do not be hard in your actions, victorious king, peace is better than fighting! Give us time to breathe!" One would here be pleased to have the Hittite view of the negotiations. It would be more matter-of-fact, although heavily biased in favor of the Hittite point of view. It could be conjectured that when it became evident that neither side would quickly gain the advantage, Muwatallis prudently decided to make the first move toward a settlement. So he sent a letter to Ramesses, couched in terms which would flatter the Egyptian king.

118-119
Rosellini's drawing of the scene in the Ramesseum showing the crucial attack by Ramesses in his chariot during which he routed the Hittites. Many of them, here named, died in the waters of the Orontes.

119 bottom
In the initial encounter between Egyptian and Hittite chariotry, the Egyptians, according to the Abu Simbel version, scattered the Hittites, leaving the field, as shown partly here, littered with shattered chariots and dead soldiers.

Ramesses II

He might even have said, "You are Seth, Ba'al in person." The tactical grovel was part of the usual procedure between rival rulers in ancient times. He would not have admitted any Egyptian claims of sovereignty over Hatti lands, and he would certainly not have conceded such sovereignty for the future. The core message was surely that which the Egyptian text offered: "Peace is better than fighting." One item in the Hittite's letter seems to convey a bitter truth. The Egyptian report has Muwatallis stating that Ramesses had spent the day before "killing hundreds of thousands. You have come today, having left no heirs." In saying this he surely was referring to the death of two brothers, whose fates are recorded separately in the relief scenes. Here was good reason for calling a truce; the future of the Hittite kingship might be seriously threatened.

Ramesses then, as reported, called off the attack and summoned his military leaders and advisers, and had Muwatallis' letter read out to them. With obvious relief, and great enthusiasm, they all agreed: "Peace is exceedingly good, O Sovereign, our Lord! There is no blame in coming to terms when you make it, for who can oppose you in the day of your fury?" Making peace from a position of strength was magnanimity. With such unanimous approval Ramesses decided to call a halt to the battle. Presumably he wrote back to Muwatallis, agreeing to the cessation of fighting, and after a suitable interval for tidying up the loose ends of battle, the Egyptian army withdrew peacefully to the south. In due course, having enjoyed a triumphant journey through the vassal states of Canaan, the king and his army arrived safely in Piramesse, the royal residence city in the Delta. So ended the passage of arms at Qadesh.

In the course of the description of the battle given above, references were made from time to time to parts of the relief representations which form an important part of the Qadesh record. Many significant facts and details can be gleaned from them to supplement the main compositions, which concentrate on the behavior, thoughts, and exploits of the Pharaoh. Most notable is the scene recording the arrival of the relief force of Nearin from Amurru. Some other scenes should be specially mentioned, along with the hieroglyphic epigraphs accompanying them. The beating of the Hittite spies is graphically portrayed, and the accompanying text explains: "Coming of Pharaoh's scout with two scouts of the Fallen One of Hatti into the presence of Pharaoh. They beat them to say where the vile Fallen One of Hatti is." In another scene the vizier is shown hurrying back to summon forward the divisions still on the march: "Hurry forward! Pharaoh your Lord stands alone in the battle." The same message is conveyed by Pharaoh's butler to the division of Ptah, and similarly by yet another emissary of the king. Meanwhile, in a scene on much grander a scale, Ramesses is shown in his chariot shooting arrows at the enemy. Variants of this scene, accompanied by differing texts vaunting the king's activity, are found in the various temples. The Hittite king, on the other hand, is given no starring role.

He is shown in his chariot, turning away

120 top
Vignette in Abu Simbel of the "vile chief of Hatti" fleeing in his chariot from Qadesh and looking back to the city. "He never came out to fight for fear of His Majesty," the text declares.

120 bottom
Presentation of prisoners after the battle, as shown in Ramesses' own temple at Abydos. They come from his victories in Hatti and Naharin "with the chiefs of all foreign lands . . . as living captives."

120-121
After the battle, Hittite captives are brought for Ramesses' inspection. The slain have had their hands cut off, and piles of severed members lie on the right, with scribes noting down the numbers.

from the town of Qadesh. In some temples a long text states, "The great, vile Fallen One of Hatti stands in the middle of his infantry and chariotry, with face turned back, trembling, his heart distressed. He never came out to fight because of the fear of His Majesty, after he had seen His Majesty overcoming those of Hatti and of the chiefs of all foreign lands who had come with him, for His Majesty overthrew them in an instant, His Majesty being like a divine falcon... ." Many of those who did engage in battle from the Hittite side are shown usually in turmoil, and the names of important Hittites among the slain, or drowned in the Orontes, are listed. One graphic vignette shows the prince of Aleppo being held upside down. The epigraph explains: "The vile Prince of Aleppo being emptied [of water] by his soldiers, after His Majesty had cast him into the water."

A number of small incidents are illustrated, in which Egyptian or Hittite soldiers are shown on the move or engaged in battle. Such scenes persuasively provide the flavor of war – the disjunctive, almost aimless, activities of small groups of soldiers, separated from their units, and not quite sure about what they should be doing. The carnage is highlighted by vignettes showing piles of hands cut off dead Hittites, in one of which a scribe is depicted noting down numbers, while prisoners are brought in by one of Ramesses' sons. A number of young sons had accompanied their father on campaign, and some are shown individually bringing captives to Pharaoh.

The remarkable value of the various relief scenes lies not only in the richness of the information they contain about one specific, identifiable battle, but also in the dramatic visual invention of the tableaux. Extensive areas of temple walls are filled with a great number of scenes, some huge, involving the king, others intimate and small-scale. The compositions are elaborate and very dramatically designed. The execution is not of the highest quality, due possibly to the fact that they were carved in the space of a very few years after the battle had been fought. Color, now lost, would have concealed much of the deficiencies in execution, and rendered the overall effect exceptionally striking, especially in the bright Egyptian sunshine. At Abu Simbel, where the color survives within the great temple, something of the effect may be appreciated, although the representations there are not at quite so large a scale as in the Theban temples. The best carvings are at Abydos, where the medium is limestone, which allows for crisper carving than the sandstone used elsewhere. Unfortunately the Abydos reliefs on the outer walls of the Ramesses

temple have lost most of their upper courses, and many of the desirable small-scale vignettes are lost. But the various representations, in mass and variety unparalleled in Egyptian temple art, present a wonderful narrative sequence of what for Ramesses II was the most momentous event of his reign. And it was all over and visually commemorated while more than fifty years of that reign remained to come.

Who in the end won? In the last chapter it was pointed out that when Ramesses and his army returned to Egypt, full of victorious bombast, the Hittites were left at Qadesh. Unopposed they moved to recover Amurru, and to annex the part of Syria known as Upe. More might have been gained had not troubles with his allies, and in particular Assyria, obliged Muwatallis to withdraw to Anatolia. He certainly believed that he had come better out of he Qadesh contest than Ramesses. It is true that his army had been mauled and some of his allies subsequently reneged in their allegiance; but he had kept Qadesh, and regained control over regions previously lost to the Egyptians. He

assuredly believed that he had won, although no record survives to signal his satisfaction, and no steps are known to have been taken to laud the triumph in word and scene. Ramesses also assuredly believed that he had won, and he spared no effort to publicize his victory. A battle had taken place on a massive scale, and Ramesses had returned to Egypt with most of his army intact. By a stretch of the imagination he could maintain that he had won. Modern historians, on the other hand, maintain that the crown of victory should go to Muwatallis. In the long term, the Hittites certainly gained an advantage, but it would be difficult to demonstrate that they had actually beaten the Egyptians. On balance, one might declare the Egyptians to be the winners of the battle; but for the campaign as a whole, they were the losers. One certain outcome of the battle of Qadesh was a realization on both sides that such a major confrontation should not happen again. Both sides might engage in minor expeditions and forays, but otherwise, an uneasy general peace prevailed, until the position was regularized by the treaty of Year 21.

122

The dominating figure of the king before the battle. He is seated in his unfinished camp informing his officials and senior officers of what seemed to be the favorable situation in which the Egyptians found themselves.

123

Ramesses II, wearing the so-called war (blue) crown and full royal regalia, and seated on a cushioned backless chair, addresses his nobles and great officials on the circumstances of the conflict to be expected at Qadesh. Rosellini's depiction.

THE GREAT BUILDER

CHAPTER 4

124
In the forecourt of the Luxor temple, a head from a colossal statue of Ramesses II confronts the visitor. Is it he, or is it usurped from Amenophis III? The answer scarcely matters: here is royalty personified.

125
The upper part of a colossal granite statue of Ramesses holding the flail and crook, the royal insignia, and wearing the double crown. It comes from the temple of Khnum on the Island of Elephantine (British Museum, EA67).

At the beginning of this book mention was made of the extraordinary impression the surviving legacy of Ramesses II makes on the modern-day visitor to Egypt. His is the cartouche most readily recognized; his is the name most readily invoked when a site is visited or a building entered. He seems to have been everywhere, and built or fiddled with most of the great structures from antiquity, with the prime exception of the pyramids. And even with the pyramids, we shall find out in due course that his son Khaemwese on his own account fiddled with many of them, but of course ostensibly in the name of his father Ramesses. When we say that a king was a great builder, what do we really mean? Certainly not that all the great temples and other structures bearing his name were necessarily built with his agreement or under his supervision. The best that can be said is that a king may be judged a great builder if there are many buildings which can be shown to have been built in his reign, and carry meaningful inscriptions about

construction and purpose, or at least examples of the king's name. But even then, the carved word or name may be misleading; for earlier texts can be modified, names recut, and steps taken to give the impression that a piece of work was carried out under a king different from the one who was actually responsible in the first place. The intention was not always *damnatio memoriae* – the deliberate attempt to destroy the memory of a predecessor who has lost his reputation. Sometimes the change seems to have been made gratuitously, to annex a building or a part of a building, just to claim it for someone other than the original builder.

When we talk of a 'builder,' as we have said, we are not referring directly to the king himself, at least not in every case. There are, however, many buildings which were undoubtedly planned and constructed at the instigation of the king, or on his agreement with what his officials may have suggested.

Generally speaking, there is rarely any specific evidence of a king's involvement in

a project, apart from those that closely affected him personally, such as his tomb and his mortuary temple. In the case of Ramesses II, however, we gain the impression that he took more than a usual interest in many of the buildings that were erected in his name, in addition to those of most intimate concern. The inscriptions of many of his high officials responsible for major projects, as we shall see later, show that they apparently worked with the positive encouragement of the king; and some of these officials were undoubtedly responsible for those features of glorification, amounting subsequently to deification, which became such a notable element in many of the temples, especially in Nubia. It is not difficult to imagine how eager his officials would have been to present proposals to the king when he visited a place like Thebes after his accession: "May I interest Your Majesty in this proposed extension to the temple of Luxor?"; "What about completing the great plans for the Hypostyle Hall at Karnak, already so nobly continued by your revered father Sethos?"

The Temple of Sethos I (seti) at ABYDOS

When he succeeded Sethos, Ramesses in name if not in fact was already engaged in works which were started by his father, and these he felt he had a special responsibility to complete. It is not possible to put in any order of priority the various undertakings, but it is possible to note especially those that had a high priority. Top of the list comes the Osiris temple at Abydos, which, as was indicated earlier, was a sanctuary of unique plan and exquisite decoration. From the great dedicatory inscription, carved in 120 lines on the western half of the wall beneath the portico leading into the first hypostyle hall, it is recorded that Ramesses II paid a visit to Abydos toward the end of the third month of autumn in his Year 1 (c. 1279 B.C.). He had traveled north from Thebes, having taken part in the important festival of Opet, possibly following his supervision of the burial of his father Sethos. Feelings of filial piety were therefore unusually strong at that time, and his visit to Abydos during the return journey to Memphis and the Delta Residence was a positive indication of his intention to fulfill one of Sethos' cherished projects. According to the text, a wretched state of affairs existed at Abydos. Earlier royal structures were in a ruinous condition, and as for "the temple of Menmare [Sethos], its front and rear parts were being built when he went forth to Heaven [died]. There was no one to finish its monuments, no one to put up its columns upon its terrace." The statue designed for the temple was unfinished and lying on the ground, and not made according to the specifications. The affairs of the temple were in a mess. So Ramesses called upon his officials to get on with the work. As he said, "A good opportunity to make provision for those who have passed on; pity is helpful, caring is good, a son should devote himself to (the memory of) his father. My heart has driven me to make

good works for Merenptah [part of Sethos' full name]." And so on and so on!

Suitably commissioned, the officials in charge of building works set about completing what had been planned in Sethos' reign. The result, a mixture of the meticulous craftsmanship of the earlier reign, and the slapdash grandeur of the later, was impressive and singularly moving. In brief, the temple consisted of two open courts with pylons and massive walls, leading the visitor from the level of the fertile valley up to the desert escarpment on which the temple proper was built.

Although the pylons are mostly destroyed and the walls reduced in height, the walk through the first and second courts, rising upward, is even now

endowed with an extraordinary feeling of anticipation. The main temple building is not a towering structure; it almost seems to squat on the first desert ridge, scarcely to be seen until the visitor passes into the second court. From a portico with square pillars, the first columned hall is entered through a single central doorway (seven were originally planned). This hall runs across the main axis and its decoration is wholly of Ramesses' reign.

126 top
View through the portico at Abydos. The square pillars carry representations of Ramesses being greeted by various gods. Here he is embraced by Isis: he wears the atef *crown, she the horned moon disk.*

126-127
A view to the west across the two courts of the Abydos temple, toward the portico marking the start of the surviving structures. The present entrance lies in the middle.

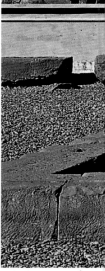

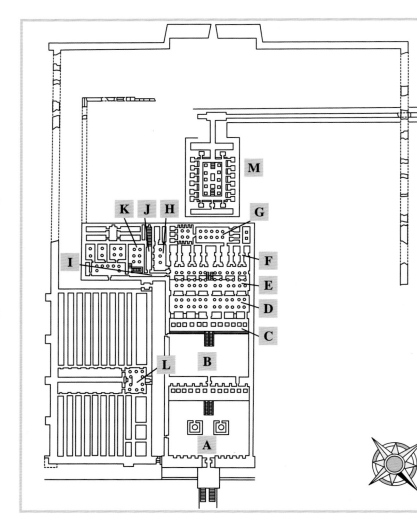

127 top left
In the first hypostyle hall at Abydos, looking through the great columns to the west wall with a scene of Ramesses, followed by the goddess Mut, adoring Ptah in a shrine who writes the king's name.

127 top right
The impressive and mysterious entry into the Abydos temple, looking west from the first hypostyle hall into the second. The decoration in the former is from Ramesses' reign, in the latter mostly from Sethos' reign.

127 bottom
View through the entrance in the Second Pylon at Abydos to the second court. Beyond can be seen the portico of the main temple. The courts were planned by Sethos, but completed under Ramesses II.

LEGEND

A	FIRST COURT	H	CHAPEL OF NEFERTUM
B	SECOND COURT		AND PTAH-SOKARIS
C	PORTICO	I	CORRIDOR OF THE LISTS
D	FIRST HYPOSTYLE HALL	J	CORRIDOR OF THE BULL
E	SECOND HYPOSTYLE HALL	K	HALL OF BARKS
F	CHAPELS OF THE DEITIES	L	PALACE
G	OSIRIS COMPLEX	M	OSIREION

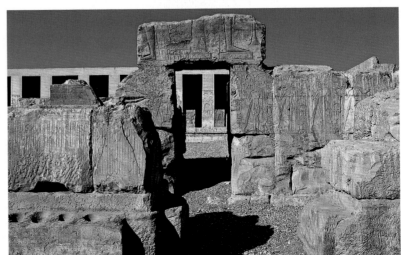

128-129
The Corridor of the Lists at Abydos, looking north. On the left the young Ramesses reads the list of royal ancestors to his father Sethos; on the right are scenes of gods and the reversion of offerings.

128 bottom
Seven chapels lead off the second hypostyle hall. Here, at the west end of the Amon-Re Chapel, is a false door, flanked by reliefs of the King offering wine to the god.

129 top left
From the small Isis chapel in the Osiris complex at Abyos, Sethos receives the jubilee elements from Isis, supported by Horus-son-of-Osiris. On the side walls, Sethos offers trays of food to Isis.

129 top right
On the south wall of the Amon-Re chapel at Abydos, the king makes multiple offerings of cloths, collars, and pectorals to the god in his living form and also as mummiform and ithyphallic.

A second hypostyle hall lies behind the first, and like the first is much wider than it is deep. Seven doors allow access to this second hall and they correspond with the entrances to seven shrines on the further side of the hall. These are dedicated to the three Osirian deities, Horus, Isis, and Osiris himself; to the three great national gods, Amon-Re, Re-Herakhty, and Ptah; and one to King Sethos himself. The Osiris shrine leads into another suite of rooms devoted to the Osirian mysteries. The second court, the complex of shrines, and some other parts of the temple lying to the south are most wonderfully decorated with painted low reliefs of Sethos' time. Adjacent rooms include the corridor in which the famous list of kings or ancestors is carved, where Ramesses apparently did not instruct his officials to ensure that the completion work and decoration should be carried out to the same standard as that achieved in his father's time. His officials or their building and decorating contractors saw no reason to expend an infinite amount of time on work which had been planned essentially for the dead Sethos.

By a happy chance the main buildings of the temple escaped the ravages of destruction found elsewhere in temples established in populous areas, and dreadfully treated by generations of squatters up until the nineteenth century. The Sethos temple became sanded up and inaccessible, apart from the stonework of the pylons and great courts, which alone provided as much building material as was needed to satisfy the demands of the relatively small local population.

129 bottom right
On the north wall of the second hypostyle hall, the king makes offerings before a shrine containing the seated Osiris supported by Isis (behind) and Ma'at and Renpet (in front). On the right are Osiris and Horus.

129 bottom left
The hall of Nefertum and Ptah-Sokaris: the king makes offerings to the deities, here to Sokaris, shown falcon-headed. The king is Sethos I, and his identity has not been usurped by his son.

The Temple of Ramesses II at ABYDOS

Less well preserved, however, was the much smaller temple built for Ramesses II himself, to the north of the Sethos temple and just beyond the small shrine put up by Sethos in remembrance of his father Ramesses I. It is possible that Ramesses II's temple was started or planned before his accession to the throne, but most, if not all, of the decoration was executed subsequent to his accession. Some of the extended surfaces of the outer walls carry records of the battle of Qadesh. The reliefs here and within the temple, especially in the shrines dedicated to Osiris and other major Egyptian deities, are very sensitively carved in the hard, fine-quality limestone with which the temple is built; much of their brilliant color has survived. By Ramesses' standard, this temple is a modest structure, and everything about it is on a modest scale. It is as if the king, in arranging for its construction, instructed his officials to ensure that it did not compete with the nobility and grandeur of his father's temple. It was, however, probably never intended to be more than a small statement of Ramesses' devotion to Osiris and the gods of Egypt. His major statement had already been made in the completion of Sethos' temple, in which, when finished, the presence of Usimare-Setpenre Ramessu-Miamun was inescapable.

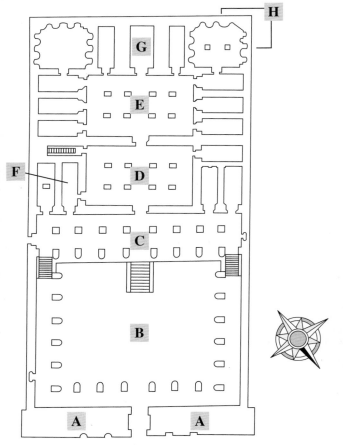

LEGEND

A SECOND PYLON
B COURT
C HALL
D SECOND HALL
E THIRD HALL
F ROOM OF THE KING LIST
G SANCTUARY
H QADESH SCENES

130 bottom
The shattered head of a black granite colossal figure of a king, probably Ramesses II, in the court of his Abydos temple; probably from one of a pair of seated statues originally placed in front of the temple's entrance.

130-131
The door into the first hall of Ramesses' Abydos temple. The texts on the jambs state that it was made "as a monument for his father Osiris... the making of a doorway in black stone."

131 bottom
View of the remains of Ramesses II's Abydos temple. The outer walls, made of fine white limestone, were carved with sunk reliefs illustrating the great triumph of the king in the battle of Qadesh.

132
One of the androgynous kneeling semi-deities representing the cities and nomes (provinces) of Egypt. They bring the produce of the land for the provisioning of the temple. Here is the representation of Hutsnofru "The Mansion of (King) Snofru."

132-133
Ramesses II wearing the afnet headpiece, makes a gesture of uncertain significance to Osiris, who is seated and holding the insignia of royal power. The colors on the reliefs in this temple are unusually well preserved.

The Temple of
KARNAK

When Ramesses had been in Thebes to bury his father and to celebrate the Opet Festival, he had the opportunity before traveling north to Abydos to make a tour of the building projects initiated during Sethos' reign, and to consider what further might be done to enlarge the great temples, thereby promoting his own importance and providing substantial wall spaces for the carving of the achievements of the new reign.

In the festival of Opet, about which more will be said later in this book, the images of the three deities of the Theban divine triad – Amun, Mut, and Khons – were taken from Karnak by river upstream about two miles to Luxor, where sacred mysteries took place, including a symbolic marriage between Amun and Mut. So Ramesses in person could observe the 'facilities' in both of the great Theban temples. Their histories were very different. Karnak had been the cult-center of the god Amun, closely associated with the great god of Heliopolis, Re. So, as Amon-Re, the god was also associated with the fertility deity Min of Coptos. The importance of Karnak greatly increased when the Theban kingdom was revivified at the beginning of the Eighteenth Dynasty; thereafter, few kings failed to leave their mark on the temple buildings. Within its great precinct, the temple was regularly enlarged by the addition of new structures and by the modification of the most sacred shrine of the great god. Many of the buildings of the early and middle reigns of the dynasty were dismantled in antiquity, and as the temple stands now, the most distinctive monumental stamp was made by Amenophis III. His plan for the development of the complex probably determined to a great extent what happened subsequently after the Amarna interlude. It was he who arranged for the construction of what is now called the Third Pylon, which was to act as a great formal entrance to the temple. It now serves as the rear wall of the great Hypostyle Hall.

134-135
Panoramic view of the sacred enclosure of the great Karnak temple complex. The main temple, which contains most of the structures of Ramesses II, runs along the center axis, with the sacred lake on the right.

134 bottom
The First Pylon entrance to Karnak is of a later date than the reign of Ramesses II, but it is approached by an avenue of sphinxes with ram heads representing the god Amon-Re, inscribed for Ramesses.

135
The central area of the Karnak temple with the massive Hypostyle Hall, the part of the temple especially noted for the work carried out in Ramesses' reign, including mural decoration and the column inscriptions.

LEGEND

A	FIRST PYLON	K	AVENUE OF THE RAM-HEADED SPHINXES
B	SECOND PYLON	L	FORECOURT
C	THIRD PYLON	M	HYPOSTYLE HALL
D	FOURTH PYLON	N	RELIEFS OF SETHOS' WARS
E	FIFTH PYLON	O	RELIEFS OF RAMESSES II
F	SIXTH PYLON	P	SANCTUARY
G	SEVENTH PYLON	Q	FESTIVAL HALL OF THUTMOSIS III
H	EIGHTH PYLON	R	SACRED LAKE
I	NINTH PYLON		
J	TENTH PYLON		

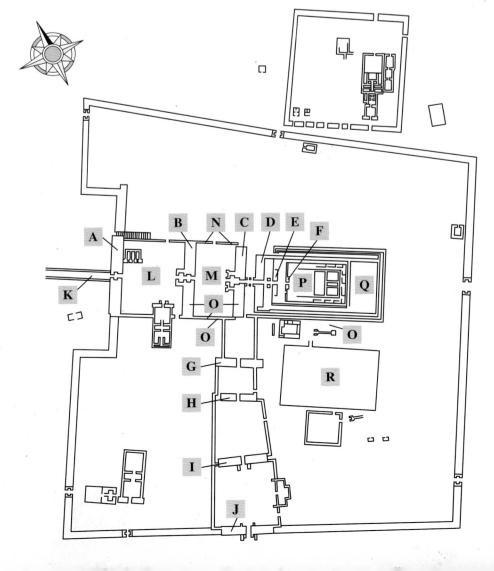

In its building many of the dismantled earlier structures were used to pack the void between the outer skin walls of the pylon. No regard seems to have been paid to the age of the demolished buildings, or to the standing of the Pharaohs in whose times they had been built; the works of even his immediate predecessors were not spared. This clearance, however, provided the space and opportunity for further development, perhaps for the laying out of the great court in front of the Third Pylon, which began to be transformed into the Hypostyle Hall by Horemheb and Sethos.

When Ramesses II revisited Karnak at the beginning of the Opet Festival in his Year I, he would have found the Hypostyle Hall structurally complete, with much relief decoration inside and out celebrating the warlike deeds of his father. The western

entrance was formed by the Second Pylon, built under Horemheb and Ramesses I, also stuffed with blocks from dismantled earlier structures, including the temples built outside the Karnak precinct in the early years of Akhenaten. Here was not much scope for great works, but Ramesses' mark was substantially placed on the elements of the hall, particularly on the inner and outer walls on the southern side, and on the columns where his cartouches appear ubiquitously.

As is so often the case, his cartouches have in many places been recut for later Pharaohs; he was not immune from the indignity of usurpation. This is evident also in the case of the sphinxes forming the monumental avenue leading from the quay, the landing place on the canal leading down to the Nile.

136 top
Colossal granite statue of Ramesses II by the entrance to the Hypostyle Hall. In front of the legs is a figure of Princess Bintanta. The statue was later inscribed for Ramesses VI, then for Pinudjem I.

136 center
The carefully carved toes of Ramesses II with those of Bintanta resting above, from the granite colossus. She was the eldest daughter by Queen Isitnofret, and later in Ramesses' reign became a great royal wife.

136 bottom
Sphinx, probably of Ramesses II, in the forecourt of the Karnak temple. Instead of front paws, human arms push forward a libation vessel, an offering to the god. The royal face is damaged and identification uncertain.

The Great Builder
136

136-137
*Ram-headed sphinxes with figures
of Ramesses II, originally part of
the avenue which led westward
from the Hypostyle Hall; after the
construction of the First Pylon they
were moved and "parked" in the
forecourt.*

From this quay the river processions to Luxor and the west bank of the river would start at the beginnings of festivals, and the evidence suggests that the quay itself was built or rebuilt under Ramesses, perhaps for the start of the Opet Festival of Year 1. The sphinxes in the avenue are not human-headed recumbent lions, but ram-headed lions – criosphinxes, as they are called. Beneath each ram head is a mummiform figure of the king, originally inscribed for Ramesses II, but later usurped by Pinudjem I (c. 1060 B.C.), high priest of Amon-Re in the Twenty-first Dynasty, virtual ruler of the Theban district who even assumed royal titles and used cartouches. This avenue now stops at the First Pylon (built c. 1350 B.C.), but it originally continued as far as the Second Pylon; the redundant

sphinxes are now unceremoniously lined up like parked cars to the sides of great First Court, again a sorry fate for monuments of Ramesses.

Within the Karnak precinct, Ramesses undertook no further structural work on a grand scale; but a considerable amount of minor building work, and a great deal of relief carving was completed. Scenes celebrating both the warlike activities of his early years and many ritual activities may be observed on the southern outer wall of the Hypostyle Hall, where Ramesses appears to have usurped himself. Here scenes and texts of the battle of Qadesh were carved in the years following the contest; subsequently the battle scenes were recarved with new scenes of warfare and triumph, although the Literary Record was

left largely untouched. It seems almost as if Ramesses' officials had run out of space to show newly commissioned scenes, and were obliged to recycle space already occupied by scenes which were better seen at Luxor and in the Ramesseum. A suggestion that the 'cover-up' may have been a tactful act to avoid embarrassing Hittite envoys at the time of the treaty negotiations of Year 21 seems wholly unlikely. Uncontroversial in every respect was the fine series of framed tableaux carved in sensitive sunk relief on the girdle wall around the eastern parts of the main temple; here Ramesses is shown as the dutiful and pious servant of the gods, making offerings to many deities, national and local. These scenes are unusually unostentatious in content and modest in scale.

138
A view at dusk down onto the Hypostyle Hall at Karnak, showing clearly the architrave beams that carried the huge roofing slabs. Outside the great entrance can be seen the colossus of Ramesses with Bintanta.

139 top
Looking through the massive papyrus-bud columns of the Hypostyle Hall to its northern wall. These columns had not yet been decorated at the time of Ramesses' accession and so received huge cartouches in heraldic devices.

139 bottom
In this view through the Hypostyle Hall, Ramesses' names and titles can be made out on the architraves; his cartouches are clearly visible on the nearest column, with a scene of Amon-Re and Amunet receiving worship from the king.

Ramesses II

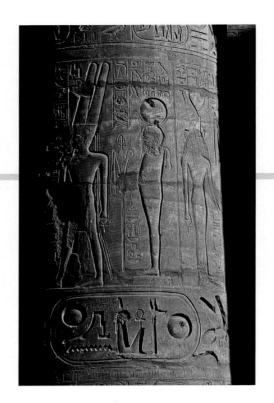

140 top
On a column in the Hypostyle Hall,
the prenomen of Ramesses II. Above
it, gods make presentations to the
king: on the left, Amon-Re, in the
center Khonsu, mummiform and
with moon disk; on the right Isis.

140 bottom left
Ramesses makes an offering of food
to the form of Amon-Re called
Kamutef "bull of his mother," shown
in the form usually associated with
the fertility god Min. Aphrodisiac
lettuce grow behind.

140 bottom right
Ramesses II, very sensitively
portrayed, offers incense to the god
in a scene on one of the columns.
He wears the blue crown and holds
an incense burner into which he
projects a stream of incense pellets.

141
On two adjacent columns, Ramesses II
makes offerings to two different forms
of Amon-Re: on the left, to the god as
Kamutef, the fertility form; on the
right, as king of the gods, his most
common designation.

The Temple of LUXOR

Moving on from Karnak to Luxor at the time of Opet, Ramesses had the opportunity to assess the possibilities for development – possibilities which were lacking at the principal Theban sanctuary. The Luxor temple, also dedicated to the gods of the Theban triad, was essentially a foundation of Amenophis III. Here the relatively small but immensely graceful temple had been extended in a northerly direction by the great colonnade in which work by Amenophis III, Tutankhamun, and Horemheb was to be seen. Perhaps more had been planned, to provide the temple with a monumental entrance and grand approach. Here then were opportunities for Ramesses' architects, and they met the challenge. A great court with side colonnades was planned, to be entered through a massive pylon, the two wings of which would cry out for majestic relief

scenes. Unusually, the axis of the temple had to be turned, so that the new entrance would line up with the avenue leading from Karnak to Luxor. It is a strange, almost uncanny, experience to enter this temple as it now exists, to pass through the great court, with an intrusive mosque built into its space on the east side, and then to turn about five degrees to the left in order to walk along the old temple axis through the great colonnade to the main buildings and sanctuary of the Amenophis structure. But try to do so when the temple is not flooded with tourists.

In a text on the great entrance pylon, Ramesses takes credit for the inspiration of this building, and he declares that he took a personal interest in the work in progress. It was certainly carried forward with speed, for this inscription states that the work was completed in the king's Year 3.

142

The device commonly found on the thrones of seated colossal figures, showing Nile deities representing Upper and Lower Egypt binding together the Two Lands with the lily of the South and the papyrus of the North. At Luxor temple.

143

The head of a colossal statue of Ramesses II (probably usurped from Amenophis II) and, in the background, a smaller seated colossus of the king. In the court of the Luxor temple.

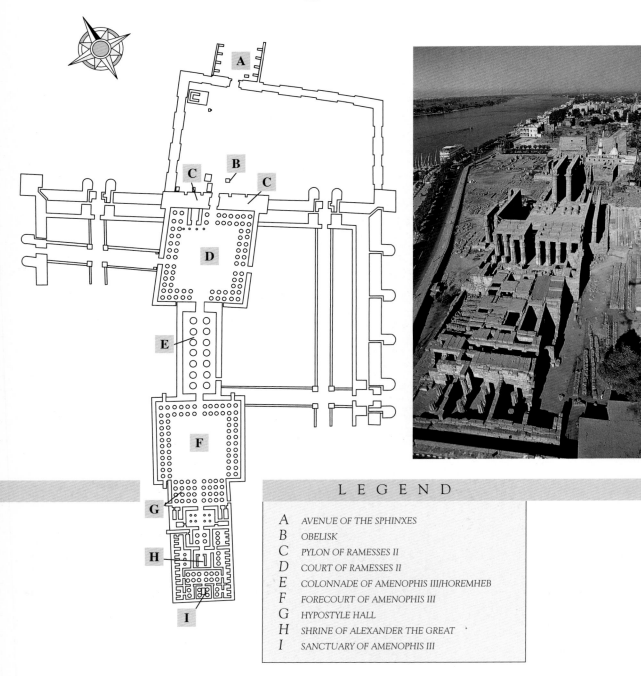

LEGEND

A AVENUE OF THE SPHINXES
B OBELISK
C PYLON OF RAMESSES II
D COURT OF RAMESSES II
E COLONNADE OF AMENOPHIS III/HOREMHEB
F FORECOURT OF AMENOPHIS III
G HYPOSTYLE HALL
H SHRINE OF ALEXANDER THE GREAT
I SANCTUARY OF AMENOPHIS III

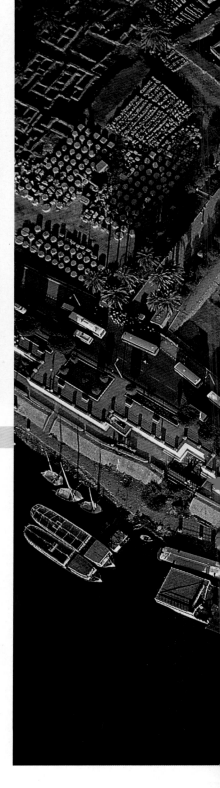

It became the first major building work in which his own hand may be detected; it bore all the hallmarks of a statement by Ramesses the Great. When it was completed, its façade presented an overwhelming sight: great flag-poles set into the niches in the pylon wings rose high with flying pennants; the entrance was flanked on each side by a colossal seated figure and two huge standing figures of the king; in front of the seated colossi were two obelisks, twenty-five meters high, only one of which remains *in situ*.

The other was presented to the French nation by Muhammad Ali Pasha; it was erected in the Place de la Concorde in

Paris in 1836. A relief carved in the southern wall of the Ramesside court shows the façade as it was planned, with pylons, flagpoles, colossal statues, and obelisks. And in this form it can be viewed today, with the absence of the flagpoles and one obelisk; some of the statues are in a ruinous state. It remains an overwhelming sight. The spaces between many of the columns in the first court are occupied by colossal granite figures, ostensibly of Ramesses II, and so inscribed; but some were certainly usurped from earlier kings. One is nevertheless greatly impressed by the sheer bulk of colossal granite statuary of this king.

144 top
Aerial view of Luxor temple. The main complex extends southwards from the great colonnade, including the buildings planned and mostly constructed by Amenophis III. The Ramesses court and pylon lie beyond the colonnade.

144-145
Aerial view of Luxor looking eastward. The change of the temple's axis to the left of the colonnade, to align the Ramesside additions with the avenue leading to Karnak, is clearly visible.

145 bottom
The great pylon built under Ramesses II for the Luxor temple, approached from Karnak along the avenue of sphinxes. The obelisk missing from the right of the entrance is now in Paris.

The Great Builder

146 top
The façade of the Luxor temple carved on the south wall of the court. It shows two seated and four standing colossal figures, two obelisks, and great flagstaves with pennants set into the pylon wings.

146 bottom
Floodlit aerial view of the pylon forming the monumental entrance commissioned by Ramesses II to the Luxor temple. Outside can be seen the top of the surviving obelisk, and within, part of earlier shrines in the court.

147
To the left of the main entrance to Luxor, a much damaged seated colossus of Ramesses II and the obelisk, set on a base with baboons raising their paws to worship the sun at dawn.

The Great City of MEMPHIS

The survival, in varying degrees of reasonable condition, of the temples in Thebes in which Ramesses' hand may be seen to have worked gives a somewhat false idea of the importance of Thebes during his reign. The political center of gravity of Egypt in the Nineteenth Dynasty lay in the north of the land. Its great cities were Memphis and Heliopolis, both not far from modern Cairo; increasingly influential was Piramesse, the Delta Residence of Pharaoh. There were other cities in the northeast of the country, the importance of which remains to be fully discovered. Memphis had from the time of the unification of Egypt in the First Dynasty been politically very important; it was also the cult-center of Ptah, and possibly the principal home of members of the royal family, as we shall see. Ptah was throughout Egyptian history one of the most respected of Egyptian deities, a creator god, with an intellectual theology much favored by thoughtful people; his great temple in Memphis with its associated shrine of the living Apis bull, was very much honored and increased in Ramesses'

160 top
The left hand of the alabaster colossus from the Ptah temple in Memphis. The fist grasps the baton often found in one or both fists of stone sculptures; it carries the prenomen of Ramesses II.

160 bottom
The alabaster colossus of Ramesses II, still lying prone in Memphis, is considered one of the most striking of royal representations. The face, in its perfect preservation, offers a serene image of the great ruler.

161 top
Granite fist from a colossal statue of Ramesses II. It was found in the ruins of Memphis by the French during the Napoleonic expedition to Egypt; it was later surrendered to the British army at the Capitulation of Alexandria, 1801 (British Museum, EA 9).

161 bottom
This colossus is one of the many found in Memphis that can be ascribed to Ramesses II with certainty, and is not an usurpation. The carving is wonderfully sensitive and remains unusually crisp.

*Small granite colossus of Ramesses,
now placed in the Memphis
sculpture park. The king is shown
with two divine standards, for Ptah
(left) and Ptah-Thoth (right), both
gods described as being "under his
moringa-tree."*

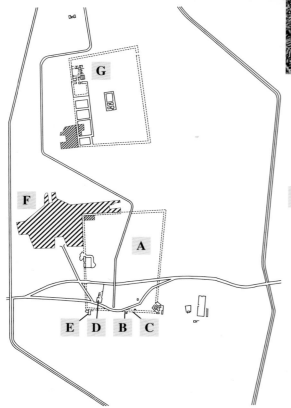

LEGEND

A	ENCLOSURE OF PTAH TEMPLE
B	ALABASTER COLOSSUS OF RAMESSES II
C	ALABASTER SPHINX
D	EMBALMING HOUSE OF APIS BULLS
E	HATHOR TEMPLE OF RAMESSES II
F	VILLAGE OF MIT RAHINA
G	PALACE OF APRIES

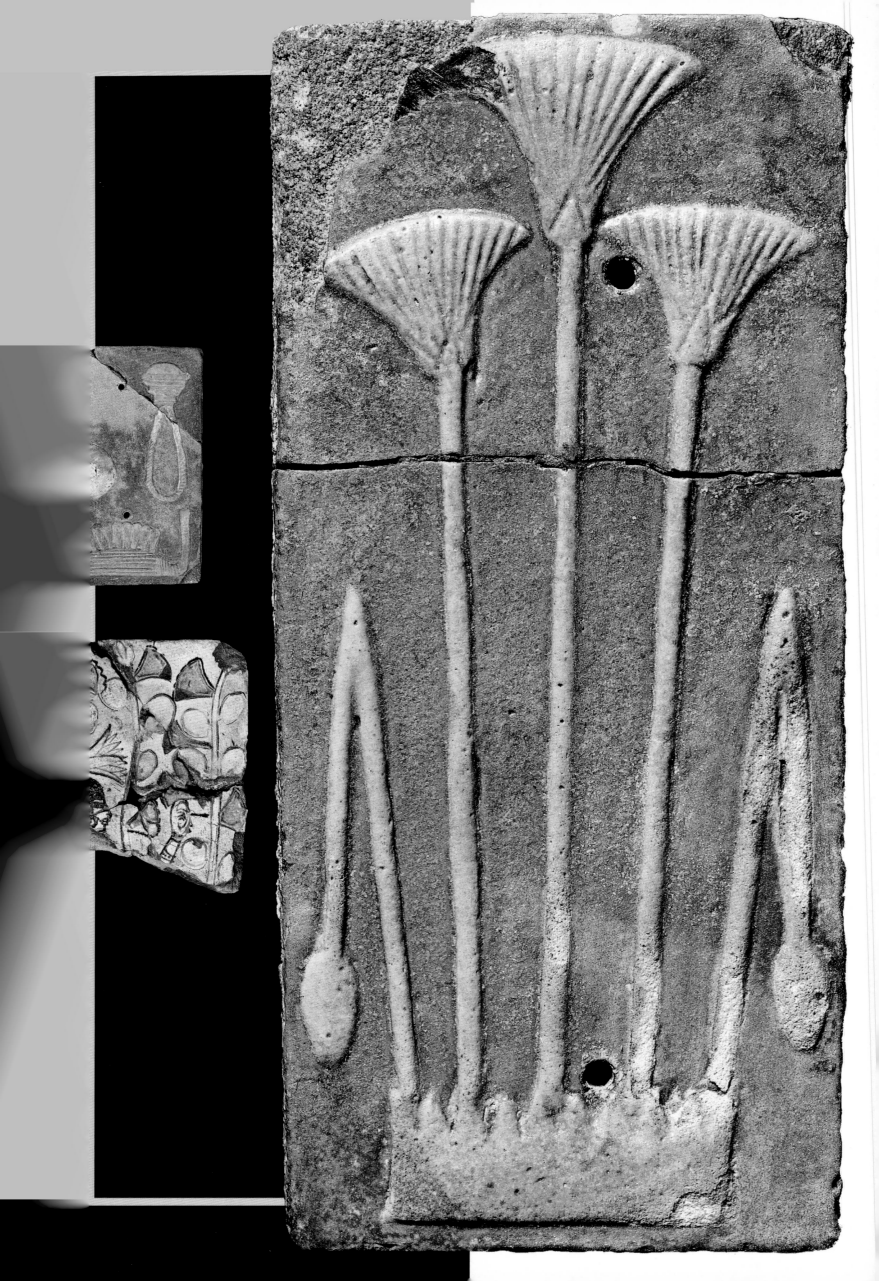

Ramesses II

172-173 and 172 bottom
*The vestibule at Bayt al-Wali showing
the two multi-fluted pillars. To the right
of the sanctuary door, a niche
containing three images: Ramesses
between two deities of the First Cataract
region, Khnum and Anukis.*

173 top left
*In the open forecourt of Bayt al-
Wali, the side walls show scenes of
campaigns in Nubia and Syria.
Here Ramesses grasps the hair
of two kneeling Syrian captives
and tramples on another.
He holds an axe.*

173 top right
*Ramesses with his khepesh-sword is
about to deliver the coup de grâce
to a Nubian kneeling before him.
The text on the right mentions the
king's oldest son Amonhiwonemef,
probably not more than seven at the
time.*

173 bottom
*The Amada temple in Nubia, built
by kings of the Eighteenth Dynasty.
Ramesses had no hand in its
construction or decoration; but it
may have inspired him or his high
officials to build temples in Nubia.*

The Great Builder

The Temple of WADI al-SABUA

The temple at Wadi al-Sabua, although a hemi-speos, was a striking structure with an avenue of sphinxes (human- and falcon-headed), pylons, and colossal sculptures. It cannot, however, be compared with the greatest of all the Ramesside Nubian temples, that at Abu Simbel, itself a speos, or, as some early Egyptologists inadequately called it, a 'grotto.' No longer can Abu Simbel be seen as it was planned; it has been raised from its original location, set back from the Nile, to a position above the waters of Lake Nasser, and approached now across a rocky forecourt, instead of, as formerly, the sloping flood plain. In moving the temple, the engineers and scholars in charge took great care to ensure that its orientation was kept precisely as it was originally, because it is believed by many scholars (and by some more vigorously than others) that the orientation was most carefully arranged in the planning of the temple. There are natural phenomena concerning the sun and possibly other celestial bodies, which seem to be explicable only in terms which, if true, would credit the Egyptians with extraordinary care in the advanced planning and the precise engineering of the temple's inner chambers. It may be said on the cautionary side that personal observation does not confirm that the appearance of the sun at dawn on the temple façade, and in its penetration of the interior of the temple, is precisely what it was before the temple was moved. In the simplest sense, the angle with which the sun, rising above the hills on the eastern horizon across the lake, strikes the façade, is less acute than it was formerly. Nevertheless, the best care was taken in the resiting of the temple, and nothing should detract from the immensity of that operation, and the remarkable success with which it was accomplished.

174 top
The inner court of the temple of Wadi al-Sabua. The colonnades on the north and south sides have pillars with engaged Osiris figures. The inner parts of the temple beyond were cut into the rock.

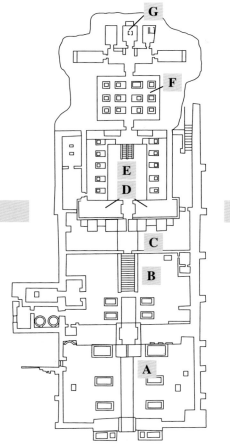

Ramesses II

LEGEND

A FIRST FORECOURT WITH LION SPHINXES
B SECOND FORECOURT WITH FALCON SPHINXES
C TERRACE WITH COLOSSUS OF RAMESSES II
D STONE PYLON
E COURT
F PILLARED HALL WITHIN THE ROCK
G SANCTUARY

174-175
Aerial view of the Wadi al-Sabua temple. The camel herd in the foreground has come from the far south of Sudan, following the routes used for southern trade since antiquity.

175 bottom
One of the six sphinxes forming the avenue in the first forecourt of Wadi al-Sabua. The royal head wears the nemes and double crown. The provincial carving may be rather crude, but the effect is powerful.

The Great Builder

The Great Temple of ABU SIMBEL

Among the Nubian temples, Abu Simbel stands out as exceptional and clearly to be included among the great works of Ramesses II. Strictly speaking, it is not a building, but an excavation and monumental sculptural ensemble. From its inception early in the reign, it was a project of truly royal proportions, supervised at all stages by senior officials in the viceroy's service, but at all times pursued with the knowledge that the king himself might decide to visit the site to check on progress, and, no doubt, interfere. As is so often the case, we have no knowledge of the temple's designer; it seems likely that its unusual form, dominated outside by the four immense seated figures of the king carved from the living rock, was one approved by the king himself. In its planning, the secondary temple at Abu Simbel was probably included at the same time; here the dedication is to Hathor and Queen Nefertari, but the king is rarely out of the picture. This Nefertari temple will be considered later under the discussion of the queen herself.

The great temple at Abu Simbel, however, was to be the focus of all the religious establishment in Nubia, and the central place for royal memorials. It was, in effect, the provincial cathedral of Nubia, although it would be wrong to consider it as being liturgically so. Its primacy depended on its size, its magnificence, and its being of personal interest to the king. Its excavation from the sandstone cliff, its decoration with relief carvings, and the making of its great sculptures took a very long time due substantially, no doubt, to the difficulty of maintaining a skilled workforce in such a remote place. The work was started early in the reign – no dates have been preserved – while Iuny was the Nubian viceroy. A revealing inscription carved near the Nefertari temple and set up by an official with the resounding name Ramesse-ashahebsed ('Ramesses-rich-in-jubilees') suggests that the king had appointed one of his intimate circle to look after the work, at least in its early stages. This official, whose name may more correctly be Ramesse-ashahebu ('Ramesses-rich-in-festivals'), was chief cupbearer of the king, an honorary title no doubt, but one that does not proclaim great power. As plain Ashahebsed (or even Ashahebu), he may be the same as a court official who visited Sinai in the reign of Sethos I. With Ramesses added to his name, he seems to have advanced in the private service of the king, not just as cupbearer, or butler, but majordomo. In the Abu Simbel inscription he states that His Majesty "brought many laborers, captives of his strong arm from all foreign lands" and that he himself was "empowered to re-establish the land of Kush in the great name of His Majesty." This elevated palace official seems to have had a roving commission in Nubia, but especially to watch over progress at Abu Simbel.

176

*The grandeur of Ramesses II
exemplified by the head of the
northern colossus at Abu Simbel.
The cuts made when the temple was
moved to its position above Lake
Nasser are clearly visible.*

177 top

*The cartouches of Ramesses II from
the base of one of the colossi; the
prenomen faces left and the nomen,
right. The former is partly written as
a rebus, with a figure of Ma'at holding
the user staff.*

178-179
Aerial view of the two temples of Abu Simbel, each in its artificial modern mountain, which were built after the temples were raised to their new positions above the waters of Lake Nasser in the 1960s.

178 bottom
A view across the façade of the great temple of Abu Simbel, looking toward the south over Lake Nasser to the rocky hills to the southeast. The king seems withdrawn, very contrary to his usual disposition.

Ramesses II

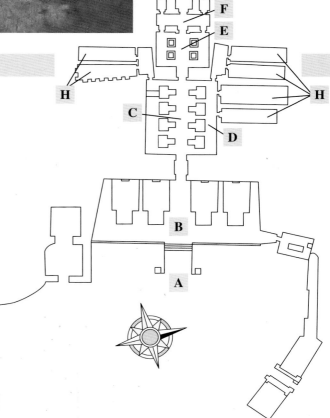

179 right
Three statues standing on the terrace in front of the colossal figures of Ramesses II: in the middle is Osiris, flanked by two Horus falcons, the divine manifestations of the king in death and life.

LEGEND

A FORECOURT
B TERRACE WITH COLOSSAL FIGURES
C GREAT HALL
D QADESH SCENES
E SECOND PILLARED HALL
F VESTIBULE
G SANCTUARY WITH FIGURES
  OF THE TEMPLE DEITIES
H STOREROOMS

It has often been pointed out that the façade of the temple with the great statues (65 feet/20 meters high) represents what would be the entrance pylon of a standard Egyptian temple of the period. In this respect it may be compared with the Luxor temple, where the pylon built by Ramesses II is fronted by six colossal statues and two great obelisks. Behind this 'pylon' the Abu Simbel temple retains many of the characteristics of the standard Egyptian temple, with two pillared halls, a vestibule, and a sanctuary, all along the main axis, with side rooms for the storage of temple equipment, offerings, and possibly for the performance of some ritual activities. The depth of the temple from front to back is 160 feet (49 meters). The cutting of the chambers and the columns with engaged statues in the first hall shows extraordinary skill, if not total mastery of the

180 left
Three of the inscriptions on the rock faces near the two Abu Simbel temples. These three are to the south of the great temple; the two larger ones have scenes of the king smiting captives before Amun.

180-181
The façade of the Abu Simbel temple flooded with the light of the morning sun. The upper part of the second colossus was tumbled down by an earthquake not long after the temple was finished.

Ramesses II

task; some of the work is crude according to the highest Egyptian standards. Nevertheless, in its completeness, it is staggeringly impressive. The initial work of cutting out the interior of the temple was completed perhaps by Year 10. This stage would have included the carving of the reliefs on the walls: scenes of the battle of Qadesh on the north wall of the first pillared hall, with other warlike scenes, mostly unspecified, on the south and east walls; elsewhere, ritual scenes which include Ramesses among the principal deities worshiped in the temple.

In the sanctuary were statues of these deities, carved out of the living rock, Re-Herakhty, Ramesses, Amon-Re, and Ptah. On two days every year (approximately 20 February and 20 October) the sun at dawn floods directly into the temple, illuminating these statues.

182

The upper part of one of the colossal figures carved against the pillars on the south side of the great hall. Such engaged figures are usually of the king as Osiris, but here he is the living king.

It is hard to deny that the temple's designers planned this phenomenon, but it is also very difficult to believe that the Egyptian surveyors were capable of such precision. The coincidence is hard to ignore, but the intention is equally hard to accept.

Once the internal work was completed, the temple was functional, although its official inauguration would have to wait until about Year 24, when the king himself, with Queen Nefertari and a great entourage, traveled south into Nubia. By then the great façade, with its colossal figures, was completed or close to completion. It was a triumph for Ramesses as king and god; and for Nefertari, her adjacent temple, probably not seen by her previously, would be a last tribute from her devoted husband; for she was to die shortly afterward. Romantics have suggested that the visit was made in February 1255 B.C. in Year 24, so as to coincide with the spring illumination of the cult statues in the sanctuary of the great temple. No conveniently dated inscription, unfortunately, supports this precise timing.

Modern visitors to Abu Simbel, viewing the façade, often wonder why when the temple was moved to its new location, the collapsed colossus to the left of the entrance was not restored. It could have been done; but it was decided to leave the fragments in the positions in which they had lain since soon after the inauguration of the temple. In about Year 31 an earthquake struck the region, causing catastrophic damage to this colossus (there was almost certainly a fault or flaw in the rock), and also serious but repairable damage to columns in the temple. No attempt was made in antiquity by the Nubian officials in charge of works to restore the great figure, as far as can now be judged. Was Ramesses himself ever informed? Who can tell? There is, however, some satisfaction to be gained from the retention of the evidence of an ancient natural disaster. Some might interpret it as divine comment on the pretensions of the king in proclaiming his divine status.

183

The great hall, first entered by Belzoni in 1817. The four pillars on either side support figures of the king wearing the white crown (on the left) and the double crown (on the right).

184 top
Scene on one of the pillars in the great hall. Ramesses offers cloths and a libation to ram-headed Khnum, who in turn bestows on the king hundreds of thousands of years.

184-185
The painted decoration on the ceiling of the great hall: the king's short titulary alternates with a representation of the vulture goddess Nekhbet, who wears the atef crown and holds ostrich feather fans.

185
View through the pillars in the great hall across the center aisle to a royal figure on the south side, wearing the white crown. Scenes of the king making offerings to various deities can be seen on the pillars.

186 top
Heads of Ramesses deified and of
lion-headed Ius'as in the great court.
A change has been made here: the
figure of Ramesses has been inserted
over an earlier figure, parts of which
can still be seen.

186 bottom
Part of a scene in the great hall:
Ramesses makes a presentation of
Nubian captives to Amon-Re,
Ramesses himself deified, wearing
ram's horns, and to Mut. The gods
are seated in a kiosk.

187
Ramesses smites Syrian captives in the
presence of Re-Herakhty. Below are
princesses, starting with Bintanta on right
(not shown), then Bekmut, Nefertari,
Merytamun, Nebttawy, Isitnofret,
Henttawy, Werenro, and Medjemmut,
not entirely in order of birth.

188
*Detail from the scene in which
Ramesses II is spearing a Libyan
while trampling on another. The
royal features, while not carved in
the best Theban manner, are
delineated strongly, and are easily
recognizable.*

189
*The head of Ramesses II from a
scene of presentation by him to gods
on the pillars in the great hall.
A change has been made in the
carving of the uraeus on his blue
crown.*

190 left
Scene on the second pillar on the left in the second pillared hall. The goddess Mut, wearing the double crown, embraces Ramesses, placing her hand behind his head in a protective gesture.

190-191
The second pillared hall of Abu Simbel. The roof is supported by four square pillars cut from the rock. The decoration shows ritual scenes and none of the warlike activities shown in the great hall.

191 top
View from the second pillared hall looking away from the sanctuary and into the great hall. In the scenes visible on the pillars, the king can be seen being embraced by various deities.

191 bottom
Scene in the second pillared hall in which Ramesses offers bouquets to Amon-Re "Lord of the Thrones of the Two Lands," and to his divine consort Mut. The king exercises his important religious function.

192-193
Ramesses offers incense and his scepter
of power while Queen Nefertari shakes
sistra before the sacred bark carrying
the image of Amon-Re. Large numbers
of priests and attendants bear the weight
of the bark.

192 bottom
The head of Queen Nefertari, from the
scene in the second pillared hall, shown
opposite. She shakes her sistra, ritual
musical instruments, and wears an
elaborate headdress, including a horned
moon-disk and tall feathers.

193 top
Four of the priestly attendants bearing
the sacred bark of Amon-Re, shown
opposite, with no apparent strain under
its great weight. They all wear the
turned-up beards usually associated with
divinity.

193 bottom
On the north wall of the second pillared
hall, Ramesses and Queen Nefertari offer
incense and shake sistra before the bark
carrying the image of the deified
Ramesses. The priests carrying the bark
have no beards.

Ramesses II

194 top
North wall of the sanctuary in Abu Simbel: right, Ramesses censes and libates before the bark of the deified Ramesses in its sanctuary; left, he stands bare-headed before his deified self.

194 bottom
South wall of the sanctuary: left, Ramesses offers incense and a libation to the bark of Amon-Re in its sanctuary; right, be annoints Amon-Re in the form of Kamutef.

194-195
The sanctuary in Abu Simbel. The three national deities, Ptah, Amon-Re, and Re-Herakhty, are joined by the deified Ramesses, wearing the blue crown, all seated and waiting to be illuminated by the sun, twice each year.

THE GREAT IMAGE-MAKER

196
The head of one of the statues of Ramesses II attached to the pillars of the great hall in Abu Simbel.

197
Ramesses as a child (mes) squats before the Syrian god Hauron, shown as Horus. Ramesses grasps the sedge plant of Upper Egypt (su). The group forms a rebus of his name: Ra (the sun), the child, and the sedge. From Tanis (Cairo, JE 64735).

1. *The Horus:* Strong bull, beloved of Ma'at (truth, order)

2. The Two Ladies [Nekhbet and Wadjet]: Protector of Egypt, who subdues the foreign countries

3. Horus of Gold: Rich in years, great in victories

4. King of Upper and Lower Egypt: Usimare-Setpenre

5. Son of Re: Ramessu-Miamun

This resounding declaration of names was used by Ramesses II in formal inscriptions from Year 2 of his reign, long before he could with some justification call himself "Protector of Egypt, who subdues the foreign countries," or demonstrate that he was "rich in years and great in victories." There was nothing exceptional in a royal titulary of such length, and so full of arrogant claims. From the time of the Old Kingdom, Egyptian kings had used five names or appellations in their full, grandiose titulary; the name 'headings' are given in italics above, and they proclaim

many of the divine associations of the Egyptian king – any Egyptian king, not just Ramesses II. For ordinary purposes, the two names which are most commonly found on monuments are 4 and 5; the first of these, known as the prenomen, is often called the throne-name, the formal, official, name taken by the king on his accession, and by which he would have been most commonly known; in the present case it was Usimare-Setpenre, or just Usimare – the Ozymandias of Shelley. As we have already seen, name 5, known as the nomen, contained the king's name from before his accession, Ramessu, with the added epithet Miamun, 'beloved of Amun,' our Ramesses.

How divine, then, was an Egyptian king? Many scholars have considered this question, and it must be said that no solution covers all the facts that are known about Egyptian sovereignty and the ways in which the king was regarded, by himself, by his court and high officials, and by the people of Egypt in general. It has already become clear in the course of this book so

far, that Ramesses II seemed to achieve a very special position *vis-à-vis* the gods of Egypt, but it is still difficult to determine the extent to which this position was recognized as being special by Egyptians, or even by Ramesses himself.

Was it a matter of being just an outstanding case of ancient propaganda, or a true reflection of what was thought to be the case during his long lifetime? What was so special about the image of Ramesses during his reign? What changes in ordinary royal behavior or practices led to the fashioning of the royal image in divine form? Was it universal throughout the whole realm, or was it limited to certain parts of Egypt and modified for different circumstances? None of the answers which will be offered will be adequate to everyone's satisfaction, largely because of the impossibility of penetrating the true thoughts and beliefs of the Egyptians, and of the uncertainty attached to the meanings of statements in texts. How does one sieve truth from hyperbole? The attempt must be made.

All kings, from the time of the earliest dynasties, were thought of as being the embodiment of Horus, the god, and therefore as having divinity as part of their being. Horus was the living king; and in due course Osiris, the dead king, and according to one strand of Egyptian divine mythology, the father of Horus, was the god with whom the king would be identified in death. But more importantly, the ruling king was described as the son of Re (title 5), and during his lifetime this relationship with the great sun god of Heliopolis was the most important of his divine connections. So the Egyptian king was heavily invested with associated, if not actual, divinity. He was Horus, he was the son of Re; these were the formal elements of royalty, which legitimized his reign, but did not seemingly make him a god in the strictest sense. The ruling king was also called the 'good god'; but again there is much doubt about the meaning of 'good' in this appellation. It was used with the prenomen often in short citations, as on a scarab, when a full titulary would have been too long. It was almost a formality, like 'your majesty'; it probably ought not to be pressed for greater significance.

The ruling king, therefore, could be seen as being divine without quite being a god, someone above all other Egyptians who could mix on fairly familiar terms with the pantheon, who had inherited duties to fulfill in his relationship with the gods, who received from the gods everything that made him a king, and who would be protected by the gods in whatever he did for as long as he reigned. And long might he reign! Such would all kings expect, and in this and in other respects Ramesses II was at the beginning of his reign no different from his predecessors. However, he undoubtedly had very high expectations, some of which were in due course amply fulfilled. At his formal accession ceremonies, which traditionally should have been celebrated in Memphis, he was invested formally and magically with the powers that would render him godlike and imbued with the authority of his unique

position. It is not certain that Ramesses' coronation actually took place in Memphis; perhaps the Delta Residence of Piramesse was chosen; it was undoubtedly the favored place for royal ceremonies later in the reign; but it seems unlikely that at the very start of his independent rule he should formally reject the traditional Memphis, which in itself surely provided some of the mystical confirmation of the royal status of the new monarch.

In the course of the coronation ceremonies the prospective king had notionally, if not actually, to perform testing activities, which would confirm his powers and put the seal on his capabilities, for example, to run a solo race between fixed markers; he would also meet and be introduced to the gods of all the nomes, or provinces, of Egypt. He was physically crowned with the white and red crowns of Upper and Lower Egypt; he was ritually washed with the water of life, in theory by the gods Horus and Thoth, whose jugs in relief representations of the rite are shown to pour forth the precious liquid in the form of chains of *ankh*-signs, of life. He was then or in subsequent ceremonies, shown frequently on temple walls, offered long life, represented by a palm stem with an infinite number of notches cut into it to show the hundreds of thousands of years he might expect. And from this palm stem were shown suspended the signs of the *sed* festival, the *heb-sed* or jubilee, the festival, which mirrored the coronation and revivified the king for the next stage of his reign. You may remember that in the great dedication text in the temple of Osiris in Abydos, which was completed by Ramesses for his father Sethos I, the dead Sethos is reported as saying that he had personally suggested to the sun god Re that he should double the length of Ramesses' life, and that in consequence Re had generously granted the young king eternity and everlastingness and millions of jubilees. And so it was to be: perhaps not quite millions of jubilees, but certainly a very long life, and rather more jubilees than any other Egyptian king had celebrated.

198 top
Scene in Karnak: Ramesses II
pouring out a libation of water to
Haroeris, a form of Horus, lord of
Sekhem (Letopolis, in the Delta),
shown here as human, but in the
text as a mummified falcon.

198-199
In the Hypostyle Hall at Karnak,
Ramesses II kneels in front of the
persea tree, receiving multiple
jubilee festivals from Amon-Re, who
is supported (but not shown here)
by Mut and Khonsu.

The practice of the celebration of the *sed*, or something similar, undoubtedly predated the establishment of the union of Upper and Lower Egypt at the beginning of the First Dynasty (c. 3100 B.C.). The death of a king and the succession were grievous matters for primitive societies to handle. How can the special powers of the king or leader of a tribe be passed on to a successor? How can these powers be sustained in an aging king, so that the well-being of the nation or tribe be secured? In some cases the answer was seen to be the ritual slaying of the ruler when his time was exhausted.

There is no evidence that this solution was ever practiced in Egypt, but there is good evidence from as early as the First Dynasty that a ceremony of renewal was celebrated, and the span of thirty years came in time to be regarded as the proper interval between accession and the first *sed* festival. In the Eighteenth Dynasty two not-so-distant predecessors of Ramesses, Tuthmosis III and Amenophis III, reigned long enough to earn a *sed* festival after thirty years; both in fact reigned even longer, which entitled them to celebrate more jubilees, at three-year intervals. These two kings were

indubitably worthy exemplars for Ramesses, the former king having been a great conqueror of enduring memory, the latter a great builder and memorialized by colossal sculptures. Ramesses may have been inspired in particular by the activities of Amenophis III, especially at Luxor and Karnak; in these two places he added to or completed buildings started by that king. In his own mortuary temple, the Ramesseum, there may have been a conscious copying of the superb architecture and decoration of the nearby mortuary temple of Amenophis III, with its great sculptures, the Colossi of Memnon. But Ramesses did not consciously need to follow either of his great royal 'ancestors' in the matter of jubilees. His thirty-year initial period of rule would not reach the halfway mark of his final tally of regnal years – not that he would have known that fact when his first thirty-year span was achieved.

Just as the accession of a new king was important for the whole country, so too was the celebration of the *sed* festival; it was a matter of great concern for the populace in general, a time for the confirmation of the king's power, and an occasion for joyous celebration. Thirty years were for a king a

significant achievement, something about which he could be truly proud; it was good for his image, and momentous for the Egyptian kingship. The jubilee needed to be prepared and it needed to be proclaimed so that suitable festivities might be organized throughout the land. If Ramesses had foreseen what his own prospects for successive *seds* were to be, he would wisely have commissioned the northern vizier or one of his older sons to set up a special department for the organization of triennial celebrations; for he was to celebrate his renewal jubilees at regular intervals up to possibly his Year 66 (c. 1214 B.C.). They were spaced out every three years from Year 30, although toward the end they may have occurred at shorter intervals, as the terminus of the reign became undoubtedly closer.

According to custom, a *sed* festival was first announced in Memphis, the traditional place of coronation. It was promoted by, or under the tutelage of, a form of Ptah, the great Memphite god. This double deity, Ptah-Tatenen, combined the nature of the principal city god of Memphis with that of another very ancient god of the earth, also local to Memphis, Tatenen. In combination

they represented the well-established cults rooted in the land of Egypt and centered on Memphis, the royal city above all when the traditions of kingship were in question.

The announcement of the *sed* festival of Year 30 was made by Ramesses' fourth son, Khaemwese, who had settled for a priestly and administrative life in Memphis, rather than one of warfare and court politics at Piramesse. In due course he was to become, as we shall see later, crown prince in about Year 51, after the deaths of his three older brothers. At Memphis he was high priest of Ptah, but for much of his career he occupied the humbler office of *sem*-priest of Ptah. He was, as it were, the Dean of Memphis Cathedral, the right-hand man of the high priest, in charge of rituals, and this position, combined with his princely status, made him the obvious choice to announce the *sed* festival, not only in Memphis but throughout the land of Egypt. Records of the announcing of *seds* have survived in rather a haphazard manner. Presumably, the royal envoy traveled to all the provincial capitals of Egypt, at least; and it might be expected that a record of the announcement would have been set up before a temple or some

important civic building. In fact, it may not have happened in that way. The surviving records of announcement suggest that a degree of informality may have attended the process, and that the physical recording may have been subject almost to chance. The only formal text for the first *sed* festival occurs on the outer wall of the Speos of Horemheb at Gebel al-Silsila, a remote place scarcely inhabited except by quarrymen. Yet it was an important place for religious reasons, as we noted earlier, connected with the flood of the Nile in the form of the god Hapy, and therefore with the concepts of renewal and fertility. The inscribed record is simple: a figure of Khaemwese himself and a short text, now slightly damaged, but originally reading, "Year 30: the first occasion of the *sed* festival of the Lord of the Two Lands, Usimare-Setpenre, given life forever. His Majesty ordered that the *sed* festival should be announced throughout the land by the prince and *sem*-priest Khaemwese, justified." The text of a laudatory hymn addressed to Ramesses, preserved on an ostracon (a sliver of limestone used for occasional writings and scribal jottings), shows that in the

200-201 and 201 bottom Processions of animals to be used in funerary rites are commonly shown in tombs of important officials from the Old Kingdom. Such processions are also found on the walls of temples during the New Kingdom, where the purpose was not funerary, but ritual. The beasts were destined for sacrifice to the temple deities, and in due course parts of the slaughtered animals would be distributed to temple staff. Here, in the temple of Ramesses II at Abydos, a fine procession of prize cattle, including an oryx and a young gazelle, is lead forward to slaughter by young attendants.

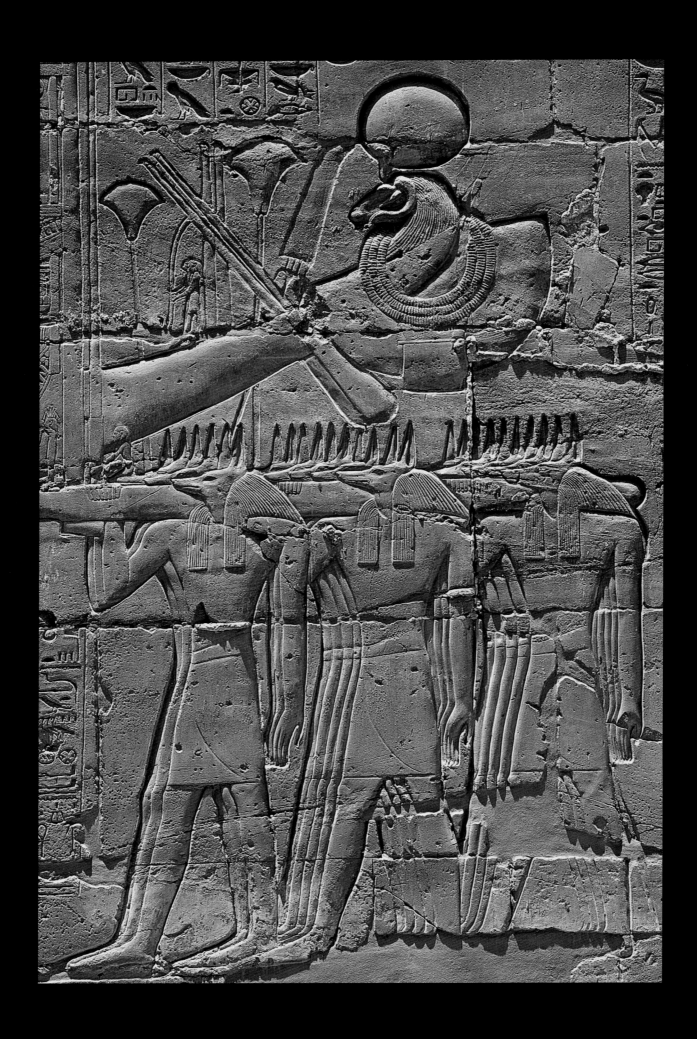

At Tanis, however, the magic of that ancestor ruler could scarcely have been so effective. Yet the greatest and most visible monuments of Piramesse, almost without exception made for and inscribed with the names of Usimare-Setpenre Ramessu-Miamun, formed the bulk of the embellishments of the great temple at Tanis. Their transference to a site more remote than that of Piramesse, and, as it happened, less affected by modern agricultural development, led to the survival of much of this monumental material. From what has been found at Tanis some ideas can be formed of how Piramesse was adorned, and how the image of the king, the long-lived Ramesses, was kept before people's sight and mind.

More striking than the rhetorical stelae were the obelisks, which were set up before the various temples in Piramesse, later to embellish the great temple at Tanis. Well over twenty obelisks, or parts of obelisks, have been identified in Tanis, all tumbled to the ground, and perhaps not all actually erected as standing monuments in that place. All bear inscriptions which contain the names, titles, and laudatory epithets of Ramesses II, and it is very evident from close inspection that not all were made during his reign, but usurped for him by the replacement of earlier royal texts, or by the addition of new texts. Attempts have been made to assign these obelisks in pairs to particular temples in Piramesse, but the evidence is as yet insufficient to identify sites on the ground, and then to distribute the obelisks with confidence to their original places. What is clear, however, is that Ramesses' temple architects enhanced the grandeur of the Piramesse temples by the placing of many soaring granite obelisks, which very definitely made visual statements about the king. One must assume that the usurpation of earlier obelisks was due to the difficulty of obtaining suitable lengths of unblemished granite from the quarries at Aswan. It is probable therefore that some completed obelisks belonging to earlier kings were shipped downstream from places like Memphis and Heliopolis. Such recycling of old monuments must be viewed as being inspired by necessity, and not by animosity toward a particular predecessor. In places other than Piramesse, obelisks already standing might be annexed for Ramesses II by the addition of texts, without the removal of the original inscriptions. This was the case with the two obelisks known as Cleopatra's Needles. They were first made for King Tuthmosis III of the Eighteenth Dynasty (c. 1479–1425 B.C.) for the temple of Re at Heliopolis. The original inscriptions containing the names and laudatory epithets of Tuthmosis were left untouched, occupying the central column on each of the four sides, the texts running from top to bottom. While they were still in Heliopolis, additional vertical lines of text were added on each side of the Tuthmoside lines; these new texts contained the names of Ramesses II and suitable epithets, for example, "a Re whom the gods made, equipping the Two Lands," "who sets boundaries wherever he wishes," "Lord of sed festivals – like his father Ptah-Tatenen," "who overcomes the peoples of the South, and lays waste [?] the land of the peoples of the North," and "who despoils Retjenu and the peoples of the desert." This pair of obelisks was subsequently moved to Alexandria in Ptolemaic times, as we have previously noted. But for many centuries they remained standing in Heliopolis, offering testimony of the greatness of Ramesses and of his worthy predecessor, Tuthmosis III.

206
The façade of the Luxor temple makes the greatest statement of Ramesses' might that was visible to the populace of Thebes. Two seated and four standing colossi of the king, and two great obelisks proclaimed his majesty.

207
One of the better preserved obelisks from Piramesse, now in Tanis. The main text proclaims "all lands make obeisance through fear of him." In the scene below, the king offers a shenes loaf to Atum.

208 and 209
The perfectly preserved face of the colossal head of Ramesses in the Luxor temple: it is regality personified, a placid exterior concealing a will of strength, which is expressed by the eyes, that are angled to look down on the observer.

The populace could focus attention on notable monuments like obelisks, whether in Piramesse or in other great cities. Similarly, the colossal statues, which were placed before temple pylons and in the open courts behind the pylons, were even more powerful demonstrations of the ruler's might, and, more specifically, presentations of the actual image of the king himself. The demand for statues of the king to enrich the appearance of the great buildings constructed in his reign undoubtedly placed a great strain on the capabilities of the royal workshops to turn out enough pieces to satisfy the demand. Yet these statues, carved in the likeness of the king, served as the best vehicles for making his image known to the people, who otherwise might never catch a glimpse of the royal person. From certain well-attested, small-scale statues, like that in the Turin Museum, discussed earlier, it can be concluded that Ramesses was endowed with good features, a strong aquiline nose, a somewhat triangular shaped face with a firm chin, shown prominently when not masked by a beard. This is, of course, an idealized representation, but perhaps not too far from being a good portrait; those who can see beyond the drawn, thin features of the king's mummy maintain a distinct likeness between it (in the king's nineties) and, for example, the face of the Turin statue (in the king's twenties). His was a distinctly recognizable face, which could well be imprinted on the minds of his subjects. Someone traveling from Thebes to Piramesse – shall we say the soldier involved in the sandal transaction, mentioned earlier – in walking about the city might see a great sculpture and say, "Usimare himself! I know him." But would he be right? In ancient Egypt a statue represented the person whose name was inscribed on it, and, as we know, it was not unusual for a king to have statues of his predecessors inscribed or reinscribed for himself. So in Piramesse, our visiting soldier might look at one of the great colossi, later

moved to Tanis, and say, "Who's that, then?" and he might ask a helpful passing scribe to read the names on the sculpture. The answer would have been, "Usimare-Setpenre Ramessu-Miamun, our noble king." Tactfully the visitor would accept the answer, but he might think, "Tell that to the marines!" or "Pull the other leg!" And he would have been right to be skeptical, for it has been shown conclusively that many of the great colossi in Tanis, moved from Piramesse, were in fact originally set up in Memphis and carved for an early Twelfth Dynasty king, Sesostris, or Senusret I (c.1965–1920 B.C.), or possibly a close successor. An embarrassing misidentification of another standing colossus as Ramesses II led to its being made the central piece in some of the showings of the Ramesses the Great exhibition in the United States in the late 1980s. The statue had been discovered in Memphis in 1962 and was visible for many years in a prone position, broken into several large pieces, among rushes in the mounds of the ancient city; it was clearly carved with the cartouches of Ramesses II. As it lay, its facial features could not be clearly seen because the nose and parts of the surrounding areas were badly damaged. When the statue was restored and shipped to America and could be seen in its magnificence for the first time, it became clear that it could not be a representation of Ramesses II; it has subsequently been closely associated with a group of early Twelfth Dynasty colossi, most of which were taken to Piramesse, and subsequently to Tanis and Bubastis, and reinscribed for Ramesses II.

Similarly, in Thebes, many of the colossal figures inscribed for Ramesses II in the great court of the Luxor temple were originally made for King Amenophis III. It is now thought that most, if not all, of these were left unfinished on the death of the great Eighteenth Dynasty king, and that they were sensibly, and economically, finished and given a new identity for

Ramesses II. It was not an inappropriate transfer of identity, for Ramesses seems to have held his great predecessor in high regard, a great builder also, the founder of the Luxor temple to which Ramesses grandly added, and the owner of the most magnificent mortuary temple in Western Thebes, a model possibly for the Ramesseum. So, as far as the Luxor statues were concerned, their reuse – scarcely usurpation – by Ramesses could have been prompted as much by esteem for an earlier king as by economy or convenience.

Colossal sculpture therefore occupied an important place in the general program of image presentation for Ramesses II, and it did not really matter very much if individual statues were made especially for the king and with his standard facial features, or usurped and adapted by inscription, and sometimes by the modification of certain facial features. There were, however, many prominent pieces, which were undoubtedly made for the king during his reign, like the colossi in the Ramesseum, including the Younger Memnon, the statue in Ramesses Square in Cairo, the wonderful alabaster colossus still at Memphis, and also the majestic figures at Abu Simbel hewn out of the living rock. Some sculptures performed an additional function, which was associated with a development in the interpretation and representing of Ramesses' image as the long reign developed.

This was the presentation of the king as divine, even as a god, more positively than just being considered as the embodiment of Horus, the living divine king.

The distinction is subtle, and was resolved in a way, which would avoid offending those Egyptians who might have scruples about worshiping the king in his actual form. Divinity in a sense was channeled through certain statues, suitably located so that they could be approached and treated as conduits for petitions and prayers.

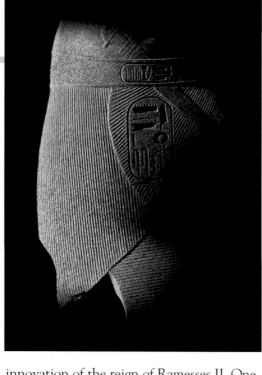

210
The head of one of the great colossi
of Ramesses at the entrance leading
to the colonnade in the Luxor
temple. It is one of the few statues
given a specific name, "Ramessu-
Miamun-Re-of-the-Rulers."

211 top
The identity of the king in statue or
relief was established by the written
name. This colossus in the Luxor
temple is stated to be Ramesses II;
his nomen is inscribed horizontally
on his belt and vertically on his kilt.

212-213
The majesty of Ramesses II is
expressed magnificently in the
colossi at Abu Simbel. Over the
temple entrance is Re-Herakhty, to
whom Ramesses is seen on either
side presenting Ma'at (Truth).

These statues were given grandiloquent titles, which identified Ramesses or associated him with particular national deities, or as a god himself. So in Piramesse there were statues of "Usimare-Setpenre-Monthu in the Two Lands," "Ramessu-Miamun, Ruler of the Rulers," "Ramessu-Miamun-Re of the Rulers," and "Ramessu-Miamun the God." In the Ramesseum the vast seated colossus was "Ramessu-Miamun-Re of the Rulers." The same name was given to the fine seated colossus in the great court of the Luxor temple placed to the right of the entrance to the great colonnade. The Abu Simbel colossi are also named, but the names do not so directly assign divinity to Ramesses, perhaps because they were made and inscribed at a time before the concept of the king's divinity had been fully developed. The divinity of the king is most clearly indicated in the temple itself, as we shall see later in this book. There may, however, be a kind of contradiction here between the inside and the outside of the temple, more significant perhaps because the statues outside were almost surely completed after the initial decoration of the temple had been planned and mostly executed. What is certain is that a huge statement about Ramesses was made by the stupendous effect of the façade with its colossi; an effect that would have done much to vaunt the greatness of the king in the eyes of anyone who visited Abu Simbel, whether in the lifetime of Ramesses II, or in a sailing *dahabiya* in the nineteenth century, or even by plane or boat after the relocation of the temple in the mid-twentieth century.

The naming of great statues was not an innovation of the reign of Ramesses II. One of the great Colossi of Memnon, set up in front of the mortuary temple of Amenophis III, is called "Nimare, Ruler of the Rulers," Nimare being that king's prenomen. The difference in respect of the named statues of Ramesses was that they were the subjects of cults, regarded as suitable recipients for personal petitions. This devotion to such statues, and probably covertly to the king himself, is demonstrated by a large group of inscriptions, said to have come from Hurbayt, a Delta town a little way to the west of Piramesse, but now thought to have been found in illicit excavations at Qantir, part of the ancient site of Piramesse. Most of these inscriptions are small and simple, and show a statue of Ramesses II receiving adoration from one or two persons. The most frequent of the named statues is of "Usimare-Setpenre-Monthu in the Two Lands." The majority of the dedicators of these stelae are unimportant people; but one stela, now in Munich, was dedicated by the vizier Rahotpe, also called Prahotpe. In the upper register it shows the king offering wine and incense to a standing statue of himself, "Ramessu-Miamun, Ruler of the Rulers, the great god, lord of heaven for ever." Behind the statue are carved four listening ears, to hear petitions. In the lower register Rahotpe is shown kneeling in adoration, with a text in which he offers praise to "your *ka*, lord of diadems, Ramessu-Miamun, Ruler of the Rulers, the great god who listens to the petitions of the whole of mankind." Rahotpe, who seems to have been the first northern vizier based administratively in Piramesse, probably in the later part of the king's reign, demonstrates in this inscription that such statue cults were not objects of devotion for simple people only. Here was the highest secular official in Piramesse making his petition to the statue of his ruler. Here indeed was recognition of the power of Ramesses, which went beyond that of an earthly ruler; here Ramesses' image in statue form had become godlike.

In his sixty-seven years of ruling Egypt, Ramesses and his advisers and close associates were able to achieve a development of the royal persona far beyond what his predecessors had been able even to attempt. His huge reputation, however, did not save him from suffering the indignity of usurpation which he had inflicted on so many of his royal ancestors. As an example of notable usurpation, consider only the huge standing quartzite royal figure now placed in the first court of the Karnak temple in front of the entrance to the Hypostyle Hall. This fine colossus shows Ramesses with his daughter Bintanta standing before his legs. On the base are added the cartouches of Ramesses IV of the Twentieth Dynasty (c.1163–1156 B.C.); the image was further usurped by Pinudjem I, high priest of Amon-Re in the early Twenty-first Dynasty (c. 1030 B.C.), who took the liberty of using royal cartouches. Perhaps Ramesses II would not have been upset by the usurpation by Ramesses IV; but he would surely have considered Pinudjem's usurpation as the impudent act of an upstart. Both probably were simply seeking a touch of greatness by associating their names with that of the Egyptian king *par excellence*. It was the image that mattered.

THE ROYAL LADIES

CHAPTER 6

214
This striking miniature portrait of Queen Tiye, found in the temple of Hathor in Sinai, reveals a woman of great strength of character, quite capable of contributing usefully to the councils of state (Cairo, JE 38257).

215
Painted limestone head of a colossal Osiride statue of Queen Hatshepsut, shown as a male ruler, but with undoubtedly female features. Powerful in her time, she was anathematized after her death, or fall from rule (Cairo, JE 56259 and 56262).

The tradition of strong queens in ancient Egypt probably existed from very early times, and can be traced especially through the Old and Middle Kingdoms. Queens may be observed accompanying their royal husbands on many occasions, although it is not clear that they were able to make substantial contributions to the politics of their periods. From the beginning of the Eighteenth Dynasty there is more evidence of the participation of queens in matters of state. Good inscriptional evidence shows how active politically were Queens Tetisheri and Ahhotpe, the grandmother and mother of Kamose, the last king of the Seventeenth Dynasty, who was responsible for taking the fight to the Hyksos usurpers. His campaigns were resumed by Amosis, the founder of the Eighteenth Dynasty, and he undoubtedly valued the advice of his mother, Ahhotpe. His principal wife,

Ahmes-Nefertari, was also a remarkable woman whose fame lasted long after her death. With her son, King Amenophis I, she subsequently shared in a cult closely associated with the Theban Necropolis, and more particularly with the inhabitants of the royal workmen's village of Dayr al-Madina.

Tetisheri, Ahhotpe, and Ahmes-Nefertari demonstrated in their time how strong, forceful women could help kings, and even direct policy in certain directions. They were admirable models for queens later in the same dynasty, none of whom would attain such power as Hatshepsut. She was herself of the royal line, a daughter of Tuthmosis I and principal wife of Tuthmosis II. On the death of her husband, she became regent of her nephew, the young Tuthmosis III, and in due course assumed the trappings of royalty. She showed no reluctance in proclaiming her legitimacy to

rule, and continued to wield power until Tuthmosis III succeeded in regaining his full regal powers, possibly at her death. Queen Tiye, favorite wife of King Amenophis III, was not of royal blood, but achieved a position of great trust and influence during her lifetime. From letters sent by Tushratta, King of Mitanni, it is clear that she had a good understanding of the politics of her husband's reign, an understanding recognized by Tushratta, who hoped that her influence might help in maintaining good relations with Egypt after the death of Amenophis III. Tiye's position subsequently at the court of Akhenaten at Amarna, seems to have been one of honor, although she may not have espoused the heresies promoted by her son. In any case, another strong-minded lady at Amarna was possibly even controlling the strings of power in both religious and political matters.

216
Quartzite head from Memphis, certainly of Queen Nefertiti. The sensitivity of the carving places it in the later Amarna Period. Eyes and eyebrows were inlaid, possibly with contrasting hard stone or glass (Cairo, JE 45547).

217
Head of Tutankhamun's queen, Ankhesenamun, from the back panel of his golden throne. The head is set against a background of gold sheet, and the inlays are of glass, faience, and semiprecious stones (Cairo, JE 62028).

Nefertiti, Akhenaten's wife, occupied a very special position during the period of Atenism. Some have even thought that she might have been the driving force of the revolution, which her husband ostensibly led. She figures almost as prominently as Akhenaten in the surviving visual and written records of the reign, and in consequence suffered as much as her husband from the vilification which followed the downfall of the Amarna regime. Some historians believe that she in fact survived Akhenaten, succeeding him to rule as Neferneferuaten.

By the end of the Eighteenth Dynasty it seems to have become quite normal for principal wives to take some part in politics, and even in diplomatic matters,

quite prepared to take some initiative when their own personal interests, or those of their families, were concerned. There was the extraordinary case of the Egyptian queen, almost certainly Ankhesenamun, daughter of Akhenaten and widow of the recently deceased Tutankhamun, who wrote to the Hittite king Suppiluliumas asking him to send her one of his sons to marry her. That the attempt to avoid marrying Ay, Tutankhamun's successor, failed, with the death of the Hittite prince when he arrived in Egypt in no way detracts from the extraordinary personal action of the queen. Ankhesenamun must have been desperate to take such action, but she must also have been confident that what she planned was not beyond the possibility of success.

Tuy,
Ramesses' Mother

Figure of Queen Tuy, mother of Ramesses. A statue by one of the Abu Simbel colossi. She is here given the longer name Mut-Tuy, and is described as "mother of the king and wife of the god."

219
The calcite top or stopper of one of the canopic jars used for Tuy's mummified entrails. This very stylized portrait was found in the queen's tomb in Thebes (Luxor Museum, J.191).

The royal ladies of the Eighteenth Dynasty showed abundant resource, and exercised notable authority in their involvement in affairs of state. It would, however, be wrong to assume that the evidence of freedom of action by particular queens implies much more than spirited individuality, except in the cases of Hatshepsut and probably Nefertiti. The independent queens otherwise showed how they could participate in the counsels of their husbands without causing constitutional problems or creating embarrassments. The Nineteenth Dynasty kings were to have some very notable queens, and few would exercise as much covert influence as Tuy, wife of Sethos I and mother of Ramesses II. She seems to have developed into a stabilizing and supporting element for the royal family in the transition to the new reign after the death of Sethos, and she remained someone on whom Ramesses could rely for good advice almost up to the middle of his long reign. It is always hazardous to draw significant conclusions from tenuous evidence, and it would be wrong to suggest that Tuy was a real power behind the throne, especially as the court at Piramesse contained several other royal ladies who were far from being ciphers. Most important, as we shall see, was Nefertari, the queen above all queens for Ramesses. At the same time there is no evidence of friction between mother-in-law and daughter-in-law. They may in fact have formed a mutually supporting alliance; Tuy and Nefertari came from non-royal parentage, and therefore may have felt slightly at a disadvantage in their relations with other court ladies, whose royal lineage was better established. But what went on in

the ladies' quarter of the royal residence may have had little significance in the more public life of the court. Tuy was a queen of experience and could therefore be a considerable ally for Nefertari, and indeed for other royal wives who may have been willing to seek her advice. She did not become a closet dowager, although it may have suited her plans from time to time to capitalize on the fact that she was the mother of Ramesses, the great conqueror of Qadesh. The degree of her acceptance as an important person within the royal family is indicated by her inclusion in sculptures, which showed her close relationship with her son. This was not common for a queen mother. The most noteworthy examples of this special treatment are to be found at Abu Simbel, where figures of Tuy are included among the other members of Ramesses' family carved as part of the great colossus groups on the façade.

Tuy, then, was part of the inner circle of the royal family, and she was even to be exploited – if that is not an unkind word – by Ramesses in the establishment of his own divine legend. The myth of the divine parentage of the reigning king had been developed during the Eighteenth Dynasty to reinforce the legitimacy of certain rulers when claims to the kingship were uncertain or shaky. Hatshepsut included a series of scenes in her mortuary temple at Dayr al-Bahri to demonstrate that Amun, the great god of Thebes, was her father. A similar series of scenes was carved for King Amenophis III in the Luxor temple. Hatshepsut had good reason to claim divine parentage in view of her irregular assumption of the kingship; Amenophis III did not labor under a similar disadvantage, but still reckoned it to be a prudent move to reinforce his undoubted legitimacy. This legitimizing of a king's right to the throne did not apparently become a matter of regular practice until a much later time in Egyptian dynastic history. The special chapels, now called *mammisi* ('birth houses'), were constructed to contain the scenes of divine birth. Nevertheless, Ramesses II or his advisers considered it to be a sensible thing to do in his own case. The evidence for such a representation of his divine birth is not as clear as it is for Hatshepsut and Amenophis III. Blocks from a dismantled building of Ramesses II were used in the construction of the mortuary temple of Ramesses III at Medinet Habu, and some of these blocks belong most probably to birth scenes showing Queen Tuy with Amun and other deities commonly involved in royal birth scenes. These blocks and many others reused at Medinet Habu came from the Ramesseum, not from the main mortuary temple of Ramesses II but from a much smaller subsidiary temple built on the north side of the hypostyle hall of the main temple. The dedicatees of this smaller temple are not wholly certain; they include Tuy and probably her husband, Sethos I, and possibly also Queen Nefertari. In this special temple Ramesses honored his mother by including her in an endowment, which would certainly have benefited from its proximity to the great mortuary temple of the king himself.

During her lifetime in the residence of her son at Piramesse, Tuy was even allowed to participate in diplomatic exchanges. At the time of the conclusion of the peace treaty with the Hittites in Year 21, as was noted earlier, she took part in the flurry of congratulatory correspondence, which passed between Piramesse and the Hittite

capital, Hattusas. Her letter, we may be sure, would not have been penned personally in her boudoir on scented papyrus, unless possibly as a draft. The actual delivered letter was in Babylonian cuneiform on a clay tablet, processed in the official Egyptian chancery. It must therefore have been sent with the full knowledge and approval of high officials; it may, of course, even have been prompted by high officials as part of the diplomatic exchanges at that important time. Nevertheless, whether she wrote as directed or on her own account, the sending of the letter in itself indicates the respect in which she was held.

Within a year or two, Tuy died, and she was further honored in death by being buried in a fine tomb, specially prepared for her in what is now called the Valley of the Queens, known in antiquity as the Place of Beauty. This valley, at the south end of the Theban Necropolis, was first used during the Eighteenth Dynasty, but began to be exploited as a suitably distinct area for the burials of queens and royal children in the Nineteenth Dynasty. The finest surviving tomb, as we shall shortly see, was made for Queen Nefertari; but the one prepared for Queen Tuy may originally have been quite as splendid. It was discovered only in recent years, sadly robbed and heavily damaged; but enough traces of decoration and of tomb furniture were found to suggest that it was wonderfully decorated and richly furnished. Sometimes during her life under her son Ramesses, her name is given as Mut-Tuy ('Mother Tuy'), which apparently

emphasized her position in the king's esteem. In the tomb she is just Tuy, as she had been when wife of Sethos I. Another close female member of Ramesses' family, who has become a little better known in recent years, is his sister Tia or Tjia, who was married to a senior administrative official also named, confusingly, Tia or Tjia. The tomb of the two Tias was excavated at Saqqara in the early 1980s, on the high plateau to the south of the Step Pyramid, overlooking the plain of Memphis. It was constructed side by side with the tomb prepared by Horemheb in the reign of Tutankhamun, while he was still a general.

The Tias' tomb is not as splendid as that of Horemheb, but it is in its superstructure almost as large, with open courts and a small pyramid. There is no suggestion from the surviving reliefs and inscriptions that Princess Tia and her husband were especially honored in their lifetime; they were presumably content to live and carry out their official duties in the Memphite region. Nevertheless, the scale of their tomb and its proximity to Horemheb's tomb – already probably the object of some posthumous veneration – suggest that they were not lacking in privilege and recognition because of the close relationship with the reigning monarch.

It seems clear that this Saqqara tomb was prepared principally for the official Tia, the husband; his wife was included, as was common, and because of her royal origin was surely able to arrange that the position and size of the tomb were consonant with her status. But she did not qualify for burial in the Valley of the Queens. Such special burial would be reserved for the royal women closest to the king, his mother and his particular wives.

The Great Royal Wife
NEFERTARI

Of the wives the most important was Nefertari, without a doubt. Like so many people in antiquity, Nefertari is extremely well known, while being at the same time almost unknown. If one is asked what was her importance in the life and reign of Ramesses II, it is not easy to provide truly adequate answers. Inference and surmise must contribute substantially to the small corpus of known facts about this undoubtedly important queen. The major pieces of evidence for her fame are two structures, the secondary temple at Abu Simbel and the tomb in the Valley of the Queens, both of which have been subjected to exceptional study and conservation in recent years. It could be said that she is important because of the temple and the tomb, and there is some truth in such a claim. Early historians of ancient Egypt, such as James Henry Breasted, make only brief references to her. Amelia B. Edwards, the Victorian novelist and traveler, was convinced on the basis of the temple (the tomb had not yet been discovered) -that there was much more to her relationship with Ramesses than a straightforward formal royal alliance.

Nevertheless, Nefertari cannot be thought of as a mere cipher. Even if for people today she is known and glamorized by her spectacular temple and tomb, it cannot be questioned that in her lifetime she was the leading lady of Ramesses' court, first in the harem of the king, but perhaps second over all, respectfully, to Tuy, who occupied a special position as dowager queen. Nefertari was the great royal wife, but sadly nothing is known of her parentage and background, which might establish more certainly on what her inherited authority, if any, rested. Unless a royal wife had royal parents it was not usual for their names to be recorded. It has been suggested that she may have been a member of the family of Ay, non-royal successor of Tutankhamun, but the evidence is very slight. It is better to think of her as belonging to the family of some high official who had been spotted by King Sethos or his 'talent scouts' as being a girl of a good family who would provide the young prince with good children. In the great dedicatory inscription of Abydos, dated in Year 1, in listing the many favors he owed to his father, Ramesses expressly mentions the setting up of his own household, chosen from the royal harem, with wives selected from the whole land of Egypt, and a suitable collection of concubines. Prince Ramessu was himself probably in his mid-teens at the time, and it is not surprising that the choice of his principal bedfellows should be made by his father. He would have plenty of time later to make his own royal selection after he became king. By the time he did become king, Nefertari was already to be regarded as great royal wife. She had by then produced an heir, to be the first crown prince, Amonhikhopshef, and had therefore established her priority among the wives of the king. From the outset of the reign, Nefertari is the queen who is almost exclusively shown attending the king in his official duties, and she was to retain this position until she died.

It will never be possible to decide whether a true love-match existed between Nefertari and Ramesses. The temple at Abu Simbel and the tomb in the Valley of the Queens may indicate great and sincere regard for a wife who had fulfilled her duties in every respect throughout many years of marriage; for a wife who participated in the activities of the state without creating problems; who may even have accompanied the royal party on the Qadesh campaign; who is at least shown in temple reliefs in many places throughout Egypt, to be at her husband's side in performing ritual acts; and who stands beside him – admittedly on a much smaller scale – in many great sculptures. There is good reason to believe that she played her part to the very best conventional standards; she could be wholly relied on. Consequently, for all this devotion to duty she earned the respect and possibly also the affection of Ramesses. But 'love' in the modern sense, as the indicator of a truly happy marriage, was probably a meaningless idea in the context of the pharaonic court. A king had ample opportunities to engage in sexual activities within his well-stocked harem, whether he might be in Piramesse or in the quite separate establishment at the place called Mi-wer, probably the modern place called Gurob on the edge of the Faiyum depression in Middle Egypt. That Ramesses took advantage of these opportunities is adequately shown by the processions of his children displayed on many temple walls; these we shall consider later. No one could ever claim that he remained faithful to Nefertari; no one in antiquity would ever have thought that fidelity in the royal marriage bed was even desirable. Let us therefore put aside the idea of Ramesses as the eternal lover of Nefertari.

221 left
A small image of Nefertari, dwarfed by the legs of her husband's colossal statue. From one of the standing figures of Ramesses with his great royal wife, at Luxor temple. Here she wears a long tripartite wig, not her characteristic vulture headdress.

221 right
This graceful elegant of Nefertari is in the vestibule of the queen's Hathor temple at Abu Simbel. The image clearly displays the gracefulness of the queen's proportions.

Nefertari's Hathor Temple at
ABU SIMBEL

Respect and gratitude are different matters. Consider first what seems to be a remarkable recognition of Nefertari's worth in the partial dedication of the small temple at Abu Simbel to the queen. It may never be known whether the small temple was included from the outset in the plans for the development of the Abu Simbel site. As seen today, which is indeed much as it would have been seen in antiquity, the small temple can almost be overlooked because of the massive grandeur of the main temple. It is set in a bay of the cliffs to the north of the main temple; but it is not insignificant in size, especially if considered in relation to most of the other Nubian temples of Ramesses II. The façade presents six standing colossi, four of the king and two of the queen, all of the same height of thirty-three feet (ten meters), by no means pygmy sculptures. As a subsidiary temple it is nevertheless not a structure to outdo the major monument at Abu Simbel. In planning what was to be done in this remote place, Ramesses, possibly on the suggestion of his senior officials, decided to follow the example of his great and much-honored predecessor Amenophis III, who had dedicated a temple to his wife Tiye at Sedeinga in Nubia between the second and third cataracts – even more remote a place than Abu Simbel. Both the temples, at Sedeinga and at Abu Simbel, were planned and executed while the dedicatees were still alive. They were therefore monuments consciously recognizing the importance of the two queens as living persons; they were not to be compared with any funerary monument which might be prepared in lifetime, but in expectation of death.

Among the bold inscriptions framing the figures of the king and queen on the façade of the small temple are clear statements of what Ramesses intended: "A sanctuary of great and mighty monuments for the great royal wife Nefertari, beloved of Mut, for whom the sun god Re shines, given life, and beloved"; and "He has had a sanctuary excavated in the mountain, of everlasting craftsmanship, in Nubia, which the King of Upper and Lower Egypt, Usimare-Setpenre, has made for the great royal wife Nefertari, beloved of Mut, in Nubia, like Re for ever and ever." Nothing could be more explicit than that.

The temple was dedicated principally to a form of Hathor, linked specifically with Ibshek, a locality in the neighborhood of Abu Simbel.

222 top
In the pillared hall at Abu Simbel, Nefertari offers a sistrum and a bouquet of flowers to Hathor, Lady of Ibshek, who is seated but raised on a podium so that the heads of both ladies are at the same height.

222-223
The façade of the Nefertiti temple, with six colossal standing figures: two of the queen, and four of Ramesses. She wears her usual feathered headdress and both are accompanied by small figures of princes and princesses.

223 bottom
The three figures on the north side of the façade. Unusually, the queen is shown as almost equal to her husband in size – but he is allowed a little extra height, as might be expected for a man.

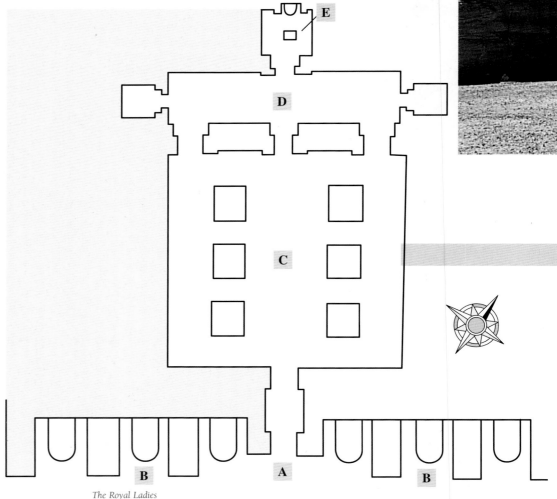

The Royal Ladies

224-225
The pillared hall: each pillar shows on one side a form of sistrum with the head of Hathor; on the other sides, figures of the queen and deities; here Thoth and the queen are visible.

Hathor was originally a sky goddess, but she acquired many functions and aspects, often represented as a cow, as she is in some places in the Abu Simbel temple. She was also, for reasons that are far from being understood, a goddess with affinities for foreign places like Nubia, and also Sinai. Hathor, Mistress of Ibshek, is, however, mostly shown in the temple as a divine lady with a moon disk and horns as her headdress. Nefertari, the other dedicatee of the temple, is not shown as a goddess, but as a queen, engaged in ceremonies associating her with Hathor and also with many other deities, both national and specifically Nubian. She is shown in the temple as a king is usually shown in a cult temple, conducting divine ceremonies. Here in the small temple she shares the ceremonies with Ramesses, except in traditional kingly scenes such as those in which the king smites his Nubian and Asiatic enemies; in these scenes she does not actively participate, but stands in attendance on Ramesses.

What is particularly noticeable in the scenes is the manner of showing the human and divine figures.

An elongation of the usual proportions for the representation of the human body imparts a distinct and striking elegance to the figures. In this departure from the standard canon, the resulting figures of women – of Nefertari, of Hathor and of other goddesses – are unusually seductive, and seem greatly to be enhanced by the long, flowing robes which that they wear. On the other hand, the male figures are not particularly more impressive than those executed according to the standard canon elsewhere. The groupings of Nefertari with another god or goddess are mostly accompanied by identificatory texts of minimal length, and the rather simple, spare effect of figures surrounded by ample space is exceptionally striking. The elongation of the queen's figure is emphasized by the headdress which she wears on top of her wig, which is tripartite, one part falling down her back, and two side lappets hanging down to her breasts. The headdress above consists of a circlet topped by a sun disk and two long and graceful horns enclosing a pair of tall ostrich feathers.

224 bottom
Inside the entrance to the pillared hall: Ramesses, followed by Nefertari, smites a Syrian captive in the presence of falcon-headed Horus of Meha. This is one of only two warlike scenes in Nefertari's temple.

225
Each pillar of the pillared hall shows on one side a sistrum with the head of Hathor and, on the other sides, portraits of the queen and deities; here Nefertari can be seen holding a flower and a sistrum.

226

Scenes of offerings to gods in the pillared hall include Ramesses more often than Nefertari, as might be expected. Here he offers a figure of the goddess Ma'at to Amon-Re.

226-227

Scenes on the north wall of the hall: Ramesses consecrates offerings to Ptah, then offers flowers and libations to ram-headed Arsaphes; Nefertari presents sistra to Hathor of Dendera and Ramesses offers wine to Re-Herakhty.

Ramesses II

While the execution of the temple reliefs is not of the highest standard, it is notably good by Nubian standards. Ramesses is the person most figured and honored in the temple, especially in the innermost shrine, where he makes a presentation to a figure of the Hathor-cow emerging from the living rock. But Nefertari, in her very striking scenes, leaves in the mind no doubt that this is her temple.

The enhancement of her status is indicated most positively by two parallel scenes. One is conventional, showing Ramesses II being empowered with royalty by the two gods, Seth of Ombos and Horus, here Lord of Maha, an unidentified Nubian locality. The two deities hold in one hand the notched palm ribs indicating infinity of reign; with the other hand they touch the double crown on the head of the king, who wears what is usually called the Nubian wig. The second scene shows Nefertari flanked by Hathor, Mistress of Ibshek, and Isis, Mother of the God; they each raise one hand to touch the queen's headdress, similarly investing her with a power which is not stated; there are no notched palm ribs, but Nefertari, unusually, carries an *ankh*-sign of life, normally carried only by deities, as here by Hathor and Isis. Nefertari also wears the Nubian wig.

Such a scene raised the queen high in status, at least in the Nubian context. It is unlikely that Nefertari had ever been to Abu Simbel before Year 24 (c.1256–1255 B.C.), when she accompanied Ramesses and a large entourage to attend the inauguration of the two temples. It must be supposed that she already knew about the temple partly dedicated to her, but it must be hoped that the reality of the temple in its dramatic setting would have come, if not as a surprise, then certainly as a matter of great satisfaction. Her visit may have been the last major official event that she attended, for within a year or two she was dead, and on her way to join some of those deities whom she was shown honoring in her own temple.

On the east wall of the vestibule, Ramesses and Nefertari give floral offerings and a sistrum to "the Great One, who gave birth to all the gods"; this is Thoeris, known best in her hippopotamus form.

In the vestibule, a scene paralleling the coronation of the king; Nefertari is consecrated by Hathor of Ibshek (left) and Isis. The gracefulness of these female figures is enhanced by the elongation of their proportions.

Looking along the vestibule at Abu Simbel with the entrance to the sanctuary on the right. The offering to Thoeris is on the left wall, and on the right, Ramesses offers wine to Re-Herakhty.

The Royal Ladies

The Tomb of NEFERTARI

The tomb prepared for Nefertari in the Valley of the Queens is now one of the best-known sepulchres in the Theban Necropolis, not only for the gorgeous quality of its reliefs, but also for the present difficulty in getting to see it. When it was discovered by Ernesto Schiaparelli in 1904, it had clearly been stripped of its funerary contents in antiquity, with scarcely a trace surviving. The state of the painted relief decoration, however, was from the first seen to be poor. The finely painted reliefs were carved into a plaster coating applied to the walls because of the poor quality of the limestone of the area. Subsequently, the action of salts in the limestone, probably activated by the humidity created by visitors, led to considerable deterioration. The tomb was closed for many years, and the reliefs in due course subjected to extensive conservation, which has seemingly stabilized them for the time being. Air-conditioning and the severe restriction of the number of visitors may delay, if not prevent, further deterioration. Sadly, therefore, it is not easy for the present-day visitor to enter the tomb and view the fine reliefs. And they are indeed very fine, of much better quality than most post-Sethos Theban tomb decoration. In death, as shown in her tomb, Nefertari is on her own to face the hazards and terrors of the journey to the afterlife. But she is not unprotected: supported by appropriate deities and friendly demons, and by the correct religious texts, she can overcome all dangers without needing the obvious support of her husband. Ramesses in no way figures in her tomb, just as in his tomb no wives are shown. The tomb is in fact very different from any prepared for private persons at this time, in which man and wife, and frequently children, participate together in the various activities represented on the walls.

230 left
One a pillar in the burial chamber: Isis takes Nefertari by the hand and offers her life (ankh). The fingers of their hands are unusually long, whereas the general proportions of the figures are conventional.

230 top right
Scene in Nefertari's tomb: Re as a mummy with ram head and sun disk, with Isis (right) and Nephthys. The texts by the mummy read: "Re is one who rests in Osiris" and "Osiris the one who rests in Re."

231
Head of Nefertari from the entrance hall. She wears her characteristic vulture headdress, topped by a circlet and a sun disk with two tall ostrich feathers. She also wears an earring in the unusal form of a cobra.

Nefertari with great dignity passes through the twelve gates of the underworld; she meets and greets many deities, she engages in a game of *senet*, a board game which figures among the activities in the passage to eternity. Throughout the tomb Nefertari is shown in royal attire, mostly wearing the vulture headdress topped by the circlet, the disk, and tall ostrich feathers found in her Abu Simbel representations, and often elsewhere; but in the tomb the slender horns of the living queen are no longer included. The common Nineteenth Dynasty canon of proportions is used for the figures, which therefore lack the elongation found at Abu Simbel. Execution and coloring are superb, the painting showing much delicacy of added shading and detailing to enhance the effect. Nefertari is not the same here as the Nefertari of Nubia, but in her different form she is equally striking, and in all respects as regal as at Abu Simbel.

In death and in her tomb Nefertari was generously honored. She had, as far as one can judge, performed her queenly duties more than adequately. She had produced heirs; she may indeed have been Ramesses' favorite. There is perhaps more than formal eloquence in the way she is described in the temple of Luxor, where, at the head of a procession of children, she shakes the sistrum before the god Amun: "Rich in affection, wearing the diadem, chantress, fair of face, beautiful with the tall two feathers, chief of the harem of Horus, Lord of the Palace; whatever emerges about her is pleasing; who has only to speak and her wish is fulfilled... just to hear her voice is living, the great royal wife, his beloved, wife of the Strong Bull, Mistress of the Two Lands, Nefertari, beloved of Mut."

LEGEND

A ACCESS STAIRS
B ENTRANCE HALL
C SIDE CHAMBER
D STAIRS TO BURIAL CHAMBER
E BURIAL CHAMBER
F ANNEXES
G VESTIBULE TO REALM OF OSIRIS

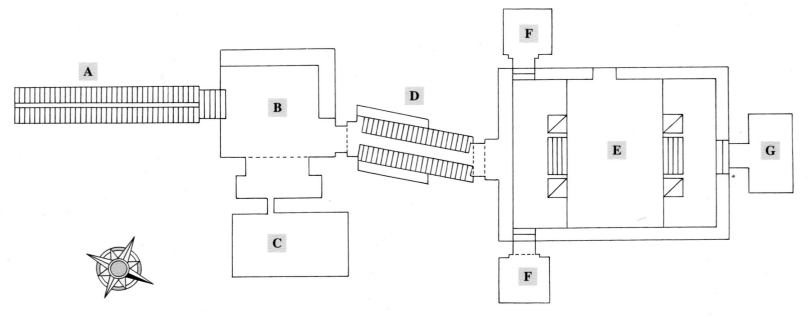

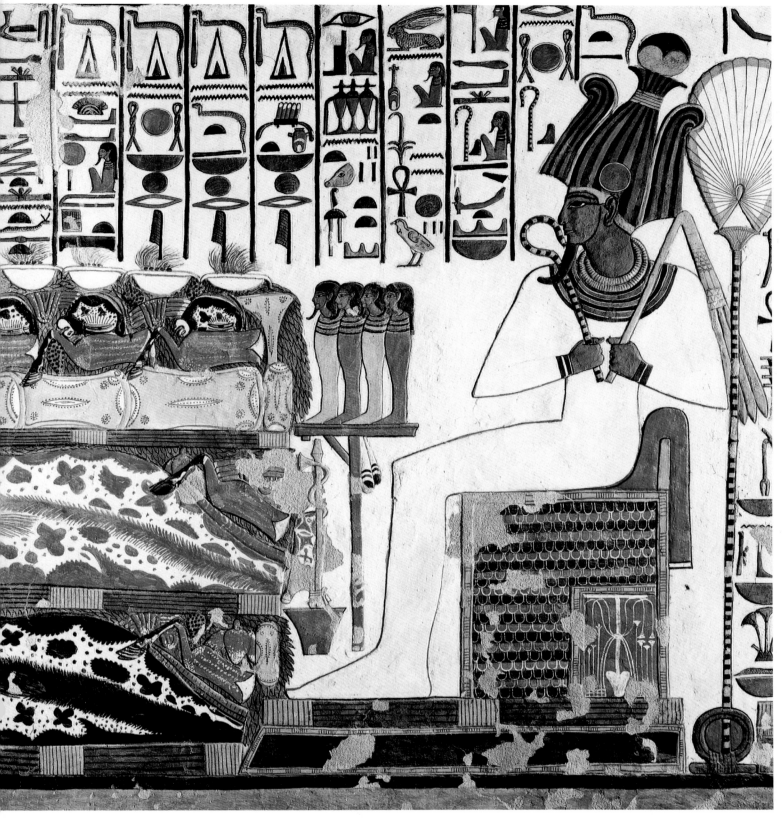

234 top left
On the left-hand wall of the stairs to the burial chamber: above, a winged serpent protects the cartouche of Nefertari; below, Anubis, the jackal god of embalming says, "I have come to you, beloved daughter...."

234 bottom
A vignette that accompanies Chapter 17 of the Book of the Dead, concerning the playing of the game senet in the afterlife. Here Queen Nefertari sits in a kiosk, competing with her destiny.

234-235
On the right wall of the stairs to the burial chamber: Nefertari offers two bowls of wine to Hathor of Thebes; to Selkis, the scorpion goddess; mistress of the holy land; and to Ma'at, daughter of Re.

235 bottom
Vignettes accompanying Chapter 17 of the Book of the Dead: Nefertari's mummy is watched over by the divine mourners, Isis and Nephthys, in the form of kites. Left, the heron (phoenix) of Re, right a Nile deity.

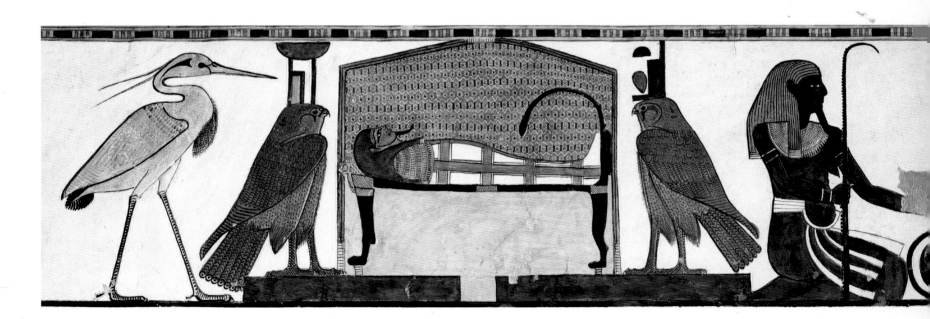

236-237
The burial chamber. Two pillars show figures of two forms of Horus: Iunmutef "pillar of his mother" (left), and Nedjiotef "avenger of his father," both depicted as living priests with leopard skin, sidelock, and, unusually, the uraeus.

237 right
In the burial chamber of Nefertari. The walls and pillars can be seen to have suffered badly from the effects of salt efflorescence. The painted reliefs in some places have successfully responded to conservation.

Other Royal Ladies

There may, however, have been constant tension, the threat of competition, in the royal harems, especially at Piramesse. From the outset of Ramesses' reign, and probably even earlier, the Queen Isitnofret lurked in the shadows of the royal presence. Like Nefertari her parentage is not known; presumably she too was the daughter of some worthy member of the court of Sethos I, chosen to be part of the initial 'stocking' of the harem, which Sethos arranged for his young son Prince Ramessu. She missed priority within the harem by failing to give birth to the first male child, who would become crown prince when Ramessu became king. But she did very well subsequently. She produced a second son, who significantly was named Ramessu after his father. Soon there was Khaemwese, son number four, of whom we shall learn much more in the next chapter. Another of her sons would ultimately succeed Ramesses, many years hence; this was Merenptah, son number thirteen. It cannot be deduced from the absence of Isitnofret on royal monuments and buildings in the first two decades of Ramesses' reign that she was deliberately put on one side, or denied her proper honor in the royal residence. She may not have lived usually at Piramesse, but in the harem establishment at Mi-wer by the Faiyum; but the regularity with which she produced children for Ramesses does not indicate that she was sidelined and neglected.

After Nefertari's death Isitnofret graduated to the status of Great Royal Wife, and there have survived a few monuments on which she is shown dressed like Nefertari, with a high, feathered headdress. The occasional depictions of the queen are not on any of the major monuments of the reign, the great temples, all of which were constructed in the early years, when Nefertari occupied the premier position. The most interesting record is a stela carved in the Speos of Horemheb at Gebel al-Silsila. It was set up by her son Khaemwese at the time of his announcing the second jubilee festival of his father in Year 33/34. On it are shown, in addition to the king, Khaemwese himself and two queens, Isitnofret described as Great Royal Wife, and Bintanta, her first daughter by Ramesses, described as "hereditary princess, great in favor, king's daughter and great royal wife." Already Isitnofret was seemingly being superseded; Ramesses had begun the process of concentrating the royal line by taking his own daughters as wives. Bintanta was the first. The stela also shows, in subsidiary positions, two further sons, Ramessu, who by then was crown prince, and Merenptah, who would eventually succeed.

In the early years of his reign Ramesses may have maintained a kind of hierarchy among his various wives. It was no doubt very important to make sure that status and priority of position were properly recognized, especially when the royal family in its widest sense was being established. So Nefertari came first, mother of the heir to the throne. Then came Isitnofret, whose position would have been enhanced by the deaths of Amonhikhopshef, the first crown prince, and most of the other sons born to Nefertari. By about Year 21 the succession had passed to Ramessu, Isitnofret's first male child. When Nefertari died shortly after, Isitnofret at last moved into first place, and she seems to have lived until about Year 34. By this time, however, there had been a small proliferation of great royal wives, the title being granted both to Bintanta, oldest daughter of Isitnofret, and also to Merytamun, oldest daughter of Nefertari. There is some evidence to suggest that the two great royal wives of the second generation graduated in status not long after the death of Nefertari; but the evidence is not convincing. It seems reasonable to suggest that the two daughters were taken into the royal harem according to no set order. Why should the great king be bound by any rule or custom, which would have no real validity? To become a king's wife may not have been such a change in status for a king's daughter, a young woman of royal birth who may scarcely have seen her father until she was of marriageable age. It is not for us to be censorious about the practices within a royal family of more than three thousand years ago. Presumably the most important matter was to secure a good succession, and to ensure that from a ceremonial point of view, legitimacy and status should be properly matched. Ramesses II, the Great, had no difficulty in securing his succession, as we shall see in the next chapter. Keeping his harem happy might have been a little more difficult; but as his reign advanced, formalities may have lost some of their force, and a relaxation of hierarchic principles may have been allowed in order to maintain what might be considered the happy home life of the monarch.

238 left

Painted limestone bust of a queen found in the Ramesseum. It is not inscribed, but it has been indentified as Meritamun, daughter of Nefertari. She became a wife of her father Ramesses II after the death of Nefertari (Cairo, JE 31413).

238 top right

The small figure of Bintanta standing in front of her father's colossal statue in Karnak. She was the oldest daughter of Queen Isitnofret, and became a royal wife after Nefertari's death, while her mother still lived.

239 bottom

The quartzite colossus of Ramesses II at Karnak, with the small figure of Bintanta in front of his legs. She is here described as "king's daughter, king's wife," but not yet "great royal wife."

A fair picture of the royal family as it seemed to be at the height of Ramesses' power, after two decades or more of rule, may be seen in the line-up of royalty on the façade of the great Abu Simbel temple. There above all are the four colossal seated statues of the king. Each colossus is accompanied by small figures of family members who mattered at that moment. The southern colossus has "the king's daughter of his body, Nebt-tawy," and "the king's daughter Bintanta"; second colossus, "hereditary prince, royal scribe, general, king's son Amonhikhopshef" and "queen mother and god's wife, Mut-Tuy"; third colossus, "king's wife Nefertari, beloved of Mut," and "royal scribe and first chief general of his Majesty, king's son of his body, Ramessu"; fourth (northern) colossus, "king's daughter of his body, his beloved Merytamun," "king's daughter of his body Nefertari," and "queen mother and god's wife, Mut-Tuy." Most notably represented is the queen mother, (Mut)-Tuy, twice shown. There is only one named queen, Nefertari. There are four daughters, Bintanta, Nebt-tawy, Merytamun, and Nefertari; and two sons, Amonhikhopshef and Ramessu. The most obvious omission from the line-up is Isitnofret, who was undoubtedly a royal wife at the time of the carving of the temple façade, but not yet a great royal wife. Bintanta was a daughter of Isitnofret, but still the senior female child of Ramesses; Merytamun was Nefertari's oldest daughter. These two, as we have seen, were to become great royal wives by about Year 34, and both were given the honor of having lavish tombs in the Valley of the Queens. These tombs are now in very poor condition, as is that of Nebt-tawy, who became a great royal wife later in Ramesses' reign. Of princess Nefertari nothing further is known, apart from her appearance in some of the lists of princesses, which will be discussed in the next chapter. She probably died prematurely, having been groomed for queenship.

It would be wrong to attribute to Ramesses any particular feeling or attitude toward those Great Royal Wives who were in fact his daughters, family members brought up in the hothouse environment of the harems at Piramesse and Mi-wer. Unlike Akhenaten, "that criminal of Akhetaten," Ramesses is never shown in intimate relationships with his children, dandling them on his knee, or allowing them to crawl indiscriminately over him. Of course, we know nothing of what happened when he visited the harems where his young children would be raised and educated. His sons, no doubt, would be introduced to the proper forms of training required for future state duty, if not for kingship. Daughters, however, could be considered suitable subjects for marriage to the king, for formal and dynastic reasons, if not necessarily for sexual purposes. It is not unlikely, however, that a wife taken from the harem as a suitable person to be at the king's side at times of formal ceremonies might not be as stimulating as someone brought in from elsewhere. Apart from considerations of propriety, which, as has been suggested, scarcely would have been of major

concern, a young woman, a daughter, would come to the royal presence heavily charged with the gossip and intrigue of the harem, with possibly too many personal axes to grind. For pleasure and gratification, concubines would serve the purposes very well; for someone more substantial and worthy of the royal dignity, a foreign bride might be the answer.

There is good evidence to suggest that Ramesses was delighted with the prospect of a Hittite bride. Surviving records from both sides indicate that the negotiations were carried out with enthusiasm and a determination to succeed. The texts describing the journey to and arrival at Piramesse are unstinting in their praise for the new queen; her Egyptian name, Mahor-neferure ('she is one who sees Horus, the beauty of Re'), suggests more than a simple renaming for Egyptian consumption. The king, after all, was the living Horus. She was subsequently treated with all honor, given the status of great royal wife, but she never lost her identity as a Hittite princess. A figure of the queen accompanying a colossal statue of Ramesses at Tanis has the inscription "Great Royal Wife, mistress of the Two Lands, Mahor-neferure, daughter of the great prince of Hatti." Scarcely anything is known of her life in Egypt. It is generally thought that she spent some years in the royal residence at Piramesse, and then retired to the harem at Mi-wer. A tantalizing fragment of papyrus found at Gurob, the probable location of Mi-wer, mentions linen belonging to Mahor-neferure. Hittite records reveal that she bore at least one child to Ramesses, a

daughter named Neferure, after her mother. Like most of Ramesses' family, Mahor-neferure disappears from the surviving records; if she were allowed a tomb proper for a great royal wife, it has not yet been found in the Valley of the Queens.

The second Hittite marriage undertaken by Ramesses happened about Year 44, ten years after the first. It has often been suggested that Ramesses had been so pleased with Mahor-neferure that he was only too ready to have a second Hittite wife. The circumstances are little known; even the name of the second foreign princess has not survived. The likelihood is that diplomatic reasons were uppermost in deciding the match. Ramesses by then was in his sixties, not beyond the age of sexual activity, but probably only at a reduced level. Mahor-neferure may already have died; at the best she may have been living a life of genteel retirement at Mi-wer. Meanwhile the position of great royal wife was occupied by Nebt-tawy, whose mother may have been Nefertari. There is little trace of her involvement in state occasions in the later years of Ramesses' reign, but apart from jubilees, there is no evidence of important happenings in these terminal years. Nebt-tawy had a substantial tomb prepared for herself in the Valley of the Queens, which she presumably occupied. But, as with so much of court life and activity at that time, the silence of the sources suggests a slow decline in which Nebt-tawy may have played just a role of comforting companionship for her father, the aged king.

240
One of the "family" figures carved beside the legs of the great colossi at Abu Simbel. Here is his great royal wife Nefertari, wearing her usual vulture headdress, and a single uraeus on her brow.

THE ROYAL PROGENY

242

Below the scene in the Ramesseum in which Ramesses receives power and jubilees from Amon-Re and Mut, is a procession of the oldest sons of the king, starting on the right with Amonhikhopshef. Not all are named.

243

Long sidelocks are commonly the sign of childhood in ancient Egypt. But they are also worn by certain kinds of priest, such as the sem-priest of Ptah, an office that Khaemwese held for most of his life. From the base of a statue in Luxor.

"He loved ease and pleasure and gave himself up without restraint to voluptuous enjoyments. He had an enormous harem, and as the years passed his children multiplied rapidly. He left over a hundred sons and at least half as many daughters, several of whom he married. He thus left a family so numerous that they became a Ramessid class of nobles, whom we still find over four hundred years later bearing among their titles the name Ramses, not as a patronymic, but as the designation of a class or rank... Ramses took great pride in his enormous family and often ordered his sculptors to depict his sons and daughters in long rows upon the walls of his temples."

One would hope that if James Henry Breasted were alive today, he would wince at reading these extravagant words, which he wrote almost one hundred years ago. The essential facts about the children of Ramesses II have scarcely changed in the intervening time, but there are few historians of ancient Egypt who would now adopt Breasted's rather puritanical approach and casual disregard for the facts. Sir Alan Gardiner, a friend and close colleague of Breasted who had a high regard for Breasted's ability as a historian, writing fifty years later, was more accurate and less judgmental in his brief comments on the great king's family:

"So proud was Ramesses II of his extensive progeny that it would be wrong to omit all reference to the long enumeration of his sons and daughters to be read on the walls of his temples. At Wadi al-Sabua in Lower Nubia over a hundred princes and princesses were named, but the many lacunae make it impossible to compute the exact figure."

It is very human to enjoy a little scandal about the great, even when the person concerned may have been dead for three thousand years. One out of the small number of facts that visitors to Egypt believe to have learned about Ramesses II is that he had a huge family, and that it was probably acquired by sexual excess in the perfervid environment of his various palaces. The spirit of Breasted lives! It is a pity to disappoint the gossips, but it seems right to declare unequivocally that there is no evidence to show that Ramesses II was a sex maniac, or that his palaces were exceptionally luxurious and decadent by Egyptian royal standards. It is, however, very evident that he was somewhat vainglorious (but not especially so in Egyptian terms), rather ostentatious (but he had plenty of time to present his image in a lavish manner), and clearly philoprogenitive. The parade of his sons and daughters, carved in relief in temples from Piramesse in the north to Amara in Nubia, is quite unusual, and it remains a phenomenon of the reign, which has not yet been satisfactorily explained. Was it done as an act of pride, or one of affection, or one of magical demonstration – to present the strength of the royal line and the certainty of strong succession?

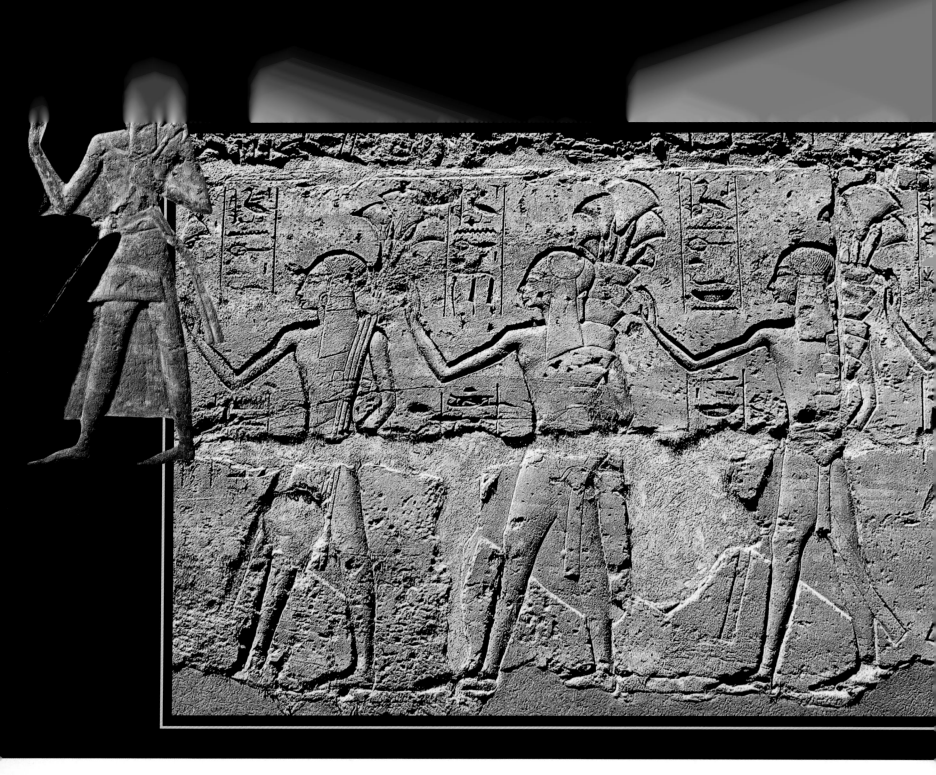

244 top left
The king's second son, Ramessu,
as shown in the Abu Simbel temple.
He had the title of "general," and
accompanied his father on
campaigns in Nubia and at Qadesh.
He was heir apparent for about
twenty years.

244-245
On the south wall of the Ramesside
court in the Luxor temple, a
procession of sons is followed by a
priest and sacrifical bull. The sons
are Nos. 15-18 in the lists:
Iotamun, Meryatum, Nebentaneb,
and Meryre II.

It is not usually possible to date with any precision when the 'progeny' reliefs were carved. Some of those in the great Theban temples – Luxor, Karnak, and the Ramesseum – are probably among the earliest. Those at Wadi al-Sabua, carved after Year 45, were almost certainly the latest. It has been suggested that the presentations in the courts of the Sethos I temple at Abydos may be of intermediate date. Even if it is not possible to put in order the many examples, it is yet clear that the practice of recording the substantial family was not confined to the early years. One must presume that at a certain point, relatively early in the reign, when Ramesses had already demonstrated his ability to father children, some palace official decided to compile a tally of princes and princesses so that there would be a record not only of the names of the royal children, but also of the order of birth, especially as far as the

boys were concerned.

One could imagine that as the years passed and the proliferation of children continued, in the confusion of the various establishments in Piramesse and at Mi-wer, the harem-residence near the Faiyum, it could have been possible to obfuscate the succession, and in other ways to cause problems within the ranks of wives, concubines, domestic officials, and others who might have personal purposes to pursue. Priority within the lists would surely have gone to the children of the principal wives; the offspring of lesser wives or concubines, still being king's sons or daughters "of his body," could scarcely be ignored, even though the prospects of a son with an unimportant mother could at the best have been very modest. Of the listed princes and princesses, only a small number have identified mothers. Careful examination of all the lists and other

monumental sources shows that at the best computation, fifty male children can be named and perhaps about the same number of female children. It might be thought that for a king in good health with a multiplicity of wives and concubines, one hundred children over a period of perhaps forty-five years of mature activity represent rather an indifferent score – and could he not have possibly fathered children after the last temple list was carved?

It may well have been thought during Ramesses' reign that the lists established after about thirty-five or forty years were more than adequate to prove that he had produced sufficient progeny to ensure the dynastic line for a long future. It is for us, however, worth reflecting that in spite of his prolific brood, Ramesses was not in the end to sire a line to last, if not for eternity, then at least for a very long time. His successor, Merenptah, was thirteenth in the

list; he ruled about ten years. Then followed a period of about twenty-five years, a time of conflicting claims to the throne, of undistinguished squabbling, and a collapse of the legacy of Ramesses' long reign. The seeds of this collapse lay possibly in the length of Great Ramesses' time on the throne. So many of his proud, and probably capable, young sons were unable to wait for their turn to come, and their own sons equally lost any possible opportunities for succession. In a sense Ramesses by his longevity had exhausted his line. It is, if true, quite a paradox.

It is interesting to note that the lists of princes retain in the main a consistent order, established apparently by order of birth, and not by queens in a hierarchic manner. The lists of princesses, on the other hand, show some variations in order, although the damaged nature of many of the label texts impedes identification in

many cases. The lists are records of progeny, not amended from time to time as sons and daughters died. They are, one might say, statements of achievement, just as in a very different field were the repeated representations and accounts of military events like the battle of Qadesh. They should not, however, be dismissed or belittled because of their inflexibility. Apart from other considerations, they present a partial picture of the size and multiplicity of an ancient Egyptian royal family, of a kind not otherwise recorded. It may be that Ramesses sired more children than any of his predecessors, but it cannot be doubted that other long-living monarchs like Tuthmosis III and Amenophis III, to go back no farther than the Eighteenth Dynasty, surely had many sons and daughters by their various wives and concubines whose names have not survived in the records.

It would be expected that of the two sides of the royal progeny, the princes would have better expectations than the princesses; but that would be only partially true, as we shall discover. Initially, however, the princes should be scrutinized, and one of the first things to emerge is how little is known about most of them; they figure in the lists, and then no further records survive. Some undoubtedly had significant prospects, and would have known that there was a good chance that succession to the throne might come their way, if mortality intervened. Who among the first five or six sons would have conceived it possible that the throne would fall to son number thirteen (Merenptah)? To

young they surely were: his oldest son, there named Amonhiwonemef ('Amun is on his right hand') can scarcely have been eight years old, while Khaemwese, son number four, may have been only five; they were the sons respectively of Nefertari and Isitnofret. They are shown taking part in the charge, each in his own chariot with attendants. Amonhiwonemef, whose name was shortly to be changed to Amonhikhopshef ('Amun is on his strong arm'), is even precociously given a speaking part: he exclaims, "I believed the sky had no limit, but the ruler [Ramesses, his father] has let us see its limit to the south. I rejoice, I am glad that my father smites his enemy; he makes his arm

in an episode recorded in the battle reliefs, where a messenger from the king comes to them, already installed in the royal camp, warning them "not to leave by the western side, and keep clear of the battle." Close by is shown Prehiwonemef, the third of Ramesses' sons, speeding in a chariot, and thought possibly to have been put in charge of the safety of his younger brothers in the camp. No other sons are shown in the battle scenes, or mentioned in the texts of the battle until the contest is over. Then a number of sons are represented, leading forward the most important foreign prisoners to be presented to the king: Horhiwonemef (son twelve), Meryre (son eleven), and Sety

begin with, all sons would as part of their education be introduced to those fields of manly activity in which a prospective king would be expected to be competent, if not excel. Consequently, princes are shown as participating in military expeditions from the earliest years of Ramesses' reign, and even from before his accession. The skirmish in Nubia, which took place late in the reign of Sethos I, but is recorded in Ramesses' early rock-cut temple at Bayt al-Wali, seems to have been the first occasion for young princes to accompany their father on campaign. And

powerful against the Nine Bows [the traditional enemies of Pharaoh]."
The reality of any participation in battle by very young princes may be considered as presence on campaign rather than actual blooding in conflict. At the battle of Qadesh in Year 5, time had advanced and several of the royal children were by then in their teens and might have accompanied their father or other divisional commanders for further experience in a major conflict. In fact, in the documentation of the battle there is mention of the presence of members of the royal family

(son nine). Later, in Thebes, a further group of sons is shown taking part in the presentation of spoils of the campaign to the Theban gods: Amonhikhopshef (son one), Ramessu (son two),... (probably Prehiwonemef, son three), Khaemwese (son four),... (probably Monthuhikhopshef, son five),... (probably Nebenkharu, son six), Meryamun (son seven), Amonemuia (son eight),... (possibly Setpenre, son ten), Sety (son nine), Meryre (son eleven), and Merenptah (son thirteen). And so the young sons were introduced to warfare and the duties which followed a successful campaign. It is, of course, impossible to tell whether things happened as depicted, but at least indications are given of how matters should be carried forward on such occasions. So, in Year 7/8, when a quick raid into Canaan was needed to remind the local rulers to whom they owed allegiance, one part of the force was put ostensibly under the command of Amonhikhopshef, who by now presumably was being seriously groomed as the heir to the throne in fact as well as in principle. A few years later, several princes took part in the Nubian foray against Irem; the names of Merenptah and Setemuia can be identified in the damaged record in the temple of

appear in the lists as the obvious next candidate in line. It has plausibly been suggested that Sethikhopshef was in fact Amonhikhopshef renamed, the northern favored deity, Seth, replacing the southern imperial deity, Amun. This solution would therefore, not unreasonably, result in the extension of Ramesses' firstborn son as crown prince. By Year 30 the second son of the lists, Ramessu, had become crown prince, to be succeeded briefly by Khaemwese in Year 52. After a few years only Khaemwese had also died, to be followed as crown prince by Merenptah. In the lists the large brood of princes are individually called just "king's son of his body, his beloved." Where additional

Amara in Nubia. Setemuia may possibly be identified with Amonemuia, son number eight.

Short and inexplicit references to the princes scarcely make up a rounded picture of the developing lives and careers of Ramesses' sons. In the lists the first three are given senior military titles, which presumably they held by the time that the lists were carved. Amonhikhopshef, firstborn son and crown prince for many years, disappears from records after Year 20, to be replaced as crown prince by a son named Sethikhopshef, who does not

references to sons occur on other monuments – and there are singularly few – it emerges that some at least fulfilled functions by which they could serve the state, and presumably justify their privileged positions. Khaemwese, the great exception, we shall encounter shortly. Merenptah, who finally succeeded his father, acquired senior military rank and other administrative functions. Meryaten, who was sixteenth son, became 'chief of seers,' the high priest of Re at Heliopolis, a most important priestly office paralleling that of Khaemwese at Memphis.

246-247
Scene from the Corridor of the Bull at Abydos, completed in Ramesses' reign. The king, along with four deities, pulls tight a net trap full of birds, which he then presents to Amon-Re and Mut, accompanied by his son Amonhikhopshef.

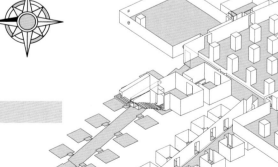

248 bottom
On rediscovery, KV5 was
not thought to be of special interest.
Burton, who had first entered
the tomb in the 1820s, was unable
to penetrate more than a few
feet because of the rubble, as
hard as concrete, that blocked
the way.

The task facing archaeologist
Kent Weeks was formidable, but
the effort was well rewarded.
As more and more of the tomb was
cleared it became evident that it had
a most unusual plan, resulting from
its use for multiple burials.
There may yet be much more
to discover.

Mortality among the princes diminished their number as the years passed, and it seems that their father, mindful of their status and possibly of the pride he had shown in them while they still lived, chose to honor them in death by providing a communal tomb in the Valley of the Kings. For his chief wives he had arranged individual sepulchres in the Valley of the Queens, as we have seen. It was inconceivable that similar treatment might be offered to his dead sons, who had in their lifetimes fulfilled such functions in war and peace as had been required of them. There was no tradition of burial for royal children in the Valley of the Kings, but the prospect of the early deaths of many princes provided the opportunity for yet another demonstration of the king's grandiose pretensions. One should allow that a degree of paternal pride and sorrow might have entered into the plan for a multiple tomb. One might also, cynically, consider that Ramesses' own tomb, vast and of an original plan (now recently cleared, but still mostly inaccessible to the public) had probably been completed by the middle of his reign, allowing the squads of royal tomb-builders the opportunity to embark on another huge excavation in the Valley.

KV5 has, in this abbreviated designation, become one of the most interesting, if not sensational, rediscoveries in Egypt of recent years. KV stands for Kings' Valley, and 5 is the number assigned to the tomb by John Gardner Wilkinson in the 1820s. The tomb was first properly noted by James Burton, an early traveler and proto-Egyptologist, who was able to enter only part of the tomb, marking his entry with his name and the date 1825. It is not impossible that some earlier entry had taken place in the eighteenth century. These early investigations were not pursued because of the massive heaps of debris washed into the tomb by floods over the millennia since antiquity. A new campaign to rediscover and clear the tomb was initiated some years ago by Kent Weeks, who has been for many years engaged in mapping the Theban Necropolis. What he has revealed in the subsequent years is a huge tomb with a network of corridors and chambers on several levels, thoroughly robbed, but still containing enough evidence in fragmentary reliefs and damaged tomb furniture to show that many of the sons of Ramesses II were laid to rest in it. The tomb entrance lies practically opposite that of Ramesses II's own tomb (KV7), and evidence suggests that it may have been an unfinished and unoccupied tomb of the Eighteenth Dynasty, taken over and exploited for the royal sons, prematurely deceased. From the evidence already collected it seems certain that some of the oldest and most important sons were buried in it, such as Amonhikhopshef and Ramessu. Quite possibly Amonhikhopshef was the first to be buried, and he is so named in the tomb, not as Sethikhopshef – the later name might not have been so welcome in the Theban context. This burial would have taken place by Year 30, an interment requiring special care and ceremony in view of this son's having been crown prince for almost three decades. Then perhaps was the opportunity taken to make use of the earlier unoccupied tomb, so close to the king's own prepared sepulchre, and later to develop it for multiple princely burials. The names of almost twenty princes have so far been retrieved on items of funerary equipment such as *shabti* figures, canopic jars, on wall inscriptions etc.

It may be many years before the full account of the tomb and its contents can be told, but the discoveries already made have provided unusual insights into the funerary activities of Ramesses' reign, and the apparent solicitude he extended to his sons in death as well as in life.

248-249
The tomb of Ramesses' sons (KV5), with Kent Weeks observing work on a mound of debris blocking part of the tomb. Since antiquity, great quantities of mud and rubble have been washed into the tomb by flash floods.

249 bottom
A corridor in tomb KV5 showing the entrances to some of the cell-like rooms, possibly the individual burial chambers for the sons of Ramesses II. The significance of much of the tomb plan remains to be discovered.

Two sons who were certainly not buried in KV5 were Khaemwese and Merenptah. The latter in due course qualified for his own individual royal tomb in the Valley of the Kings (KV8), and his career as king lies beyond the scope of this book. The career of Khaemwese, however, is quite another matter. He made his mark in no uncertain terms during his father's reign and achieved such a reputation that he became a figure of great wisdom and authority, about whom fantastical tales were told long after his death. There might be some justification in considering that Egypt would have fared extremely well had Ramesses not lived out his sixty-seven years of rule, but died when Khaemwese had advanced to be crown prince. All the surviving evidence points to Khaemwese's having been an exceptional person, an excellent administrator, a concerned conservator of ancient monuments, and a learned priestly official in Memphis who was undoubtedly entrusted with important responsibilities by his father.

Khaemwese was fourth son, the second born to Isitnofret. His birth predated Ramesses' accession to the throne, and in his early years Khaemwese was schooled, as were the other young sons, in the practices of warfare. As noted above, he is shown in the reliefs in the temple of Bayt al-Wali, in a chariot attending the skirmish conducted by his father in Nubia during the last years of Sethos I. He was also included among the sons shown making the presentation of offerings to the Theban deities after the battle of Qadesh. But the military life was not for him. In the listings of sons he receives no military titles; in fact, like most of the later sons, he is mostly described as "king's son of his body, his beloved"; only in the later list in the temple of Wadi al-Sabua (after Year 44) is he described also as "*sem*-priest of Ptah," a title he had held since he was about twenty years old. We shall never know how Khaemwese managed to extricate himself from a predictable military career. Was he no good in the arts of warfare, and in the handling of troops in battle? Was he simply more interested in intellectual matters? It would be good to think that some perspicacious palace official

250 bottom left
Mask of sheet gold found on a
mummy, possibly that of
Khaemwese, in the Serapeum at
Saqqara. Other objects associated
with this mummy and with the
burial of Apis bulls are inscribed for
Khaemwese (Louvre, 536).

250 bottom right
An amulet of falcon-headed Horus,
of lapis lazuli set in gold, inscribed
with Khaemwese's name. Found
on the body that is possibly
Khaemwese in the Serapeum
(Louvre, N.744).

250-251
Pectoral found on the masked
mummy in the Serapeum. Within a
pylon shape, the primary motif
consists of the vulture and uraeus
together with wings, with the
prenomen of Ramesses II above.
Gold with glass inlays
(Louvre, N.767).

252 top
Alabaster canopic jar made to contain
the mummified entrails of an Apis bull
buried in Year 16 or 30 of Ramesses II:
"A monument made by the sem-priest
and king's son Khaemwese."
From Saqqara. (Louvre).

252 bottom
An amulet of Khaemwese found with
the burial in the Serapeum. This tyet,
the "knot of Isis," could be used
according to the Book of the Dead
to invoke the power of Isis
(Louvre, N.753).

recognized his interest in religious and
domestic matters and aversion to the
military life, and recommended that he
serve a kind of apprenticeship among the
priesthood of Ptah at Memphis, under the
tutelage of Huy, high priest of the god. In
whatever way it happened, it turned out to
be a good move, for Khaemwese remained
in the service of the god throughout the
remainder of his life.

The cult of Ptah at Memphis was one of
the oldest and most respected of Egyptian
religious institutions. Heliopolis (Re),
Thebes (Amun), to a lesser extent
Hermopolis (Thoth), and Memphis were in
the New Kingdom the distinguished
centers of religious influence, and of these
Heliopolis and Memphis could claim the
priority. Ptah was a creator god, an earth
god, a god of intellectual status, always
honored from at least the time of the
unification of the two lands of Upper and
Lower Egypt under Menes at the beginning
of dynastic Egypt. His cult was highly
respected, his influence essentially non-
political, his authority awesome. Because of
him, as much as for the location of the city,
Memphis retained a position of pre-
eminence among Egyptian cities, always a
major center of administration and trade,
well established long before upstart Thebes
rose to a kind of prominence in the New
Kingdom. Ramesses II, as we have seen,
saw in Memphis and in its primal cult of
Ptah a vital hinge on which his power
could turn. The temple of Ptah was greatly
extended in his reign, massively
embellished with colossal sculptures. It is
no surprise, therefore, that he saw the
importance of maintaining the distinction
of the city, and the need to ensure that its
governance and administration should be
overseen by officials who could be trusted.
Who better, then, to establish in Memphis
as his principal representative than his
fourth son, whose inclination lay
apparently in the direction of non-military
activities?

As *sem*-priest of Ptah, Khaemwese was
subordinate to the high priest of the god,
but as time passed he became someone

upon whom many of the principal duties of
the priesthood devolved, and he seems to
have acquired a position of very
considerable authority in Memphis, which
was not confined to religious matters. For
example, there was the supervision of the
subsidiary cult of the Apis bull, which was
maintained within the complex of the Ptah
temple. The Apis, the living animal of part
of the essence of the god Ptah, was selected
according to certain specified markings,
and throughout its life lived in a special
compound, pampered and worshiped. At
death its body was mummified and taken
for burial to the royal necropolis of Saqqara
just to the west of Memphis. Up to the
reign of Ramesses II, the mummified Apis
bulls were buried individually at Saqqara.
Khaemwese, however, introduced a new
arrangement according to which the
mummified bulls were buried in a catacomb
of chambers served by a single chapel in
which rituals could be celebrated. In the
Late Period further catacombs were
developed, and it is these that are now
open to tourists and are known,
erroneously, as the Serapeum. It is not
impossible that Khaemwese himself was
buried in or close to the bull catacomb
which he initiated, but the evidence is very
confusing. It is certain that he was buried
at Saqqara and not in tomb KV5 in the
Valley of the Kings. Unfortunately, the
remains of a mummy and a coffin, which
probably came from his Saqqara burial, do
not appear to have survived after their
discovery by Auguste Mariette in the mid-
nineteenth century. The circumstances of
their finding seem to have been unusual –
not in a regular tomb – but there can be
little doubt that he was buried in or near
the bull burials at Saqqara. He had himself
supervised the burials of dead Apis bulls in
Years 16 and 30, and initiated the new
catacomb with a burial in, possibly, Year
42/43. Burials in Years 55 and, again
possibly, 65/66, were conducted by
Merenptah. Khaemwese remained at
Memphis for the rest of his life,
undertaking many duties in addition to his
priestly function. He established a

remarkable reputation during his lifetime, laying the basis for a posthumous renown for sage wisdom. He has sometimes been described in modern times as an archaeologist, even the first Egyptologist, a title which he probably would have found very puzzling. The appellation has arisen out of the activities he undertook to examine and rehabilitate some of the older monuments in the Memphite Necropolis, particularly pyramids. The extent of his 'antiquarian' activities are not fully understood because the memorial texts he arranged to have carved into the facing stones of the rehabilitated pyramids have in many cases been lost along with the stripping of the outer skins of fine limestone from the structures in medieval and modern times.

From the fragments of surviving texts it is clear that although the work on the pyramids was carried out in the name of Ramesses II, the credit for its implementation, and probably its inspiration, must go to Khaemwese: "Very greatly did the *sem*-priest, the king's son Khaemwese desire to renew the monuments of the kings of Upper and Lower Egypt, because of what they had done, and of their solidity, which was falling into decay." Such work was carried out at North and South Saqqara, at the sun temple of Neuserre at Abu Gurob, and possibly elsewhere. We may allow Khaemwese the credit. Concern for the monuments of past ages was something that the Egyptians liked to claim as the inspiration for such works. There is no doubt that when it suited their purpose, Egyptian kings and also provincial officials were pleased to look after what had been erected by their great predecessors. But they were equally ready to change or destroy the works of their ancestors if they wished to make use of sites occupied by older structures. It is perhaps a little excessive to consider what Khaemwese did with the pyramids as being antiquarian or archaeological as we would understand these words; the inscriptions he had carved on these monuments with their somewhat vainglorious claims, can hardly be thought

of as early 'museum labels,' as they have sometimes been described. Nevertheless, there was merit to be gained from looking after the works of the past. In the general standard text of restoration, quoted above, Khaemwese could indeed claim credit for what had been done: for him the glory, for the dead, the honor.

Khaemwese remained ostensibly in the service of Ptah, the god of Memphis, until he died in Year 55 of Ramesses' reign. For a year or two only, at the very end, he became high priest of the god, but for the many years preceding, forty or more, he was content with the rather modest office of *sem*-priest. We must admire his order of priorities in that he did not require the highest Memphite priestly office until the very last years of his life. He was, after all, one of the senior sons of the king, although he did not achieve the position of crown prince until about Year 50. Nevertheless, his power only partially derived from his priestly position, and he certainly acted in administrative matters as if the royal authority was there to support him. Memphis remained an important place, probably second only to Piramesse at that time, the place where coronations should be celebrated, and where jubilees should be proclaimed. As we have seen, the many jubilees celebrated by Ramesses II were acted out at Piramesse, but it also seems clear that Memphis remained the key place from which these notable events should be initiated. To that end Khaemwese served as the principal agent in proclaiming each jubilee throughout the land, and was initially involved in the proclamations of the first five jubilees, up to Year 42. He traveled the length of the country in making his proclamations; at least that is the impression gained from a consideration of the places where inscriptions record the proclamations. It must be thought possible, however, that in some of the more remote places where records have been found, like the island of Biga in the First Cataract, the task of proclaiming the jubilees may have been done in his name and not personally, as the records suggest.

253
Sandstone kneeling statue of Khaemwese, found in the Karnak cachette in 1904. He is shown holding before him a shrine containing a figure of the god Ptah-Tatenen, usually associated with Memphis. (Cairo, JE 367220).

When Khaemwese died in Year 55 (c. 1225–1224 B.C.), he was succeeded as crown prince by his younger brother Merenptah, a son, like Khaemwese, of Isitnofret, and originally number thirteen in the tally of royal sons. Not a great deal is known about his career up to that point. He held senior military titles, and certainly participated in some of the punitive expeditions of the earlier years of Ramesses' reign. He may have been too young to have attended the Qadesh campaign, but he subsequently made sure that his name was included among those sons who made presentations to the Theban gods after the campaign. It is thought likely that even before he became crown prince, Merenptah had become Ramesses' right-hand man at Piramesse, and that after Khaemwese's death he moved easily into the position of prince-regent for the remaining years of the reign. He also took over some of his brother's Memphite duties, including, as was mentioned earlier, conducting the obsequies for dead Apis bulls in Khaemwese's new bull catacomb. Merenptah was probably in his mid-fifties when he became crown prince, and happily he had enough stamina to survive until he could succeed his father. By then he had ample experience of government, and could move easily to become the new living Horus, King of Upper and Lower Egypt.

254 left
Shabti *figure for "the king's son, sem-priest Khaemwese." Here as usual he is shown wearing the side-lock mostly associated with childhood, but also worn by the sem-priest and the Iunmutef form of Horus. (Louvre, N.461).*

254 right
Sandstone shabti figure of Khaemwese from the Serapeum at Saqqara. These figures, whose duty was to work in place of the named deceased in the afterlife, usually carry agricultural tools. This figure holds tyet *and* djed *symbols (Louvre, SH74).*

255
Granite bust of King Merenptah from his funerary temple at Thebes. Thirteenth son of Ramesses II, he became king when he was over 50. On his shoulder can be seen his prenomen as Pharaoh, Baenre-Merenamun. (Cairo, JE 31414).

Generally speaking, daughters were not as well regarded in ancient Egypt as sons. Nevertheless, there is plenty of evidence to show that women were not without respect even in the families of unimportant persons. Women had their own particular spheres of activity in Egyptian life, and they were not thought to be of small importance, to be ignored. Daughters are usually included in representations of families on funerary stelae, and in the tombs of private officials. Their domestic functions were important, and their matrimonial prospects of considerable potential value. Within the royal family, women might play very important roles, as was seen in the last chapter: daughters could become the wives of kings, and could be given as wives to foreign rulers or princes as elements in the political game. None of these considerations were applicable to Egypt alone in the ancient world, but an impression is gained that in Egypt, women, especially princesses, were far more highly regarded than elsewhere. In the reign of Ramesses II his daughters did very well.

The lists of the daughters represented in the temples of Egypt and Nubia, parallel to those of the sons of Ramesses II, show that the recorded female progeny was about the same in number as the male progeny. As has been pointed out, there is not such strict consistency in the order of daughters as there is for the sons. But many of the lists are badly preserved, and the names of many princesses are lost or indecipherable. However, the order of the earliest born is reasonably well established. The harem establishment of Mi-wer has been mentioned before as having been a place where a large part of Ramesses' collection of wives and concubines lived in relative domestic isolation, many miles away from the Delta Residence of Piramesse. No records have survived which give information about the division of wives and children between the two establishments, but it may be thought likely that at least one of Ramesses' great royal wives kept him company in Piramesse, and that within her entourage there might be secondary wives, concubines, and even some children, particularly boys. Most of the girl children would surely have been nurtured and educated at Mi-wer. But as they grew to maturity their royal mothers might consider bringing them to the attention of their father, if only for the self-interested reason of retaining influence. In this way the daughters of Nefertari, the first and most influential of the great royal wives, were promoted, and also those of Queen Isitnofret, whose own status apparently remained inferior to that of Nefertari until the latter's death.

Four daughters at least became royal wives, and were eventually honored with burials in the Valley of the Queens. The two most senior daughters – the firstborn girls of Isitnofret and Nefertari – were Bintanta and Merytamun. It is not certain which of these was first to become a great royal wife, but they were both described as such after Nefertari died, but before the death of Isitnofret. It is not possible to tell which of them had precedence, but the recent discovery of colossal statues of Ramesses II and Merytamun at Akhmim, an important provincial capital, provides the suggestion that this queen might have acquired the priority which had certainly been possessed by her mother. Unexpected discoveries, however, are always open to extravagant interpretations, especially when evidence is exiguous. Two further princesses at least became great royal wives later in the reign, Nebt-tawy, who was fifth in the lists, and Hentmire, who does not occur in the lists, but is now thought certainly to be a daughter of Ramesses II, and not, perhaps, of his father King Sethos I. Nothing substantial is known about these two great royal wives, but both qualified for burial in the Valley of the Queens. A fifth daughter, Hent-tawy, number seven in the lists, presents a problem: she is nowhere recorded as a consort of her father, yet she was allowed a tomb in the Valley of the Queens. There clearly remains much to learn about the lives and fates of the daughters of Ramesses II. Those who were not married to their father, to a brother, or to a foreign prince were destined for the sheltered life of the harem. They could not expect personal tombs in the Valley of the Queens, or even the kind of communal tomb provided for Ramesses' sons, unless one such is still to be discovered. In life, however, they were condemned to a kind of benevolent incarceration; their royal genes could not be wasted on non-royal husbands.

256 left
Rosellini's strongly colored illustration of Bintanta offering a bouquet and a sistrum to the goddess Anukis (not shown); on one of the pillars in the great hall of Ramesses' temple at Abu Simbel.

256 right
Figure of Merytamun, daughter and wife of Ramesses II, from the first hall of her tomb in the Valley of the Queens. In this scene she stands in front of the djed pillar, symbol of stability. Illustration by Rosellini.

257
Figure of Nebt-tawy by Prisse d'Avennes, from her tomb in the Queens' Valley. In the tomb she is rightly described as "great royal wife," but here she is shown wearing a headdress associated with royal concubines.

THE KING'S REALM

CHAPTER 8

258
Ceremony during the festival of Min, on the second pylon of the Ramesseum. Birds are released, and a lector priest issues instructions to two subordinates raising standards before Ramesses, who wears a circlet of uraei *around the double crown*

259
Khaemhet, a royal scribe and official in charge of granaries, supervises the grain harvest. Scribes note the results, which are reported by their supervisors to Khaemhet. This Eighteenth Dynasty scene reflects official duties typical for the New Kingdom.

Continuity in administration and confidence in its efficiency are the secure bases upon which good governance is founded. The politics of rulers and the intrigues within palaces might be unsettling or eccentric, but all will be well if there is a good civil service to keep the course of the ship of state steady. In ancient Egypt, long periods of untroubled government led to remarkable administrative confidence and regularity. A highly efficient system of internal bureaucracy was developed during the Eighteenth Dynasty, which provided the Pharaoh with a settled base upon which he could develop his particular policies, especially in regard to foreign affairs. The divine ruler was unquestionably the fount of authority, and the indisputable master of the fates of his people; but the management of affairs lay under the control of those officials who were appointed expressly to carry out the will of the ruler. There is much evidence to show that in ancient Egypt the tentacles of administration embraced every activity in the land, and

that few ordinary Egyptians could live lives free from the interference of officials. Up until the Middle Kingdom (c. 1800 B.C.), local affairs were in the hands of noble provincial families, – nomarchs – who were mostly hereditary and ruled the provinces, or nomes, like minor princelings. Their power was greatest in the nomes far from the royal residence and capital, which was usually in the region of Memphis. The fairly independent administrations of the nomarchs were abolished during the Twelfth Dynasty, and a more centralized regime developed, in which the highest official in the land, usually called the vizier, acted as the king's representative in most internal matters. The power of the vizier, established at that time, formed the core around which was constructed the highly developed system of officers and senior officials, which evolved during the Eighteenth Dynasty.

It was possibly the existence of this powerful, well-established administration, which prevented the country from falling utterly apart during the reign of Akhenaten – the Amarna Period. Some senior officials

migrated from Thebes to Amarna and maintained some general control over the country. In the north of the land, administration based in Memphis seems to have been less affected, being untainted in the eyes of the Atenist regime by the dire influence of the Theban deities and their priesthoods. Senior officials like Horemheb were well placed in Memphis to avoid the greatest and most damaging effects of the rule of the Aten, and were able to appreciate the possibility of a return to what could be called 'normality' when Akhenaten might die. And so it seems to have happened. After the demise of Akhenaten and his immediate successors, it remained for Horemheb as king to rebuild the Egyptian administration and restore the kind of internal bureaucracy that had proved so successful before Akhenaten's brief revolution. One may conjecture that the essential framework had survived the intervening period, and that with the help of senior officials, Horemheb, and later Sethos I, were able to re-establish the excellent system, which had made Egypt such an efficiently run country.

260 left
Kneeling sandstone statue of Paser,
Viceroy of Kush, found by Belzoni in
the Abu Simbel temple. He holds a
pillar topped with a ram-head of
Amon-Re, with a prayer to the god
"residing in Piramesse."

260 right
Shabti-figure of Paser. It does not
carry the usual formula calling on
the figure to work for Paser in the
afterlife, but just a full titulary of
Paser as vizier.

By the time of Ramesses' accession, the machine of state was running smoothly, and it appears to have been the case that for the whole of his long reign there were no serious problems in the system. It is, of course, hazardous to make such a claim, because it was not in the nature of official Egyptian inscriptions to draw attention to the failings of the system. It was usually left to a succeeding regime to point out the weaknesses of a preceding period in order to demonstrate the efficiency and success of what was achieved under new management. In the case of Ramesses II, however, the emphasis in the great Abydos dedicatory text is on completion, on carrying to a successful conclusion the works and projects initiated in his father's relatively short reign. To this end there is an emphasis on continuity, and no suggestion of substantial change. As was to be expected, the administration would be supervised from the top by the two viziers, of South and North – Theban and Memphite, the latter to become based subsequently at Piramesse. The southern viziers are better documented than those of the north, and in particular Paser, who had received his appointment under Sethos,

serving him for about five years before the new king ascended the throne. Paser then continued in office for perhaps another twenty-five years. He seems to have been an exemplary chief of staff for his sovereign, and apparently viewed his role in the tradition of the great viziers of the Eighteenth Dynasty, like Rekhmire and Ramose. A strong indication of his conservative approach to the exercise of his office may be found in the tomb he constructed in the Theban Necropolis, begun under Sethos and completed under Ramesses.

Paser's family was well established in Thebes, although in origin it probably came from the north. His father, Nebnetjeru, was high priest of Amun, and his mother, Merytre, was head of the harem of Amun. He belonged therefore to the highest level of Theban officialdom, and his elevation to the position of vizier bears the stamp of strong family tradition, if not of nepotism. He did not disappoint; and his tomb, richly decorated with painted reliefs now greatly damaged, testifies to his importance and to his attachment to the status quo. Among the texts in the great columned transverse hall of the tomb chapel, completed and

probably decorated during the reign of Sethos, are the sad remains of a composition outlining the duties of the vizier. It is an ancient text; scholars still argue about the date of its composition. It occurs in a number of Eighteenth- Dynasty vizier tombs, and it is now thought that it was most probably composed early in that dynasty. There are, however, good grounds for considering it of earlier date, possibly of the late Middle Kingdom (c. 1750 B.C.), when successive viziers were exceptionally powerful, maintaining some stability for a royal regime of very uncertain power. This debate over composition need not concern us in considering the importance of this text to the mind of Paser. For him it clearly represented the traditional statement of the vizier's duties, written down a long time ago; it scarcely would have mattered if it were three hundred or five hundred years earlier. It was the text found in the tombs of the great Eighteenth Dynasty viziers, and that fact would have been enough to set the seal of authority on it.

All aspects of administration were placed under the control of the vizier, and a few extracts from the text may give the flavor of the whole.

261 left
Blue faience cup placed by Paser in
an Apis buial. Such objects were
commonly part of funerary
equipment. The text here calls on all
scribes to perform their proper
functions for the vizier Paser
(Louvre).

261 right
Two amuletic carnelian beads from
an Apis burial in the Serapeum.
They have a funerary purpose and
were deposited by Paser, who here is
"the Osiris, overseer of the city
[Thebes] and vizier" (Louvre).

Although the Paser version is only very partially preserved, it appears to have followed closely the version found in, for example, the tomb of Rekhmire, the great vizier of King Tuthmosis III. It is an impersonal document, not aimed specifically at any named vizier. The composition starts with instructions on how the vizier should dress and present himself in his hall:

"The sealing of the strong-rooms... should be reported to him... . The condition of fortresses of the Delta and the North should be reported to him... . He should greet the lord [the king]... every day when the affairs of the Two Lands have been reported to him... . If any agent whom the vizier may send on a mission to any official... let him not be enticed, and let him not be bullied by an official... . Anybody who petitions him about lands, the vizier should order him to appear before him... . All conveyances [of property] should be brought to him, and it is he who shall seal them... . It is he who dispatches any courier and any expedition of the king's house. It is he who appoints from the magistrates those who are to be the administrators of the North, the South, the Head of the South [Southern Upper Egypt]... . It is he who should arrange the mobilization of troops and their movement

in the suite of the Lord when he travels downstream and upstream [i.e., within Egypt]... . It is he who should dispatch regional officers to construct dykes throughout the whole land... . Every plea should be reported to him... . Nome records should be lodged in his office for the hearing of cases concerning any land... . It is he who should make every public proclamation and hear every complaint... . It is he who should hear all pleas... ."

This poorly organized but very comprehensive document provides a kind of blueprint of the vizier's role in Egyptian administration. It is by no means an accurate outline of the program of any particular vizier, but perhaps a reminder of the all-embracing nature of his responsibilities. It was the kind of reminder, which an earnest official might keep on his desk, but not necessarily follow or even read from time to time. Having it in one's tomb was just an indication of being committed in principle to the best practices of the past. Nevertheless, it would not be wrong to see in this document and in its placement in Paser's tomb the idea that he accepted the blanket responsibility for Egypt's internal administration in all its complexities. The full text is amazingly detailed in its specification of the vizier's duties, of which the extracts given above

provide just a flavor, and it may be properly deduced that most of the duties were carried out by subordinates in the vizier's office in Thebes or Memphis and by local officials in the provincial capitals. But the vizier was in the end responsible and answerable to the king alone.

It must be supposed that the vizier's office was daily bombarded with reports, pleas, complaints, and every kind of document. Egyptians were much given to putting things 'on paper,' but it is only occasionally that some glimpses may be obtained into the complexity and abundance of official documentation. A letter, a copy of which is preserved on a limestone flake from Thebes, sent by a scribe called Mose – a person of no real importance – to Paser, declares that he (Mose) is fulfilling all the duties assigned to him, mentioning in particular certain agricultural matters of a very local nature. Another ostracon copy of a letter was written by the scribe Nebre to Paser reporting the condition of the workmen's village at Dayr al-Madina: "Everything is in order, all the walls are in good shape, and all the workmen are receiving everything that is owed to them." Such trivialities no doubt made up the bulk of the incoming submissions to the vizier. There is little to suggest that Egypt was anything other than well administered during Paser's long tenure of the viziership.

262 top
Gold kiosk-shaped pectoral with faience and stone inlays, from the Serapeum. The lapis lazuli heart scarab has a text invoking the heart of Paser to help him. The scarab is supported by Isis and Nephthys (Louvre, N762).

263 top
The lapis lazuli reverse of the gold pendant. The texts are from the Book of the Dead, that on the scarab being the special text to invoke his heart to act for him in judgment. From an Apis burial in the Serapeum.

263 bottom
Gold-faced pendant inscribed with the name and title of the vizier Paser. It is pylon-shaped and has figures of the goddesses Isis and Neith worshiping a large lapis lazuli scarab (Louvre, N762).

Paser was succeeded as vizier by Khay before Year 30, possibly as early as Year 25. He inherited an administration, which seems to have remained highly efficient throughout Paser's term, and there is little evidence to suggest that matters deteriorated subsequently. One area in which Khay acquired additional responsibilities was that of organizing the royal jubilees. Up until the fifth jubilee, in Year 42/43, Khay was commissioned to proclaim the celebrations along with Khaemwese, and for the sixth jubilee he seems to have been the sole proclaimer. It may further be assumed that his jubilee duties were not restricted to proclamation. It is interesting to note that in all cases Khay is charged to carry out the duty of proclamation in the South and in the North, and one must speculate whether he therefore was for a time acting as vizier for the whole country. One small fragment, possibly from his Theban tomb, describes him as "mayor and vizier of the South and the North." It could be the case, however, that the authority of the Theban vizier subsumed that of the northern vizier as well. It would have been very surprising if the northern vizier had no part to play in successive *sed* festivals (jubilees).

The names of a number of northern viziers during the reign of Ramesses II are known, but unfortunately exact dates for their tenures of office cannot be established with any certainty. Two had the same name, Prahotpe or Rahotpe, of whom the second may have been the last to serve Ramesses in his long reign. One stemmed from Abydos and the other from Heracleopolis in Middle Egypt, and they may have been distantly related. There remains much confusion in the discrimination between these two senior officials, largely because the surviving documentation is not sufficiently detailed to solve the problems of identification. One man was buried at Sedment, near Heracleopolis, the other possibly at Saqqara. The earlier in office was serving Ramesses II in Year 42; the second, as stated above, served later, but probably not directly after the first. A great granite stela found at Saqqara shows a vizier named Rahotpe making adoration to Osiris and the Apis on one side, and Anubis and Ptah on the other. The texts are primarily eulogistic in respect of the vizier, but some sentences give an idea of how he considered his duties. Among other titles and epithets, he describes himself as "judge of the Two Lands, shield of the sovereign... greatest steward of the Lord in the Hall of Jubilees, who issues orders to everyone, chief of works, overseer of crafts, supervisor of the laws of the Good God in the Hall of Justice, spokesman of the King of Upper Egypt, herald of the King of Lower Egypt... who works out all the revenues in the whole land." These claims are no doubt excessive, and there is much more, Rahotpe asserting that he holds most of the senior religious appointments in the land. Overstating the case was not uncommon for Egyptian officials at all levels in the civil and religious fields. Presumably, if you were as grand as Rahotpe (Prahotpe), you could claim to be almost anything, provided that it was done in the name of the king.

While the stability of the king's realm depended to a great extent on the efficiency of the administration of the country, the continuation of stability was substantially secured by the prosperity of the country and the successful system of

taxation by which the financing of the whole could be maintained. The wealth of Egypt derived not so much from foreign tribute or the plunder acquired by warfare as from agriculture. A prosperous Egypt was an Egypt in which the progression of the seasons through the year was successfully exploited by good land management and by the complex system of taxation – by no means fully understood – which maximized the return of wealth to central treasuries. The good exploitation of the land was in turn dependent on the regular behavior of the river Nile, and on the widespread system of canals and dykes which controlled flooding and conserved water after the annual Nile flood. By the time of Ramesses' reign, the Egyptian state bureaucracy had many hundreds of years' experience in managing the land, and a clear appreciation of the importance of river and land management. Well-trained officials could estimate the effects of the annual flood, predict with some accuracy the outcome of harvests, and in consequence make fairly reliable assessments of what should be paid in taxes. It need not be supposed that the

system was free from abuse; there would always be officials who would take personal advantage of their privileged positions. A scribal exercise paints a miserable picture of the vulnerable peasant, whose crops have been devastated by snakes, hippopotamuses, mice, locusts, even cattle. Sparrows have assisted, and thieves have stolen cattle: "Then the scribe has landed at the riverbank, and sets about assessing the harvest tax; his assistants carry staves and palm rods. They say, 'Give corn,' although there isn't any. He is beaten severely, tied up and thrown into the well. His wife is bound and his children put in manacles."

As this is part of a scribal exercise, it ends with a professional encouragement: "A scribe, on the other hand, is the controller of everything.

He who writes is not taxed; he has nothing to pay." This, no doubt, was a common experience for the defenseless peasant, but it should not have been so, and would most surely have been deplored by the vizier had he known about such abuse.

Blind eyes may well have been turned, for the general good of the economy of the country.

264-265
The timeless activities of Egyptian agriculture are best shown in Eighteenth Dynasty tombs. Here, episodes in the barley harvest: treading the grain, winnowing, and recording the results. From the Theban tomb of Menna.

265 top right
Stela of the vizier Rahotpe, who may have been buried at Saqqara. He is shown, above, worshiping Osiris and the living Apis. The text below includes a self-justification. On the reverse, a text about the viziership (Cairo, JE 48845).

Closer to the system were the senior treasury officials, who supervised at the highest level the operation of the system, although they too may have been somewhat distant from what happened in the remote corners of the land. In the absence of general texts specifying the duties and outlining the activities of these and other officials, one can only deduce from occasional documents the magnitude of the responsibilities they carried. Equally, only rarely can one catch a glimpse of the extent of the wealth of the land, and of the immensely rich estates belonging to the great religious establishments throughout Egypt. A rare, but very extensive document of the Twentieth Dynasty provides astounding details of temple holdings in the reign of Ramesses III. Nothing of this kind has survived from Ramesses II's reign, but one copy of a letter on a Theban limestone ostracon gives some indication of the position in the earlier reign. It is a letter from the chief treasury official, the overseer of treasuries, Panehsy, addressed to Hori, a priest of Amun in the Southern City (Thebes). Panehsy writes from the north, giving a situation report on the land and other holdings of the great Theban temple situated in the Delta, and particularly specifying the people employed on the estates of Amun, along with their families. He states that he is submitting a list "of every man according to his occupation, together with their wives and children." Unfortunately only fragmentary pieces of information can be extracted from the central text, which includes a summary of the information collected. There are, for example, 8,760 farmers, 13,080 goatherds,

22,530 men in charge of fowl, 3,920 donkey-men, and so on. Even without precise details, it is still possible to comprehend the scale to which the land of Egypt was closely administered at the time. In a sense Egypt was easy to control; all the land that mattered agriculturally – and therefore fiscally – was flat, for the most part easily accessible from the Nile or the major waterways in the Delta. Farmers could not disappear into mountain valleys to hide from prying officials; they could not easily escape the long arm of the scribe and his bailiffs, who probably took some pleasure in enforcing the law and extracting at the same time something for themselves to pocket.

A striking feature of Egyptian administration in general is the theoretical ease with which quite humble petitioners were able to gain access to high authority when they needed to pursue matters of personal concern. The approach of the humble to the great has, it seems, always been an attractive characteristic of civil life in the Near East. While the law and its exercise by petty officials has rarely seemed to be on the side of the small individual, there always appeared to be the possibility of personal petition, even to an official as high as the vizier. So it would seem to be from a reading of the duties of the vizier, and so it would seem to have been from the few documents, which concern complaints addressed directly to high officials. No text throws such light on the workings of the Egyptian legal administration in the New Kingdom as that written up in his tomb by the treasury scribe in the temple of Ptah, called Mose.

The text contains the details of a case involving Mose's family and the ownership of a piece of land; the matter had its origins as early as the reign of King Amosis, first of the Eighteenth Dynasty rulers, approximately three hundred years before the reign of Ramesses II. A ship's captain, Neshi, was granted land in the region of Memphis by King Amosis as a reward for services rendered during the war of liberation, which saw the expulsion of the upstart Hyksos from Egypt and the establishment of the Eighteenth Dynasty and what is now called the New Kingdom. The piece of land was to be kept as a unit and not divided by inheritance, and it seems that no problems arose to disturb this arrangement until the reign of Horemheb at the end of the Eighteenth Dynasty. After the death of the contemporary administrator of the estate, the lady Sheritre, legal proceedings allowed a division of the land between a daughter, Werenro, and her brothers and sisters. For the time being, Werenro was to administer the estate, still as a unit, on behalf of her siblings. This decision was challenged by a younger sister, who succeeded in having a declaration made so that each child should have its own share. This decision in turn was challenged by Werenro and her son Huy, and it seems that without the matter being properly settled, Huy continued to cultivate the land as a unit until he died. His widow, Nubnofret, was then evicted from the land by an individual named Khay, whose position seems to have been to act as an agent for other members of the family. In Year 18 of Ramesses II, Nubnofret returned

Ramesses II

to the courts, bringing her case before the vizier in Heliopolis and calling for an examination of Treasury records to prove that she was indeed a descendant of Neshi and that her husband had regularly paid his taxes on the land and its produce. The appropriate documents were collected from central archives in Piramesse and produced in court for scrutiny. They did not, however, substantiate Nubnofret's claims, and she lost the case. It was shown that Huy's tax payments were not recorded, and that Nubnofret was not mentioned in the documents. So she remained evicted, and the land was parceled out to the so-called legitimate descendants of Neshi. The matter did not end there. In due course Mose, the son of Huy and Nubnofret, grew up and reopened the case, claiming that Khay had managed to have the documents from Piramesse falsified, in collusion no doubt with the officials who had collected them from the archives. These officials, probably at the suggestion of Khay, could see something to their own advantage in organizing this deception. Mose changed the direction of his and his mother's defense, relying now on the evidence of witnesses who established beyond argument that Huy had cultivated the land, paid his taxes, and was a legitimate descendant of Neshi. At last, judgment was made in favor of Huy's widow and son, and Khay was declared to be in the wrong. From Mose's point of view justice at last had been done, and the inclusion of the account of the extended affair, along with copies of some supporting documents, in the texts in his tomb serves to record his triumph and perhaps his excessively self-satisfied attitude.

In this tangled and long drawn-out matter, it is the side of Mose and his mother that is presented in the tomb. One may wonder whether it all stopped there. Perhaps other descendants of Neshi returned to the courts at a later date; they too would have had reason to feel aggrieved at having been denied part of Neshi's inheritance. As is so often the case, one's sympathies naturally lie on the side of the one who is the last to present the matter, namely Mose. There is now no way of discovering the ultimate outcome; but there is no reason to believe implicitly in Mose's statement of the case. Nevertheless, the contents of the texts in Mose's tomb throw light on many aspects of Egyptian law and administration during the New Kingdom. It can be seen that resort to law, even to the court of the vizier, was something within the capability of fairly ordinary people. In law, Egyptian women were treated equally with men in matters of land tenure and inheritance. It was possible to reopen a case if new evidence could be produced. Records existed and were preserved in central archives, in this case at Piramesse, the Delta capital of Ramesses II. The court, presided over apparently by the vizier himself, was prepared to take time over reaching a decision, and very ready to summon documentation for inspection. Nothing was arbitrary. The impression is gained of a system, which worked not just to the advantage of the bureaucracy and the administration, but even for the interests of the individual. It would be good to believe that the impression is close to the truth.

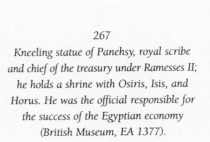

267

Kneeling statue of Panehsy, royal scribe and chief of the treasury under Ramesses II; he holds a shrine with Osiris, Isis, and Horus. He was the official responsible for the success of the Egyptian economy (British Museum, EA 1377).

The secret of the success of the ancient Egyptian system of administration was to a great extent the efficiency of the scribal class. "Be a scribe!" was surely the call that most Egyptian mothers with pretensions for improvement would repeat again and again to their sons. To be a scribe was to be in effect a civil servant; it was a safe and steady calling, and one that brought with it all kinds of advantages. It was, moreover, highly respectable as a profession, to such an extent that no great person in the land objected to being called a scribe. Among other things, being a scribe implied being literate, being able to write, whether in hieroglyphs or in the cursive hieratic script, the form used for most writing on papyrus. It also involved the ability to read, and that meant not just knowing how to interpret the great inscriptions on the mighty buildings and monuments throughout the land, but also the capacity to scrutinize documents, read letters, and comprehend calculations. Literacy was a very valuable tool. A scribe could control the papers, interpret the documents, check the accounts, or simply act as an intermediary between individuals who were not literate. It was a serious matter to be a scribe, and while the texts emphasize his responsibilities and praise his impartiality, there is no reason to believe that some scribes might find it convenient on occasion to bend the rules, or engage in a little falsification.

Some of the student exercises contain the elements of accepted practice and the outlines of the scribal ethic. Such texts were written out by student scribes and were written wholly from the scribal point of view. Nevertheless, it is possible to consider them as proper statements of how

the profession and practices of scribes were estimated in the Nineteenth Dynasty. On training:

"I have placed you in the room of instruction together with the children of magistrates, to inform and teach you about that promising profession. Let me tell you how the scribe goes on, saying, 'Jump to your place! Write in front of your fellows! Tidy your clothes and see to your sandals!' You should bring your book every day with good intent; do not be idle... . Do your sums quietly, without noise from your mouth being heard. Write with your hand, read with your mouth, and seek advice. Don't be tired, don't waste time idly, or look out for your limbs! Follow the ways of your teacher, and listen to what he has to say. Be a scribe!"

So if the student paid attention and became a good scribe, his future would be good. If he came from a scribal family, he would almost certainly find a good position, possibly even following precisely in his father's footsteps. Otherwise patronage or nepotism might help. In such matters the ancient Egyptian would have seen no impropriety. And the advantages of being a scribe were not insignificant: "It saves you from hard work and protects you from all kinds of manual labor. You don't have to carry the hoe and the mattock, and therefore, no basket. It separates you from having to pull on the oar, and spares you afflictions, for you are not subject to many lords and many masters." The writer then lists a great many professions and trades which are essentially disagreeable: the child put to be a soldier, the old man, a farmer, the cripple, a doorkeeper, the blind man to look after cattle. Even the priest has a tough time, endlessly engaged in

religious services and soaking himself in water three times a day, in winter and summer, in rain or shine. The baker is endlessly baking bread, his head right in the oven, while his son hangs onto his feet – and if the son lets go, he falls right into the oven. And so the writer comes to the obvious conclusion: "But the scribe, he is way ahead of every kind of labor in this world."

In addition to escaping hard work and avoiding paying taxes, the scribe had the real possibility of position and wealth in Egyptian society. He could become the trusted official of the king, with power to open treasuries and granaries, to issue the necessary offerings on days of festival, "dressed in fine clothes, accompanied by horses, and with [his] own boat on the Nile." He might have assistants, a splendid house, a powerful position, and all the king's gifts. Who would be a soldier? All the evidence points to scribal advantages, but, as we noted, all the evidence comes from texts written and probably composed by scribes. What was the other side of the coin? Were scribes regarded with respect by illiterate Egyptians? Were they seen to be the officers of a repressive, centralized state who could exploit the system to their own advantage? We shall probably never know, but it is hard to believe that scribes – that is, civil servants – were always objects of affection and respect in ancient Egypt. They were certainly not greeted with enthusiasm in the countryside, as we have seen; and the likelihood is that those who were in a position to do favors, or even just be helpful, would expect reciprocal favors. There is nothing to suggest that the official was not as venal in antiquity as he may be today in certain societies.

269 top
This Fifth Dynasty unnamed sculpture perfectly expresses the qualities expected in the Egyptian scribe. Holding his papyrus on his tightened kilt, he radiates confidence, but avoids the smugness of his Ramesside successors (Cairo, JE 30273).

269 bottom
Two New Kingdom scribes bend earnestly over their open papyrus sheets, writing accounts for their superiors. Scribes formed the backbone of the ancient Egyptian civil service, and enjoyed great privileges as a result.

The king's realm, strictly speaking, was just the land of Egypt, the Nile Valley from Elephantine (Aswan) in the south to the Mediterranean Sea in the north. It was Upper and Lower Egypt, each part organized into provinces, or nomes. Throughout dynastic history no serious attempt was made to change these limits, to extend the land area of Egypt, to incorporate, for example, the territories in Asia, which became subservient to the Egyptian king from time to time, and often for long periods. Such lands were not Egypt as it was conceived by the ancient Egyptians themselves; the inhabitants of these lands could never be Egyptians. One region, however, was specially regarded, and during the New Kingdom closely administered, and treated almost as if it were part of the mother territory of Egypt.

This was Nubia, the land of Kush, the extension of Egypt southward along the course of the river Nile, the river which provided a thread of unity to the relationship. Nubia was a source of mineral wealth, a home to tribes, which could be hostile, and the conduit for exotic products brought by caravan from equatorial Africa, an account of which was given earlier in this book. Nubia had always been a land of concern and interest to the Egyptians. It was deeply penetrated by the kings of the Twelfth Dynasty, and strong fortresses were constructed along the Nile, especially in the region of the Second Cataract. Nubia was lost to Egypt in the troubled time called the Second Intermediate Period (c.1750–1650 B.C.), but reoccupied by the forces of the kings of the Eighteenth Dynasty. As formerly, no move was made to incorporate the region into the land of

Egypt proper, the king's realm; but it was seen to have a much closer relationship to Egypt than any of the other occupied lands in the Near East. It was seen to belong within the ambit of the Egyptian crown, and was consequently more closely administered than other subject countries. The head of the Nubian bureaucracy was called the 'king's son of Kush,' and often 'overseer of the southern deserts,' 'fan-bearer on the right of the king,' and 'king's envoy to every foreign land.' He was not of royal blood, and the title of king's son was honorific. This high dignitary, virtual ruler of Nubia, is now usually called the viceroy of Kush, and during the reign of Ramesses II a series of apparently very active and efficient viceroys served the king's interests in this extension of his realm.

Apart from the day-to-day administration of Nubia, the supervision of the collection of tribute, the maintenance of security, and the development of Egyptian settlements throughout the region, the viceroys were deeply involved in the promotion of the royal image, especially through the construction of the Nubian temples, in which, as we have seen, the divine aspect of the king was promoted. The first viceroy of the reign was Iuny; he had been appointed toward the end of the reign of Sethos I, when Ramesses was already effectively co-regent. He was responsible for the commencement of the work at Abu Simbel, no doubt on the instruction of the king, but he did not remain in office to see the completion of the work. This responsibility fell to his successor, Hekanakhte, who supervised the arrangements for the visit to Nubia by Ramesses and Queen Nefertari in about

Year 24. Not long afterward Hekanakhte was followed by a new viceroy named Paser, in no way related to the vizier Paser, whose career was outlined earlier in this chapter. The viceroy Paser had the misfortune of being in office when the disastrous earthquake struck Abu Simbel in Year 31 or 32, inflicting huge damage, some of the results of which may still be observed today in the fallen colossal head and the ancient repairs to statues and pillars within and outside the great temple. As mentioned earlier in this volume, it is not known whether Ramesses ever heard about this disaster, although it is hard to believe that Paser could have successfully hushed it up. He did retain his office until about Year 34, a few years after the earthquake, using the time to repair at least some of the damage. It is not impossible, however, that the Abu Simbel disaster prompted his replacement. Among the inscriptions set up by Paser at Abu Simbel, one placed between the two temples, contains a 'dialogue' with the king, which could be considered rather piquant in the context of the great temple and the earthquake. Ramesses II greets his viceroy "You are a wholly trustworthy person, useful to his lord." Paser obsequiously answers, "One does everything as you have stated, O Horus, beloved of Ma'at!" He might have added, "It wasn't my fault that your statue fell down."

By Year 34 Paser had been replaced by Huy, a senior military officer who had been part of the company charged with escorting the Hittite princess from her homeland to Piramesse and marriage to Ramesses. It must be presumed that the successful

outcome of the journey and the subsequent marriage commended Huy to Ramesses. It was surely so, and Huy's elevation to the high status of viceroy of Kush represented his reward. Paser, it seems, was just relieved of his office. Sadly we rarely know how careers finished, or what were the subsequent fates of displaced officials. It is not surprising that a copy of the great marriage inscription celebrating the Hittite-Egyptian matrimonial alliance was placed in the great temple at Abu Simbel. It was a text which served as a kind of testimonial for Huy. His tenure of office did not last long.

By Year 38 he was followed by Setau, a man of great energy who remained viceroy almost until the end of Ramesses' reign – perhaps a term of twenty-five years – and was then buried in a large, but now badly damaged, tomb in the Theban Necropolis. He may or may not have died in office. Setau was generous in leaving ample records of his activities in Nubia during his tenure, and the most informative of these memorials is a large stela which was set up in the temple of Wadi al-Sabua – one of more than a dozen inscriptions and statues – a temple for the construction of which he was largely responsible. If we can pick out details of his career, which seem to be trustworthy, it emerges that he rose from relatively modest beginnings and owed his rise to mighty office to his own abilities and diligence. He makes no mention of his parentage (known, however, to have been Siwadjyt and Nefertmut), but claims to have been brought up as a ward in the royal household. He distinguished himself as a young scribe and was in due course appointed chief scribe of the vizier. In this

position he was responsible for assessing taxes throughout the land, and he performed this task so well that all the national granaries were bursting with grain. He was then appointed by the king to be chief steward of the god Amun, in which position he again did so well that his abilities were recognized by the King, and he was made viceroy of Kush. As such, he claimed, "I collected all the revenues of this land of Kush twice over. I made the tribute of this land of Kush like the sand of the shore; no other viceroy of Kush has ever achieved so much since the time of the God." He was successful as a military commander, organized the building of the temple at Wadi al-Sabua, and restored all the temples in Nubia which had fallen into ruin, "in the great name of His Majesty, his name carved on them for ever." By his own estimation, Setau had been a good choice for viceroy. Much of what he says about his career may be accepted, and it suggests that merit and hard work, and probably close attention to those matters which would be noted especially by the king, would secure preferment. His initial piece of luck was to have been brought up at court, where he would have been but one of many who enjoyed such a privileged beginning. His career certainly bears out the view that talent could bring success in the bureaucracy of ancient Egypt. It also bears out the frequently maintained assertion that to be a scribe could be the making of a man. On such principles was the administration of Egypt based, and in their execution was the success of the King's realm established during the reign of Ramesses II.

271

Lid of the granite sarcophagus of Setau, Viceroy of Kush, with a distinctive, but strangely naive, head. Probably from his Theban tomb. The inscription invokes the goddess Nut as protectress (British Museum, EA 78).

THE KING AND THE GODS
IN LIFE AND DEATH

272

Anukis, "lady of Elephantine," one of the cataract deities, suckles Ramesses II, who is not shown as a child. He is "the Great King, lord of the Two Lands." Note the hieroglyphic sign of a mother suckling her child. In Bayt al-Wali temple.

273

Ramesses, the triumphant king, presents the fruits of victory to the gods of the Theban triad, Amon-Re, Mut, and Khonsu, and also Ma'at: quantities of precious vessels and captives (not shown). From Luxor.

CHAPTER 9

Ancient Egypt is generally thought of as having a culture dominated by religion, and the land of Egypt as being a place of temples and tombs. For many people the attraction of Egypt lies in these temples and tombs, and a visit to the country tends to emphasize this religious obsession. Even when an opportunity occurs to visit some ostensibly non-religious site, the visitor's attention is commonly diverted from secular considerations to religious reflections. A prime case is Amarna in Middle Egypt, the site of Akhenaten's 'new city,' Akhetaten. There is more to see at Amarna than a brief visit may reveal, but it is perhaps inevitable that the remains of Akhenaten's religious foundations, the unfinished tombs of his great officials, and the remote and evocative tomb of the king himself, should monopolize attention. And the talk and chat will mostly be about Akhenaten's religious revolution and the significance of the place in this respect. Someone may even read out parts of the great hymn to the Aten, and everyone will stand around solemnly, as if at a burial or important memorial occasion. There then will rarely be time for a wander about the city, to contemplate the remains of houses, important villas, industrial areas. For people lived in Amarna and spent their days mostly ignoring the religious aspects of life at the highest level. The case is rather less clear when a visit is made to the workmen's village – 'the Place of Truth' – at Dayr al-Madina, where for four hundred years the craftsmen, scribes, and artisans who worked on the royal tombs lived, and for whom a mass of documentation has survived. It is even more evocative to walk through the well-marked lanes of the village, to enter the stone houses, the names of whose owners are in some cases known. Here, as we shall hear later, lived people whose careers in some cases are better known than those of the great officials of Ramesses' reign. But the visitor today is rarely told about the village and its ways of living; generally some of the small but well-preserved tombs of the workmen are shown and a visit made to the small temple near the village, which has nothing much to do with the village. Then it will be off to another group of tombs in the Theban Necropolis, or to a temple, perhaps the splendidly preserved mortuary temple of Ramesses III at Medinet Habu, or the Ramesseum, the great mortuary foundation of Ramesses II, not as well preserved as the Medinet Habu temple, but full of interest for the visitor for very particular reasons connected with the life, achievements, and legends of Ramesses the Great. The Ramesseum was without a doubt the most important religious building constructed in Ramesses' reign, although this claim must be tempered by the fact that not nearly enough is known about the temple of Ptah at Memphis, greatly enlarged (if not a new foundation) by him, or the lost sacred establishments in the Delta Residence of Piramesse. The certainty that the king would be buried in the Valley of the Kings, and the knowledge of the large and splendid individual royal mortuary temples already existing in Western Thebes, rendered the Theban area particularly important in the course of the king's life from accession to death.

This progress was in Egyptian terms essentially a religious one in which the king at his coronation became the living form of the god Horus, in his oldest form of a sun god, shown as a falcon. His life thereafter was a steady progress toward death, when he would join the pre-eminent sun-god Re in the heavens, and also become assimilated with Osiris, the divine but dead king, whose martyrdom in life (mythologically) provided him with his justification to exist after death as the monarch of the afterlife – the Chief of the Westerners.

The three great temples of ancient Thebes, which provide evidence for the involvement of Ramesses II with the worship of the gods and the various rituals and ceremonies connected with them, are the Luxor and Karnak cult foundations and the Ramesseum. It is in these temples that the presence of the king is dominant, in such a way that modern-day visitors become persuaded of his power and even religiosity. The scenes of warfare and triumph are mostly placed on the parts of the temple buildings, which might be seen by Egyptians allowed to enter the sacred enclosures. Within the temples, where access was strictly limited and increasingly linked in the approach to the innermost sanctuaries, the scenes are almost wholly ritualistic in character. The king is shown in close association with the gods, making offerings to them corporately and individually, receiving reciprocal favors from them, participating in ceremonies connected with the temple and the cult, and involved in the periodic festivals in which the gods take part. The pervasive presence of the king in these temple scenes is neither a mark of his overweening pride nor an indication that he spent his whole time engaged in religious activities. It was the king's duty, even his

justification, to act as the go-between for the gods and the people of Egypt, not to be just the representative of the gods on earth, but in a sense the conduit for their powers. In the earlier chapter on Ramesses the great image-maker, something has already been said about the Egyptian king and his relationship with the gods, and particularly with those gods who embodied the ideas of royalty and majesty, investing the ruling king with his special powers, spiritual and terrestrial. Ramesses was no exception in accepting the gifts of the gods, especially those of divinely granted authority, of long life and many *sed* festivals. A fine and explicit scene in the Ramesseum portrays the rite by which the sun god of creation, Atum, supported by ibis-headed Thoth and Sefkhet-abu (a form of Seshat, goddess of writing), inscribes the name of Ramesses on the leaves of the *ished* tree (possibly the persea), thereby granting the king a multiplicity of jubilees. Ramesses sits on a block throne in front of the tree, wearing the horned *atef* crown. From the branches of the tree hangs the sign for *sed*, with the symbol for 'million' below.

Such scenes demonstrate the king's dependence on the gods, and the advantages he obtains from his inheritance of royal power and from his carrying out of the many ceremonies by which the gods in turn are honored and serviced in daily and periodic ritual activities. In theory, these services for the gods in all the temples of Egypt were carried out by the reigning king. Quite evidently, such a fulfillment of ritual obligations was quite beyond the capacity of a single person; even if he were to attempt to carry out all the ceremonies in one place only, for example, Piramesse, Memphis, or Thebes, the task would be impossible. But by delegation to the priestly officials in every

temple and sanctuary, the king could theoretically fulfill his ritual obligations, and in this way be seen to be involved. And so by representations and texts, the sacred duties could be seen to be accepted and by magic carried out according to the calendars of festivals and ceremonies. Such a theoretical arrangement was undoubtedly a great convenience, inasmuch as it gave the king complete freedom to carry out his ritual role whenever and wherever he wished, and to ignore it if attendance at a particular shrine was not convenient.

A king who chose to be unobservant of his religious duties might then not feel that he was being particularly undutiful; but lack of attendance to duty would not pass unnoticed, and a wise king would realize that proper performance by him was truly expected. He would therefore feel the need from time to time to proceed to a particular temple to assume his proper duties and carry out the appropriate ceremonies. It is unlikely that he would act in this way without giving ample notice of his intention to attend. The nature of religious observance in ancient Egypt was altogether different from what is now seen to be proper practice. For a Pharaoh to visit a temple for a ritual purpose was not the same as a visit by a modern king or head of state to church on a Sunday for the celebration of the Eucharist, or to a mosque for the participation in Friday prayers. Regular services in which the generality of the populace might join in formed no part of the religious life of the ancient Egyptians. The daily rituals, which served as the basis of the religious activity in a great temple, were conducted in private, and, if the king were present, he would be the principal actor in the sacred performance.

274
Wearing the atef crown, Ramesses sits in front of the persea tree. Atum, behind, and Sefkhet-abu and Thoth in front, write his name on the leaves of the tree. From the Ramesseum, drawn by Lepsius.

275
Ramesses II, kneeling on a basket and in front of the persea tree, receives the jubilee symbols from the hand of Re-Herakhty, while Thoth writes his name on the leaves of the tree. From Abu Simbel.

The King and the Gods in Life and Death

There is no way by which we can now discover whether Ramesses, or any other New Kingdom Pharaoh apart from Akhenaten, was particularly diligent in the exercise of his pontifical duties. Mentions of actual attendances at temples or at particular festivals are not common, and when they occur it is not always certain that the reports are factually true. The presence of the king in a temple is proclaimed perpetually by the scenes and inscriptions on the temple walls. Ramesses need not have felt guilty if he rarely made personal appearances at the great shrines of the land. Nevertheless, it may rightly be assumed that whenever he made progress from Piramesse southward to Thebes and even farther, for example to Abu Simbel, he would have taken the opportunity to visit the principal temples on his way. If the visit could be timed to coincide with a particular festival, so much the better. It would have been good for the Pharaoh, the Good God, Lord of the Two Lands, to be seen at festivals like that of Sokaris at Memphis, or the Osiris mysteries at Abydos.

The most important and spectacular divine celebrations about which much is known were the Opet Festival and the Valley Festival, both at Thebes, and both concerned with the cult of the imperial god Amun and his divine family, the goddess Mut and their child, the moon god Khonsu. Such celebrations were important not only for the temples and the services they maintained, but also for the ordinary people of Egypt. From the religious point of view, they provided opportunities for everyone to see the deity, in the form of its cult statue, brought out from the innermost shrine in the temple and paraded about with suitable pomp. From the political point of view, it might provide opportunities for everyone to see the great officials who controlled their lives, and even Pharaoh, who could intervene on their behalf with the gods. And most particularly, for most people, from the point of view of entertainment, the festivals were occasions for all kinds of festivities, both connected directly with the sacred performances and organized separately, apart from the official activities. There was, for example, a huge provision of food and drink, made generally available from the massive slaughtering of animals and the copious brewing of beer. Accounts of what went on at festivals elsewhere and at other periods make it clear that in Egypt a good festival was a time of plenty and a time of license, when controls were relaxed and a blind eye turned to excess.

The pattern of royal progresses on the Nile and the paying of visits to temples is in rare, specific cases made clear, as in the great dedicatory inscription of Ramesses II in the Osiris temple of Sethos I at Abydos. It happened in his first year of reign. The text describes the king leaving Thebes and traveling north, back to Piramesse. When the river flotilla reached the Thinite nome, Ramesses made a detour "to inaugurate offerings to Unennefer [an epithet of Osiris], the good things that his *ka* loves, and to greet Onuris, his brother [the god of the Thinite nome]." Here it seems certain that in doing this, in performing the other ceremonies in the temple of Sethos at Abydos, and in seeing to the various building activities, which he had himself initiated in that sacred place, Ramesses was in his own person performing acts which might usually be carried out by others in his name. And these activities at Abydos came only a very few days after he had been in Thebes, celebrating his coronation and supervising the ceremonies of the Opet Festival. Again there is no reason to doubt that Ramesses himself took part in the celebrations, an act of conspicuous and auspicious importance at the very beginning of his reign. Would he ever do the same again during his long reign? It might be expected that he would from time to time, but certainly not on an annual basis.

In the calendar of Theban festivals, the Opet represented the most important festival event in the year. It began during the second month of *akhet*, the season of inundation, on the evening of day 18, and continued for about three weeks, ending on day 12 of the third month of *akhet*. During Ramesses' reign this period would have been in the month of

September in the modern calendar. The festival gave its name to the month, Opet, in which it took place, and the name gains additional significance in that its core event was a journey from Ipetsut (Opet-sut) 'most favored of places,' the Karnak temple, to Ipet-resyt (Opet-resyt) 'the southern hidden place' or 'southern harem', the Luxor temple. Egyptian gods lived a busy social life and were much given to visiting each other in their respective shrines. Sometimes long distances might be involved, as in the case of the annual trip made by the goddess Hathor from her temple at Dendera to the temple of Edfu, 108 miles (174 kilometers) by river to the south, where her sacred marriage to the local deity Horus was celebrated. This is perhaps the best described of regular divine travel, the relevant texts at Edfu, of Ptolemaic date, providing a wealth of evidence about the official ceremonies and of the wild participation in the festivities by the general population. There can be no doubt, however, that the Opet Festival was in all respects more important in significance and greater in scale; it is just less well documented than the Edfu festival.

There are, however, splendid and extensive visual representations of the major public events of the festival on the walls of the Theban temples. Those most artistically composed and informative in detail are in the processional colonnade in the Luxor temple; they were possibly begun in the reign of Amenophis III, completed under Tutankhamun, and usurped by Horemheb. There are further scenes added by Ramesses II in the first court of the same temple. The "Beautiful Festival of Opet," as it was called, began in Ipetsut, Karnak, when Amun, the principal deity, was brought out of the temple, his effigy in a divine bark, which was placed in a riverboat to be conveyed upstream to Ipet-resyt, the Luxor temple. He was accompanied by his divine consort Mut and their child Khonsu, each of whom was similarly conveyed in a separate boat. The journey was conducted with great ceremony, with many boats on the river and huge crowds on land. After a journey of about two miles, the divine barks were brought to the quay of the Luxor temple and taken into the innermost, secret (hidden) rooms of the shrine. There various ceremonies and rituals were performed in private; and then, after about three weeks, the gods were conducted back to Karnak and deposited in their shrines.

The second great Theban festival in which the king might have been expected to participate, if he were in the south at the right time, was the Valley Festival, the "Beautiful Festival of the Valley." It took place in the second month of the season *shomu* ('summer'), at the time of the new moon. In early days it was associated with the royal mortuary temples in the valley of Western Thebes leading up to Dayr al-Bahri.

Ramesses II

276-277
Scenes on the granite shrine of Philip Arrhidaeus at Karnak showing the sacred barks ready to take part in the Valley Festival. Two rest on stands, and two are carried by priests, preceded by the king with a censer.

278 left
Quartzite shrine from Tanis, originally from Heliopolis, showing Ramesses offering bowls to Khepri "who is in his bark," a cake to Atum, "lord of Heliopolis," and wine to Re-Herakhty, "lord of Heaven" (Cairo, JE 37475).

278-279
Part of the lintel of a shrine in the temple enclosure at Dayr al-Madina, showing Ramesses II protected by the Hathor cow in a papyrus marsh. The lintel was dedicated by the royal scribe Ramosi (Louvre, E 16276a, b).

In the Nineteenth Dynasty, the three gods of the Theban triad, Amun, Mut, and Khonsu, were involved in a sacred progress which began with a river-crossing from Karnak to the west bank of the Nile, followed by a water progress along canals to the desert edge, to the land of the Theban Necropolis and the royal mortuary temples. On coming to land, the procession formed up and proceeded to visit the temples in the eponymous valley, and then to other temples along the desert edge. It did not, apparently, go to the Valley of the Kings, where there were no shrines to visit and no suitably equipped priestly establishments to welcome the visitors and entertain them. It was again a spectacular occasion, offering at the superior level of the celebrations opportunities for the great and the good to meet the deities and receive favors from them, and at the lower level of the event, the chance for the populace to view the gods and indulge in a degree of license not commonly granted them.

In the tomb of Paser, the distinguished vizier whom we have already met, there is a significant mention of the Valley Festival in an inscription on one of the pillars in the tomb's broad hall. The text is phrased like a spell from the *Book of the Dead*, empowering Paser to come forth from his tomb so that he may greet and adore Amun "when you arrive at the western desert of Kheft-hir-nebes [a name of Thebes as a whole, in all probability], I shall be first of those who follow you in your beautiful Festival of the Valley." In his lifetime Paser, as vizier and governor of Thebes, had an important role to play in the conduct of the festival, especially in the absence of his Pharaoh, and he might expect that in his afterlife he could enjoy the privilege of participating in the festival by having his image included among those which joined the Theban triad in the procession. The same text includes the words "O my lord, my city god, Amun, Lord of the Thrones of the Two Lands, grant that I may be among the ancestors, the excellent honored ones." The practice of including

images of previous kings in the procession developed during the Nineteenth Dynasty, and it would seem that the privilege of joining the festivities posthumously was later extended to notable officers of state. Apparently the Valley Festival attained special importance during the reign of Ramesses II, and the Ramesseum was used as the overnight stop for the Theban deities. This was in no way inappropriate, for the temple was then best equipped to offer comfortable lodging to the gods, who would already have found themselves the subjects of regular daily rituals in that temple. There is further evidence from the early Ptolemaic granite shrine in the Karnak temple, which carries scenes of the celebration of the Valley Festival, that this use of the Ramesseum as a kind of grand way-station, or overnight billet, was still observed one thousand years after Ramesses' reign.

The presence of the king at the Valley Festival, as at the Opet Festival, was assumed but rarely expected. There are no certain

records that Ramesses II ever traveled to Thebes specially to preside at any of the great festivals after his initial attendance at the Opet in Year 1. And yet there must have been many occasions when he came south: to make presentations of tribute, booty, and prisoners after the campaigns of his early years, to inspect progress on his mortuary temple and tomb, to inaugurate the temples at Abu Simbel, and even just in periodic progress up the Nile. As part of the Ramesseum complex, a special palace for the king was built abutting the western side of the first court. It is now a complete ruin, but much of its plan can be traced. In size it was large (about fifty by fifty meters or 160 by 160 feet), but not excessively large, providing accommodation for the king and a small party of family members and attendants for short stays. Other royal mortuary temples in Thebes also provided relatively modest accommodation for the visiting monarch. It seems unlikely that such provision would have been made unless it was expected that it would be occupied from time

to time. But the existence of a grandiose rest-house does not imply that it was frequently occupied by its intended visitor. It may well have been used by privileged officials and even representative members of the royal family, and particularly on occasions like the celebration of the Valley Festival. It was probably an occasion looked forward to and therefore enjoyed occasionally by royal 'deputies.' It was an especially joyful event, much mentioned in private as well as official texts, and great celebrations involving the populace took place on the night following the main progress of the gods around the temples in Western Thebes – a change, no doubt, from life at Piramesse.

The absence of specific mentions and descriptions of the king's taking part not just in the periodic festivals in the great religious centers in Egypt, but also in general, regular religious activities, such as the daily rituals, prevents our making a proper assessment of his practical relationship with the gods. It has been

pointed out already that a complete fulfillment of his ritual obligations was impossible, and could be made valid only by the magical force of representations of the sacred activities on temple walls. The fact that some of the scenes of the regular and important ceremonies showing Ramesses II engaged in his necessary activities with the gods have not survived does not mean that such scenes never existed, or that Ramesses did not perform the particular rituals. Massive destruction in the principal temples, at Karnak and the Ramesseum in Thebes, and in the northern cities, accounts for the absence of much of the original visual record. Nevertheless, in all those temples in which work was initiated during Ramesses' reign, there are many scenes of his conducting minor ceremonies and engaging in close relationships with the gods. He may be seen as being on very familiar terms with all the great deities of Egypt, and with many who fulfilled minor divine functions or represented provincial cults.

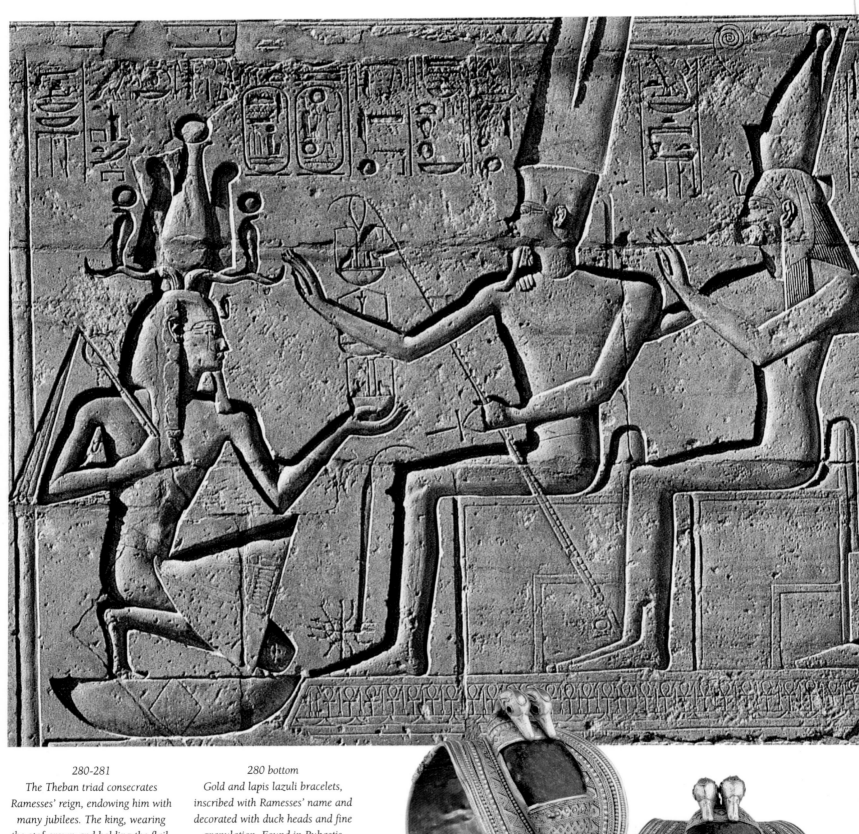

280-281
*The Theban triad consecrates
Ramesses' reign, endowing him with
many jubilees. The king, wearing
the atef crown and holding the flail,
kneels and receives the sed symbols
from Amon-Re, Mut, and Khonsu.
In the Ramesseum.*

280 bottom
*Gold and lapis lazuli bracelets,
inscribed with Ramesses' name and
decorated with duck heads and fine
granulation. Found in Bubastis
in the Delta in 1906 and thought
to be part of a temple treasure
(Cairo, JE 39873).*

A very good idea of the range of these activities and contacts can be found at Karnak on the girdle wall enclosing the principal shrine, the Central Court, and Tuthmosis III's Festival Temple. The wall dates to the reign of Tuthmosis III, but it carries on its outer face a great series of scenes in which Ramesses II engages with a great many deities. A selection of 'episodes' gives a fair idea of their range: Ramesses presents bread to Re-Herakhty; he consecrates offerings to Amun; he presents flowers to Neith; he offers incense and a libation to Amun of the Saite nome; he runs with *sed*-festival symbols toward Bastet; he offers a haunch of meat to Horus; he presents a miniature Sokar-bark to Ptah-Sokar-Osiris; he anoints the lioness-headed Mehyt; he holds up the heavens before Onuris-Shu; he measures up the temple with scribal deity Sefkhet-abu; he raises the pillar of Heliopolis before Atum; he raises two obelisks and offers incense before Re; he makes purification before Horus of Letopolis, a city in the southern Delta; he stands before Queen Ahmes-Nefertari, wife of Amosis and mother of Amenophis I of the early Eighteenth Dynasty, who was especially revered with her son in the Theban Necropolis; he pours a libation to Sakhmet; in the company of Khonsu-Neferhotep he receives the symbol of jubilee from Amun. All these scenes – and they are but a selection from the whole series – occur on the outer south side of the girdle wall. There was no limit to his divine relationships, and a great many of them are excellently recorded on this wall in very

well-designed and executed sunk relief. Further scenes are carved on the east and north sides of the same wall, and there are many similar depictions elsewhere at Karnak and in the Luxor temple and the Ramesseum. They would not have been absent from other temples throughout Egypt built by Ramesses or added to or embellished by him. A rather more limited range of activities is to be found in the Nubian temples, in which, as we have seen, Ramesses had a somewhat elevated position vis-à-vis the imperial gods and the particular gods of the cataract region and Nubia.

Whether or not Ramesses II conducted his life according to the best Egyptian ethic, we can never know. All the outward signs of piety were in place to remind him of his divine being and divine duties. Certainly in the surviving record of his reign there is much to suggest that the royal obligations were regularly fulfilled, even if the agent was not regularly the

281 bottom right
A remarkable silver vessel with gold mounting and a gold handle in the from of a goat, from the Bubastite Treasure. The decoration contains Asiatic elements, but its dedication is by the royal butler Atumemtaneb (Cairo, JE 39867).

king himself. There were plenty of deputies or representatives to act on behalf of the king, and it was surely the case that it was the carrying out of a ritual activity that mattered, not who carried it out, provided that he was properly authorized. Nevertheless, the proper service of the gods throughout life was the proper preparation for death and a proper burial. From the moment of birth every Egyptian would have had his or her eye on the ultimate goal, although it is unlikely that the prospect of death and burial would have become a matter for serious concern until an individual had reached a position in life when anything more than the simplest of burials would have been contemplated. For the Pharaoh the position was rather different. From the moment of coronation, his destiny became a matter of high concern. Up to that point the prospective king was an ordinary, if specially privileged, Egyptian. At accession he became the living Horus, and so he would remain until his death, when he would move into a different state of divinity and by the appropriate rituals, including the provision of the appropriate texts, pass from his terrestrial existence to a posthumous celestial state and also to his identification with Osiris in the underworld realm.

In considering his death and burial, a newly crowned Pharaoh would necessarily instruct his officials to arrange for the cutting of his tomb. It might be thought that the subject would be on the agenda of the first 'Privy Council' meeting of the new reign. There is some evidence from the work on other royal tombs of the New Kingdom that traces parts of the course of construction in particular cases. If a king began his reign at an advanced age, then it was imperative that work should begin as soon as possible and pursued with the utmost vigor. If the king was young on accession, then it might be thought unnecessary to start work on his tomb for some years. Whatever the circumstances at the start of a reign, there was always the chance that things might go wrong. Such seems to have been the case with Tutankhamun. He was very young on accession, and scarcely out of his teens when he died. His planned tomb, probably no. 23 in the Western Valley of the Kings, was by no means ready, and his successor, Ay, arranged for him to be buried in a small tomb prepared, no doubt, for some important official like Ay himself or for some member of the royal family. So Tutankhamun missed his proper interment by dying young and probably unexpectedly. Ay, on the other hand, becoming king at an advanced age with a small expectation of life, took over Tomb 23 and had it completed and prepared for himself within the three or four years of his reign.

282
In his relationship with the gods, Ramesses is regularly shown making offerings to, or receiving gifts from the gods, especially Amon-Re in Karnak. Here he offers the god a tray of incense pots.

283
Ramesses II, wearing the cap crown bends forward with a tray of varied offerings to the god in Karnak. He is "presenting things to his father Amon-Re," a very general designation of his offering.

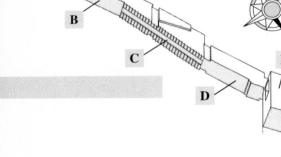

284-285

Ramesses II's tomb was once a monument of great magnificence. Sadly, the depredations of man, but mostly of nature have reduced it to a profound wreck. But much clearance work remains to be done. Here is the burial chamber after clearance.

Ramesses II

The King and the Gods in Life and Death

In Ramesses II's case the arrangements worked well. Firstly, he became Pharaoh when he was young; secondly, he lived to a ripe old age. Never, presumably, did it seem that work on his tomb should be accelerated. It may therefore be assumed that his tomb was finished in form and decoration well before he was ready to occupy it. In many royal tombs of the Eighteenth and Nineteenth Dynasties there is good evidence that the work was uncompleted at the time when they had to be closed, after the funerals of the dead monarchs. Of Ramesses II's immediate predecessors, his grandfather Ramesses I (one or two years' reign) had a relatively small tomb without much decoration, while his father Sethos I (fifteen or sixteen years' reign), had a tomb with much uncompleted decoration, although in sum it is all of exceptional quality. Of his immediate successor, Merenptah (ten or eleven years' reign), unfortunately the present condition of his tomb is such that the completeness of its decoration at the time of the king's death cannot be adequately assessed. The same should be said of Ramesses II's tomb. It has been open in part since late antiquity; it has suffered flooding on a number of occasions; it has only in recent years been systematically cleared, cleaned, conserved, and recorded. The damage it has suffered over the millennia has left much of its decoration in a sorry state, but as far as one can gather from recently published reports, the tomb was finished and ready to receive the royal burial many years before Ramesses found it necessary to take the long and hazardous path to his divine destiny.

The position of Ramesses II's tomb and the character of the rock and shale through which it was cut provide good reasons for its unfortunate fate, structurally, in subsequent times. It is not known how the position for a royal tomb in the Valley of the Kings was chosen. Presumably, high officials – possibly including the vizier, the mayor of Thebes, and the high priest of Amun – inspected likely positions, advised by local officials who knew the nature of the Valley and the hazards that might endanger a badly sited tomb. The king himself may have been shown the selected site and even visited it on occasion when he came to Thebes. It could have been included in his itinerary along with the Ramesseum, which would probably have been of greater interest to him. The two places, tomb and mortuary temple, formed a complex for the care and protection of the royal body after death and for the nurturing of the royal spirit by services and offerings. In earlier periods, tomb and temple were physically joined. At Thebes, however, once the Valley had been chosen as the resting place for the royal bodies, the temples had to be constructed elsewhere within the necropolis. In the tomb in the Valley, appropriate inscriptions and scenes ensured the safe progress of the dead king through the dangers of the underworld until he was born again into the celestial company of Re, the sun god, at dawn every day. In the mortuary temple, in the company

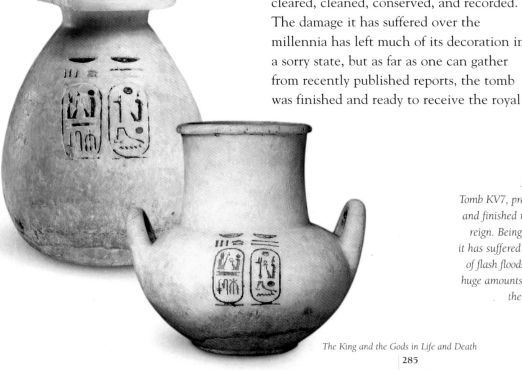

285 top
Tomb KV7, prepared for Ramesses II and finished relatively early in his reign. Being a deeply cut tomb, it has suffered badly from the effects of flash floods which have washed huge amounts of debris into it over the millennia.

285 bottom
Two alabster vessels inscribed with the names of Ramesses II. Such vessels were commonly placed in royal burials, and many fragments of similar pieces have been found during the clearance of KV7 (left: Cairo, JE 46712; right: Louvre, N.440).

The King and the Gods in Life and Death

of the Theban gods and of the other great gods of Egypt, the king could continue his relationship with these deities, so long as the services and offerings for his spirit were maintained.

In area, Ramesses' tomb is the largest in the Valley, although possibly exceeded by KV5, the tomb constructed for the king's sons, across the road into the Valley, which is not yet fully cleared. When the two tombs were cut, they were the first to be met on entering the Valley by the principal path. The king's tomb consists of a long descending corridor with two sets of stairs leading to the well or sump designed for protection and the collection of flood water; a pillared hall interrupts the continuing progress of the corridor, and at the end of the corridor a large suite of rooms, including the burial chamber, lies at approximately right angles to the corridor. The royal funerary texts inscribed on the walls of the corridor and the various chambers include *The Litany of Re, The Book of What is in the Underworld, The Book of Gates, The Book of the Divine Cow*, and parts of The *Book of the Dead*. On the upper walls of the well and on the many pillars in the larger halls, the king is shown with various deities in familiar meetings; they seem to recall the scenes of similar intimacy found in the temples, where the living king could consort with the gods. In the tomb scenes it is almost as if the gods are bidding farewell to one of their number, passing from life to death and then to reunion with the pantheon in his afterlife.

When Ramesses died in his Year 67, the end could scarcely have been considered unexpected. One may wonder how often in the last decades of his reign there had been crises in his health and warnings of imminent death. One may also surmise that on such occasions, word would be sent to Thebes to prepare the tomb for occupation and to make preparations for the royal funeral. Although no king had been buried in the Valley since the death of Sethos I, there would have been in the long interim plenty of activity, with the construction of the new royal tomb, the subsequent cutting of the tomb intended for the royal sons, and the periodic funerals of many of the sons. Merenptah, who eventually succeeded his father, was the thirteenth son, and many others younger than he would have died before his accession. Whether the sons' tomb continued to be used after Ramesses' death is not yet apparent, and it may never be decided when it received its last burial. So from time to time there would have been burial ceremonies in the valley in KV5, opposite the royal tomb-in-waiting. Presumably, this tomb, KV7, was inspected regularly, and not just closed up until the day when it would receive Ramesses, and he would pass from the kingdom of the living to the realm of the gods.

286 bottom
Four blue faience vessels, made possibly for Ramesses' burial, but rescued from destruction when his body was moved in antiquity. His names are supplemented with texts invoking forms of Amon-Re and Mut.

287 top
A low relief of a clump of lilies from the tomb of Ramesses II. The lily, an alternative to the lotus, symbolized Upper Egypt.

287 bottom
Relief carving from Ramesses' tomb showing the goddess Ma'at with outstretched wings kneeling on a basket. She is "daughter of Re" and announces her intention to protect the king. She holds the shen sign of universality.

288
Cedar coffin that contained the
mummy of Ramesses II on discovery
in 1881. It was probably for a
predecessor, possibly Ramesses I.
An inked text on the front has an
account of the vicissitudes suffered
by the body in antiquity
(Cairo, JE 26214).

289 top
Pendant of gold and semiprecious
stones in the form of a ram-headed
falcon, the kind of jewel to have
been placed on Ramesses' mummy.
None of his actual funerary jewelry
has survived. Found in the
Serapeum (Louvre, N.764).

289 bottom
Upper part of the mummy of
Ramesses II as he may be seen in
the Cairo Museum: a remarkable
triumph for the uncertain art of
mummification in ancient Egypt
(Cairo, JE 61078).

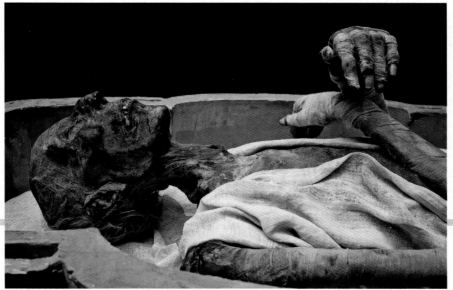

No account has survived of Ramesses' death and burial. From evidence obtained when his mummy was examined in Paris in 1975, it seems that the body was prepared for burial in the north of Egypt, not in the Theban area. It could properly be expected that he died in Piramesse, and that the process of mummification would necessarily have been carried out there. Long travel south would have led to rapid putrefaction of an unembalmed body, and the impossibility of successful subsequent preservation. And so, after the prescribed time required for embalming, the seventy days of the records, the royal body was conducted south by river, brought to Thebes, conveyed to the Ramesseum for a period of rest and final rites, and then taken to the tomb where the interment took place. The proceedings at all stages were accompanied by suitable pomp and extravagant scenes of mourning, and the whole series of events supervised by the new king, the new Horus, Merenptah. After the placing of the royal mummy in the burial chamber and the introduction of a great quantity of funerary equipment, the tomb was closed up and sealed. It became Ramesses' 'house of eternity.' But that was not to be.

By a strange irony, almost more is known of Ramesses' movements after death than for much of his lifetime. His tomb was to be his dwelling place forever, but it became the subject of a number of intrusions and robberies, which greatly disturbed the continuity of his posthumous existence. In Year 29 of Ramesses III (c. 1155 B.C.), scarcely fifty years after the burial of his illustrious predecessor, an attempt, or possibly two separate attempts, were made to enter the tomb, although it does not appear that any serious damage was done at that time. During the later Twentieth Dynasty, evidence came before the Theban authorities that the royal tombs in the valley had been or were being robbed. While Herihor was high priest of Amun at Thebes and the virtual ruler in that region, the legitimate Pharaoh in Piramesse being Ramesses XI (c. 1099–1069 B.C.), the mummy of Ramesses II was rescued and rewrapped and temporarily placed in the tomb of his father Sethos I, whose body was also rewrapped. Clearly both tombs had been seriously violated by this time. Further moves took place in later years: in Year 10 of Siamun of the Twenty-first Dynasty (c. 968 B.C.), a number of royal mummies, including that of Ramesses II, were deposited in a remote tomb in the hills of Dayr al-Bahri, originally made for Queen Inhapy, wife of Seqenenre-Taa II of the Seventeenth Dynasty (c. 1570 B.C.); and then, finally in or shortly after Year 11 of Osorkon I of the Twenty-second Dynasty (c. 924–889 B.C.), Ramesses' mummy, along with many other royal mummies, was placed in another tomb at Dayr al-Bahri, originally made for the burials of the high priests of Amun of the Twenty-first Dynasty. And so, three hundred years after he was conducted to meet his fellow gods in the afterlife, Ramesses found a secure resting place in which he remained undisturbed for about 2,780 years; and then in about 1870 the secret cache was discovered by Egyptians from the nearby village. In 1881 the coffin containing Ramesses' mummy was removed by the Antiquities Service to the Cairo Museum. And there it has remained ever since, apart from two excursions. For a short period in the 1930s all the royal mummies were transferred from the Cairo Museum and put on display in the mausoleum of Sa'd Zaghlul, the greatly esteemed Egyptian nationalist politician of the early twentieth century. In 1975 Ramesses made a visit to Paris, where he was met and treated like a visiting head of state; his body was subjected to extensive scientific examinations and carefully conserved.

The complicated history of the wanderings of Ramesses II and of other Egyptian kings has been pieced together mostly from dockets written on their coffins and bandages. Ramesses, confusingly, was not in his original coffin when he was placed in the Dayr al-Bahri cache. It is thought on stylistic grounds that the cedar coffin in which he was placed, now scraped clean of all original decoration, was originally made possibly for his grandfather, Ramesses I. The lid is inscribed in ink with the later king's two cartouches and a long hieratic text outlining some of the history of the royal peregrinations. Hieratic texts on his bandaging confirm his identity and some of his movements. It is sad to contemplate what survives of the great king's mortal remains. He no longer has the trappings to help him secure his continuing posthumous existence in the company of the gods with whom he was destined to spend eternity. And yet he has in a sense achieved a greater posthumous existence, and certainly a greater fame than most of his fellow Egyptian kings. His body may be deprived of its amuletic protection, but his face retains a magnificent dignity, providing striking confirmation of his terrestrial power. And indeed, his name lives. His gods have not wholly deserted him.

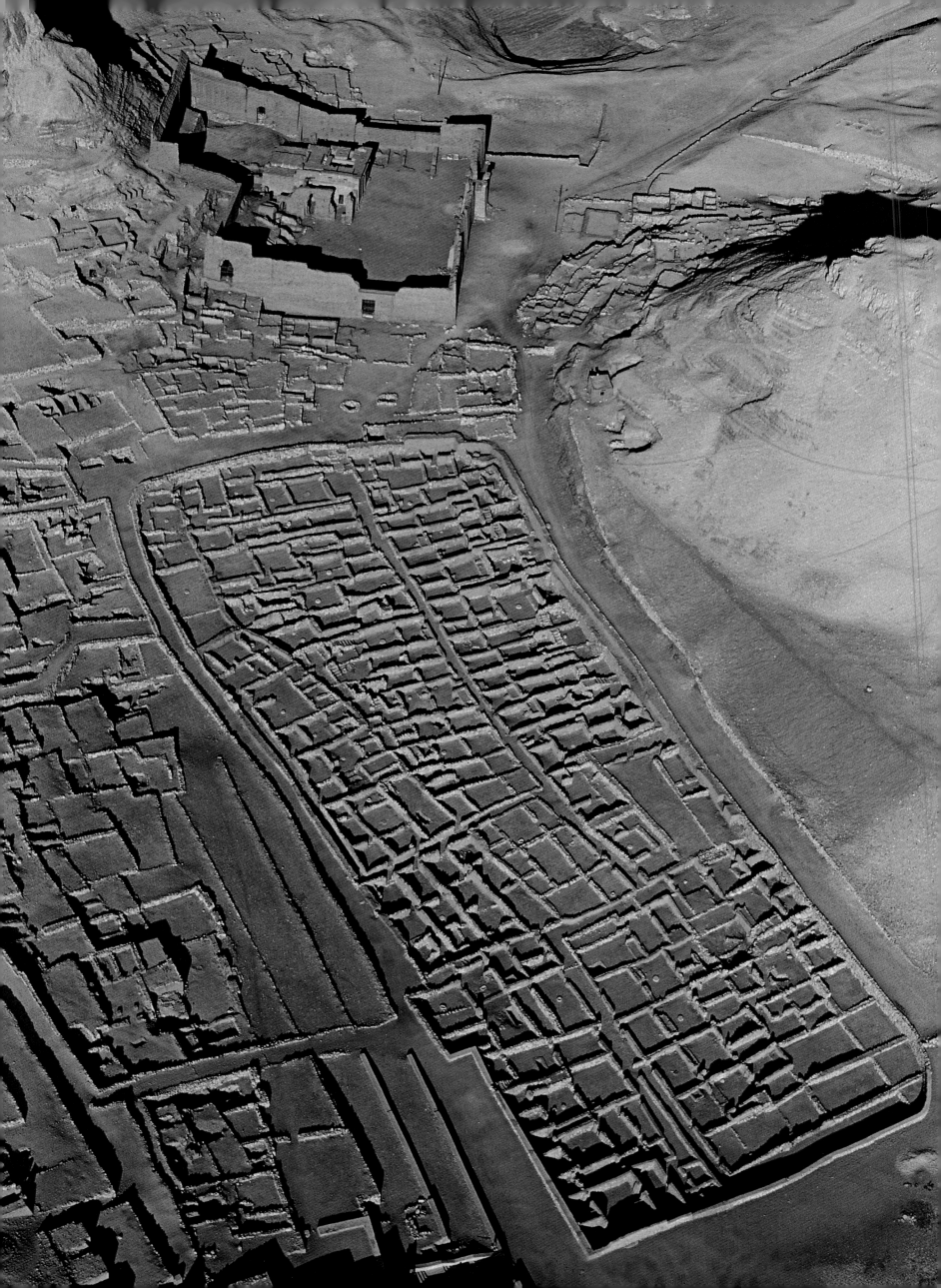

RAMESSES' PEOPLE

CHAPTER 10

290

The workmen's village at Dayr al-Madina, established within walls from about 1500 B.C. until its ending in about 1070 B.C. Extensions beyond the walls can be seen, and at the top is the temple enclosure containing some building commissioned by Ramesses II.

291

Scenes of agriculture from the tomb of Sennedjem: above, with his wife Iyneferti, he plows; below, he harvests barley with sickles, and flax by pulling. Such was actual life on the land in Ramesses' reign.

"Pendua: First month of *akhet* [inundation], day 14: drinking with Khonsu."

A black mark (in fact a red note) therefore against the workman Pendua, who failed to turn up for work on that day in Year 40 of Ramesses II (c. 1239 B.C.). On day 16 of the third month of *akhet*, Siwadjet was away because his daughter was ill. For the same reason, Wadjmose was absent from duty on day 23 of the fourth month of *peret* (sowing), and he was away again on day 6 of the fourth month of *shomu* (summer) because he was building his house. Horemuia absented himself on the eighth day of the second month of *peret* to brew beer. Aapehty signed himself off duty for a run of days in the third and fourth months of *akhet* because he was ill, and on the same days Pehery-pedjet was absent, the reason noted "with Aapehty." Pehery-pedjet is also marked down as being away from duty "with Khonsu, dispensing remedies" and "dispensing remedies for the scribe's wife"; he clearly had secondary, medical duties, probably officially arranged.

Other reasons for absence are given as "eye trouble," "offering to his god," and "wrapping his mother"(that is, preparing her body for burial).

These details are extracted from a register of the workmen who formed part of the élite corps employed on the making and decorating of the royal tomb and the tombs of other privileged persons in the Theban Necropolis; they lived in the village community at the place now called Dayr al-Madina. The corps and its village were established in the early Eighteenth Dynasty (c. 1500 B.C.), and the corps remained active and the village inhabited until the end of the Twentieth Dynasty (c. 1070 B.C.). The members of this workmen's corps were not only privileged in being favored protégés of the Pharaoh, but unusually literate. Their company included scribes, and there is some evidence that the ability to read and write was possessed by many who were not classified specifically as scribes. A huge quantity of written material has been discovered in the area of the workmen's village, the greatest part of it

written on smooth limestone flakes, for which the term ostraca is used. Many of these ostraca carry simple texts dealing with the everyday affairs of the workmen and their families, and in aggregate they make up a formidable dossier of information about a small, but special, community, of humble status, the lives of whose members were far divorced in all respects from those of the royal family, the high officials of the land, and even of the lesser officials in a place like Thebes. But because of the survival of so many written texts concerning the daily activities of the villagers, more is known about them and their way of life, their personal habits, and the manner in which they conducted their affairs than about the members of any other stratum of Egyptian society.

The register of workmen is written on an unusually large ostracon (41 by 35.5 centimeters or 104 by 90 inches), with the text extending over both sides. The names of forty workmen are listed, practically the whole of the gang as it was constituted in the middle of the reign of Ramesses II.

By Year 40 it is most probable that the royal tomb in the Valley of the Kings was completed, and also the greater part of the sons' tomb (KV5), so that the workforce had been scaled down or reduced by natural wastage (old age or death). Pressure on the gang, therefore, could not have been as great as it would have been when major works were being undertaken, and the apparently casual attitude of individual workmen to their regular attendance was seemingly tolerated as long as clear abuse was not extensive. There is nothing in the register to indicate the imposition of any penalties. Apart from the existence of this register (and of others of later date), in itself a remarkable example of ancient Egyptian bureaucratic practice, what is so striking about it is the range of reasons listed for absence, which were apparently seen to be acceptable. Today they might add "going to a football match" or "spending the day fishing," but "recovering from a hangover," "attending a funeral," "looking after a sick wife," "tending the vines," or "taking part in wine making" are excuses as appropriate for today as for antiquity. Few documents demonstrate in so clear a manner the perennial concerns of the working man and the wonderful continuity of the ordinary human anxieties.

There are in fact many thousands of ostraca surviving from the occupation of the workmen's village. There was no shortage of limestone chips that could be used for casual documentation. Every tomb excavation in the better areas of the Theban Necropolis, and particularly in the Valley of the Kings, yielded these flakes, and they could presumably be picked up and used in a very informal way. Yet it is hard to believe that there would not have been some person delegated by the leaders of the gang to select and put on one side those pieces, which could be best employed for official purposes. But anyone with the intention to write a short note or memorandum would have had no difficulty in acquiring suitable chips of limestone as he walked about the whole district of Western Thebes. The contents of many of the notes that can be dated to the mid-Nineteenth Dynasty, even specifically to the reign of Ramesses II, are relatively trivial; a piece from which the names of the writer and the recipient are lost refers to the sending of cakes and incense by the hand of a policeman named Pesaro: an additional five measures of incense were sent "on the day of the offering that you made to Amun during the Festival of the Valley." The writer adds, "They are not taken from anything that you sent me," presumably meaning that the commodities sent were a new consignment. From this brief note it can be seen how a simple workman of the royal-tomb gang could involve himself in the festivities connected with the Valley Festival, one of the two most important annual Theban celebrations, discussed in the last chapter.

Much matter of personal concern is included in these informal communications; the outline-scribe (draftsman) Prahotpe writes to his boss, the well-known scribe Qenhikhopshef:

"Why are you behaving toward me in this wretched way? As far as you are concerned I am a donkey. If there's work – bring the donkey; if there is food – bring the ox; if there is beer – I am not included. But when there is work, then I am sought. Indeed, if I am badly behaved because of beer, don't call for me. Listen to this in the House of Amon-Re, King of the Gods, life, prosperity, and health.

P.S. I am someone with no beer in his house. I look for satisfaction in writing to you."

Simple transactions seem often to have been conducted in writing, especially when workmen were on duty in the Valley of the Kings and away from the village. Letters were sent on what seem to have been trivial matters. But such letters provide vivid evidence of the system of barter by which most transactions in Egypt were conducted before the introduction of coinage, many centuries later. Paser writes to a woman named Tutuia:

"What's the meaning of your reproach to me? When your mother was still alive, you sent for me and I came, and I gave you a garment. And I gave you the... [?], and I told you, 'take possession of these,' and they became yours. You brought three bunches of vegetables and I asked 'Where from?' and you replied, 'I didn't get them from my mother, Sitamun.' I came again after your mother had died, and I gave you a *takhbes* basket, asking you to buy a goat with it, and you said, 'One *takhbes* basket is not enough.' So I said, 'Add on a bunch of vegetables to it and buy the goat.' But now you write to say, 'I have bought you a... [?] goat, the price being one *takhbes* basket and vegetables, and another *takhbes* basket to

292 bottom
Laborers make mud bricks: water is drawn from a pool to mix with earth; molded bricks are set out to dry; a wall is built and dried bricks carried away. From the tomb of Rekhmire (c. 1450 B.C.), drawn by Prisse d'Avennes.

293 top
The building of a structure with a ramp: laborers bring materials and a master mason sees to surfacing the

ramp with stone slabs. The ramp itself is of stone with matting for reinforcement. From the tomb of Rekhmire, drawn by Prisse d'Avennes.

complete the purchase. I have bought it.' And look, I gave you... [?], saying, 'Buy oil with it. Make use of it [for the transaction]. Don't use the bunch of vegetables; use that to buy oil.' I am your good brother who cares for you, my sister."

Some transactions were concerned with burial preparations, which no doubt were regularly in train in what was essentially a lower-class, but not quite peasant, society. The outline-scribe Pay writes to his son Pra-emheb, also an outline-scribe:

"Please see about acquiring the two faience hearts [amulets] that I spoke to you about [saying], 'I will pay their owner whatever price he asks.' And you should set about finding this fresh incense, which I told you about, needed for varnishing your mother's coffin. I shall pay the owner for it. And you should get hold of that wreck of a kilt and wreck of a loincloth, to have the kilt made into a sash [?], and the loincloth into an apron [?]. Don't neglect anything I've told you, watch it!"

Sickness and death were constant concerns, and many letters deal with problems of health. Again the outline-scribe Pay writes to his son Pra-emheb:

"Don't abandon me; I am not well. Don't hold back your tears for me, for I am afflicted with eye trouble [?], and my lord Amun has turned his back [?] on me. Please bring me some honey for my eyes, and also ochre newly made into sticks and genuine eye-paint. See to it properly! Surely I am your father, but now I am out of action, straining for my sight, but [my eyes] are not well."

A great many of the ostraca carry texts dealing with very mundane activities – the provision of rations, the arrangements for laundry in the village, the completion of all kinds of petty transactions which involved the inhabitants of the village and their families. A few deal with the primary activities of the workmen; such is the large ostracon with the register for Year 40 of Ramesses II. The majority, however, deal with small personal matters. The scribe Pabaki writes to his father Maaninakhtef:

"I have paid attention to what you said: 'Let Ib work with you.' Now see, he takes all day long bringing the water jug, no other duty having been given him all day long. He has paid no attention to what you advised: 'What have you done today?' [or, perhaps, 'What will you do today?']. See, the sun has already gone down and he is still away with the water jug."

Occasionally the writer of a begging letter seems to draw excessively on divine support for his request. The outline-scribe Khay writes to a colleague whose name is lost:

"In life, prosperity and health, and in the favor of Amon-Re, King of the Gods, your good lord, daily. See, I invoke [Amon-Re, Mut, Lady of Asheru and Khonsu in Thebes] and all the gods of Karnak, that you may be healthy, and continue in life, and be held in the favor of Amun, King [of the Gods], and of the King of Upper and Lower Egypt, Lord of the Two Lands, Usimare-Setpenre [Ramesses II], may he live, be prosperous and healthy, your good lord, that you will prosper in the service of

the city [Thebes]. Please pay attention, and obtain some ink for me, and some rush brushes ['pens'], and some sheets of papyrus, very urgently."

A further paragraph, badly damaged, gives a reason for this peremptory request: Khay is lying at home sick, and is without fresh food or anyone to bring him provisions.

Trivial such documents may be, but they bring to life quite vividly the humdrum daily round of the inhabitants of one small, although superior, working community. Here in Dayr al-Madina is a distinctive group of Ramesses' people, exposed in great detail because a high proportion of them could read and write and found it convenient to correspond with one another by means of ostraca; also recording lists of objects and small commercial transactions, while at the same time exposing their thoughts, wishes, and anxieties to sympathetic (and sometimes unsympathetic) family members and colleagues. One wonders, for example, what trouble might have prompted the note sent by the woman Werel to the scribe Huynefer:

"In life, prosperity, and health, and in the favor of Amon-Re, King of the Gods: Look! Every day I speak to every god and every goddess who is in Western Thebes, that you may be healthy, may live, and be in the favor of Pharaoh, life, prosperity, and health, your good lord. Also, take care for your brother; don't neglect him. And again, for Neferkhay – take care for your brother Khay; don't neglect him."

It is not surprising to see how frequently the major Theban gods are invoked in these brief communications, especially Amon-Re, the great imperial god of Karnak. Such divine invocations are undoubtedly routine; a proper letter would invariably start with the naming of the great local gods, but in communications from the workmen's village, it is very common to have other, less important deities mentioned. For example, in this last note the woman Werel calls on "every god and every goddess who is in Western Thebes" (the text actually has "in the district of the west"). Indeed, there were a great many gods and goddesses who claimed allegiance from the inhabitants of the village. Perhaps the most commonly invoked divine personage was the early Eighteenth Dynasty king Amenophis I (c.1525–1504 B.C.) together with his

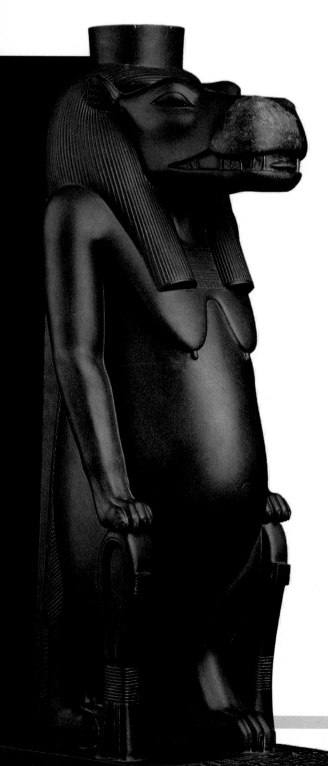

mother, Queen Ahmes-Nefertari; they were regarded as the patrons of the workmen. It remains uncertain why precisely these two historical figures achieved such local divine status; by the time of Ramesses II, at least, no indication is given in surviving texts of an appreciation of why the king and his mother were such objects of devotion. It is now generally thought that the veneration arose from the possible founding of the élite corps of workmen by Amenophis I, although it seems that the village, as the corps' base and home, was not established until the reign of Tuthmosis I, the successor of Amenophis. The royal mother Ahmes-Nefertari was in her lifetime a person of great consequence in state affairs, and, again for unknown reasons, was frequently associated closely with her son Amenophis. Perhaps because of their former human status, both were thought to be more approachable than the gods of Karnak. Additionally, in the local cult, Amenophis could be consulted as an oracle for the solving of local problems, just as Amon-Re could be at a much higher level.

Hathor, as a goddess of the West, was, not surprisingly, venerated by the workmen; and of the other national deities, Ptah of Memphis, 'Lord of Truth,' as patron of craftsmen, had a special place in the devotions of the villagers. A particularly local goddess, associated with the rocky peak of al-Qurn, which overlooks the Valley of the Kings, was Meresger. Her name means 'she who loves silence,' and she was shown usually as a cobra with a female human head. Ramose, in a letter to a priest Amenhotpe in the Ramesseum, invokes Meresger in particular as:

"Mistress of the West, to keep you healthy and living, to allow you to achieve a long life and a prosperous old age, and to pursue the office of your father, and to allow your children to succeed you after an infinity of time, while you remain in the favor of Amun of the temple 'United-with-Thebes' [the Ramesseum], your good lord."

The lesser domestic deities, like the female hippopotamus Thoeris and the leonine dwarf Bes, were very popular within the village, and certain foreign deities were worshiped, probably introduced by Asiatic craftsmen, and stamped with the attraction of exoticism. Among them were Astarte, Anat, Qudshu, and, strangely, Reshep, essentially a war god. In the village itself, cults in which the family ancestors were revered formed a significant part of the most intimate, domestic worship conducted within individual houses. The piety of these people of Ramesses is abundantly shown in the personal devotional objects found during the excavation of the village, in the textual evidence of the ostraca, and particularly in many small limestone stelae. These stelae carry carved inscriptions with representations of revered deities; many were placed in shrines in the precinct of the village, in rough shrines established in the heights of the hills, along the paths leading to the Valley of the Kings, and in the tombs prepared for the burials of the workmen and their families. Because of the wealth of talent available among members of the corps, these stelae are in many cases very well carved. The same is the case with many of the tombs, in which superior skills in painting provided unexpectedly well-decorated chambers for the not-very-important people who were to benefit from them in their afterlives.

It would be wrong to deduce from the way of life and the special advantages enjoyed by the villagers of Dayr al-Madina that the same conditions would have been found in other less-favored communities in Egypt. The privileged status of the villagers derived from their particular involvement in the making of the royal tombs in the Valley of the Kings, and in their employment in similar work for members of the royal family, for high officials, and others who might be granted special funerary favors. The workmen of Dayr al-Madina formed a protected species out of the genus 'Ramesses' people,' trapped in a closed environment, but spared most of the problems of life in the countryside, especially in the remote nomes of Middle Egypt and the distant reaches of the Delta. These 'servants in the Place of Truth,' as the royal-tomb workmen were called from the time of the mid-Eighteenth Dynasty, are the best-known ancient Egyptians of any period before Ptolemaic times. They are exceptional in having their lives exposed by texts, by the physical remains of their houses, and by their devotional stelae, and in some cases their tombs. Even their disputes have been recorded on ostraca, with details of local court cases, some of which were heard and settled in the special tribunal established for the villagers – another mark of their unusual status. A case concerning donkeys, which can with great probability be dated to the reign of Ramesses II, provides a good example of the practice of the law for such people. The beginning of the ostracon text is lost, and with it the names of some of the litigants, one of whom declares, "Return the female donkey which I delivered to you, because it belongs to the chief of police Sobkhotpe." I said to him, "Send someone for the handover. Then return my donkey and the garment which I paid for the she-donkey

that you sold." The local court questioned what was said by the water-carrier Tjay: "Were you given the donkey and the garment?" He said, "Indeed, I have them, and on this day I gave the she-donkey for the chief of police Sobkhotpe." The local court declared, "The workman Nefersenut is in the right, and the water-carrier Tjay is in the wrong." The matter was not settled by this judgment, and it was three years before Tjay had a she-donkey brought back to him. Still the affair was not settled; further items, including fields in Armant (to the south of Thebes) were thrown into the negotiation, which now included a woman litigant. The text ends, "I shall not accept the fields, but only return the she-donkey itself."

No doubt the case involving Sobkhotpe's she-donkey would be more understandable if the whole of the background and the full course of the proceedings were known. But it scarcely matters. What is of interest in a case of this kind is to observe the form of the proceedings and to be able to determine how simple disputes might be handled, how local

affairs could drag on for years, and how accessible a certain level of legal support could be secured by workmen in the village. We saw in an earlier chapter how the case over land and inheritance, reported in the texts in the tomb of Mose in Saqqara, could drag on for many centuries. One may hope that the existence of the local court or tribunal ensured that local disputes, not serious enough for the vizier's court, could be heard and settled in reasonable time. Justice, however, was not easy to obtain, especially as modern rules of evidence do not seem to have been recognized. There was apparently always the possibility of reopening a case and overturning, temporarily at least, a judgment. From the great many texts, which refer to legal disputes or give apparent transcripts of parts of trials, it is clear that the inhabitants of the village were a litigious lot, much given to wrangles over small matters and inclined to take an opponent to law, possibly because the facility of the local court was there and prepared to hear evidence and make judgment.

294 left
The female hippopotamus, Thoeris, a household deity, protector of pregnant women and revered by all people. This Late Period schist statue, inscribed for the god's wife of Amun, Nitocris, was found in Thebes (Cairo, JE 39194).

295 left
Decoration on the child's chair of Princess Sitamun (c. 1400 B.C.). The hippopotamus Thoeris, and leonine Bes, with knives and tambourine, were used as protective deities on beds and other personal objects (Cairo, CG 51113).

295 right
Stela of the necropolis workman Bay, who worships the hearing ears of Amon-Re, shown above as a ram and described as "the good ram." Such stelae expressing personal cults are common at Dayr al-Madina (Cairo, JE 43566).

In many respects the necropolis workmen were different from the workmen and peasants who formed the bulk of the population of Egypt during the reign of Ramesses II, perhaps most notably in the matter of burial and provision for the afterlife. Unlike the majority of what may be called the 'common folk,' the necropolis workmen carried their privileged status beyond the life on earth. Many were able to be buried in the neighborhood of the village itself, some tombs even being linked closely to houses and maintained as family sepulchres over several generations. A very good representative tomb of this kind was that established by the workman Sennedjem and used for the interment of family members over three generations at least. In the numbering of the private tombs in the Theban Necropolis, it has been assigned the number one (TT1) on geographical grounds, in that the systematic identification and numbering of the Theban tombs began at Dayr al-Madina in the early years of the twentieth century, and the first ten tombs were numbered at Dayr al-Madina. Tomb 1 was discovered in 1886, and by a most unusual chance was in a virtually intact condition. It has, therefore, served as an invaluable example of what a workman's burial might contain. Above all there were the bodies.

Sennedjem himself had a large rectangular sarcophagus of wood containing a mummiform coffin and a mummy-case containing the embalmed corpse. This ensemble was remarkably fine for someone whose formal title was simply 'servant in the Place of Truth,' that is, just 'workman' or 'member of the gang.' The forms and decoration on these intimate pieces in general follows those of the kinds of coffins provided for much more important burials. Sennedjem clearly knew the current practice for a high-class burial, and he was able, through his own technical abilities and those of his sons (also workmen) and of fellow members of the gang, to prepare an equipment far better than he could have expected if he had lived and worked elsewhere in Egypt. His tomb is situated very close to the southwest corner of the village, where his own house has been identified.

There is a great temptation to surmise that Sennedjem and perhaps many of his colleagues were able to exploit their positions and professional abilities by engaging in lucrative extramural activities connected with tomb-preparation. In this way they could greatly improve the way of life of themselves and their families, and also, very importantly, make good provision for a handsome burial.

296 top left
Outer face of the door to Sennedjem's tomb at Dayr al-Madina. Sennedjem, a workman in the Place of Truth, with his wife Iyneferti, plays senet *against destiny. The texts are from the Book of the Dead.*

296 top right
Inner face of Sennedjem's door showing the locking device. Upper scene: Sennedjem, Iyneferti, and their daughter Irunefer worship Osiris and Ma'at; below: seven named sons worship Ptah-Seker-Osiris, a funerary god, and Isis (Cairo, JE 27303).

297
Head of Sennedjem's outer coffin. Necropolis workmen of Dayr al-Madina were of modest status, but highly talented, and able to obtain funerary equipment far beyond what they might otherwise have expected (Cairo, JE 27308).

298-299
Burial chamber of Sennedjem's tomb, looking north to a wall covered with scenes of his life with his wife in the Field of Reeds after death and judgment. Ritual scenes cover the other walls.

One may also wonder whether burials of the kind enjoyed by Sennedjem would have been considered suitable by the majority of superior Theban officials. The relative remoteness of the village, tucked away in a fold in the Theban hills out of sight of the main Theban Necropolis, together with the protected status of the villagers, enabled them to get away with behavior and activities that would have been considered unforgivably presumptuous elsewhere.

In addition to Sennedjem's burial, the tomb also contained the burials of eight family members, including his wife Iyneferti, their son Khonsu, and his wife Tamaket, and of Isis, wife of their elder son Khabekhnet (whose own tomb was close by). Some of Khabekhnet's funerary furniture, including *shabti* boxes, were there also. A number of more simply prepared burials were found in the tomb – possibly of lesser members of the family. Among items of funerary equipment included in the burial chamber were pieces of furniture, pottery (some painted to represent rare

stone and glass vessels), and copies of tools of the kind used by Sennedjem in his work on earth: a cubit rod for measuring, a right-angle with plumb-bob for leveling, and a vertical level with plumb-bob for establishing the correct vertical line of a wall. Sennedjem presumably hoped to pursue his professional activities in the afterlife. Such activities, however, would be undertaken only when he and his wife were relieved from the necessary duties of plowing, sowing, and reaping in the fields of Iaru – duties brilliantly portrayed in paintings on the east wall of the burial chamber. Most of the other well-preserved, brightly painted scenes in the burial chamber depict Sennedjem and Iyneferti engaged in acts of worship and ritual acts, which in a simple way reflect contemporary paintings in royal and very senior official tombs, and particularly the tombs of the royal wives like Nefertari. There are no scenes of daily life, which were common in Theban tombs of the Eighteenth and early Nineteenth Dynasties.

298 bottom
Most private tombs of the New Kingdom at Thebes have ceilings decorated with attractive patterns. Sennedjem's vaulted ceiling has a series of scenes in which he and his wife adore funerary deities.

299 top
Figurine of Sennedjem, not truly a shabti figure as it lacks the tools carried by a true shabti. Its text speaks speaks of "all that comes forth from the offering table of Amun in Karnak for the ka of Sennedjem justified" (Cairo).

299 bottom
View looking south in Sennedjem's tomb. Many workmen's tombs were dug near the village enclosure of Dayr al-Madina. Their decoration is wholly funerary, with no scenes of daily life, probably considered inappropriate for such humble people.

The conditions enjoyed by Sennedjem and his family and colleagues in life and, by expectation and proper provision, in death, were not to be expected by the vast majority of Ramesses' people. Those who lived and worked on estates belonging to the great religious foundations throughout the land enjoyed various privileges, which to some extent would have changed from place to place. The great inscription inscribed on a rock face at Nauri in Nubia during the reign of Sethos I, Ramesses' father, deals with the affairs of the Osiris temple at Abydos, which was completed during Ramesses' reign. Among the provisions are quite stringent regulations concerning the conditions under which the large temple staff and workers on the temple estates should operate, including many exemptions from activities, which usually involved most of the unprivileged population of Egypt, like military service, the annual corvée, taxation, and the general exploitation by superiors. Such special ordinances were almost certainly made for other temples at other times, and it may reasonably be assumed that the servants and laborers on the lands of foundations like the temple of Ptah in Memphis, of Re at Heliopolis, and of the

many new temples in Piramesse were accorded similar protections and exemptions. The appropriate decrees of Ramesses II have not, unfortunately, been found, and their actual promulgation can only be postulated. Nevertheless, it would probably be a mistake to assume that workers in these and other temples and on the extensive temple estates throughout Egypt would have had particularly easy lives in spite of being spared military service and the harassment of local officials.

No ordinary Egyptian peasant or workman would have been able to read and write in the manner of the élite inhabitants of Dayr al-Madina. In the northern part of the country, where the papyrus plant was most common, the paper made from it was subject to monopoly control and difficult to come by even for

trained scribes not employed in governmental or temple administrations. Furthermore, the conditions for the preservation and survival of papyrus documents in the wetlands of the Delta were far inferior to those of the drier environment of the Theban district. Consequently, very few papyrus documents have survived from Lower Egypt, dating to the reign of Ramesses II, and of these the ones that deal with commerce and agricultural matters throw very little light on the lives and conditions of the ordinary inhabitants of Egypt. The term, which seems generally to describe such people is *rekheyet*; it is written, significantly, with the hieroglyph of a lapwing with its wings locked together – pinioned and unable to fly away. So was the bulk of the population in a sense pinioned and certainly not able to fly away.

300 left
The regular form of transport on land in ancient Egypt was the donkey. Expeditions were equipped with large numbers for carrying equipment, and they were the common working farm animal. From Dayr al-Bahri temple, drawing by Prisse d'Avennes.

300 right
Egyptians enjoyed hunting in the desert, a sport reserved for the highest ranks of society. In this Theban tomb scene, a servant brings back the results – an oryx and a hare – accompanied by a tired hound. Drawing by Prisse d'Avennes.

301
The marshy lands on the Delta and the Faiyum are still fine hunting grounds for wildfowl. In antiquity Egyptian peasants used clap-nets to trap wild birds, as shown here by Rosellini.

Some indication of the servile, depressed condition of ordinary people, Ramesses' people, may be obtained from those passages composed for scribal training, in the collections called Miscellanies. One striking piece deals with the peasant, the writer being eager to point out how much better the life of the scribe was. Parts of this piece have already been quoted in dealing with the bureaucracy of the country, in Chapter 8, where the peasant's misery at the hands of the tax assessors and collectors is vividly described. Farmers have never been slow to complain of their misfortunes, but in Egypt their lot was in general rather favorable, when they were not being harassed by petty officials. Living conditions were more comfortable than in countries where winters were cold and where rain could make working conditions miserable; famine was not common, and

cultivation was very much easier, and therefore more profitable, than in most of the other countries of the Mediterranean and the Near East. Egyptian peasant farmers should have been able to extract a reasonable living from the land, even if their tenancies were vulnerable, or even non-existent. But they were open to gross abuse by officialdom. Apart from taxes, there was the business of the corvée, in which men were conscripted for long or short periods to work on state projects, and especially on the annual rehabilitation of the country following the Nile flood. The maintenance of canals, ditches, and dykes and the re-establishment of marked boundaries were crucial for the continuance of successful land management and good agriculture. The annual call-up for these necessary tasks was undoubtedly to the advantage of everyone who worked on the

land, but that did not make it welcome to those whose names came out of the corvée-master's hat. It is more than suspected that the process was open to abuse and corruption, and that those peasants at the bottom of the human heap would suffer greatest exploitation. The distaste aroused by the corvée and the fear that its application might extend into the afterlife were serious considerations for Egyptians at all levels of society, and account in part for the existence in burials, even of kings, of *shabti*-figures which were designed to rescue the great and the good from having to dirty their hands in annual ditch-clearing and dyke-mending. The *shabti* could by magic act for a named individual if the name came up in the corvée-list of the fields of Iaru. Such a way of escape was certainly not available for the humblest in the land, whether in life or in death.

Service in the army was similarly a fate which peasants would have found hard to escape. Precise details of how Egyptian forces were recruited are quite unknown. What is clear, however, from surviving records is that a large part of the army was made up of mercenary troops, recruited possibly under duress from Nubians, Libyans, and other foreign settlers, and also from the ranks of foreign prisoners of war, who would have had little option but to serve a new master. Soldiers in all such categories might have had some training or experience of the battlefield, and in consequence were of immediate use for active service. Untrained native Egyptians were also recruited, probably by a form of corvée, no doubt administered with great unfairness by low-rank officials. There may have been volunteers, possibly including young men dissatisfied with the life on the land and the absence of prospects for the future, and even renegades escaping from

justice. The romance of life in the army was undoubtedly an attraction, but it was not an attraction that could last. As ever, the scribe could sneer at the fate of the soldier, not to be compared with the comfortable, privileged life of the petty bureaucrat. The scribe Amenemope writes to the scribe Pabes, pointing out the superiority of their profession:

"Let me tell you of the position of the soldier – he who is tormented. He is carried off as a child, 2 cubits tall [about 1 meter, or 3.25 feet], and shut up in barracks. His body is thrashed, his eye is smashed, his brow cracked, his hand split with a wound. He is floored and pounded like papyrus... . And what about his going to Palestine and marching through the hills? He carries his bread and his water like a donkey, his neck ridged like that of a donkey. His backbone is distorted; he drinks foul water and stops marching only to go on guard duty. When he comes to battle, he is already like a

plucked bird, drained of all strength. When he returns to Egypt, he is like a worm-eaten stick; he is ill, utterly exhausted, riding on a donkey, his clothes stolen, abandoned by his attendant."

I do not think that Amenemope the scribe would have been used as a recruiting agent for the Egyptian army. And yet what he wrote was probably not very far from the actuality of military service. Throughout the ages, the life of the soldier may have been thought to be romantic, but in reality has been hard and dangerous, especially for the humble infantryman. The Qadesh reliefs do not conceal the misery of battle.

The lack of evidence of the kind that illuminates the lives of the inhabitants of the workmen's village at Dayr al-Madina for the rest of Egypt prevents reliable assessments from being made about the existence of the members of the lowest strata of Egyptian society in Ramesses' reign. While the physical conditions of life

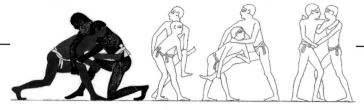

may have been reasonably tolerable, the town dwellers – those engaged in the most unpleasant industries and in the back-breaking activities of commerce – undoubtedly suffered from squalor and neglect, unregarded by the great, exploited by junior officials and uncaring masters, exposed to disease, and with a very modest life-expectancy. No matter what you were or what you did, there were particular hazards. Another scribal essay, written in the north of the country, possibly in the region of Memphis, points out starkly the reality of life for most ordinary people:

"Man issues from his mother's womb and runs [at once] to his master; the child serves the soldier, the youth is a marauder. The old man is obliged to be a farm-hand, and the grown man to be a soldier. The cripple becomes a doorkeeper, and the blind man a fattener of cattle. The bird-catcher takes position on the threshing floor; the fisherman is submerged. The god's servant

is also a farmer; the priest carries out his duties, and spends much of his time immersing himself in the river, for his duties recur three times a day; it is the same, winter and summer, wind and rain. If the stable manager relaxes his work, his team becomes abandoned in the field, his wife is put to measuring barley, his daughter is working on the dykes, his maidservant is conscripted [?] to the gang, and his assistant is [sent] to the quarries. The baker is always baking, putting bread on the fire, with his head right in the oven, his son hanging on-to his feet; if he slips from his son's grasp, he falls down into the oven."

That is the kind of thing you must expect if you are out in the rough, unkind world. As ever, how much better to be a scribe!

The one aspect of life in which tension might be relieved and some entertainment enjoyed, was, as has been pointed out in an earlier chapter, the celebration of the

periodic religious festivals and the grander occasions of the jubilee festivals during Ramesses' long reign. It is perhaps just as well that we do not have written records of the excesses, which undoubtedly accompanied such festivities. If there were registers of absentees from work drawn up throughout the land, there would surely be very many entries on the days following festivals in which the reason for absence would be 'illness,' or more specifically, 'recovering from the festival.' One would hope that even the strictest overseer would appreciate the compelling need to observe a festival with full participation. Festivals were among the few things in life to which the *rekheyet*, the ordinary Egyptians could look forward, and happily, in Ramesses' long reign there were many festivals, and they could be enjoyed without the problems of external threats or internal disturbances upsetting their proper observance.

302 top
Rosellini's drawing of a troop of Egyptian bowmen returning to Thebes after another victorious campaign. Some carry objects that appear to be booty, but texts do not speak of such benefits for the ordinary soldier.

302-303
Soldiers preparing for battle. An Egyptian with a shield and battle axe is followed by eager Nubian bowmen, stringing their bows and flourishing their arrows. In the New Kingdom, Nubian mercenaries were used for warfare and civil security. By Rosellini.

303 top
Young men engage in wrestling, in preparation, no doubt, of having to take part in hunting and warfare when their time came. From the tombs of Beni Hasan, drawn by Rosellini.

THE LEGEND
OF RAMESSES II

CHAPTER 11

304
Limestone slab from a structure in the Apis complex at Saqqara, built by or associated with Prince Khaemwese; his head is shown wearing the sidelock commonly worn by the sem-priest of Ptah.

If a sovereign reigns for a great many years, there is a good chance that he may be remembered in later times partly because the name is one that has become indelibly printed on the tablets of people's minds. The name may even be used to characterize a whole period. Today one can think in particular of Victoria, who was the British queen from 1837 until 1901 and whose name conjures up the culture of the greater part of the nineteenth century and is used in this respect not only in Britain itself, but commonly in America, and even in some European countries. 'Victorian' is not always used in a complimentary way; in moral matters, it suggests a very old-fashioned approach to the conduct of life; in artistic matters, it has often a pejorative force; in industrial and business matters, it regularly invokes scientific invention and commercial enterprise. 'Victorian' can be good and bad; it can represent a virtuous way of life, or

one unutterably dreary and outdated.

What about Ramesses II? Egyptologists have often characterized his reign as being one of special qualities, to be considered almost an era in itself. He is commonly called Ramesses the Great, and his reign, taken with those of his successors to the end of the Twentieth Dynasty, is called the Ramesside Period. It can be given this sobriquet quite simply because most of the kings who reigned during this time carried the nomen Ramesses. But it was not a coherent period in which the characteristics of the reign of Ramesses II continued to be evident for the next 150 years. The name Ramesses served as the link, but scarcely as the model for most of the kings of the later Twentieth Dynasty, similarily named. The only king Ramesses who bears in any way comparison with the great predecessor was Ramesses III, second king of the Twentieth Dynasty (c. 1184–1153 B.C.). He was the first Egyptian ruler to carry the name

Ramesses after his illustrious namesake, and he also took the prenomen Usimare, by which Ramesses II was particularly known in much later times in the Greek form Osymandyas. Ramesses III undoubtedly saw himself as a worthy successor and endeavored during his reasonably long reign of thirty years to pursue policies in foreign and in domestic affairs which were aimed certainly at trying to restore the successes of the earlier reign. That he achieved only partial success in his purposes was not entirely his fault. The pattern of external pressures on Egypt from Asia, Libya, and the Mediterranean world had radically changed, while within Egypt the even tenor of life was seriously disturbed by tensions within society and unfavorable harvests. Still, he was Usimare Ramesses, and in a sense he must have hoped that the magic of the names would bring him success. To emphasize his close following of his illustrious (but not quite direct) ancestor,

he even built at Medinet Habu a great mortuary temple roughly on the same plan as the Ramesseum, which at the time was probably the best preserved and certainly the most impressive of the surviving mortuary temples. Ramesses III also included in his temple a special chapel for the cult of Ramesses II's image in its divine bark.

Although no kings later than the Twentieth Dynasty carried the nomen Ramesses, a significant number during the Twenty-second and Twenty-third Dynasties took as part of their prenomen the significant Usimare, the name by which the original Ramesses II should, in Egyptian tradition, be better known. While the names of Ramesses II still resonated to a certain degree at the highest level of Egyptian society, a fading memory of his greatness and importance remained in the memories of Egyptians generally. An educated scribe of the latest Pharaonic times, skilled in the demotic script, might not have been able to recognize Ramesses' cartouches if he had walked past the great but probably ruined temples in the Delta cities, or in Memphis or in Thebes, but he could be well acquainted with the stories told about the great Pharaoh Usimare and his son Khaemwese.

Tales written on papyrus in the demotic script, the very cursive successor to the hieratic script (the form used on the ostraca of the Theban workmen), have as their principal character a priestly prince called Setne Khamuas. Setne is a corruption of an old priestly title, *setem* or *sem*, used in the case of Khamuas (Khaemwese) as if it were a first name. The stories are preserved on papyri in the Cairo Museum and the British Museum and are ostensibly set in the time of the great Pharaoh Usimare. The principal figure is Setne Khamuas, who retains something of his historical character of wise man or magician, although in the stories he is made to appear less than worldly-wise, or even noble.

The most entertaining episode involves magic, seduction, retribution, and a happy ending. Setne Khamuas learns of a magical book in the keeping of the spirit of a priest called Naneferkaptah in his tomb in Saqqara. By trickery, Setne Khamuas steals the book from the tomb and carries it off in triumph, although warned by Naneferkaptah that terrible things would happen to him. Setne's father, the Pharaoh Usimare, advises him to return the book, protecting himself with powerful charms. He ignores this advice and falls into an adventure which threatens to destroy him. Walking one day in the precinct of the temple of Ptah, he notices an attractive lady whom he attempts to woo. She turns out to be a priestess of Bastet, the cat goddess of Bubastis, who, having at first rejected Khamuas' advances, then arranges an assignation in her house in Bubastis. In due course Khamuas travels to Bubastis and seeks out the house of the priestess, whose name is Tabubu. He is eager to achieve her seduction, but she teases him and then persuades him to make a will in her favor. She pursues her advantage and gets Khamuas to summon his children and have them sign away their rights to any inheritance. Finally, in order to secure his purpose with Tabubu, he agrees to have his children killed, and while he and the priestess settle down to the consummation of their passion, they can hear the noise of dogs and cats tearing at the children's corpses in the court below. Even then Khamuas is denied his hard-won reward; as he stretches out his hand to touch Tabubu, she lets out a great cry and he wakes up in a state of sexual excitement, with no clothes on, in the open country. At that moment he sees a company approach with a great man carried in a litter; he turns out to be Pharaoh, his father. Embarrassed because he is in the nude, Khamuas finds it difficult to get up; but Pharaoh spots him: "Setne why are you in this state?"

"It is Naneferkaptah who is responsible," says Khamuas. Pharaoh tells him to go to Memphis, where he will find his children waiting for him. "How can I go to Memphis with no clothes?"

Usimare orders a servant to bring him clothes. Back in Memphis, he is asked by Pharaoh whether he had been drunk. He then tells of his adventure with Tabubu, and his father advises him to take the magic book back to Naneferkaptah. Protected by a forked stick and with a lighted brazier on his head, Setne Khamuas takes the book back to the tomb in Saqqara and hands it over to the spirit of Naneferkaptah.

"It is the great god Ptah who has brought you back in safety," says the spirit's wife Ahwerre.

"I told you so!" says the spirit itself. And they parted on friendly terms.

This wholly fanciful story is a product of literary invention, but peopled with identifiable characters placed in an identifiable setting. Setne Khamuas was one thousand years earlier, Khaemwese, favored son of Ramesses II and the high priest of Ptah in Memphis. In this city he was at home, and in the adjacent necropolis of Saqqara he would be buried. Of Tabubu nothing is known, but it is known that there was a small temple dedicated to the goddess Bastet in a district of Memphis called Ankhtawy, which is mentioned in the story. Bubastis lay about one hundred kilometers (sixty-two miles) to the northwest of Memphis, and was easily accessible by water. Nothing else in the story corresponds with the reality of the times of Ramesses II, the Usimare of the narrative. It is a romance, and part of a series of romances based on the imaginary happenings involving a person of historical reality who might still have been remembered in a shadowy form, along with his father, the great Ramesses II, whose sculptures were still to be seen in the city of Memphis.

A rather different kind of remembered event, and involving a more clearly defined royal person, is recorded on a fine stone stela over 7 feet tall (2.22 meters), discovered in 1829 in Karnak near the temple of Khonsu, within the precinct of the great temple of Amon-Re, and now in the Louvre Museum in Paris. It is carved and set out as if it were an inscription of the time of Ramesses II, but it was undoubtedly made toward the end of the Pharaonic Period, possibly in the Twenty-seventh Dynasty (Persian) in the sixth century B.C., but before the arrival of Alexander the Great in 332 B.C. It is an unusual creation for this time, and there has been much debate about why it should have been made. Every effort seems to have been employed to produce a convincing pastiche of a Nineteenth Dynasty royal inscription. Even the language is a reasonable copy of the grammar, syntax, and spelling of an authentic text of Ramesses' time. Some kind of propaganda purpose may be suggested as the reason for its making, possibly political, possibly religious, involving the cults connected with the Khonsu temple. It is clear, however, that it was considered necessary to invoke the memory of the great Ramesses, a real presence at Karnak, the site where he could still be recalled by those who could read the multifarious inscriptions set up in his name. But who could, or would, read this stela with the story of Bentresh, Princess of Bakhtan? It is altogether an enigma. The scene at the top of the stela is in two parts: on the right, Ramesses II makes offering to the bark of Khonsu in his form 'Contriver in Thebes';

on the left, a priest named Khonsuemhet-netjerneb carries out a similar presentation. This double scene establishes the relevance of the monument to the cults of Khonsu in Karnak, which, as emerges from the text, include that of Khonsu-Neferhotep. The text begins with a full royal titulary, including the names Usimare-Setpenre and Ramessu-Miamun, prenomen and nomen of Ramesses II, quite correctly, but with other royal names, which refer specifically to King Tuthmosis IV of the Eighteenth Dynasty (c. 1400–1390 B.C.). After a florid royal encomium, the main text begins with a retrospective preamble telling of Ramesses' annual visit to the land of Naharin (northern Syria), where he receives tribute from many foreign princes, including a special gift from the Prince of Bakhtan, is eldest daughter. Ramesses is delighted and makes her a great royal wife with the name Neferure and brings her back to Egypt, where "she did everything appropriate for a queen." Now follows the account of events, which closely involve the cults of Khonsu. A precise date establishes the time of a visit by an envoy from the Prince of Bakhtan: Year 23, second month of summer, day 22 (supposedly c. 1257 B.C. in the real reign of Ramesses). At this time Ramesses is in Thebes celebrating the Opet Festival. The envoy presents gifts, and then reveals the real purpose of his visit: Neferure's younger sister Bentresh is seriously ill – can an Egyptian doctor be sent to help? The royal scribe Djehuty-emheb is recommended and duly sent; he diagnoses an evil spirit in possession of Bentresh's body, and the Prince of Bakhtan writes to Ramesses

requesting a visit from an appropriate god to wrestle with the evil spirit. This is in Year 26. Being again in Thebes, Ramesses consults Khonsu-Neferhotep, the principal form of the god, and he suggests Khonsu-the-Contriver, "the great god who drives out sickness demons." Fortified with extra magic, Khonsu-the-Contriver (that is, his cult-image) is sent with great ceremony and an impressive retinue to Bakhtan, which he reaches after a journey of one year and five months.

As soon as Khonsu-the-Contriver has been welcomed in Bakhtan, he is taken to the sick princess, and in no time drives out the evil spirit, who submits without a struggle, saying, "Be welcome, great god who drives out evil spirits. Bakhtan is now your city, its inhabitants are your servants, and I too am your servant. Now I shall return to the place from where I came, so as to satisfy your wish in the matter for which you came to this city. May your divine majesty order the celebration of a festival in which I and the Prince of Bakhtan can take part." While these private exchanges are being made in the princess's chamber, the Prince of Bakhtan and his entourage remain outside in terror at the terrible noises coming from within. When the cure is revealed, the prince arranges the great festival as the spirit suggested, but secretly plans to keep the image of Khonsu-the-Contriver for a little more time; in fact it turns out to be for three years and nine months. Then the prince has a dream in which he sees the god leave its shrine as a golden falcon and fly away in the direction of Egypt. Ashamed at what he has done in delaying

307
Heraldic device of a kind found on
columns in buildings of the reign of
Ramesses II. The nomen and
prenomen of Ramesses are set over
the sign for "gold," topped with
sun disks, and flanked by uraei,
also with sun disks.

its return, he calls the god's priest, saying, "It seems that your god is still here in Bakhtan with us. It is high time that he went back to Egypt. Get his chariot ready." And so the god leaves Bakhtan, greatly honored and weighed down with many rich gifts. The whole population of Bakhtan turns out to send him on his way. When he is back in Thebes, Khonsu-the-Contriver goes to report to the shrine of Khonsu-Neferhotep, and gives him all the gifts from Bakhtan. By then it is Year 33, second month of winter, day 19 of the King of Upper and Lower Egypt, Usimare-Setpenre. The episode has lasted ten years.

This extraordinary inscription, which is of its kind not unique among ancient Egyptian monumental texts, is a fantasy, almost a romantic fiction, and could be classified as such were it not to be seen as having connections with the cult of Khonsu-Neferhotep in Thebes and having a purpose other than fictional. It is significant that the events should be placed in the reign of Ramesses II, who had perhaps as much as seven hundred years before the text was carved, ruled over the land of Egypt. The main intent seems to be the boosting of the prestige of Khonsu by invoking long-past events, which can be linked only tenuously to the reign of Ramesses. The king's marriage to a foreign princess took place in his Year 34 (c. 1246–1245 B.C.), not Year 23, as the Late Period text has it. The foreign wife was given the name Mahor-neferure, while in the later texts she is just Neferure. The historical foreign wife was Hittite; the later has always been taken to be a princess of Bakhtan. This country is otherwise not known, and Egyptologists in the past have usually thought the name to be a version of the Egyptian word for Bactria, a country in the farthest reaches of Central Asia. Recently, however, it has been suggested that there was a misinterpretation of a crucial hieroglyph in the writing of the place name, and that what the composer of the text had intended was Hatti, the land of the Hittites. Such a solution would greatly help to equate the 'legend' on the stela with the historic events surrounding Ramesses' Hittite marriage. The idea of having medical exchanges between countries in the ancient world is well founded. In even earlier times, the king of Babylon sent the cult-image of Ishtar of Nineveh to assist the ailing King Amenophis III of the Eighteenth Dynasty. Hittite sources record that medical help was sought from Egypt during Ramesses' reign. In general, Egyptian physicians were famous in antiquity, practicing specialization and often traveling to other countries when required. The possibility of a request for help from the Hittites is therefore by no means out of the question, and even the sending of a divine image not contrary to ancient practice. It would be possible to point to a number of apparent errors in the account of the whole episode, but these would not amount to a significant weakness in the account. For us now, it is significant to observe the persistence of the memory of Ramesses II, and the use of his name and some events of his reign to support the cult of Khonsu-Neferhotep at a time of strain in Egyptian affairs, when Persians dominated the land.

The memory of Ramesses II continued to resonate in the writings of Greek authors, who knew nothing first-hand of the great king but relied on the faded recollections and stories of native Egyptians. Herodotus, the Greek historian, traveled in Egypt in the mid-fifth century B.C., and in Book II of his *History*, he includes his findings on the history, culture, religion, and other aspects of ancient Egypt at a time when Egypt was under Persian domination (the Twenty-seventh Dynasty, in the reckoning of Manetho). Although there had been a Greek-assisted revolution in the Delta not long before his visit, and the Persians generally were still more than suspicious of Greek, particularly Athenian, intentions, Herodotus seems to have had little difficulty in entering Egypt and traveling throughout the country for several months. There had been a considerable Greek presence in Egypt since the seventh century B.C., and not all Greek communities were necessarily anti-Persian, or particularly pro-Athenian. Herodotus picked up his information in an apparently casual manner, and does not describe or comment on the monuments of antiquity in a regular or geographically systematic manner. He does, however, talk of the king named Rhampsinitus, and of his particular monument, which was the western gateway to the temple of Vulcan, that is, the Ptah temple in Memphis, which had two colossal figures standing before it. These, according to the comments of the priests, were called Summer and Winter, the former being an object of devotion to ordinary Egyptians and the latter, the opposite. The name Rhampsinitus is now generally thought to be a corruption of Ramesses with the added epithet sa-Neith, 'son of Neith' (the goddess of the Delta city Sais). This epithet was never part of the formal titulary of Ramesses II, but was a common royal epithet for kings of the Twenty-sixth Dynasty and later. Scholars are not at all sure that Rhampsinitus is Ramesses II, or even a conflation of Ramesses II and Ramesses III; and there is no reason to think that Herodotus had any particular Egyptian king in mind. He was purveying priestly information, and it is not clear whether he himself had been to Memphis and seen the Ptah temple and the colossal statues in that city. Herodotus also seems not to have visited the great funerary temples of the Ramesseum and Medinet Habu (Ramesses III), in the first of which he would have seen colossal statues greater than those in Memphis and on which he could hardly have failed to comment. In fact he gives no general account of Thebes and its monuments, and some scholars have doubted, probably erroneously, that he ever traveled in Upper Egypt. He says more about Rhampsinitus, however, in presenting at length a story concerning him which might contain vague recollections of the prosperity of the years when Ramesses II was king, and even of his great mortuary temple, the Ramesseum. According to the story, Rhampsinitus was immensely rich, with a vast store of precious objects, for which he built an apparently impregnable treasure-house. The builder, knowing the reason for the structure, incorporated in it a loose stone, by the removal of which he might be able to enter and steal treasure from time to time. He himself never took advantage of the loose stone, but he passed on the knowledge of it to his two sons on his deathbed. They immediately began to exploit the possibility of wealth, and continued to do so until the king, aware that thefts were taking place regularly, set traps. One of the sons got caught, and he persuaded his brother to cut off his head so that his body might remain unidentified. The king, astonished at finding the headless body, there still being no sign of obvious entry into the treasure-house, had the body displayed publicly in the hope of discovering its identity by the appearance of a weeping mother. She, in great distress had her surviving son retrieve the body by tricking the guards and making them drunk. Again the king was angered and more determined than before to catch the other thief; he used one of his daughters as bait, installing her in a brothel and requiring her to ask any client what had been the cleverest and most wicked thing he had ever done. Once again the thief saw through the trick, visited the brothel, duped the daughter, and escaped, leaving her holding on to the arm of a newly dead man. The king then gave up, offered the thief a rich reward, and when he surrendered, he was offered the king's daughter as his wife., and Rhampsinitus declared: "The Egyptians are wiser than the rest of the world, and this man is wisest of them all." One may assume that if Rhampsinitus were indeed Ramesses II, he could easily have spared one of his large number of daughters, especially as the one in question had become what might be called 'soiled goods,' for whom he might not easily find a respectable husband.

Some scholars have thought that the whole story refers to Ramesses III, and that

309
Marble bust of Herodotus of Halicarnassus, Greek historian of the fifth century B.C., whose account of Egypt, in the second book of his History, *contains the story of Rhampsinitus, apparently Ramesses the Great.*

the treasure-house was the temple of Medinet Habu, or one of its subsidiary buildings. It is much more likely, however, that the Ramesseum, the mortuary temple of Ramesses II, is the intended site. There is good evidence to suggest that in the late Pharaonic Period, the Ramesseum was the more striking complex of buildings, in spite of the fact that the Medinet Habu temple was in a far better state of preservation. But Medinet Habu had by then already become a busy township in itself, the main temple being almost engulfed by domestic and other buildings. It remained so, and became even more cluttered with mud-brick structures until it was extricated from its engulfment in mud-brick by excavators in the early decades of the twentieth century. It was never visited in modern times by early travelers and archaeologists to the same extent as the Ramesseum, where an uncluttered precinct offered more open access to the structures of its founder. Furthermore, within the precinct at the back of the temple, there is an impressive range of vaulted mud-brick buildings, storerooms for temple goods, and possibly seen in late antiquity as the positive evidence for the treasure-house of Ramesses II; and these storerooms were only a few hundred meters from the small palace built within the precinct for the king's occasional visits to Thebes.

It will never be possible to determine satisfactorily who Rhampsinitus was, or to confirm the details of the story recounted by Herodotus. The amiable Greek historian ends his account of the Egyptian king by reporting the priestly opinion that up to the time of his death, Egypt was well governed and prospered greatly. These judgments

would apply better to the long and generally successful reign of Ramesses II than to that of Ramesses III, when the country suffered from internal as well as external problems. It would, however, be quite a mistake to place too much reliance on all that Herodotus recounts. He follows the reign of Rhampsinitus with that of Cheops, the builder of the Great Pyramid, who in fact reigned about thirteen hundred years before Ramesses II. Nevertheless, there remain in the account of Rhampsinitus' reign faint suggestions, which can quite properly be traced to memories of the great king.

Even more positive resonance may be found in the work of the later Greek writer Diodorus the Sicilian, who composed his *History* in the first century B.C. Although he never traveled in Egypt as far south as Thebes, he includes descriptions of Theban monuments, including what he calls "the tomb of Osymandyas." This "tomb," as described, bears a close resemblance to the Ramesseum, especially in respect of the colossi of the great king which littered the precinct, and were clearly to be observed in the first century B.C. Diodorus writes in particular of one vast seated colossus of the king carved from a single piece of the black stone of Syene, that is, the so-called black granite (more properly described as granodiorite) from the quarries at Aswan. He gives a summary description of the statue, which he calls the biggest in Egypt, and he paraphrases the inscription on it: "King of kings, Osymandyas am I. If anyone wishes to know how great I am and where I lie, let him surpass my works." Osymandyas has very reasonably been identified as a Greek

corruption of Usimare, Ramesses II's prenomen. The Ramesseum is described as the "sacred precinct of Memnon" by the Greek geographer Strabo, who was a contemporary of Diodorus. The use of Memnon to describe the maker of the Ramesseum (whether tomb or temple) clearly suggests that Strabo, and other classical authors who use the name (probably following Strabo), were ignorant of the historical Ramesses and employed the name of the mythical Greek hero as being a suitable candidate for the ownership of this great structure. For much the same reason, the two great statues of King Amenophis III, which dominate the flood plain not far from the Ramesseum, were called the Colossi of Memnon – and still are, erroneously but affectionately, to this day. Confusion over identification reveals the ignorance of these Greek writers about the Ramesseum and its builder, and the use of the name Memnon makes it evident that they were floundering in a morass of part information, part legend, part romantic invention. If they visited Egypt they had to rely on what they were told by Egyptians or by Greek inhabitants of Egypt, or what they may have read in the writings of earlier Greek authors. They could not read hieroglyphs, and if they had been able to do so, they would still have had difficulty in extracting information that they could properly comprehend. What they gleaned surely came to a great extent from what the local folk-memories purveyed, and we all know how unreliable such memories can be. If Diodorus was close to the truth in calling the Ramesseum the tomb of Osymandyas, his fellow writers like Strabo were well off the mark in bringing Memnon into the story.

310
A reconstructed view in full color of
the inside of the small Ptolemaic
temple at Dayr al-Madina, as
envisaged by the artists of the
Description de l'Égypte. It is
probable that Egyptian temples were
even more brightly painted.

But it was Memnon who stuck in later tradition, so that when the engraved scenes of the Ramesseum were published in the massive French *Description de l'Égypte*, one of the most important products of the Napoleonic invasion of Egypt (1798–1801), the great mortuary temple of Ramesses II is described as the tomb of Memnon, the Memnonium. The connection with Ramesses II was not made, and even if the name of Osymandyas was also sometimes used, it could not have been understood that it concealed the true prenomen of the great king, Usimare. It would be some years before the name Ramesses in hieroglyphs would be identified by Jean-François Champollion, to whom must go the greatest credit for the decipherment of the Egyptian script.

At the beginning of the nineteenth century, scholars were about to step from the ignorance of the past into the knowledge and clarity of the future, as far as Egypt was concerned. At that point, the name Ramesses was known from the chronicle of Manetho as having been a long-lived king of the Eighteenth-Nineteenth Dynasties. The name was also known from the Old Testament as that of an Egyptian town (in fact, probably Piramesse) on which the Children of Israel had toiled. The name could not yet be recognized in its hieroglyphic form, and buildings that carried the name could not be dated. When Henry Salt and William John Bankes came to Ramesses' great temple at Abu Simbel in 1818, one year after it had been opened for Salt by Giovanni-Battista Belzoni, they had no idea when the temple had been carved out of the rock or who was represented by the great seated colossi on the façade. Bankes, standing on the sand-drift in front of the entrance, noted a Greek inscription high on the leg of one of the colossi referring to a campaign in Nubia during the reign of a king named Psammetichus. From classical sources Bankes knew that there were kings named Psammetichus in the Twenty-sixth Dynasty. They ruled in the seventh and sixth centuries B.C., and Bankes deduced that the builder of Abu Simbel must have lived many years earlier. The carver of the Greek text must have stood on a sand-drift high above the pavement leading to the temple entrance in order to reach the point on the leg that he had chosen for his inscription. The name of the temple owner would be known within ten years of the Salt-Bankes visit, but before the decipherment of hieroglyphics, scholars and travelers could only guess at the identity of kings.

It is not surprising, therefore, that Memnon was accepted in the early nineteenth century, but it is surprising that the name may still be used even today. Diodorus wrote about the great seated colossus in the Ramesseum. In 1801 William Hamilton, an envoy of Lord Elgin, traveled through Egypt, and in the Ramesseum noted the bust of a colossal statue: "It is certainly the most beautiful and perfect piece of Egyptian sculpture that can be seen throughout the whole country. We were struck by its extraordinary delicacy; the very uncommon expression visible in its features." He goes on to say, "The place in which it is to be found exactly answers to the sacred precinct of Memnon [Hamilton uses the Greek of Strabo here]." A little over fifteen years

later, this bust was removed from the Ramesseum by Belzoni on behalf of Henry Salt and the Swiss orientalist Jean-Louis Burckhardt, who together presented it to the British Museum. In London it was known as the Memnon, or the Younger Memnon, being smaller than the great Colossi of Memnon (a different king) or the shattered granodiorite monster in the Ramesseum. Even now the bust in London is sometimes affectionately called the Younger Memnon, although its true identity has been well known for almost two hundred years.

The Young Memnon arrived in London in 1817 and was soon included in the display of Egyptian and other ancient sculptures, although not, as one unsympathetic trustee pointed out to Salt some years later, "among the works of Fine Art… . Whether any statue that has been found in Egypt can be brought into competition with the grand works of the Townley Gallery [that is, Greek sculpture] remains to be proved." Nevertheless, the bust made its mark in London and received much favorable publicity. At about the time of its arrival, the poet Percy Bysshe Shelley was writing his sonnet "Ozymandias," and it has often been claimed that its inspiration was this bust from the Ramesseum. Few scholars, whether of ancient Egypt or of English literature, now believe this attribution is correct in spite of the temporal coincidence of the bust's arrival and the sonnet's composition. The king represented in the bust was never identified with the Osymandyas of Diodorus, and it is now supposed that the source for Shelley's sonnet, apart from Diodorus (for Shelley

was a good classical scholar), was William Hamilton. He had written about the Ramesseum and the Memnon, and may have even talked to Shelley about the great fallen colossus in the temple. Hamilton indeed may be the person involved in the opening lines of the poem:

> I met a traveller from an antique land
> Who said: "Two vast and trunkless legs of stone
> Stand in the desert. Near them, on the sand,
> Half sunk, a shattered visage lies… ."

Diodorus is undoubtedly the source for the lines:

> And on the pedestal these words appear:
> "My name is Ozymandias, King of kings:
> Look on my works, ye Mighty, and despair!"

And so was Ozymandias (Osymandyas), Usimare, introduced by way of a poem to the British public, and at the same time the noble features of the great Ramesses were revealed in the British Museum under the alias of 'Memnon.' There is nothing to connect the two 'revelations,' nothing to suggest that that at that time (1817), Ozymandias and the Younger Memnon were one and the same person, although not the same sculpture. But it would be only a few years before the hieroglyphic cartouches of Ramesses II were identified. In no time would the extent of his building works throughout Egypt be appreciated, and his presence identified in the impressive battle scenes of Qadesh in the temples of Thebes and at Abu Simbel. John Gardner Wilkinson, in his *Manners and Customs of the Ancient Egyptians*

(1837), compares at length Diodorus' description of the Memnonium with the actual surviving features of the Ramesseum, and concludes very properly that Ramesses II was its builder. He notes, further, that the long reign ascribed to this king by Manetho (sixty-six years) is practically confirmed by the dates in Year 62 already discovered on his surviving monuments. In France, Champollion had identified the name Ramesses among the first royal cartouches he deciphered, and he was soon to reveal the extent and importance of his monuments, including the great obelisk from Luxor, which he recommended for removal to Paris. It was, after many delays, taken down and transported to the French capital, where it was re-erected in the Place de la Concorde in October 1833. In Italy, by about the same date, the fine seated statue of the young Ramesses II from Karnak was established in the Egyptian Museum in Turin. At the same time, many monuments of that king and of his reign were entering the great collections of Europe and bringing the myth of the great Ramesses to practical view. The legend of Ramesses II was thus being renewed with knowledge drawn from ancient sources that could provide a new age with a profile very different from the one that survived to the late Pharaonic Period; Ramesses would soon be invested with a new glamour. No matter what the scholars may say about the impossibility of getting close to the great kings and queens of ancient Egypt, there are many people who see the monuments of Ramesses II, especially the resited temples of the king and of his wife Nefertari at Abu Simbel, and feel that they know him more than a little.

afnet Tight-fitting cap crown with a short "tail," and on the brow, the *uraeus*.

ankh Egyptian word for "life;" written with a sign similar to a cross with a loop at the top; carried by gods and offfered to kings.

Apis Sacred bull, incarnation of Ptah, the god of Memphis. Kept in the temple precinct of Ptah in Memphis and buried in Saqqara, in a place called now the Serapeum.

atef A crown incorporating ram's horns, the sun-disk and ostrich feathers, worn by Osiris, and sometimes by the king.

blue crown Crown with *uraeus*, shaped something like bishop's miter, usually colored blue, and worn by the king in battle.

canopic jars Four containers placed in a burial, containing the embalmed entrails of the deceased.

cap-crown A tight-fitting crown, sometimes thought erroneously to be a form of the blue crown; worn by the king in carrying out certain functions.

cartouche Oval rope-shape with tie, used to enclose the prenomen and nomen of the king.

djed Pillar-like sign, sometimes described as Osiris' backbone; often used amuletically with the sense of "endurance," and decoratively with the *tyet*-sign.

faience Glazed quart frit, a material much used in ancient Egypt for moulded vessels, small figures and colored inlays.

flail One of the two signs of power regularly held by the king; its origin is uncertain, but may be agricultural.

hemi-speos Temple of which part (e.g. the sanctuary) is cut into the rock, and part built free-standing.

heqa Crook-shaped scepter, one of the two signs of royal power.

hypostyle Hall in a temple, the roof of which is supported by many pillars.

Iunmutef "Pillar of his mother," a form of Horus, and also of a priest representing him, and associated with the *sem*-priest.

Iusa'as Heliopolitan goddess, 'She who becomes great as she comes,' a divine expression of the female principle.

ka The element of a person's being, often, but inaccurately, equated with the "soul." Its function was specially important after death, in representing the deceased.

Kamutef "Bull of his mother;" the name of Amon-Re in that of the god Min, mummiform and ithyphallic.

khepesh Curved scimitar-like sword, symbol of royal power, often shown being presented to the king by a god.

Ma'at Egyptian word for "truth, order," and personified as the goddess Ma'at, shown with the feather of "truth;" often presented as a small figure with the feather on the squatting goddess's knee.

mammisi Birth-house; a room or separate building in a temple in which the divine birth of the king is shown and celebrated.

Memnon Classical here incorrectly identified with the Egyptian king of the Colossi of Memnon (Amenophis III and of the Ramesseum (Ramesses II).

Memnonium Tomb of Memnon, erroneously applied by early travellers and scholars to the Ramesseum.

Menhit Protective goddess, in origin possibly the cobra, but later often shown as a lioness-headed woman.

moringa Tree with oil-yielding fruit, associated with certain deities, who are described as being "under" or "in his moringa tree."

nemes The most common royal headdress, made possibly of cloth, pleated, with "wings" and lappets, with the *uraeus* on the brow.

nome Term used for the provinces of ancient Egypt, of which there were 22 in Upper Egypt and 20 in Lower Egypt.

nomen Names contained in the second cartouche of a king's titulary; his birth name.

Opet The greatest annual Theban festival, when the gods of Karnak, the Theban triad, Amon-Re, Mut and Khonsu, traveled by river to Luxor to celebrate a sacred marriage.

Osiride pillar Square pillar in a temple with an attached figure of Osiris, mummiform, usually with the identity of the appropriate king.

ostracon Sherd of pottery or sliver of limestone, used for casual writings.

persea The tree *Mimusops schimperi*, on the leaves of which the gods traditionally wrote the name of reigning monarch.

prenomen Name contained in the first cartouche of the king's titulary. His throne name.

Renpet Goddess, the personification of the year, especially in connection with the years of the king's reign.

sed The royal jubilee, the festival of renewal, celebrated after thirty years of rule, every three years following.

sem-priest Priest especially in the service of Ptah in Memphis, shown wearing a leopard skin and with a long sidelock.

Serapeum Name given to the part of the Saqqara necropolis where the embalmed Apis bulls were interred.

shabti Funerary figurine placed in a burial to act as the deputy of the deceased when called upon for certain menial tasks in the afterlife. Often called *ushabti* or *shawabty*.

speos Rock-cut temple, such as Abu Simbel.

stela Inscription, usually in the form of a freestanding monument, with funerary, historical or celebratory texts.

tyet Object in the form of a knot, used amuletically and associated with Isis; sometimes called "blood of Isis;" often used decoratively in alternation with the *djed*-pillar.

uraeus The cobra placed on the brow of a king, representing the protective goddess Wadjet of Buto in the Delta.

user-staff Staff with the top often in the form of an animal's head, representing "power;" usually carried by gods.

Weret-hekau Goddess often in serpent form, "Great one of magic," closely associated with Isis and the protective power of the king.

INDEX

BIBLIOGRAPHY

Baines, J. & Malek, J., *Atlas of Ancient Egypt*. Oxford, 1980

Bierbrier, M.L., *Tomb Builders of the Pharaohs*. London, 1982; Cairo, 1989

Bietak, M., *Avaris: Capital of the Hyksos. Recent Excavations*. London, 1996

Bleiberg, E. & Freed, R., eds., *Fragments of a shattered visage. Proceedings of the International Symposium on Ramesses the Great*. Memphis, TN, 1991

Desroches-Noblecourt, C. & Kuentz, C., *Le Petit temple d'Abou Simbel*. Cairo, 1968

Freed, R.E., *Ramesses the Great. His Life and Works*. Exhibition Catalogue. Memphis, TN, 1987

Gardiner, A.H., *Egypt of the Pharaohs*. Oxford, 1961

Gardiner, A.H., *The Kadesh Inscriptions of Ramesses II*. Oxford, 1960

Gurney, O.R., *The Hittites*. London, 1952 (latest revision, 1999)

Habachi, L., *Features of the deification of Ramesses II*. Glückstadts, 1969

Kitchen, K.A., *Pharaoh Triumphant. The Life and times of Ramesses II*. Warminster, 1982

Kitchen, K.A., *Ramesside Inscriptions*. Vol. I *Ramesses I Sethos I and Contemporaries*: Texts, Oxford, 1968-9; Translation, Oxford 1993; Annotations, Oxford, 1993.

Kitchen, K.A., Vol. II, *Ramesses II, Royal Inscriptions*: Texts, Oxford, 1969-1979; Translations, Oxford, 1996; Annotations, Oxford, 1999.

Kitchen, K.A., Vol. III, *Ramesses II. His Contemporaries*: Texts, Oxford, 1978-80; Translations, Oxford 2000; Annotations, forthcoming.

Menu, B., *Ramesses the Great. Warrior and Builder*. London & New York, 1999

Murnane, W.J., *The Road to Kadesh*. Chicago, 1985

Tanis, L'Or des pharaons. Exhibition Catalogue. Paris, 1987

Tyldesley, J., *Ramesses. Egypt's greatest Pharaoh*. London, 2000

Weeks, K.R. *The Lost tomb. The greatest discovery at the Valley of the Kings since Tutankhamen*. London, 1998

Weeks, K.R., ed., *Valley of the Kings. The Tombs and Funeral Temples of Thebes West*. Vercelli, 2001

ACKNOWLEDGMENTS

THE PUBLISHERS WOULD LIKE TO THANK:

H.E. Farouk Hosny, The Egyptian Minister of Culture;

Zahi Hawass, Secretary General of the Supreme Council for Antiquities;

Nabil Osman, President of the Egyptian Information Center;

Gamal Morsi, Director of the Cairo Press Center;

Sabry Abd El Aziz Khater, General Director of Antiquities of Luxor and Upper Egypt;

Mohamed A. El-Bialy, General Director of Antiquities of Thebes West;

Kent Weeks;

Christian Leblanc;

Gamal Shafik of the Cairo Press Center;

The Mena House Oberoi Hotel;

Alessandro Cocconi and Guido Paradisi.

THE PUBLISHERS WOULD ALSO LIKE TO ACKNOWLEDGE:

Ashmolean Museum;

Bodleian Library, Department of Western Manuscript, Oxford;

Tanya Watkins of the British Museum, Dept. of Egyptian Antiquities, London;

CNRS Phototeque, Paris;

Robert Partridge of the Egypt Picture Library;

Sue Hutchinson of the Griffith Institute;

Rebecca Akhan of the Metropolitan Museum of Art, New York;

Musèe du Louvre, Dpt. des Antiquites Orientales, Paris;

Cristiana Morigi Govi of the Museo Civico, Bologna;

Matilde Borla of the Museo Egizio, Turin;

Hikmet Denizli of the Museum of Anatolian Civilization, Ankara;

Carla Hosein of the Oriental Institute, Chicago University;

Reunion de Musees Nationaux, Paris;

Patricia Spencer of the The Egypt Exploration Society;

Steven Snape of the University of Liverpool.

Abbas Ataman;

Ersu Pekin.

PHOTOGRAPHIC CREDITS

Page 1 Alfio Garozzo/Archivio White Star

Pages 2-3 Araldo De Luca/Archivio White Star

Pages 4-5 Araldo De Luca/Archivio White Star

Pages 6-7 Giulio Veggi/Archivio White Star

Page 8 Alfio Garozzo/Archivio White Star

Page 9 Alfio Garozzo/Archivio White Star

Page 10 Hervè Lewandowski/Photo RMN

Page 11 Alfio Garozzo/Archivio White Star

Pages 12-15 Araldo De Luca/Archivio White Star

Pages 16-17 Alfio Garozzo/Archivio White Star

Pages 18-19 Araldo De Luca/Archivio White Star

Page 20 Alfio Garozzo/Archivio White Star

Page 21 Alfio Garozzo/Archivio White Star

Page 22 top R.& V./Contrasto

Pages 22-23 center R.& V./Contrasto

Page 23 top left Photos12

Page 23 bottom left Photos12

Page 23 right Giulio Veggi/Archivio White Star

Page 24 top right T.G.H. James

Page 24 top left T.G.H. James

Pages 24-25 Archivio Images Service

Page 25 top British Museum

Page 26 top Archivio White Star

Page 26 bottom Archivio White Star

Page 27 left Archivio White Star

Page 27 right Antonio Attini/Archivio White Star

Page 28 top Alfio Garozzo/Archivio White Star

Page 29 top Alfio Garozzo/Archivio White Star

Page 30 top Archivio White Star

Pages 30-31 Archivio White Star

Page 31 bottom left Archivio White Star

Page 31 bottom right Archivio White Star

Page 32 Archivio White Star

Page 33 top left Alberto Siliotti/Archivio Geodia

Page 33 top right Archivio White Star

Page 34 T.G.H. James

Pages 38-39 Alfio Garozzo/Archivio White Star

Page 40 Araldo De Luca/Archivio White Star

Page 41 top Araldo De Luca/Archivio White Star

Page 41 bottom Araldo De Luca/Archivio White Star

Pages 42-43 Archivio White Star

Page 44 left Araldo De Luca/Archivio White Star

Page 44 top right Hervè Lewandowski/Photo RMN

Page 44 bottom right Hervè Lewandowski/Photo RMN

Page 45 Araldo De Luca/Archivio White Star

Page 46 top left Araldo De Luca/Archivio White Star

Page 46 top right Chuzeville/Photo RMN

Pages 46-47 Archivio Scala

Page 47 left B. Hatala/Photo RMN

Page 47 right Araldo De Luca/Archivio White Star

Page 48 top Alfio Garozzo/Archivio White Star

Page 48 center left Alfio Garozzo/Archivio White Star

Page 48 center right Alfio Garozzo/Archivio White Star

Page 48 bottom Alfio Garozzo/Archivio White Star

Page 49 left Antonio Attini/Archivio White Star

Page 49 right Araldo De Luca/Archivio White Star

Page 50 Araldo De Luca/Archivio White Star

Page 51 top Araldo De Luca/Archivio White Star

Page 51 bottom left Araldo De Luca/Archivio White Star

Page 51 bottom right Araldo De Luca/Archivio White Star

Pages 52-53 Araldo De Luca/Archivio White Star

Pages 54-55 Araldo De Luca/Archivio White Star

Page 55 top Araldo De Luca/Archivio White Star

Page 56 top Archivio White Star

Page 56 bottom left Archivio White Star

Page 56 bottom right Archivio White Star

Page 57 Araldo De Luca/Archivio White Star

Page 58 left Alfio Garozzo/Archivio White Star

Page 58 top right Antonio Attini/Archivio White Star

Page 58 center right Antonio Attini/Archivio White Star

Pages 58-59 Archivio White Star

Page 59 bottom Hervè Lewandowski/Photo RMN

Page 60 bottom Archivio White Star

Pages 60-61 Alfio Garozzo/Archivio White Star

Page 61 top Alfio Garozzo/Archivio White Star

Page 62 top left Archivio White Star

Page 62 bottom right Archivio White Star

Pages 62-63 Archivio White Star

Page 63 bottom Archivio White Star

Pages 64-65 Alfio Garozzo/Archivio White Star

Page 65 top Alfio Garozzo/Archivio White Star

Page 65 right Antonio Attini/Archivio White Star

Page 66 top Antonio Attini/Archivio White Star

Pages 66-67 Archivio White Star

Page 67 Archivio White Star

Page 68 top Antonio Attini/Archivio White Star

Page 68 bottom left Antonio Attini/Archivio White Star

Page 68 bottom right Antonio Attini/Archivio White Star

Page 69 Antonio Attini/Archivio White Star

Page 70 top Antonio Attini/Archivio White Star

Page 70 center Antonio Attini/Archivio White Star

Page 70 bottom British Museum

Page 71 Antonio Attini/Archivio White Star

Page 72 Araldo De Luca/Archivio White Star

Page 73 Archivio White Star

Page 74 bottom Hervè Lewandowski/RMN

Pages 74-75 Archivio White Star

Pages 76-77 Araldo De Luca/Archivio White Star

Page 77 Archivio White Star

Page 78 bottom left Archivio White Star

Page 78 bottom right Archivio White Star

Page 79 Archivio White Star

Page 80 Antonio Attini/Archivio White Star

Page 81 Archivio White Star

Page 82 top left Hadiye Cangokce-Cem Cetin

Page 82 top right Hadiye Cangokce-Cem Cetin

Page 83 top Hadiye Cangokce-Cem Cetin

Page 84 top Hadiye Cangokce-Cem Cetin

Page 84 center Hadiye Cangokce-Cem Cetin

Pages 84-85 Ekrem Akurgal

Page 86 top Archivio White Star

Pages 86-87 Archivio White Star

Page 87 bottom Archivio White Star

Pages 88-89 Araldo De Luca/Archivio White Star

Pages 90-91 Alfio Garozzo/Archivio White Star

Page 90 center Archivio White Star

Page 90 bottom Archivio White Star

Page 92 Alfio Garozzo/Archivio White Star

Pages 92-93 Archivio White Star

Page 93 bottom Archivio White Star

Page 94 Araldo De Luca/Archivio White Star

Page 95 Araldo De Luca/Archivio White Star

Pages 96-97 Araldo De Luca/Archivio White Star

Pages 98-99 Archivio White Star

Pages 100-103 Araldo De Luca/Archivio White Star

Pages 104-105 Archivio White Star

Page 105 top Araldo De Luca/Archivio White Star

Page 105 bottom Araldo De Luca/Archivio White Star

Page 106 Araldo De Luca/Archivio White Star

Page 107 top Archivio White Star

Pages 108-109 Archivio White Star

Page 110 top Araldo De Luca/Archivio White Star

Page 110 bottom Araldo De Luca/Archivio White Star

Page 111 top Araldo De Luca/Archivio White Star

Page 111 center Araldo De Luca/Archivio White Star

Page 112-113 Araldo De Luca/Archivio White Star

Page 113 top Archivio White Star

Page 113 bottom Archivio White Star

Page 114-115 Archivio White Star

Page 116 bottom Araldo De Luca/Archivio White Star

Page 117 Archivio White Star

Pages 118-119 Archivio White Star

Page 120 top Araldo De Luca/Archivio White Star

Page 120 bottom Antonio Attini/Archivio White Star

Pages 120-121 Araldo De Luca/Archivio White Star

Page 122 Araldo De Luca/Archivio White Star

Page 123 Archivio White Star

Page 124 Antonio Attini/Archivio White Star

Page 125 British Museum

Page 126 Alfio Garozzo/Archivio White Star

Page 126 bottom Drawing by Angelo Colombo/Archivio White Star

Pages 126-127 Alfio Garozzo/Archivio White Star

Page 127 top left Alfio Garozzo/Archivio White Star

Page 127 right Alfio Garozzo/Archivio White Star

Page 127 bottom Alfio Garozzo/Archivio White Star

Pages 128-129 Alfio Garozzo/Archivio White Star

Page 128 bottom Alfio Garozzo/Archivio White Star

Page 129 center left Antonio Attini/Archivio White Star

Page 129 center right Antonio Attini/Archivio White Star

Page 129 bottom right Antonio Attini/Archivio White Star

Page 129 bottom left Antonio Attini/Archivio White Star

Page 130 top right Drawing by Angelo Colombo/Archivio White Star

Page 130 center Alfio Garozzo/Archivio White Star

Page 130 bottom Alfio Garozzo/Archivio White Star

Pages 130-131 Alfio Garozzo/Archivio White Star

Page 131 bottom Giulio Veggi/Archivio White Star

Page 132 left Alfio Garozzo/Archivio White Star

Page 132-133 Alfio Garozzo/Archivio White Star

Page 133 Alfio Garozzo/Archivio White Star

Pages 134-135 Marcello Bertinetti/Archivio White Star

Page 134 bottom Alfio Garozzo/Archivio White Star

Page 134 bottom Drawings by Angelo Colombo/Archivio White Star

Page 135 Marcello Bertinetti/Archivio White Star

Page 136 top Giulio Veggi/Archivio White Star

Page 136 center Giulio Veggi/Archivio White Star

Page 136 bottom Marcello Bertinetti/Archivio White Star

Pages 136-137 Giulio Veggi/Archivio White Star

Page 138 Marcello Bertinetti/Archivio White Star

Page 139 top Alfio Garozzo/Archivio White Star

Page 139 bottom Antonio Attini/Archivio White Star

Page 140 top Marcello Bertinetti/Archivio White Star

Page 140 left Alfio Garozzo/Archivio White Star

Page 140 right Antonio Attini/Archivio White Star

Page 141 Alfio Garozzo/Archivio White Star

Page 142 Alfio Garozzo/Archivio White Star

Page 143 Giulio Veggi/Archivio White Star

Page 144 Marcello Bertinetti/Archivio White Star

Page 144 top Drawing by Angelo Colombo/Archivio White Star

Pages 144-145 Marcello Bertinetti/Archivio White Star

Page 145 bottom Giulio Veggi/Archivio White Star

Page 146 top Antonio Attini/Archivio White Star

Page 146 bottom Marcello Bertinetti/Archivio White Star

Page 147 Marcello Bertinetti/Archivio White Star

Page 148 top Alfio Garozzo/Archivio White Star

Page 148 bottom Marcello Bertinetti/Archivio White Star

Pages 148-149 Alfio Garozzo/Archivio White Star

Page 151 Alfio Garozzo/Archivio White Star

Pages 152-153 Marcello Bertinetti/Archivio White Star

Page 152 bottom Archivio White Star

Page 152 bottom left Drawing by Angelo Colombo/Archivio White Star

Page 153 top Marcello Bertinetti/Archivio White Star

Page 153 bottom Archivio White Star

Page 154 top Antonio Attini/Archivio White Star

Page 154 bottom right Marcello Bertinetti/Archivio White Star

Pages 154-155 Alfio Garozzo/Archivio White Star

Page 155 bottom left Marcello Bertinetti/Archivio White Star

Page 155 bottom right Alfio Garozzo/Archivio White Star

Page 156 Antonio Attini/Archivio White Star

Page 157 top Antonio Attini/Archivio White Star

Page 157 center Antonio Attini/Archivio White Star

Page 157 left and right Archivio White Star

Pages 158-159 Antonio Attini/Archivio White Star

Page 160 top Alfio Garozzo/Archivio White Star

Page 160 bottom Alfio Garozzo/Archivio White Star

Page 161 top British Museum

Page 161 bottom Antonio Attini/Archivio White Star

Page 162 left Alfio Garozzo/Archivio White Star

Pages 162-163 Alfio Garozzo/Archivio White Star

Page 162 bottom Marcello Bertinetti/Archivio White Star

Page 162 bottom left Drawing by Angelo Colombo/Archivio White Star

Page 163 top Alfio Garozzo/Archivio White Star

Page 163 bottom Alfio Garozzo/Archivio White Star

Page 164 top Alfio Garozzo/Archivio White Star

Page 164 center Alfio Garozzo/Archivio White Star

Page 164 bottom Alfio Garozzo/Archivio White Star

Page 165 top Alfio Garozzo/Archivio White Star

Page 165 bottom Alfio Garozzo/Archivio White Star

Page 166 top Alfio Garozzo/Archivio White Star

Page 166 bottom Alfio Garozzo/Archivio White Star

Page 167 Alfio Garozzo/Archivio White Star

Page 168 right Hervè Lewandowski/Photo RMN

Page 168 left Gerard Blot/Photo RMN

Page 168 bottom left Araldo De Luca/Archivio White Star

Page 169 top Araldo De Luca/Archivio White Star

Page 169 bottom Araldo De Luca/Archivio White Star

Pages 170-171 Alfio Garozzo/Archivio White Star

Page 170 bottom Alfio Garozzo/Archivio White Star

Page 171 Alfio Garozzo/Archivio White Star

Page 172 top Alfio Garozzo/Archivio White Star

Page 172-173 Alfio Garozzo/Archivio White Star

Page 172 bottom Alfio Garozzo/Archivio White Star

Page 173 right Alfio Garozzo/Archivio White Star

Page 173 left Alfio Garozzo/Archivio White Star

Page 173 center Alfio Garozzo/Archivio White Star

Page 173 top Antonio Attini/

Archivio White Star

Page 174 bottom Drawing by Angelo Colombo/Archivio White Star

Pages 174-175 Marcello Bertinetti/Archivio White Star

Page 175 bottom Antonio Attini/Archivio White Star

Page 176 Giulio Veggi/Archivio White Star

Page 177 top Araldo De Luca/Archivio White Star

Pages 178-179 Marcello Bertinetti/Archivio White Star

Page 178 bottom Antonio Attini/Archivio White Star

Page 179 right Alfio Garozzo/Archivio White Star

Page 179 bottom Drawing by Angelo Colombo/Archivio White Star

Page 180 Araldo De Luca/Archivio White Star

Pages 180-181 Antonio Attini/Archivio White Star

Page 182 Araldo De Luca/Archivio White Star

Page 183 Araldo De Luca/Archivio White Star

Page 184 Araldo De Luca/Archivio White Star

Pages 184-185 Araldo De Luca/Archivio White Star

Page 185 top Araldo De Luca/Archivio White Star

Page 185 bottom Araldo De Luca/Archivio White Star

Page 186 top Araldo De Luca/Archivio White Star

Page 186 bottom Araldo De Luca/Archivio White Star

Page 187 Araldo De Luca/Archivio White Star

Page 188 Araldo De Luca/Archivio White Star

Page 189 Araldo De Luca/Archivio White Star

Pages 190-191 Araldo De Luca/Archivio White Star

Page 190 left Araldo De Luca/Archivio White Star

Page 191 top Araldo De Luca/Archivio White Star

Page 191 bottom Araldo De Luca/Archivio White Star

Pages 192-193 Araldo De Luca/Archivio White Star

Page 192 bottom Araldo Dè Luca/Archivio White Star

Page 193 top Araldo De Luca/Archivio White Star

Page 193 bottom Araldo De Luca/Archivio White Star

Page 194 top Araldo De Luca/Archivio White Star

HAIKU PAINTING

Leon M. Zolbrod

Half-title page: *The Maiden Flower* (detail; see pl. 15).
Title page: *Song of the Yodo River* (detail; see pl. 13).
Copyright page: *Master Bashō* (see fig. 14).
Contents page: *Bashō's Narrow Road to a Far Province* (detail; see pl. 18).

Note to the Reader: Japanese names in the text are given in the customary Japanese order, surname preceding given name.

The publisher is indebted to the Shūeisha and Heibonsha publishing companies for kindly providing photographs.

Distributed in the United States by Kodansha International/USA Ltd., through Harper & Row, Inc., 10 East 53rd Street, New York, New York 10022.

Published by Kodansha International Ltd., 12–21, Otowa 2-chome, Bunkyo-ku, Tokyo 112 and Kodansha International/USA Ltd., 10 East 53rd Street, New York, New York 10022 and 44 Montgomery Street, San Francisco, California 94104.

copyright © 1982 by Kodansha International Ltd.
all rights reserved
printed in Japan
first edition, 1982

LCC 82–48792
ISBN 0-87011-560-X (U.S.)
ISBN 4-7700-1044-3 (in Japan)

Library of Congress Cataloging in Publication Data
Zolbrod, Leon M.
  Haiku painting.

  (Great Japanese Art series)
  Bibliography: p.
  1. Haiga. I. Title. II. Series.
ND2462.Z6   1982   759.952   82–48792
ISBN 0-87011-560-X

CONTENTS

1.   Ryūho (1595–1669). *Was It True or Not True?* [*Ari-ya nashi-ya jigasan*]. Hanging scroll, 28 cm. by 51 cm. Faint blue and pink tint with ink on paper. Text:

> *When she saw the full moon of the eighth month, fifteenth day, reflected in the lake, she recognized the idea that what seems like reality may be unreal, that what seems unreal may not really be unreal. Creating a world from the depths of her imagination, she wrote chapter after chapter, so that for succeeding generations her work might stand as the jewel of romances.*

> | | |
> |---|---|
> | *Was it true or not true?* | Ari-ya nashi-ya |
> | *From what's false may grow what's true—* | uso mo makoto-no |
> | *Seeds of the flower.* | hana-no tane. |

> [Signed] *By Ryūho. From about my sixtieth year I started doing a new kind of painting. Here is an effort now that I am in my seventy-third year. Please look upon it with indulgence.* [seal]

According to legend, Lady Murasaki, early in the eleventh century, began to write the *Tale of Genji*, the supreme masterpiece of Japanese literature, while she was in retreat at the Ishiyama-dera temple by the southern shores of Lake Biwa, near the capital of Kyoto. She is said to have started with the chapters that tell of Prince Genji's adventures in exile by the seaside at Suma and Akashi, near present-day Kobe. This legend, reported in various medieval commentaries, has been handed down as traditional lore.

Ryūho cleverly works on the ambiguity of language and indeed of truth itself. On the one hand, he questions the legend, and on the other he praises the great romance. His painting possesses a fresh quality in contrast to the apparent lifelessness of many Tosa-style representations of ancient Japanese poets, which formed a subgenre of portraiture known as "poetic immortal pictures" (*kasen-e*).

Although heir to this tradition of fanciful figure paintings of poets, Ryūho instilled fresh life into the form by depicting a youthful and vivacious Lady Murasaki, her brush poised in a saucy manner, ready to write on the white scroll, still untouched on the desk in front of her.

The stiff lines of the garments reflect the older traditions of *kasen-e*. The subdued tints suggest the understatement and abbreviation characteristic of the new haiku movement. Ryūho, who did this work in 1667, just two years before his death, deserves to be remembered as the founder of haiku painting.

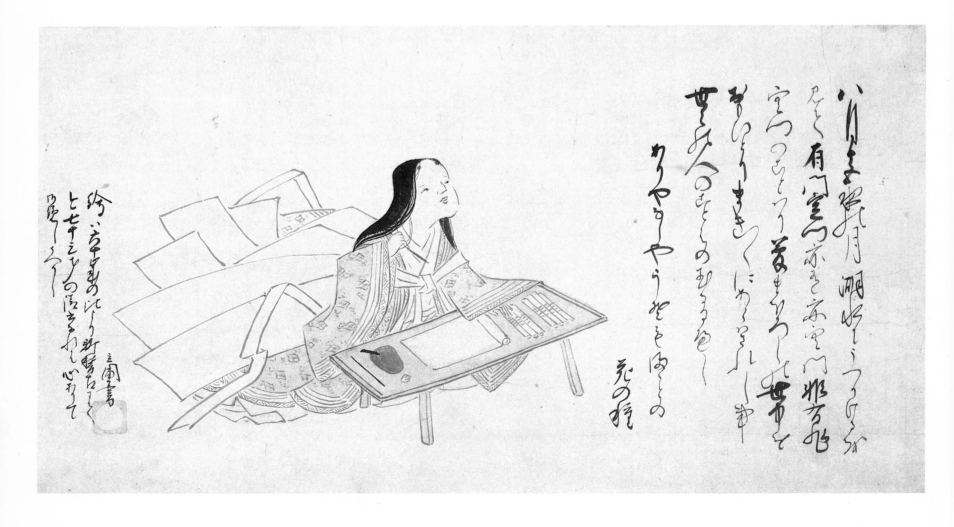

2. Ichū (1637–1711). *Oto-Goze* [*Oto-Goze jigasan*]. Hanging scroll, 69.2 cm. by 28.5 cm. Red and yellow pigment and ink on silk. Text:

Another name for Oto-Goze was Madam Wealth. Indeed, where laughter comes, riches follow. Remembering that Lady Murasaki wrote, "Class alone is not important," I composed a verse:

Class and looks alone	Shina katachi
Are good, but even better,	yoshi-ya Yoshino-no
When you take a wife,	yama-no kami
Is the flower of the heart,	kokoro-no hana-no
With a fragrance of its own.	iro shi-niowaba

[Signed] *Painted as Ichijiken's plaything*

The legend of Oto-Goze, who also had many other names, was based on a tale of a tradesman's wife, who despite being as plain as plain can be, was virtuous, hardworking, and good-natured. She helped her husband gain great wealth and happiness, and for this she came to be worshiped as a household deity. Images of her became popular in the form of masks, dolls, and paintings, a collection of which is still to be found in the Sembon Shakadō, an old temple in the Nishijin area of Kyoto. As shown in Ichū's representation, Oto-Goze almost always has a high forehead, fat cheeks, and a flat nose. Saikaku (1642–93), famous haiku poet, author, and illustrator, did a version of her that looks similar to Ichū's.

The expression *yama-no-kami* in the Japanese text, literally "mountain god," is a colloquial term for wife. "Yoshino" is a place name used both as a poetic epithet for *yama*, "mountain," and with the semantic sense of "good," yielding the meaning in translation "good, but even better."

Ichū's text has its point of departure in the second chapter of the *Tale of Genji*, where the strengths and weaknesses of various kinds of women are being discussed on a rainy night in early summer, and one of the men in the group praises the sort of woman whose beauty is hidden inside and does not take a showy form. The verse is a thirty-one-syllable *waka*, rather than a seventeen-syllable haiku, belying the fact that Ichū was an early haiku master prominent in the Danrin or "Literary Forest" circle around Sōin (1605–82), of which Saikaku was also a member. The prose preface and verse together convey a light tone of irony, which is a central feature of haiku poetic technique. Ichū's work belongs to what is now called haiku painting, and his overall contribution to the growth and development of the haiku movement deserves further study.

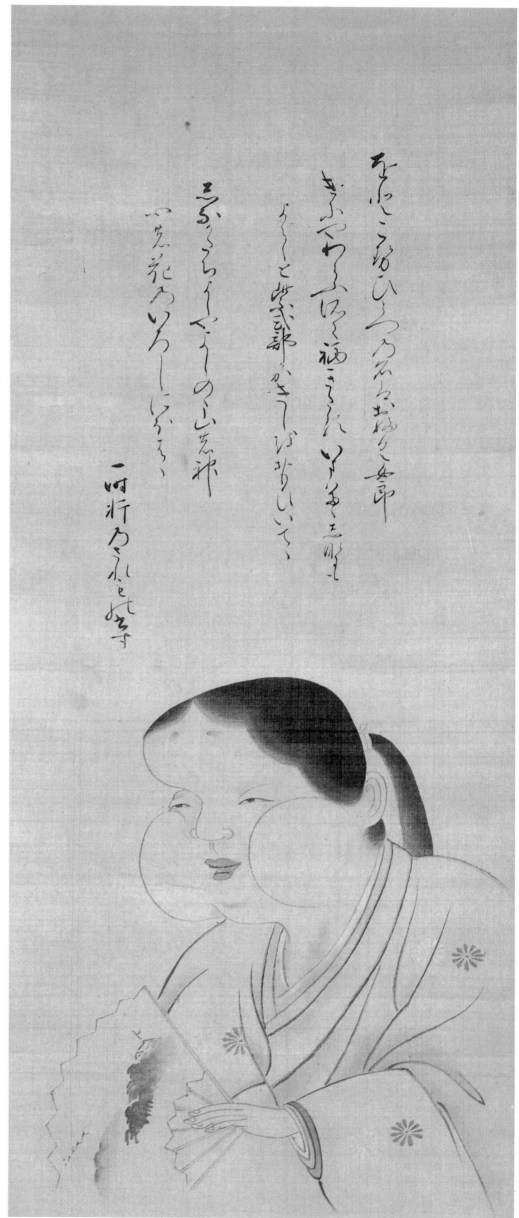

3. Bashō (1644–94) calligraphic text. *Prose Poem on Stopping in the Rain and Autumn Crow Verse* [*Kare-eda karasu, Kasa-yadori gasan*]. Hanging scroll, 32.5 cm. by 82.5 cm. Vermilion and green pigment and ink on silk. Text (from right to left):

On a withered bough	Kare-eda-ni
A flock of crows has perched—	karasu-no tomaritaru-ya
Autumn is over.	aki-no kure.

Stopping in the Rain

With a sedge hat on his head, old man Mr. Slope[1] in his straw raincoat walked under cloudy[2] skies by the bays and the ocean. In out-of-the-way places, with the sedge hat that he wore on his lonely way, Saigyō[3] took shelter from the rain. A sedge hat made of plum blossoms, such as bush warblers are said to weave, would surely help to hide the signs of old age. In a sedge hat that you wear when you go to visit girls, you would be loathe to pass by without stopping, so you take shelter from the rain.[4] When you get soaking wet, with only your elbows to keep off the rain, you can say that you've really been drenched. You would think that a sedge hat made of lotus leaves might look spick and span. Yet one like that would be neither charming nor handsome. Rather, it would resemble one abandoned in a mountain paddy on a scarecrow placed there to guard the fields, torn by the wind and exposed to the rain.

You who own a sedge hat—wait for the wind and the rain. Feel the full force of these elements:

I am old and weary,	Shigururu-ya
Like Sōgi[5] walking in the rain—	ware mo kojin-no
Is there any place to stay?	yo-ni nitaru.

[Signed] *Mr. Stopping-on-Boats, Old Man Bashō*

Not a haiku painting in the narrow sense of the term, this striking scroll is rather a combination of a picture in the Kanō style with two verses by Bashō, the second being part of a haiku prose poem (*haibun*). The period of composition is uncertain, but analysis of the calligraphy suggests a date around the early 1680s; Bashō's verse "On a withered bough" was first published in 1681. Although there are claims to the contrary, both recent and ancient, the painting has traditionally been accepted as being by Bashō. It now seems more likely, however, that someone commissioned a trained artist to collaborate in a joint production. The result exemplifies the deep-rooted Japanese impulse to combine text and picture.

The forlorn and somewhat eerie motif of late autumn crows on a withered bough matches that of the poet as lonely traveler, his sole protection against the elements being the sedge hat he is carrying. As a result, bird and man are seen as one, the sedge hat and the flimsy shelter of the tree equated. In terms of what may be called the cultural code of this piece, the idea of Zen permeates the literary and pictorial elements of both halves of the composition. From the suggestion of pairs and parallels—crow and branch, man and raincoat, left and right, picture and poem—a unitary impression emerges, which may be equated with the essential oneness of life and diversity.

Notes: [1] Ha-ō, referring to Su Tung-p'o (1036–1101), a Chinese poet and official of the Northern Sung dynasty. His name (Tung-p'o, or "Eastern Slope" in Chinese) came from fields that he worked in his temporary home near Huang-chou, overlooking the Yangtze river. He traveled widely, mostly as an exile, finding himself out of favor with the government of his day. [2] Difficult to decipher; may also be read as "snowy." [3] Saigyō (1118–90), traveling poet and monk, who went about the countryside praying and composing verse. Remembered for his simple way of life, his belief in art, and his fondness for peace, not war, he was one of Bashō's most revered spiritual ancestors. [4] In Bashō's day, men visiting the pleasure quarter customarily wore sedge hats as a sort of disguise. "Taking shelter from the rain" is a poetic way of suggesting that someone stopped to enjoy the company of women. [5] Sōgi (1421–1502), traveler and linked verse poet, was another of Bashō's spiritual ancestors or predecessors.

4 (overleaf). Bashō. *Hibiscus* [*Michi-no be-no jigasan*]. Hanging scroll, 62 cm. by 25.2 cm. Olive gray and light pink pigment on paper. Idemitsu Art Museum. Text:

> *There beside the road,* Michi-no be-no
> *A hibiscus, and a horse* mukuge wa uma-ni
> *Has chewed it all up.* kuware keri.
> [Signed] *Bashō* [seal]

The verse comes from Bashō's poetic diary *Records of a Weather-Exposed Skeleton (Nozarashi kikō)*. Composed in 1684, it was first recorded in the portion of this diary describing Bashō's journey between the Ōi river and Sayo-no-nakayama post station, in present-day Shizuoka Prefecture, about a day's walk from the famous inn described in Oliver Statler's *Japanese Inn*.

The painting, judged to date to the late 1680s, is praised as one of the best examples of Bashō's efforts to combine poetry and painting in a harmonious unit exemplifying the spiritual ideals of haiku. The overall composition has grace and simplicity with the barest minimum of color—pale rose and a dark olive that borders on gray. The calligraphic text at the top runs from the upper left toward the lower right, the reverse of the normal right to left pattern. The line of vision moves from lower right to upper left, from where the text brings it back toward the center to an imaginary point, or boundary, between text and picture. The seal impression is placed slightly aslant, emphasizing the symmetry of asymmetry, an established aesthetic principle in East Asian painting and calligraphy. A few deft strands of grass in the lower right-hand corner introduce a contrastive element, parallel as a common everyday image to the horse, which is mentioned in the verse but not represented in the picture. Abbreviation and suggestiveness, ubiquitous qualities of haiku painting, are thus observed. Paradoxically, while the horse of the verse is not shown, the flower to be consumed is preserved for posterity.

5 (overleaf). Bashō. *Bush-Clover and Sun* [*Aka-aka-to jigasan*]. Hanging scroll, 82 cm. by 29.2 cm. Pale pink and olive-gray pigment with ink on paper. Tenri Central Library. Text:

> *Red as red can be,* Aka-aka-to
> *The sun shines mercilessly—* hi wa tsurenaku mo
> *Breeze in the autumn.* aki-no kaze.
> [Signed] *Bashō* [two seals]

Gracefully bending before the light of the sun, the flowering plant in the foreground is the bush-clover (*hagi*), an elegant emblem of autumn, feminine beauty, and transitoriness. In a different context, bush-clover covered with a film of morning dew carries erotic overtones of sexual love.

Bashō's verse, which comes from his poetic diary *Narrow Road to a Far Province (Oku-no hosomichi)*, was composed in 1689 on the way to Kanazawa, in present-day Ishikawa Prefecture. Its juxtaposition of hot sun and cool breeze is expanded upon in the painting, where the bush-clover, bending before an unseen force, reveals the action of the refreshing wind. By the modern calendar the bush-clover blooms in the summer, but lingering associations from the past continue to make it suggestive of the autumn. The verse evokes the dog days of August, recording a subtle moment when one feels two seasons at the same time. A pair of conflicting sensations are thus revealed—discomfort and relief.

The faint touch of pigment conveys the sense of understatement and openendedness so highly regarded in traditional haiku. The motif of the sun, rising or setting, appears in a number of Bashō's surviving paintings (see pl. 7), and the bush-clover is represented in others. Here the two idioms are effectively joined. For a verse by Bashō associating bush-clover with feminine beauty and a faint suggestion of eroticism, with painting and calligraphy by Buson, see plate 19.

4. Bashō. *Hibiscus* (see page 9 for caption).

5. Bashō. *Bush-Clover and Sun* (see page 9 for caption).

6. Bashō. *Melon Blossom* [*Yūbe-ni mo jigasan*]. Hanging scroll, 32.8 cm. by 48.5 cm. Olive and ochre tones with ink on paper. Text:

Neither to evening   Yūbe-ni mo
Nor to morning does it belong— asa-ni mo tsukazu
The melon blossom.   uri-no hana.
[Signed] *Painted by Bashō* [three seals]

Painting and calligraphy combine to give an overall impression of subdued charm and careful execution. The composition opens out from the lower left, starting with three jagged calligraphic strokes, and ends on the right with several lines that represent tendrils (see figs. 5, 13 for similar treatment of slender, coiling appendages of climbing plants).

Most likely, the verse was composed in the summer of 1690. It first appeared in *Sarō yama* (preface, 1692, tenth month), an obscure anthology probably issued early in 1693 (see Yamamoto Yuiitsu, *Haibungaku-no keifu*, Kyoto: Hōzōkan, 1978, pp. 339–43).

The meaning of the verse comes from the association of the morning glory (*asagao*) with the morning (*asa*), and likewise the gourd, or "evening face" (*yūgao*), with the evening (*yū*, or *yūbe*). The melon blossom (*uri-no-hana*), however, to which both plants are botanically related, is ambiguous—it belongs to neither morning nor evening.

Flower and verse alike may be taken as an imaginary projection of the self, suggesting a free spirit, appropriate for a self-styled hermit, as Bashō was at the time. Morning-glory and "evening face" both have associations with characters in the *Tale of Genji*, but the melon blossom has none.

7. Bashō. *Solitary Traveler in Winter Shower* [*Kyō bakari jigasan*]. Hanging scroll, 95.2 cm. by 27.4 cm. Ink monochrome, modified with tint of crimson on paper. Masaki Art Museum. Text:

On a day like this   Kyō bakari
It makes you feel a year older— hito mo toshi yore
First winter shower.   hatsu-shigure.
[Signed] *Painted by Bashō, the Wandering Old Man*
[two seals]

The verse was composed on the third day, tenth month of 1692, when Bashō called on his disciple Kyoriku (1656–1715), who was living in a house on the Edo estate of the Hikone clan. On this occasion Bashō and three fellow poets also did a thirty-six-verse "poetic immortal" (*kasen*), an abbreviated form of linked verse that Bashō and his group had pioneered and preferred over the one-hundred-verse form. The three companions with him were all considerably junior to Bashō.

His verse may be seen primarily as a call for young people to put themselves in an older person's shoes and feel the loneliness of a time of the year and weather that suggests solitude and patient endurance of discomfort.

In the painting the winter squall has not yet hidden the sun, which hangs low in the sky and gives a touch of color to the prevailing gray hue. The verse, signature, and seal on top, the sun and shower in the middle, and the human figure in the lower right form a composition of subtle dignity. In abstract terms the viewer finds a combination of twos and threes. First, there is picture and text, man and nature, darkness and light, which make pairs of their own. There is also text, signature, and seal; sun, rain, and cloud; top, middle, and bottom; five, seven, and five (the syllabic rhythm); sun, storm, and man; rain hat, clothes, and feet. Such an analysis by no means exhausts the possible implications of the simple yet complex code of this work of art.

8. Bashō. *Banana Tree and Gate to Banana Tree Hut* [*Mino-mushi-no jigasan*]. Hanging scroll, 93.3 cm. by 29.3 cm. Olive tones and ink on paper. Idemitsu Art Museum. Text:

The sound of bagworms—	Mino-mushi-no
Come over and listen	ne-o kiki-ni koyo
At my thatched cottage.	kusa-no io.
[Signed] *Bashō* [seal]	

Bashō's name means Mr. Banana Tree. The plant and the man were poetically equated ever since one of his disciples built a hut for him on the outskirts of Edo, and there, in a riverside garden, Bashō planted this tree that he loved. The painting is an unpretentious depiction of the gate to the Banana Tree Hut (Bashō-an) and the tree itself, its wind-tattered leaves both fragile and yet resistant, but not of bananas, for the tree bore no fruit in the rigorous Japanese climate. The degree of abstraction and abbreviation points to qualities that later became the hallmark of haiku painting. This work probably dates from about 1692–93, after Bashō and Kyoriku became associated, while the verse was composed earlier, in 1687, as a combined autumn greeting and poetry-party invitation sent to a disciple of Bashō's living in retirement by the name of Sodō (1642–1716), an extremely talented man who practiced not only *haikai* but calligraphy, tea ceremony, classical Japanese verse (*waka*), and Chinese verse as well.

The quality of Zen found in this verse's paradoxical evocation of a silent insect's voice bears comparison with that of the incorporeity of a noisy insect's voice penetrating impenetrable rock in another of Bashō's verses: "Still as still can be— / Penetrating the boulders, / The cicada's cry" (*Shizukesa ya / iwa-ni shimi-iru / semi-no koe*).

Buson also has a verse: "The canny bagworm / Wisely finds itself a home— / First winter drizzle" (*Mino-mushi-no / etari kashikoshi / hatsu-shigure*). This verse suggests a model of how to get along in a hostile world. When the natural elements rage against living things, they slip into their nests just as snug as can be. As long as a traveling poet has a straw raincoat, he is as free from worries as a bagworm, or "raincoat insect," rolled up in a leafy cocoon.

9. Buson (1716–84). *Benkei and Young Bull* [*Ushiwaka Benkei jigasan*]. Hanging scroll, 48.7 cm. by 25.9 cm. Red, gray, yellow, olive, and flesh-toned pigment with ink on paper. Itsuō Art Museum. Text:

Snow, moon, and blossoms—	Setsu-gekka
And then a pledge for three lives,	tsui-ni sanze-no
Faith and loyalty.	chigiri kana.
[Signed] *By Mr. Purple-Fox Hut* [two seals]	

Humorous and appealing, *Benkei and Young Bull* is one of the most masterful of Buson's haiku paintings. On first glance the pale washes of pigment give an impression of timidity, but on closer inspection one finds richness and variety. The scene depicted here, in which a huge ungainly warrior with a halberd follows a slip of a boy, is part of a legend about late twelfth-century events surrounding the conflict between the Taira and Minamoto clans for control of Japan. In particular, it recalls the Noh play *Benkei at the Bridge* (*Hashi Benkei*), which tells the story of how Yoshitsune, the future Minamoto military leader who was to be brilliant but ill-fated, met and defeated the warrior-monk Benkei in a hand-to-hand fight resembling that between Robin Hood and Little John, and this when Yoshitsune was only a boy of twelve or thirteen. The encounter forged a bond between the two, and Benkei went on loyally to serve Yoshitsune in good times and bad, till the moment of death in battle.

Buson's Benkei has a grotesquely funny face, vaguely like that of the Beshimi mask in Noh, which on rare occasions may be used by an actor playing Benkei. He wears armor, carries a halberd, and moves in a lumbering gait. Slight and boyish and in a plain robe, Young Bull (Ushiwaka, Yoshitsune's boyhood name) walks in front. Benkei's head is like a melon, Young Bull's like a pea. Benkei carries a paper lantern and a pair of wooden clogs tied to the staff of his halberd, as if spoofing military preparedness. The sheath of Young Bull's sword sticks out behind him like a fox's tail, as though this mischievous animal had transformed itself into the form of the hero.

The verse is partly derived from the Noh play and partly from a line of Chinese poetry by Po Chü-i (772–846), "In the season of snow, moon, and blossoms I think mostly of you." Buson's favorite combination of qualities, elegance and plainness, are neatly harmonized. Just as Young Bull—noble, courtly, youthful—comes first, and Benkei—common, burly, crude—follows, so elegance predominates. The signature, Shikoan (literally "Purple-Fox Hut"), suggests a date prior to 1777 for the painting, because in that year Buson allowed his disciple Tōgai to use the name. The overall composition has a triangular effect, allowing the viewer's eye to start almost anywhere and move freely to the three general focal points.

雪月花
つねに三世の
なく達の
朱荷竜書

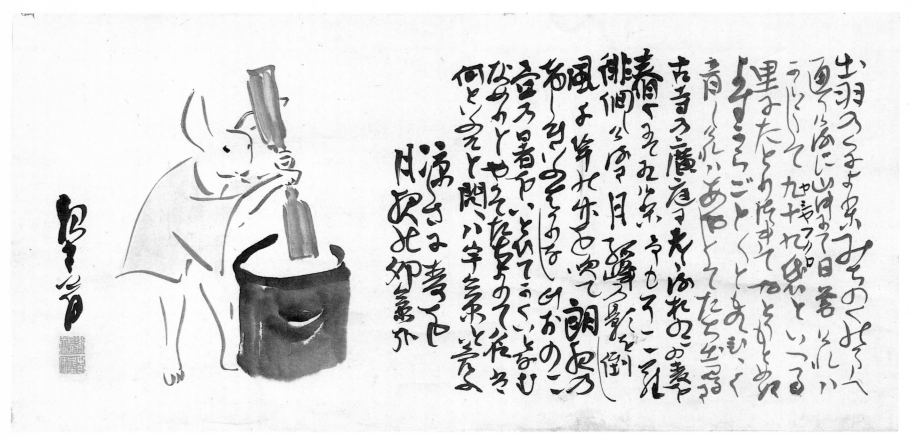

10. Buson. *Mr. Hare on a Moonlit Night* [*Tsukiyo Uhei jigasan*]. Hanging scroll, 30.8 cm. by 61.7 cm. Faint blue tint and ink on paper. Text:

> *When I was traveling in the province of Dewa on my to Michinoku, I was passing through the mountains when it began to grow dark. Eventually I managed to get to the hamlet of Yashabukuro and find a place to stay. During the night I repeatedly heard a heavy thumping sound. Wondering what it could be, I got up and went to look. In the large temple garden an old man was pounding barley. As I stood in the shadows I saw the moon shining through the groves of bamboo, lending the bright night an eerie beauty. I guessed that the old man was working then so that he might keep out of the midday heat. At last I went up to him and asked his name, and he said, "Uhei."*

It's better when it's cool,	Suzushisa-ni
To pound barley on a moonlit night—	mugi-o tsukiyo-no
That must be Mr. Rabbit.	Uhei kana.
[Signed] *Old Man Midnight* [seal]	

In contrast to the prose text, where it is given phonetically, in the verse Buson has written the name Uhei with a character that means "hare" or "rabbit," thus transforming the scene into the realm of legend. According to folk belief, the image of a hare or rabbit pounding rice appears on the moon. The idea comes from a Buddhist tale about how the hare once sacrificed its life so that an old man (really Buddha in disguise) might have something to eat. As a reward, it was reborn on the moon to remind everyone of its generosity.

In a harmonious mixture of prose, poetry, and picture, Buson has combined a setting, a season, and a faint suggestion of denial of self. The event described here in imaginative and poetic terms presumably took place during the 1730s or 1740s, when he traveled in Bashō's footsteps to the northern provinces and beyond, reaching the farthermost shores of Honshū. The painting is from much later, most likely after 1777, when he recorded memories of earlier days. Calligraphy and painting are vintage Buson. The signature Yahan-ō ("Old Man Midnight") was a favorite after he passed the age of sixty and added ō, for "old man" and also for "master," to his poetic name of Mr. Midnight Pavilion (Yahantei), which he began using in 1771.

11. Buson. *Rocks Scattered Here and There* [*Ishi jigasan*]. Hanging scroll, 58.5 cm. by 36.5 cm. Light tint of reddish-brown and gray with ink on paper. Itsuō Art Museum. Text:

> *In the earlier and later* Prose Poems on the Red Cliffs, *every single word is lovely, but my favorite passage is, "The mountains rise high, the moon looks small, and the water falls between the rocks." This image stands out like a solitary crane among a flock of chickens.*
>
> *Long ago, when I was on my way to the province of Michinoku, underneath the Pilgrim's Willow Tree, I thought of a verse on the topic of rocks strewn about:*

Willow leaves are gone,	Yanagi chiri
The fresh brook has now run dry—	shimizu kare ishi
Rocks scattered here and there.	tokorodokoro.
[Signed] *Buson* [seal]	

Like *Mr. Hare on a Moonlit Night* (pl. 10), the subject is poetic reminiscence of times long past. With a slightly different preface this verse is included in an anthology titled *Scrap Sheets from a Screen* (*Hogo-busuma*), edited in 1752 by Gantō (d. 1773) and other early poetry companions. "Willow leaves are gone" has been praised as the finest of Buson's early haiku from his period of wandering in Edo and the northeast during the 1730s and 1740s, before settling down in Kyoto. The preface mentions Su Tung-p'o's prose poems commemorating a famous battle in the third century A.D., on the Yangtze river in China. Buson's verse, in turn, alludes to a *waka* verse by the poet-monk Saigyō: "At the side of the road, / Where fresh water is flowing, / By a shady willow, / I'll take a rest for a while / Before going on my way" (*Michi-no be-ni / shimizu nagaruru / yanagi kage / shibashi-tote koso / tachi-tomaritsure*).

The same willow tree also figures in a Noh play, the *Pilgrim's Willow* (*Yugyō yanagi*). When Bashō visited the same site as part of his journey described in the *Narrow Road to a Far Province*, he had composed the following verse: "A whole paddy field / Is planted, and now good-bye / To the willow tree" (*Ta ichi-mai / uete tachi-saru / yanagi kana*).

Buson's casual placement of five or six rocks forms a tranquil yet far from static composition, balancing with the calligraphic text, signature, and seal. The rocks by themselves remind the viewer of the so-called dry landscape gardens (*karesansui*), such as that of Ryōanji temple in Kyoto. The choice of subject and the execution of the theme reflect the austere spirit of Zen Buddhism. Although the verse is one of the earliest by Buson that has survived, the painting dates from the period after 1777, when Buson recorded memories of his travels more than thirty years earlier. The slight touch of red-brown tint, modifying the predominantly gray hue of the rocks, adds to a sense of movement amid stillness, an appropriate complement to the idea of water amid dryness.

16. Buson painting and calligraphy, Bashō text. *Bashō's Records of a Weather-Exposed Skeleton: Flowering Plums at Shūfū's Cottage at Narutaki [Nozarashi kikō emaki, Shūfū besshō bairin]*. Handscroll, 23.4 cm. by 872 cm. (part shown, about 55 cm.). Light pigment, mostly of flesh tones, green, gray, and white with ink. Text:

I went to Kyoto and called on Mitsui Shūfū at his mountain cottage by Narutaki waterfalls:

White blossoming plums—	Ume shiroshi
Yesterday perhaps the crane	kinō-ya tsuru-o
Got stolen away.	nusumareshi.

Bashō's own text of the earliest of his famous poetic diaries exists in several editions, including one with twenty-one haiku sketches by him. Bashō's pilgrimage started in Edo and followed the Eastern Sea Post Road to Ise, to his birthplace in the province of Iga, and to Nara, Lake Biwa, Nagoya, and other places before he returned once more to his birthplace, to Nara, and to Kyoto. It lasted for about nine months, from the summer of 1684 till the following summer. The brief passage and verse here illustrated refer to Bashō's visit in early spring 1685 to the country home of a wealthy Kyoto merchant and generous patron of the arts, Mitsui Shūfū (1646–1717). There he enjoyed the flowering plums at their best.

The verse was a fanciful way of acknowledging Shūfū's hospitality and flattering him for the breathtaking beauty of his garden by means of allusion to a Chinese poet-monk of the Southern Sung dynasty, Lin Ho-ch'ing (967–1028), who had a legendary fondness for cranes and plum blossoms. On seeing the plum blossoms, Bashō suggests that a crane, which Lin was supposed to have kept like a pet, could surely not be far off.

Of eleven scenes that Buson illustrated for his calligraphic scroll of Bashō's text, this is the ninth and the aesthetic high point of the whole. By summer 1778, when he did this scroll, Buson was a past master of handling the theme of plum blossoms and the motif of a mountain hut and rustic fence. This work, along with the scrolls and screens of *The Narrow Road to a Far Province* (see pls. 17–19), represents Buson's veneration of Bashō as the god of haiku.

15. Buson painting and calligraphy, Bashō verse. *The Maiden Flower [Ominaeshi gasan]*. Fan painting mounted as a hanging scroll, 17 cm. by 43.7 cm. Tints of brown, blue, and yellow with ink on paper. Text:

So tall and slender	Hyoro-hyoro-to
And looking fresh as the dew—	nao tsuyukeshi-ya
The maiden flower.	ominaeshi.
(Bashō)	

[Signed] *By Buson* [with seal, lower left]

Bashō's verse is primarily about a flowering plant, actually a kind of wild carnation. Buson takes the literal meaning of the flower's name, "courtesan bloom," and in a few deft strokes gives it human shape as the figure of a woman. The exaggerated serpentine line imparts a sense of fullness. The figure is reduced virtually to the utilitarian minimum needed to identify a female form, making the fan painting a primer of what is basic in haiku painting. The roundness of the figure, fan, and calligraphy are contrasted with the geometrically radiating ribs of the fan.

Buson's picture parodies Bashō's verse. Elsewhere Buson's disciple Kitō parodied the verse and picture alike by changing the last line to read, *otoko-beshi* ("How manly a flower").

19

17. Buson painting and calligraphy, Bashō text. *Bashō's Narrow Road to a Far Province: Departure Scene* [*Oku-no hosomichi emaki, Tabi-dachi*]. Part of two handscrolls, 28.2 cm. by 812 cm.; 28.2 cm. by 1057 cm. Light pigment, mostly gray, tan, blue, and yellow, with ink on paper. Itsuō Art Museum. Text (partially illustrated):

My closest friends, who had been with us since the night before, came on the riverboat to see us off. We disembarked at a place called Senju, and my heart was heavy at the thought of the miles that lay ahead. And though this ephemeral world is but an illusion, I could not bear to part from it and wept.

> Loath to let spring go,   Yuku haru-ya
> Birds cry, and even fishes'   tori naki uo-no
> Eyes are wet with tears.*   me wa namida.

Over a span of three years, from 1777 to 1779, Buson did several scrolls and screens of Bashō's *Narrow Road to a Far Province*, each one being illustrated with cartoon-like drawings. Following Bashō's own practice, he emphasized not the natural splendors along the way but events of human interest. Buson expressed his pride in these scrolls and screens to various patrons and haiku masters. By leaving visual interpretations of Bashō's ultimate classic, Buson helped to spread the memory of the great master. These scrolls and screens thus had a devotional purpose, as well

as contributing toward making Bashō's poetic diary one of the most widely read Japanese classics. The so-called Korekoma text, from which this illustration is taken, and which is named after Buson's disciple for whom it was done, shows fourteen scenes such as the one given here.

The departure depicted here actually took place on the twenty-seventh day, third month, 1689 by the traditional Japanese calendar, spring ending on the last day of the month. Bashō and his traveling companion, Sora, are shown on the left, and five people are illustrated on the right, representing probably a much larger group who bade good-bye to the master on his most famous journey. It was part of the technique of abbreviation that led to Buson's depicting only a limited number of people and to his decision not to show any sign of the natural features of Senju, such as the bridge, the river, or the boats that were part of the actual scene. The sorrow of parting is expressed partly in showing Bashō and Sora walking on without looking back. Their faces are solemn, whereas one finds a trace of a smile on two of the figures in the party of well-wishers. The coloring is highly subdued, with deep olive, gray, and a slight touch of brown pigment along with the black ink.

*Dorothy Britton, trans. and intro., *A Haiku Journey: Bashō's Narrow Road to a Far Province*, 2nd ed. rev. (Tokyo and New York: Kodansha International, 1980), p. 30.

19. Buson painting and calligraphy, Bashō text. *Bashō's Narrow Road to a Far Province: Ichiburi Barrier* [*Oku-no hosomichi, Ichiburi-no seki*]. Size of scrolls same as plate 17. Itsuō Art Museum. Text (only partially illustrated):

We were exhausted and went to bed early, but in a nearby room I heard voices I judged to be those of two young women. The voice of an old man mingled with theirs. I gathered they were ladies of pleasure from the port town of Niigata, in Echigo, on a long pilgrimage to the Grand Shrine at Ise. The man had come with them as far as this barrier, and they were writing letters for him to take back to Niigata the next day and giving him sentimental messages to deliver. . . .

I fell asleep listening to their chatter, and the next morning, as we were about to set off, one of the young women approached us.

"We do not know the way," she said. "We are helpless and afraid. May we follow you . . . ?"

"I fear we stop too often along the road," I replied. "But there will be others to follow, who are going your way. May God protect you." For a long time after we left them, my heart overflowed with pity, and I could not get them out of my mind.

> 'Neath the selfsame roof   Hitotsu ya-ni
> I slept with a courtesan! like moon yūjo mo netari
> With bush-clover, forsooth.   hagi-to tsuki.

I told Sora my poem and he wrote it down.

For the significance of the bush-clover in the verse, see the discussion of Bashō's *Bush-Clover and Sun* (pl. 5). The text here, despite its apparently simple surface, is culturally complex. Two elements especially deserve mention. First, there is Bashō's self-identification with the poet-monk Saigyō, as mentioned and noted in *Prose Poem on Stopping in the Rain* (pl. 3). On his pilgrimage Bashō was following Saigyō's footsteps. One famous episode in the earlier poet's life and legend involved his similarly spending the night under the same roof with a courtesan—the idea suggesting fickle love, transitoriness, and the emblems of moon and bush-clover. This particular incident figured as well in a famous Noh play, *Eguchi*, the title of which was taken from the name of the place where the incident was said to have happened.

The second element involves an interpretation of Bashō's poetic diary as a rendition in a mixed prose-poetry form of a chain poem or linked verse. One requirement of linked verse was to have a love scene somewhere in the sequence, and this is fulfilled by the *Ichiburi Barrier* section.

Buson's pigmentation in the figure of the woman shown weeping includes a yellowish hue, a touch of lavender, and a brighter green than in many of the other scenes. Despite the overall restraint, it thus suggests a faintly amorous and erotic tone. The *Ichiburi Barrier* scene is the tenth of the fourteen that Buson illustrated. This pair of scrolls, known as the Korekoma text, was completed in the tenth month of 1779.

*Britton, *Haiku Journey*, pp. 72–73.

20

18. Buson painting. *Bashō's Narrow Road to a Far Province: Little Girl on Nasu Moor* [*Oku-no hosomichi emaki, Nasuno kohime*]. Size of scrolls same as plate 17. Itsuō Art Museum. Text by Bashō (to right of painting but not illustrated here):

He lent us his mount. No sooner had we set off than two children came running after us. One was a little girl who said her name was Kasane, which means "Manifold." It was such an unusual and charming name that Sora composed the following lines:

> *Were she a flower,*   Kasane-to wa
> *She would be a wild, fring'd pink,*   yae-nadeshiko-no
> *Petals manifold.**   na naru beshi.

The illustration conveys the sense of motion and freedom of line of Buson's best haiku paintings. The scene comes from the second of fourteen illustrated in the pair of scrolls. The text describes in part how Bashō traversed the Nasuno highlands on a borrowed horse while two small children followed behind. Buson depicts the little girl holding tightly to her elder brother's hand. He, waving a stick in his other hand, is a sturdy boy in a short green tunic. Bashō is shown as a frail figure on a horse that is disproportionately small. His traveling companion, Sora, carries their few belongings. In the overall composition the human figure is emphasized to the exclusion of the natural surroundings described in the text. The strong, leftward-facing diagonal slant in the children's figures becomes less pronounced in that of Sora and is practically nonexistent in Bashō's figure. This suggests a stoppage of eye movement when one gets to the poet, who is here the focus of attention.

*Britton, *Haiku Journey*, p. 35.

20. Buson. *Young Bamboos* [*Wakatake jigasan*]. Hanging scroll, 112.3 cm. by 28.3 cm. Faint touches of blue or green pigment with ink on paper. Text:

> *Yes, the young bamboos—*   Wakatake-ya
> *And Hashimoto courtesans,*   Hashimoto-no yūjo
> *Are they there or not?*   ari-ya nashi.
> [Signed] *Buson* [two seals]

Through stalks of thin bamboo with trunks like broken lines, leaves like dots, and color so faint as to be almost nonexistent, two simple huts are shown in ink outline. The subdued tone of the composition matches the mood of early summer, as do the girls of Hashimoto, young and fresh from the countryside and as pliable as new bamboo. Long ago they stood ready to serve travelers on the Yodo river between Kyoto and Osaka near the Iwashimizu Hachiman shrine and Otokoyama, or literally "Man Mountain."

The idea of love-making, mystery, and supple bamboo gives rise to a magnificent haiku painting. A Chinese tradition of painting bamboos developed during the Sung dynasty, and in Japan as well bamboo became, like chrysanthemums, one of the standard themes in virtually all schools. By giving this theme an erotic touch, Buson imparts the breath of haiku into an otherwise academic and spiritual exercise.

21. Buson. *Matabei at Cherry-Blossom Time* [*Hana-mi Matabei jigasan*]. Hanging scroll, 103.8 cm. by 26.3 cm. A touch of red pigment with ink on paper. Itsuō Art Museum. Text:

When the blossoms in the capital begin to fall, it's like the undercoating on a Kōshin painting that starts to peel away:

> *Yes, you will meet him—*   Matabei-ni
> *Matabei at Omuro*   ō-ya Omuro-no
> *Cherry-blossom time.*   hana-zakari.
> [Signed] *Buson* [two seals]

On the box in which the scroll is stored there is an inscription by Tomioka Tessai (1836–1924), the most famous Nanga artist of his day: "In this Buson, one senses the ultimate scenery of Kyoto in the late spring." All nonessential elements are left out, entrusting to the viewer's imagination a background of fluttering petals, temple halls, and mountain scenery. The uneven stride, or drunken dance, of the disheveled figure, and the presumably empty drinking gourd beneath it, tell mutely of the Dionysian side of flower-viewing in Japan. The idea of the world of art, rather than that of actuality, is amplified by the inscription. The metaphor of pigment coming off an old painting by Tosa Mitsunobu (Kōshin; 1434–1529) stands for the fading beauty of spring. The verse names the dancing figure as Matabei, the pioneering *ukiyo-e* artist Iwasa Matabei (1578–1650). Buson's Matabei was surely inspired by fanciful representations of Hotei (Chinese Pu Tai), one of the seven gods of good fortune, such as that by Ogata Kōrin titled *Pu Tai Playing Kickball* (*Hotei kemari zu*). Omuro, the place in northwestern Kyoto where the Ninnaji temple stands, is famous for its late-blossoming cherry trees. After the passing of springtime there, the world of the cherry blossoms is gone for another year. The overall impression of lateness, of time past, and of the end drawing near, goes well with a work which seems, on the basis of the calligraphic style and treatment of the subject, to be one of the last of Buson's haiku paintings.

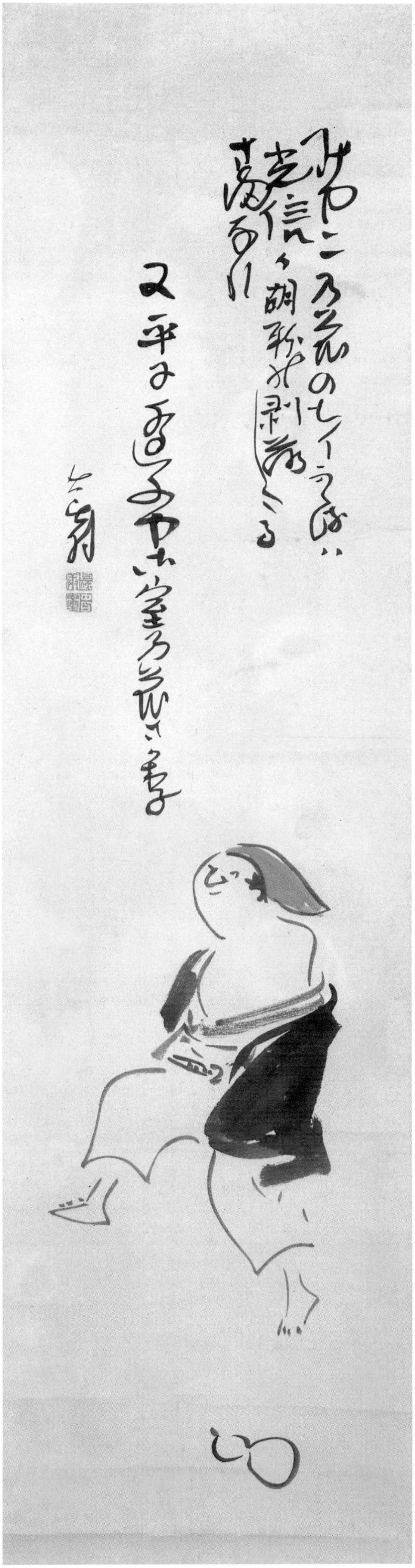

22. Ike Taiga (1723–76). *Hare Dancing with Bells in Hand* [*To-ji suzu mai-no zu*]. Hanging scroll, 78 cm. by 29 cm. Pale yellow, rose, and light blue pigment with ink on paper. Text:

> May there be great joy,   Kei ari-ya
> Rabbit dear, oh rabbit dear.   usagi usagi.
> [Signed] *Kashō* [two seals]

Not a haiku painting in the narrow sense, Taiga's work shows that the borders of any genre are fuzzy and uncertain. When the *Hare Dancing* is compared with Buson's *Mr. Hare* (pl. 10) and Gekkei's *Tiger and Hare* (pl. 26), one notices that the Buson and Taiga show a remarkably similar degree of abstraction and abbreviation. Gekkei's hare reveals marginally greater detail around the ears and whiskers and a fuller set of clothing. Of the three variations on the theme of hares acting like humans, Taiga's version looks the most like an animal, because of his treatment of the legs. Gekkei's and Buson's are like human caricatures with an animal's face. Taiga's coloration is the showiest. The three examples suggest how the Nanga artists shared the same impulse to reduce the complexity of the actual world of nature to meet aesthetic conventions and expectations. Kashō was one of Taiga's most widely used signatures.

23. Gekkei (1752–1811) painting and calligraphy, text from the *Tale of the Heike*. *Only a Deer Is Stirring* [*Dairi shika gasan*]. Hanging scroll, 104.7 cm. by 27.5 cm. Reddish-tan pigment and ink on paper. Itsuō Art Museum. Text:

> *Toward evening on the day of the full moon in the Godless Month, a rustling sound was heard in the garden, as if someone were approaching through the fallen leaves of the oak trees.*
> *"I wonder who might visit us in such a place?" said the former empress, who was living there in retirement. "Please go and see. If it is someone I ought to hide from, I'll do so."*
> *Her companion, the Assistant Lady-in-waiting to the Chief Councillor, went out to check quietly and saw that it was only a deer that had been passing by.*
> *"Who was it?" the empress asked, and the lady, her eyes filled with tears, recited a poem:*

> Tramping rock and root   Iwa-ne fumi
> Who comes to us, you ask;   tare-ka wa towan
> But through the oak leaves,   nara-no ha-no
> Only a deer is stirring,   soyogu wa shika-no
> As it passes on its way.   wataru nari keri.
> [Signed] *The year of wood and the dragon* [1784], *first day of autumn, at the Dragon Gate, painting and calligraphy by Gekkei* [seal]

Gekkei's deer, which has a stylistic pedigree that traces back to his master, Buson, and to Hyakusen (1698–1753), is a young animal with a humped back, a furry tail like a rabbit, and a face as meek as a mouse. Using a passage from the *Tale of the Heike* (*Heike monogatari*), which relates the rise and fall of the Taira (or Heike) clan in the twelfth century, Gekkei captures the essence of the situation in the figure of an animal that stands for an emotionally charged moment in human life. The empress had lost her child and all that she loved in the world, and was forced to take refuge in a lonely mountain temple, where the incident described took place.

The Dragon Gate mentioned in the signature was the Kyoto residence of Kyōtai (1732–92), a Nagoya poet, who with Buson helped bring about a revival of the haiku movement late in the eighteenth century. Besides being an influential master in his own right, Kyōtai was a generous patron of Buson and Gekkei. Partly because of the circumstances of its composition, this piece is treated as a haiku painting, despite its association with a medieval chronicle rather than with a haiku text.

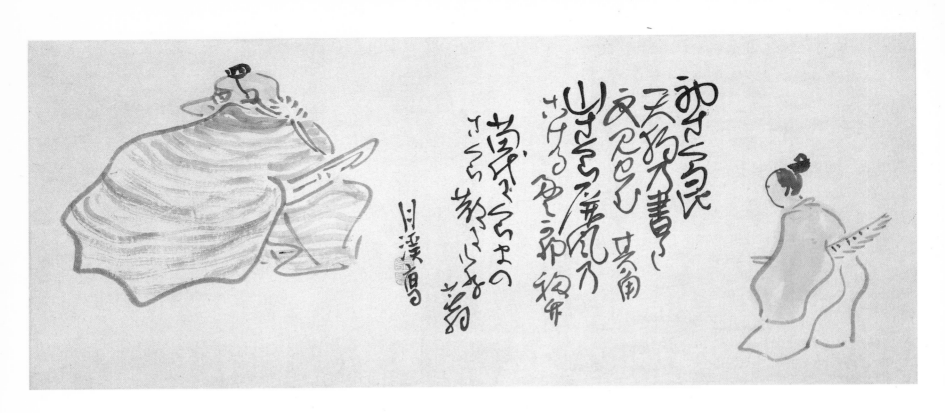

24. Gekkei painting and calligraphy; Kikaku, Ichiku, and Buson verses. *Young Bull and the Goblins* [*Ushiwaka-maru gasan*]. Hanging scroll, 24.7 cm. by 59.7 cm. Faint tan, blue, and gray pigment with ink on paper. Itsuō Art Museum. Text:

First cherry blossoms—   Hatsu-zakura
Let me show you a letter   tengu-no kaita
That the goblins wrote.   fumi misen.
(Kikaku)

Mountain cherry blossoms—   Yama-zakura
Like a screen that's blown over   byōbu-no kokeru
On a tatami mat.   tatami kana.
(Ichiku)

On rice-seedling beds   Nae-shiro-ni
Kurama cherry blossoms   Kurama-no sakura
Are all scattered now.   chiri-ni keri.
(Buson)

[Signed] *By Gekkei* [seal]

There is a legend about "Young Bull," or Minamoto no Yoshitsune as a boy (see pl. 9), that tells of how a kind of goblin (*tengu*) associated with the martial arts and the disaster of war taught him swordsmanship while he was growing up in the mountains in the northern hills of Kyoto, as the ward of the abbot of the Kurama temple. The mystique of the mountain temple, the legend of Yoshitsune, and the spring theme of cherry blossoms, symbolic of the passing of youthful beauty, are treated in the Buson manner, as is the figure of Young Bull. Yoshitsune's frail appearance is probably due in part to the convention in the Japanese theater of always having a child actor play Yoshitsune's part. The figure on the left suggests a cross between the abbot of the Kurama temple, dressed as a monk of the mountain sect of Buddhism (Shugendō), and a long-nosed goblin, usually shown as part bird and part human, somewhat like a griffin or gargoyle.

Gekkei has presented three verses, one by his master, Buson, one by Ichiku (1710–60), who until his death was associated with the Buson circle in Kyoto, and one by Bashō's disciple Kikaku (1661–1707), who they looked to with special reverence as their teacher's teacher and as a direct hereditary link with the great master, Bashō. Of the three verses, Kikaku's is the most difficult. Perhaps it suggests a visit to a place such as Kurama for a cherry-blossom viewing picnic. Ichiku's verse emphasizes the wildness of such a place, and Buson's describes a scene involving the transition from one season to the next, combining the world of nature and the activities of man.

Unfolding from right to left, with the text separating the two complementary figures, the composition has a rhythm and aesthetic meaning of its own. The viewer may note, especially, the parallel treatment of the swords, which counterbalances the predominant left-right axis.

25. Gekkei painting and calligraphy, Kikaku verse. *Tsuna Going to Rashōmon Gate* [*Futari-no musha gasan*]. Hanging scroll, 26.5 cm. by 26.4 cm. Pale blue, flesh-colored, and gray pigment on paper. Itsuō Art Museum. Text:

Tsuna is now leaving,   Tsuna tatte
Tsuna is on every tongue—   Tsuna ga uwasa-no
On a rainy night.   amayo kana.
(Kikaku) [Signed] *By Gekkei* [seal]

This is another example of Gekkei's preference for using a text by others to accompany his own inimitable drawings. The situation represented in painting and verse alike comes from the Noh play *Rashōmon*, which in turn draws on events that brought on the collapse of the Heian court and the rise of military rule.

During a long spell of spring rain, with no sign of letup, a group of warriors, including Watanabe no Tsuna (953–1024) and Sakata Kintoki, got together to drink and tell stories. One of the group told of a demon haunting Rashōmon gate, at the south entrance to the capital. Tsuna challenged the report, saying he would go that very night to find out the truth.

Gekkei's sketch and Kikaku's verse suggest a scene near the end of the first act in the Noh play, when Tsuna, on the left, is about to leave (*Tsuna wa . . . tatte ide keru*) and also a passage at the end of the play, "Tsuna, indeed, has made his name famous" (*Tsuna wa na-o koso age-ni kere*). The season word, "rainy night," in the verse has a counterpart in the play, "This indeed is a rainy night tale" (*Kore zo amayo-no monogatari*). Gekkei's powerful line, with thick horizontal strokes in the garments, matches the bravado of the subject. In haiku and almost every aspect of Tokugawa popular culture, elements of the Noh theater may be found just below the surface.

26. Gekkei. *Tiger and Hare* [*Tora-u jigasan*]. Hanging scroll, 28.1 cm. by 45 cm. Light tan, gray, and blue pigment with ink on paper. Text:

When someone who has been ill gets up again, it feels like a clear dawn morning after a rainy night.

To bed with the rat,   Ne-ni fushite
Up with the tiger and hare—   tora-u-ni manako
Just like New Year's Day.   ake-no haru.
[Signed] *Gekkei* [two seals]

In the picture Mr. Hare has fixed Miss Tiger a sea-bream to congratulate her for getting better. The fish, which is eaten especially on New Year's Day and other happy occasions, stands for good wishes. This clever painting with its cryptic yet witty verse may well have been a present to someone who had just recovered from an illness, perhaps a woman whom Gekkei knew.

Formerly in Japan people told time by using the twelve animal signs of the Chinese zodiac, which were applied to hours, days, and years. The rat (*ne*), which is also a pun on *ne* meaning "sleep," was the first of the series, the tiger (*tora*) the third, and the rabbit (*u*) the fourth. The second animal of the twelve, the ox (*ushi*), is suggested by the phonetic similarity with *fushi*, meaning "to lie down" or "go to bed"; this allusion does not appear in the translation. Although the word play and ambiguity of the haiku verse make the meaning nebulous and, almost defy translation, the illustration is one of the most vivacious and compelling examples of early modern haiku painting. When Buson recommended Gekkei to one of his patrons, he said, "He has wondrous hands and is beyond compare." His painting alone "is enough to strike me with fear." Notice the stylistic similarity between *Tiger and Hare* and Buson's *Gods of Wealth and Long Life* (pl. 14).

27. Hakuen (1741–1806). *Retiring from the Stage [Shibaraku jigasan].* Hanging scroll, 90.7 cm. by 27 cm. Light reddish-tan pigment with ink on paper. Itsuō Art Museum. Text:

> On leaving my robes and my long sword to my son:
>
> | The world of the stage, | Shibaraku-no |
> | At last I've left behind me— | yo-o nogare keri |
> | Holed up for winter. | fuyu-gomori. |
>
> [Signed] *Ichikawa Hakuen*

Hakuen is the haiku name of the Kabuki actor Ichikawa Danjūrō V, a leading stage personality of his day. Ever since Danjūrō II (1688–1758), of an earlier generation, became a disciple of Kikaku, the Ichikawa family had maintained contact with the haiku movement. The first word of the verse, *Shibaraku*, here translated as "at last," is also the name of the most famous of the eighteen favorite Kabuki plays in the Ichikawa family repertory. In fact, the actor in our illustration, shown in a side and rear view as he bows his last farewell with extended fan, wears a kimono bearing the distinctive mark of this particular play.

28. Hōitsu (1761–1828). *Triptych of Dolls with Weeping Willows and Weeping Cherry Blossoms [Hina-ningyō, yanagi, itozakura sampuku-tsui].* Hanging scrolls, each 105.7 cm. by 29.2 cm. Bright pigments of gold, crimson, green, pink, and brown with ink. Text:

[center]	How about some pearls	Tama mo iza
	To gather along with dolls	hirowan hina-no
	Beside the seashore?	iso-zutai.
	[Signed] *By Hōitsu Kishin* [seal]	
[left]	If you were to play,	Hiku-naraba
	It would take twenty-five strings—	nijū-go-gen-ya
	Weeping cherry blossoms.	itozakura.
	[Signed] *Hōitsu* [seal]	
[right]	They are all twisted,	Mata musubi
	They are all twisted again—	mata musubitaru
	Weeping willow strands.	yanagi kana.
	[Signed] *Hōitsu* [seal]	

Better known as a great artist in the tradition of Kōrin and as the younger brother of Sakai Tadazane (d. 1790), the Lord of Himeji castle, Hōitsu was also a haiku poet, practicing under the name of Ōson. In 1797 he retired into monastic life at the Edo branch of the Nishihonganji temple and took the name Kishin. As a painter he had training under Utagawa Toyoharu (1735–1814), of the *ukiyo-e* school, and under Kanō teachers, but he came to favor the Rimpa manner, and for the centennial of Kōrin's death he edited albums of his work and erected a monument in his honor.

In terms of style, the triptych illustrated here belongs to a different world than that of most haiku paintings. Nevertheless, by virtue of Hōitsu's interests, activities, and attainments, formal paintings such as these may also be classified in this eclectic genre.

30–32 (above and overleaf).   Watanabe Kazan (1793–1841). *Absorption in Pleasure* [*Yūgi-zammai gasan*]. Album, seventeen leaves, 28.9 cm. by 32.2 cm. each. Illustrated here are leaves 8b (pl. 31), 9b (pl. 30), and 15b (pl. 32). Various light pigments with ink on paper mounted on paperboard. (See also fig. 30 for leaf 17b.) Text:

[pl. 31]   *Ryūho's painting style.* [two seals] *Mr. Doll's House has a fragrance of Pine Flower Hall.*

[pl. 30]   *With morning glories,*   Asagao wa
The clumsier you draw them   heta-no kaku sae
The more pathos they have.   aware nari.
[seal]

[pl. 32]   *Buson's painting style.* [two seals] *Master Midnight's paintings resemble Old Valley Stream.*

29.   Hōitsu and Tani Bunchō (1763–1840). *Bellflower and Autumn Grass* [*Kikyō-zu gasan*]. Hanging scroll, 49 cm. by 39.8 cm. Blue, rust, gray, and green pigment with ink on silk. Text:

Wildflower viewing—   Hana-no-mi-ya
Why do you bring pampas grass   nani-o obana ga
Back with you in your sleeve?   sode-miyage.
[Signed] *Ōson* [and] *painted by Bunchō* [seal]

Another example of the intermixing of formal painting and the informality of haiku, this piece was created by Hōitsu in collaboration with Tani Bunchō, one of the most versatile, talented, and influential painters of his day. After Hōitsu became a monk and settled into life as a cultivated townsman, he often enjoyed literary and artistic pursuits with his younger friend, Bunchō, and other people in literary and art circles. This piece is a product of such activities.

In the topsy-turvy spirit of haiku, the commonplace and weed-like pampas grass comes in front, and the more elegant and delicate bellflower is placed in the background. Not even mentioning the blossom, the poet imagines an eccentric sort of person, who might go picking wildflowers and bring back only a sprig of grass instead of something nice and showy. Actually, this idea reflects the Japanese aesthetic preference for restraint, understatement, and hidden value. Hōitsu's haiku activity and his collaboration with Bunchō reveal how, in the shogun's city of Edo, townsman and samurai occasionally shared in what has been called the "democracy of haiku."

"Mr. Doll's House" (Hina-ya) is another name by which Ryūho is known. "Pine Flower Hall" refers to Shōkadō (1584–1639), a painter, calligrapher, and Buddhist monk, who was familiar with literary men and tea masters in Kyoto. He was a contemporary of Kōetsu (1558–1637) and a member of his circle. "Old Valley Stream" denotes Kokan (1653–1717), a Kanō-style painter and illustrator, who besides working under masters of that school also studied the style of Sesshū (1420–1506). Although they do not reflect current academic opinion, Kazan's associations of Ryūho's and Buson's haiku paintings with obscure masters is nevertheless of interest. His morning glory verse, actually by Bashō and written as an inscription for a picture by Ransetsu (1654–1707), offers an amusing parody on the appeal of haiku painting.

A gifted and innovative artist, Kazan was probably the first person to use an expression (*haikai-e* in Japanese) that may be translated directly as haiku painting. Among Kazan's formal paintings, several examples are classified as national treasures and important cultural properties.

31

立圃畫意

雞屋八松花堂ト
新香宮二似タリ

31. Watanabe Kazan. *Absorption in
Pleasure* (see page 31 for caption).

蕪村ノ字ヲ
夜半蕭画八古洞
ノ畫ヲ耶二似タリ

32. Watanabe Kazan. *Absorption in
Pleasure* (see page 31 for caption).

32

Fig. 1. Bashō. *There, in the Old Pond* [*Furu-ike-ya jigasan*]. Hanging scroll, 22.8 cm. by 52.5 cm. Ink monochrome on paper. Text:

[seal]	*There, in the old pond—*	Furu-ike-ya
	A frog has just jumped in	kawazu tobi-komu
	With a splash of water.	mizu-no oto.
	[Signed] *Bashō Tōsei* [seal]	

Bashō's most often quoted and translated verse, composed in 1686, is combined with an informal sketch. The cry of the frog had been traditionally regarded as part of the elegant world of classic *waka* verse, but Bashō's combination of movement, sound, and silence was startling and fresh. In the painting, the frog is poised to leap, contrasting with the idea of the verse and giving a sense of before and after.

Fig. 2. Bashō. *Bowl-beating* [*Hachi-tataki jigasan*]. Hanging scroll, 34 cm. by 19 cm. Ink monochrome on paper. Tenri Central Library. Text:

Will he even go	Chōshō-no
To visit Chōshō's grave?	haka mo meguru-ka
A bowl-beating monk.	hachi-tataki.
[Signed] *Bashō*	

A child-like bowl-beater (*hachi-tataki*) looks over his shoulder toward the waning moon through a rift in the clouds, the moon and the text seeming to form a roof over him. The occasion for this painting occurred late in 1689 when Bashō visited Kyoto, where he and Kyorai renewed their friendship. On the twenty-fourth day of the twelfth month of Genroku 1 (early 1690 by the Western calendar), Bashō went to Kyorai's place in the western hills of Saga, the Fallen Persimmon Hut (Rakushisha), hoping to hear the bowl-beating monks. As the hour grew late and it seemed they would not come, Kyorai composed a verse in jest: "Just lend me a broom—/I'll show you imitations/of bowl-beating monks" (*Hōki kase / manetemo misen /hachi-tataki*).

At last they came, whereupon Bashō composed his verse. The Chōshō mentioned therein is Kinoshita Chōshōshi (1570–1650), who was related through marriage to the great warlord Toyotomi Hideyoshi (1536–98), and remembered not only as a talented poet but also as the former lord of Obama castle. After defeat in the Battle of Osaka (1615) he retired to Ōhara, in the hills northeast of Kyoto, the same area referred to in Gekkei's painting in plate 23. Bashō admired Chōshōshi, or Chōshō, as a spiritual predecessor in poetry and life.

Bowl-beating was a ritual that took place every winter on the anniversary of the death of Kūya (903–72), a Buddhist monk and popular teacher of the Pure Land sect, who wandered about to spread the faith among common people. He taught that a simple chant in praise of the Bodhisattva Amitābha was enough to bring eternal salvation. For forty-eight nights of each year, starting from the thirteenth day of the eleventh month, his followers renewed their devotion by dressing as monks and going about tinkling small bells, beating on gourds with bamboo sticks, ringing gongs, or the like, as they recited Buddhist verses about the transitory world. This devotional practice caught the imagination of Bashō, Buson, and other poets. (See also figs. 16, 23.)

Fig. 3. Bashō. *Arrowroot Leaves* [*Kuzu-no ha-no jigasan*]. Hanging scroll, 27.7 cm. by 42.7 cm. Faint green, pink, and gray pigment and ink on paper. Text:

The arrowroot leaves	Kuzu-no ha-no
Are showing all of their fronts—	omote mise keri
In the morning frost.	kesa-no shimo.
[Signed] *Bashō* [two seals]	

The arrangement of vines of arrowroot (*kuzu*) and bamboo (*sasa*) in the upper right, and the placement of the verse in the lower left, is an example of one of Bashō's characteristic compositional schemes. This unconventional reversal in position—the illustration normally being low and the text high—matches a similar reversal of the traditional poetic image in which arrowroot leaves show their undersides (*ura-mi kuzu-no ha*, "seeing the backs of the arrowroot leaves"). The verse gives the reason for the shift in image: the leaves are laden down with white frost so as to prevent their turning over. Legend has it that the verse celebrated Bashō's having patched up a disagreement with his disciple Ransetsu (1654–1707), thus explaining the paired ideas of front and back on the one hand, and the purity of white frost on the other. The painting has only the faintest touch of green and red pigment, mixed with a thin wash of ink. The verse was composed in 1691, the painting probably dating from the following year.

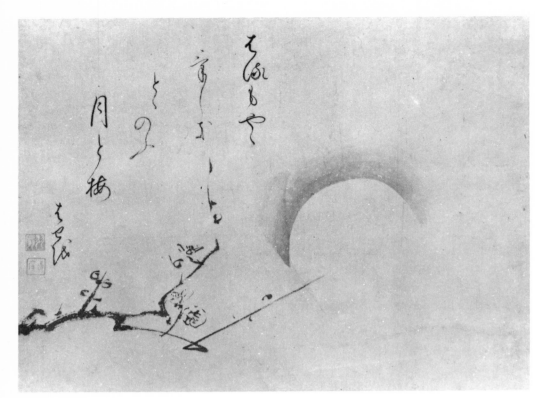

Fig. 4. Bashō. *Finally It Is Spring* [*Haru mo yaya jigasan*]. Hanging scroll, 32.8 cm. by 42.2 cm. Ink monochrome on paper. Kōno Shin'ichi Memorial Hall. Text:

> *Finally it is spring,*　　Haru mo yaya
> *And things are all together—*　keshiki totonou
> *Moon and plum blossoms.*　tsuki-to ume.
> [Signed] *Bashō* [two seals]

On the fifteenth or sixteenth of the first month of 1693, Bashō visited Kyoriku in Edo, where they enjoyed themselves with painting and poetry and creating pictures to go with Bashō's verse. It being the time of the full moon, they picked the painting topic of plum blossoms and the moon. The phrase "Finally it is spring" brought these two images together in a verse.

Bashō's version shown here (one of several), displaying a horizontal orientation, is composed of the empty space on the right and the three elements of an arc-like moon just rising, rather stiff plum blossoms, and flowing calligraphy of five uneven lines. The two seals, slightly askew, complete the composition.

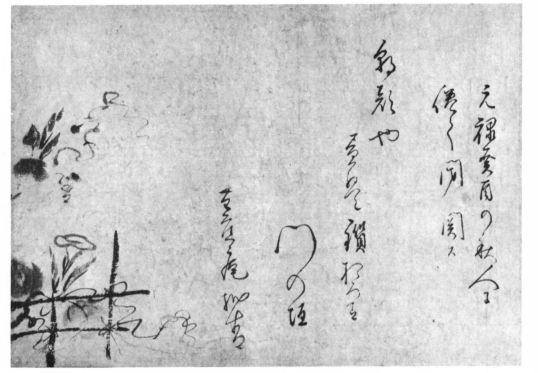

Fig. 5. Bashō. *The Lock Is Shut* [*Heikan jigasan*]. Hanging scroll, 30.4 cm. by 42 cm. Ink on paper. Idemitsu Art Museum. Text:

> *In the autumn of the year of water and the cock of Genroku [1693], I grew tired of meeting people, and shut my gate:*
>
> *Morning glories bloom—*　Asagao-ya
> *All day long the lock is shut*　hiru wa jō orosu
> *On my fence and gate.*　kado no kaki.
> [Signed] *Bashō-an Tōsei* [seal]

For about a month in early autumn of 1693 (still summer by the modern calendar), Bashō kept his gate locked and did not welcome visitors. The painting shows fanciful morning glories clinging to a makeshift fence, and a bit of abstract foliage above them. There is a suggestion here, in verse and painting, that a short-lived flower may somehow control people's lives, which might be compared with a similar theme in Chiyo-ni's verse (fig. 12). There may also be a remote association with a character in the *Tale of Genji*, namesake of the same flower, who was a retiring person and rebuffed Prince Genji's advances. This work is thought to date from 1694, the year of Bashō's death, the verse appearing in 1696 as part of a prose poem in *Bashō-an kobunko*, an anthology edited by Fumikuni.

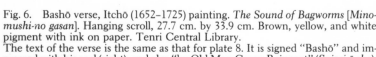

Fig. 6. Bashō verse, Itchō (1652–1725) painting. *The Sound of Bagworms* [*Mino-mushi-no gasan*]. Hanging scroll, 27.7 cm. by 33.9 cm. Brown, yellow, and white pigment with ink on paper. Tenri Central Library.

The text of the verse is the same as that for plate 8. It is signed "Bashō" and impressed with his seal (right), and also "by Old Man Green Raincoat" (*Suisai-ō sho*), namely Hanabusa Itchō, with his seal (lower left). One of the most original painters to emerge from the Kanō school, Itchō was born in Osaka, went to Edo where he studied under a Kanō master, and established an independent studio of his own. He maintained a friendship with Bashō, Kikaku, and Ransetsu, doing a group portrait of Bashō and his two popular disciples. Kazan mentions Itchō as one of the pioneer haiku painters (see fig. 30, text and discussion).

Subdued and mellow, this tiny piece is a far cry from the sort of work Itchō is best known for—street scenes, strolling singers, and habitués of the gay quarter. Here, the world of people has been reduced to the realm of a hibernating insect hanging precariously to the branch of a withered tree.

Fig. 7. Bashō verses, Kyoriku (1656–1715) painting. *Sparrows [Suzume gasan]*. Hanging scroll, 28.7 cm. by 76.4 cm. Blue-gray and black ink on paper. Text (right to left):

Amid fields of rape,	Na-batake-ni
Like people viewing flowers—	hana-mi-gao naru
Sparrows dance and chirp.	suzume kana.
Dancing under cherry blossoms—	Hana-ni asobu
Now, don't eat up the horseflies,	abu na kurai so
Big crowd of sparrows.	tomo-suzume.
Little baby sparrows—	Suzume-ko-ya
They're exchanging songs and cries	koe naki-kawasu
With a nest of mice.	nezumi-no su.
Sparrows in the rice field	Ine suzume
Always have groves of tea plants—	cha-no ki-batake-ya
Where they can escape.	nige-dokoro.
End of the year calls—	Seki-zoro-o
Even the sparrows would laugh	suzume-no warau
To see such a sight.	de-tachi kana.

[Signed] *Bashō-an, Old Man Peach* [two seals by Kyoriku]

A pair of sparrows and a pair of poets are brought together in a way that neatly conveys the light and playful side of the two arts and two like-minded practitioners. In each of Bashō's verses some aspect of human society is touched upon in terms of bird life. Each of the verses resists full and immediate understanding in English translation. In the fourth, for instance, sparrows in rice fields were legitimate prey for hunters who sold them as food, but such people were not permitted in tea groves. "End of the year calls," the last verse, refers to a mummer-like people who went about in outlandish costumes, a custom related to bowl-beating (figs. 2, 16, 23) and New Year's dancers (pl. 12).

Fig. 8. Sampū (1647–1732). *Chrysanthemum [Kiku jigasan]*. Hanging scroll, 68 cm. by 25.5 cm. Ink monochrome on paper. Itsuō Art Museum. Text:

White chrysanthemum—	Shira-giku-ni
Even a big tall cockscomb	takaki keitō
Would be scared of it.	osoroshi-ya.

[Signed]-*Sampū* [seal]

Painting chrysanthemums was a conventional exercise in the Kanō school, and a number of such works with haiku inscriptions have come down to us. Sampū's brushwork deserves comparison with that of Bashō in figure 5 and his subject with that of Buson in figure 17. The refined beauty and elegance of the chrysanthemum, praised in China and Japan as the last and therefore dearest flower of the year, is emphasized by being contrasted with a gaudy flower, the cockscomb, which, unlike the chrysanthemum, has the strength to stand on its own stem.

Buson has a verse, "Hundred-house hamlet—/There is not a single gate /Without chrysanthemums" (*Mura hyaku to/kiku naki kado mo/mienu kana*), so popular was their cultivation.

Fig. 9. Shikō (1665–1731). *Figures in a Round Window [Ensō jimbutsu jigasan]*. Hanging scroll, 98 cm. by 26.8 cm. Ink monochrome on paper. Itsuō Art Museum. Text:

Whether they look up	Aomuku mo
Or down, they're still lonely—	utsumuku mo sabishi
Lilies flowering.	yuri-no hana.

[Signed] *Kyōshi Rōjin* [written seal]

Poets are here likened to the lilies of the field, and similarly, as in the case of the flower, depending on the species and the stage of development, some look up and others down. The master at his haiku desk, known as a *bundai* and serving as a lectern, is shown with his head low and a round fan held over it. Does he have a hangover? Is he thinking of a verse, perhaps about lilies?

Surely the implication of a round rather than square window may be related to the reversibility suggested by the words of the verse and the circularity of the haiku activity. The idea of solitariness amid plurality is emphasized by the triad in the picture, as opposed to the possibility of a pair, which more easily suggests friendship and communion of the spirit (see fig. 7).

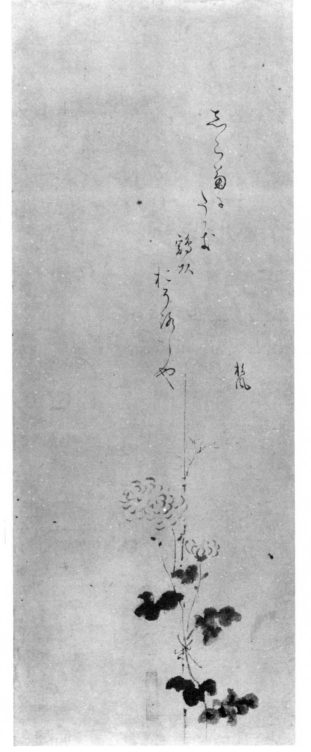

35

Fig. 10. Hyakusen (1698–1753). *White Heron* [*Shira-sagi jigasan*]. Hanging scroll, 104.4 cm. by 28.8 cm. Ink monochrome on paper. Text:

One year at Shimayama in Noto, I was asked for a verse about snow. I took an idea from Wang Shih-chen about a boat moored to a bridge among pine trees, and a moon as big as a white heron seen on a snowy night:

White herons flying—	Shira-sagi-no
A young one might go astray	mayoi-go-mo ari
In the evening snow.	yuki-no kure.

[Signed] *Hassen Kankyō* [three seals]

The place was Noto peninsula, now part of Ishikawa Prefecture, extending like a finger pointing north into the Sea of Japan, where winters are heavy with snow. The person mentioned in the inscription, Wang Shih-chen (1526–90), was a Chinese scholar and poet of the late Ming dynasty. Hyakusen himself was one of the pioneers of the Nanga style of painting derived from China, and Buson looked to him as a kindred spirit (see pl. 12, signature).

Both text and picture reveal an impulse to take direct influence from abroad (China in this case) and find fresh inspiration to expand older Japanese traditions. The idea of a white heron and a bridge is as old as early Japanese court poetry, but Hyakusen's treatment is novel, spectacular, and quintessentially in the haiku mode.

Fig. 11. Yayū (1702–83). *Picking Fresh Young Shoots* [*Wakana tsumu jigasan*]. Hanging scroll, 94 cm. by 26.2 cm. Touches of brown pigment with ink on paper. Text:

Picking fresh young shoots	Wakana tsumu
In the fields—for a salad	no ya su-miso-ni wa
It's really too cold.	mada samuki.

[Signed] *Rain* [seal]

The title of this piece gives the seasonal element, referring to an ancient custom of going out into the fields on the first day of the rat early in the New Year to pick seven different kinds of herbs to serve to the court in a kind of consommé. Originally treated as a religious observance, with young women doing the picking, it later became a recreational activity associated with the coming of spring.

Irony in the situation is exploited, both in picture and verse. The verse tells of the discomfort of the season. People might prefer to stay inside and keep warm instead of chafing their hands in the frosty fields. In the illustration the clothing suggests a summer scene rather than the coldest time of the year. A binary world is presented, with warmness and coldness, maturity and youth, male and female, poetry and painting.

Placement of verse and sketch, as with many haiku paintings, contributes to the overall design. The verse moves downward from right to left. Likewise, the figures move from right to left as well, but upward; their placement, together with that of the calligraphy, describes an incomplete arc coming together at an imaginary point between the seal and the head of the woman.

Yayū, who began as a samurai and who later retired to devote himself to poetry, is best known for a collection of haiku prose poems, *Rags and Tatters* (*Uzura-goromo*). He respected Shikō and tried to emulate him. One of his surviving haiku paintings, done in collaboration with Hyakusen, had the same design of figures in a round window as Shikō's work in figure 9.

Fig. 12. Chiyo-ni (1703–75). *Willow* [*Yanagi jigasan*]. Hanging scroll, 100 cm. by 18 cm. Brown pigment and ink on paper. Itsuō Art Museum. Text:

Though leaving its roots,	Ne-o oite
Today again, no return—	kyō mo modoranu
Just like a willow.	yanagi kana.

[Signed] *Chiyo* [seal]

A cryptic verse, and a painting so abstract as to be barely identifiable as a referential object, are combined in a rhythmic composition. This sense of balance is created by three frail tips of the willow intermingling with three lines of calligraphy at upper left, and the gnarled trunk moving out of the picture frame at lower right.

The neutral agent, translated as "it," stands first for the freely swaying tendril-like tips of the weeping willow. In a metaphorical sense, "it" may also represent a person or a sentiment—a husband unwilling or unable to come home, a child that goes wandering at play, a heart that strays from religious commitment. Although it is impossible to know what the actual intent of the poet and artist may have been, Chiyo in real life bore a child and lost it, had a husband who left her a widow, and experienced a turn to religious life.

Fig. 13. Chiyo-ni verse, Yata Shijoken (dates unknown) painting. *A Morning Glory* [*Asagao gasan*]. Hanging scroll, 43.5 cm. by 58.3 cm. Blue-gray pigment and ink on paper. Shōkōji temple, Ishikawa Prefecture. Text:

> *A morning glory*   Asagao-ya
> *Twining around the well rope—*   tsurube torarete
> *I'll borrow water.*   morai-mizu.
>
> [Signed, lower left] *Chiyo-ni* [two seals]
> [Signed, upper right] *By Shijoken* [seal]

The best-known verse by the most popular woman writer of haiku during the early modern period is tastefully illustrated with a simple painting by Yata Shijoken, an artist who worked for the Maeda clan's studio and was a contemporary of the poet. The degree of abbreviation in the painting matches perfectly with that of the verse. The lines of the tendrils across the lower right-hand corner accentuate the downward and slanting thrust of the calligraphy. The heaviness of the first and third lines of the verse balances that of the two solid shapes near the right-hand margin. Similarly, the signatures and seals of artist and poet are balanced in the two corners.

In the verse the unspoken part expresses the feeling and motivation that inspire the composition: fleeting beauty is too fragile and sacred to disturb. Walking for a pail of water is a small price to pay for the pleasure and enjoyment of such beauty.

Fig. 14. Buson. *Master Bashō* [*Bashō-ō zō*]. Hanging scroll, 98.8 cm. by 32.1 cm. Light pigment of gray, brown, flesh-tone, and green with ink on paper. Itsuō Art Museum. Text:

> *Do not speak of other people's faults. Do not brag about your own strengths:*
>
> *When I say something,*   Mono ieba
> *I feel a chill on my lips—*   kuchibiru samushi
> *The cold autumn wind.*   aki-no kaze.
>
> [Signed] *By Old Man Midnight Buson* [two seals]

This is probably the outstanding example of a number of Buson's surviving figure paintings of Bashō. The figure overflows the space, suggesting the still powerful spiritual presence of the master, though nearly a century had passed since his death. These paintings suggest a link between master and pupil, following an authentic tradition.

Buson said to a patron in Ōtsu that his work was like Sampū's image of the master but with an added touch of commonness. Surely Buson's portrait makes Bashō look far older than he appeared in actuality. This, however, followed a convention, and what Buson called the "bone-cold and lonely" aspect was to show that the master had cast off "everyday life." Even so, Buson depicts a face that seems two or three decades older than that in representations by Kyoriku, Sampū, and Yaha (1663?–1740).

Fig. 15. Buson painting and calligraphy, Bashō verse. *Master Bashō* [*Bashō-ō zō*]. Hanging scroll, 96 cm. by 32.1 cm. Light pigment of gray, flesh-tone, and tan with ink on silk. Text:

> *On visiting the monk Ninkō at the Saiganji temple:*
>
> *Right down on my sleeves—*   Waga kinu-ni
> *Let the peach-blossom dew fall,*   Fushimi-no momo-no
> *Here at Fushimi.*   shizuku seyo.
>
> *The sad cuckoo bird—*   Hototogisu
> *Through a great field of bamboo,*   Ō-take-bara-o
> *Moonlight penetrates.*   moru tsukiyo.
>
> *Banana leaves in the storm—*   Bashō nowaki shite
> *Listening at night to rain*   tarai-ni ame-o
> *Dripping in a tub.*   kiku yo kana.
>
> *As the sea grows dark,*   Umi kurete
> *The faint cry of the wild ducks*   kamo-no koe
> *Brings a sound of white.*   honoka-ni shiroshi.
>
> *Mornings and evenings,*   Asa yosa-ni
> *Anyone's favorite place*   tare Matsushima-zo
> *Would be Matsushima.*   kata-gokoro.
>
> [Signed] *Respectfully by Buson* [two seals]

Five verses by Bashō are placed in a calligraphic text in the upper half of the composition. As if an afterthought, the last verse in two staggered lines of text is written in a smaller script. The verses form a seasonal progression, spring, summer, autumn, winter, and either New Year's (sometimes referred to as a separate season in haiku poetry) or a non-seasonal one. Bashō's features are softer and more relaxed than in the portrait in figure 14, and the face appears somewhat less lean and gaunt. Likewise, the garments and head covering here are treated differently, with a bit more detail. Nevertheless, both portraits are unique products of Buson's imagination and project his idealization of the master. Each is an original owing little to the work of Buson's predecessors.

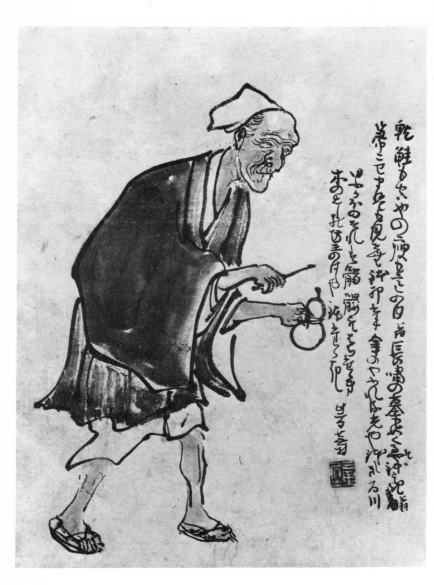

Fig. 16. Buson painting and calligraphy; Bashō, Kyorai, Hyakusen, and Buson verse. *Bowl-beating* [*Hachi-tataki*]. Hanging scroll, 33 cm. by 24.7 cm. Flesh-tone and gray wash with ink on paper. Text:

Like salted salmon,	Kara-zake mo
And Kūya all shriveled up—	Kūya-no yasuru mo
The coldest season.	kan-no uchi.
(The Master)	

[same verse as in fig. 2, "Will he even go"]
(The Master)

[same as in fig. 2, discussion, "Just lend me a broom"]
(Kyorai)

A torn umbrella	Kara-kasa-no
May look just like a halo—	yabure gokō-ya
On bowl-beating monks.	hachi-tataki.
(Hyakusen)	

The flower is gone,	Yūgao-no
Only a skull-like shell remains—	sore wa dokuro-ka
Bowl-beating season.	hachi-tataki.

The stump of a tree,	Ki-no hashi-no
Of monks, the lowest of low—	bōzu-no hashi-ya
Bowl-beating again.	hachi-tataki.

[Signed] *These last two verses by Buson* [seal]

Although one of the smallest of the haiku paintings presented here, covering little more than the area of a standard-sized sheet of typewriter paper, this figure of a bowl-beating monk with six haiku verses, two by Bashō in the first line from the right, one each by Kyorai and Hyakusen in the second line, and a pair by Buson in the third and fourth lines, is one of the most poignant and memorable that has been preserved from the early modern period. The bent and wizened figure, tapping his gourd (see the fifth verse above), represents not only the devoted monk Kūya but also his followers, as well as the poets who responded to such an enduring sense of piety and all of the old and tired people who continue to walk the face of the earth.

Fig. 17. Buson. *Chrysanthemum* [*Ippon-giku jigasan*]. Hanging scroll, 112.7 cm. by 30 cm. Ink monochrome on paper. Itsuō Art Museum. Text:

I went to visit a friend in the mountains, and I admired his chrysanthemums. He took out some paper and an ink-stone and asked me for a verse:

Chrysanthemum dew—	Kiku-no tsuyu
Just put it in an ink-stone,	ukete suzuri-no
And it comes to life.	inochi kana.

[Signed] *Buson* [two seals]

An ink-stone is a kind of inkwell, used with an ink-stick and water to mix the fluid for painting and calligraphy. Buson recalls a Chinese inscription on an old ink-stone, "The life of a brush is measured in days, the life of an ink-stick in years, the life of an ink-stone in generations."

By tradition in China, Korea, and Japan, the Chrysanthemum Festival was held on the ninth day of the ninth month of the year. In celebration of friendship, a special wine, "Chrysanthemum Dew," was served. According to legend, there had once been a boy living in the mountains who drank the dew of chrysanthemums and stayed young for seven hundred years, somewhat like the ink-stone mentioned above.

To go with his verse Buson drew a single stalk of flowers tied to a slender bamboo stake. Poetry, prose, and painting combine to suggest how art and life may yield an auspicious vision. Buson takes an unconventional approach to a conventional topic (see fig. 8), in which his painting skillfully harmonizes with the calligraphy. The verticality of the stake and flower stalk is duplicated in that of the inscription and verse. A subtle combination of asymmetry and balance may be found in the two lines of the picture portion and the three lines of the textual part. The three lines of text, in turn, consist of two units, prose inscription in slightly smaller script and verse in slightly larger. The signature and seals at the bottom are like the roots of the text above, and this element in the lower left-hand corner offsets the two blooms in the upper right. The entire composition evinces an impressive sense of aesthetic wholeness and a unique beauty.

Fig. 18. Buson painting, Basho text. *The Broken Hammer* [*Kine-no ore*]. Hanging scroll, 110.7 cm. by 28.3 cm. Ink monochrome on paper. Itsuō Art Museum. Text:

This implement, which is called the "Broken Hammer," was treasured by an eminent person. It is indeed one of the rarities of our land.

Broken Hammer, what mountain were you born on? What lowly person in what village used you for pounding? Before you were an ordinary tool, but now you are called a flower vase. Renamed as you are, your place was over the head of a noble person.

It is the same with people. When you are in a high position, you must not be haughty. When you are lowly, you must not be envious. It is best in this world to be an ordinary hammer.

What was this hammer?	Kono tsuchi-no
Was it once a camellia,	mukashi tsubaki-ka
Or was it a plum?	ume-no ki-ka.
(Bashō)	

[Signed] *By Shunsei, on the full moon of the sixth month, in the year of fire and the cock* [two seals]

For a prose poem by Bashō published posthumously in 1756, Buson did a calligraphic text and added the simplest imaginable representation of the object that presumably inspired Bashō's original composition. The "year of fire and the cock" corresponds to 1777, when Buson was involved in making his illustrated versions of Bashō's best-known poetic diaries as well as in other activities to honor his memory. Buson has given reign to his imagination in depicting the object in the painting, which resembles a fulling block or mallet, used to pound clothing to make it soft for winter use, a practice which was mentioned in the *Tale of Genji*, Noh, and Chinese poetry. There is no way of knowing the actual shape of the wooden flower vase about which Bashō fancifully wrote as if it had actually been a broken hammer.

In the posthumous collection in which Bashō's text appeared, a note tells that the implement was handed down in Ōtsu, by the shores of Lake Biwa, and that later a Kyoto merchant owned it. It is now lost.

Bashō's text tells poetically of the vicissitudes of people high and low and of the objects they use for work and play. The didactic tone reflects one aspect of the haiku tradition that often makes modern critics and commentators feel uncomfortable. The extreme simplicity of Buson's handling of the text serves, by means of understatement, to emphasize his respect for the words of the master, much as a judge at the bench might use his gavel to call the court to order or announce a decision.

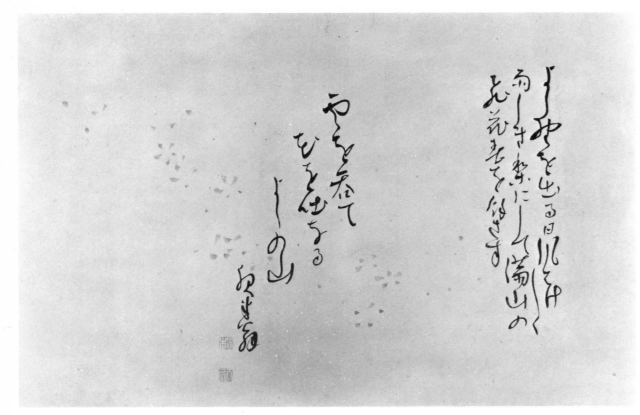

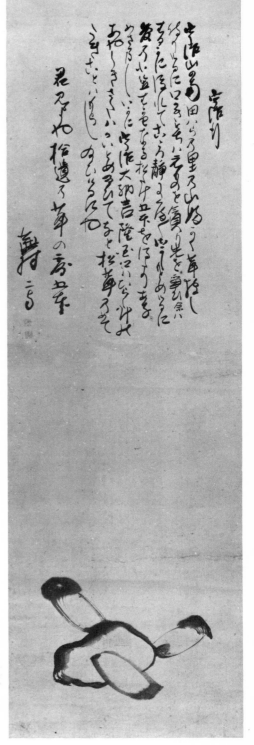

Fig. 19. Buson. *Yoshino Cherry Blossoms* [*Yoshino-yama hana-mi kaishi*]. Hanging scroll, 27.2 cm. by 40.2 cm. Ink monochrome on paper. Itsuō Art Museum. Text:

> *On the day we left Yoshino the wind blew so hard and it rained so fiercely that the blossoms were flying all over the mountains as a reminder that spring cannot last long:*
>
> *They drank in the clouds,*   Kumo-o nonde
> *And they spit out*
>   *the flowers—*   hana-o haku naru
> *Yoshino mountains.*   Yoshino-yama.
>
> [Signed] *Old Man Midnight* [two seals]

A passage from a letter written after an excursion in the spring of 1782 to a famous area south of Nara, rich in historical and literary associations, has been transformed into a calligraphic composition set against falling cherry-blossom petals that could suggest snowflakes or animal tracks as easily as flowers.

This piece exemplifies a characteristic of haiku painting and Japanese aesthetics, namely the use of a part of an object to represent the whole. This piece and that in plate 21 are like the reverse sides of a single coin, the one showing petals and no people, the other people but no petals.

Fig. 20. Buson. *Song of Uji* [*Uji-kō jigasan*]. Hanging scroll, 93.3 cm. by 27 cm. Ink monochrome on paper. Itsuō Art Museum. Text:

> *In the southern part of the Uji hills, in the deep mountains near the hamlet of Tawara, I went on a mushroom-picking party. The young people were greedy to get as many as they could, and they hurried on ahead. I lagged far behind and took my good old time looking in every possible spot. I found five mushrooms that were as large as a small sedge hat.*
>
> *Oh, what a revelation! How could the Major Counsellor of Uji, Lord Takakuni, have written about miraculous mushrooms and failed to mention the kind that I found? Could I miss a chance to tell of my luck with them?*
>
> *Just look, my good sir,*   Kimi miyo-ya
> *Mushrooms that you left behind—*   shūi-no take-no
> *Five of them, with dew.*   tsuyu gohon.
>
> [Signed] *By Buson* [two seals]

Part of a prose poem in a letter to a host at a picnic held late in 1783, barely three months before Buson's death, is joined with a calligraphic and pictorial composition. The three mushrooms at the bottom of the scroll are presented so abstractly that the text is necessary to clarify the object of reference.

"The Uji hills" refer to a place southeast of Kyoto, the main setting for the last ten chapters of the *Tale of Genji*. Despite being close to the large city, even today some of the area retains its rustic charm. "The Major Counsellor" alludes to an anecdote in *A Collection of Tales from Uji* (*Uji shūi monogatari*), a fourteenth-century text.

The relaxed style of the composition projects the idea of leisurely activity, of finding happiness in the small pleasures of life, and of expressing thanks for hospitality. Besides being one of Buson's representative haiku paintings, it is probably the last such work of his life.

Fig. 21. Ōemaru (1722–1805). *Citron Bean-Paste* [*Yu-miso jigasan*]. Hanging scroll, 35.8 cm. by 47.2 cm. Light touches of blue and tan pigment on paper. Kōno Shin'ichi Memorial Hall. Text:

> *Look-alike faces—*   Nita kao-no
> *Citron bean-paste and seven-step*   yu-miso shippo-no
> *Poems to make you weep.*   shi-o naku ka.
>
> [Signed] *Ōemaru* [four seals]

Amusing in its own right as calligraphy and painting, *Citron Bean-Paste* is hard to explain as poetry. "Seven-step poems" and the idea of weeping come from a Chinese tale about Emperor Wen-ti (T'sao P'ei, 186–226) of the Wei dynasty, in which he orders his younger brother, Ts'ao Chih (192–232), to compose a poem within seven steps or else face execution. Chih succeeded in producing an allegoric verse that chastized his brother for lack of the natural love and respect that siblings ought to feel. Chih's poem told of beans that came from the same root and were boiled in the same pot, an idea suggesting that brothers in the same stew ought not to quarrel. The verse and anecdote were well known in Japan, especially since the fourteenth century, figuring in a widely read collection of anecdotes, comments, and observations on life known as *Essays in Idleness* (*Tsurezuregusa*).

Perhaps the point in Ōemaru's verse is that citron bean-paste tastes sour and bitter, and the girl bending over and blowing through a bamboo tube to fan the fire feels as uncomfortable tending her boiling beans as Chih did centuries before. The puffed-up face of the girl, something like a citron itself, and the round lines of her bottom help to turn pity for her task into ridicule of her posture. Note the general similarity between Ōemaru's serving girl, or good-natured wife, and Oto-Goze in plate 2. Most readers will find the cultural code of this haiku too complex for ready understanding.

Besides being an Osaka haiku master who had contacts with such Edo counterparts as Ryōta (1718–87) and the itinerant master Ryōtai (Takebe Ayatari, 1719–74), Ōemaru managed a family courier business. He traveled the Eastern Sea Road more than fifty times, and he also had periodic contact with Buson.

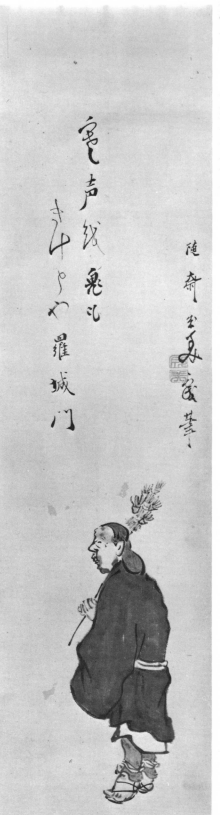

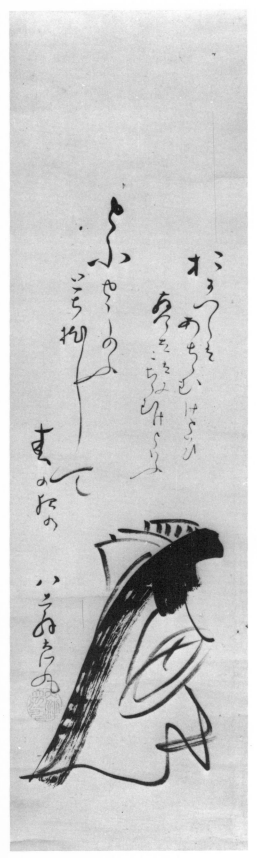

Fig. 23. Seibi (1749–1816). *Cold Prayers* [*Kan-nembutsu jigasan*]. Hanging scroll, 98.9 cm. by 25 cm. Touches of tan and blue-gray pigment with ink on paper. Itsuō Art Museum. Text:

> *A cold kind of voice—*   Kansei-o
> *Might a devil hear it too,*   oni mo kike-to ya
> *At Rashōmon?*   Rashōmon.
> [Signed] *By Zuisai Seibi* [two seals]

"A cold kind of voice" comes from the set haiku topic of *kan-nembutsu*, or "cold prayers," another name for "bowl-beating" (see figs. 2, 16). Seibi, an Edo haiku master, has treated his "monk" in a frumpish and lighthearted way, which goes with the spirit of haiku. This haiku painting is one of those with rather little of the abbreviation of line and feature that has come to be thought typical of the genre.

The place, Rashōmon (see pl. 25), is here associated with the eerie sounds of bowl-beating "monks." Seibi's droopy and forlorn figure, with his slightly stooped back, appears reluctant to make his rounds, like a would-be Halloween prankster afraid of ghosts.

Fig. 24. Sengai (1751–1837). *Mount Fuji and the Rising Sun* [*Fuji kyoku-jitsu jigasan*]. Hanging scroll, 33.2 cm. by 56.3 cm. Ink monochrome on paper. Text:

> *Even with no caw,*   Nakazu-to mo
> *Our land of the rising sun*   waga hi-no-moto-no
> *May have the first crow.*   hatsu-garasu.
> [Seal]

Sengai is not normally treated as a haiku poet. He was a Buddhist monk of the Rinzai sect of Zen, who is remembered as an educator and as a painter of ink-monochrome drawings and calligraphic inscriptions, such as that shown here. Many of the inscriptions are in the form of haiku. Certainly, his extreme abbreviation of line and form, as well as his playful tone, have much in common with the work of poets and artists who were directly involved in the haiku movement.

From the usual vantage points for seeing Mount Fuji, this scene would suggest not the rising but the setting sun. Only from places such as the Kōfu plains, in Yamanashi Prefecture, would such a view be possible, and only then with foothills in the foreground. Eccentric and fanciful, after all, Sengai is dealing with poetry and art, not verisimilitude.

His verse deals with the haiku seasonal topic of "the first crow" (*hatsu-garasu*), and the poet relates this to the sunrise on New Year's day in terms that suggest one of the poetic designations of Japan, "land of the rising sun" (*hi-no-moto-no* [*kuni*]). On a deeper level the relation of crow and rising sun calls to mind associations in Japanese mythology with the "eight-headed crow" (*yata-garasu*) that the Sun Goddess sent to guide the legendary first emperor, Jimmu, on his conquest of the east. In Chinese mythology this term refers to an imaginary three-legged bird that inhabits the sun and also to the sun itself. The verse brings such associations together in a clever and ironical way. Mount Fuji in the illustration may suggest the land that is implied but not specifically mentioned in the verse. The sun in the painting may be equated with the crow, which is denoted in the verse but not actually shown.

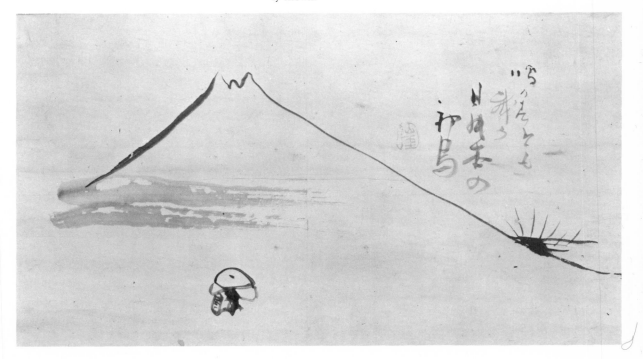

Fig. 22. Ōemaru. *On a Night in Spring* [*Haru-no yo-no jigasan*]. Hanging scroll, 90 cm. by 28.8 cm. Ink monochrome on paper. Kōno Shin'ichi Memorial Hall. Text:

> *Onitsura said, "Face it that way." Ryōta said, "Face it this way."*
>
> *Oh, what can I do,*   Dō-shiyō-nō
> *Which way should my*
> *   pillow go—*   dochi makura shite
> *On a night in spring.*   haru-no yo-no.
> [Signed] *Eighty-one-year Old Man, Ōemaru* [seal]

The logical way to see this picture is as a view from the ceiling, because the woman is supposed to be lying down, with a pillow—represented by one horizontal line and five vertical lines—under her head. The short text and verse refer to a difference of opinion, presumably about poetry, between the old master Onitsura (1661?–1738) and Ryōta, who Ōemaru looked to as his own haiku teacher. Ōemaru says in terms of haiku poetry, "How can I choose between them?" He achieves an additional degree of wit by alluding to an old *waka* verse on the same topic, and by using diction that suggests the persona of a woman who cannot pick between two lovers.

Fig. 25. Gekkei. *Scarecrow* [*Kakashi jigasan*]. Fan painting, 17.2 cm. by 47 cm. Ink monochrome on two-tone paper of light olive green and cream. Text:

> *Leaves on the rice plants*   Ine-no ha-no
> *May still be all fresh and green—*   aokarishi yori
> *But a scarecrow's up.*   kakashi kana.
> [Signed] *Gekkei*

This is one of Gekkei's unusual works, in that he is dealing with his own verse rather than someone else's. He treats the illustration as part of the text, thereby creating a kind of acrostic. The verse tells in a lighthearted way of the farmer's concern for his crops.

Fig. 26. Sobaku (1758–1821). *The Most Famous Moon* [*Meigetsu-no jigasan*]. Hanging scroll, 99 cm. by 25.5 cm. Faint tones of yellow and gray with ink on paper. Kōno Shin'ichi Memorial Hall. Text:

> *In the city:*
>
> *The most famous moon,*   Meigetsu-no
> *The very first sight of it—*   hatsu kage kakaru
> *There against the eaves.*   nokiba kana.
> [Signed] *Sobaku* [seal]

Not the moon but the people are shown, making this piece another of the many haiku paintings that suggest the whole subject by means of a part of it. The tender age of the children suggests the freshness of the newly risen moon. Likewise, their form duplicates the roundness of the full moon, and the reduplication of similar children suggests the barely noticeable movement of the moon itself.

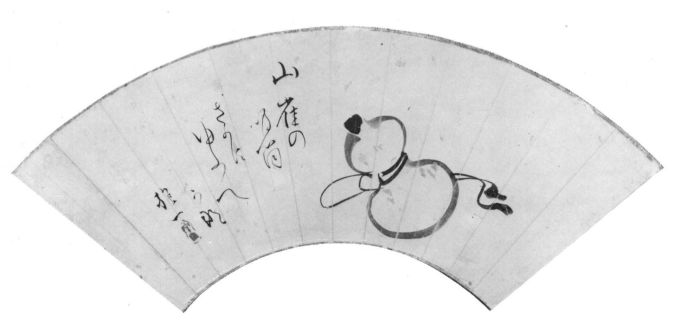

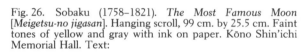

Fig. 27. Hōitsu. *Even a Titmouse* [*Yamagara-no jigasan*]. Fan painting mounted as a hanging scroll, 16 cm. by 48.6 cm. Ink monochrome on paper. Text:

> *Even a titmouse*   Yamagara-no
> *Might look for a*
>   *drinking gourd,*   sui-zutsu sagasu
> *Now that it's evening.*   yūbe kana.
> [Signed] *Hōitsu* [seal]

The gourd suggests a container for wine (see pl. 21) and also a place where a tiny titmouse might try to nest, the two ideas coming together. During the early modern period titmice were kept as pets, like canaries. Here the choice of an illustration to go with the verse resembles a technique used in linked poetry, whereby one semantic element in a given unit became the focal point and was presented in such a way that it might lead to a new idea in the next unit, perhaps to that of a person who wants a drinking companion with whom to spend an autumn night.

Fig. 28. Issa (1763–1827). *Mr. Pigeon* [*Hato jigasan*]. Hanging scroll, 97.3 cm. by 29.9 cm. Ink monochrome on paper. Text:

Mr. Pigeon gives a scolding:
   Look here, Mr. Owl,   Fukurō-yo
   Brighten up that face of yours—   tsura kuse naose
   Spring rain is falling.   haru-no ame.
    [Signed] *Verse also by Issa* [written seal]

Pigeons are born optimists, always looking happy, while owls always seem to have a scowl. Spring rain is supposed to make you feel good, because winter is over, which is the reason for Mr. Pigeon's advice.

Many of Issa's verses, in comparison to the work of other poets, deal with birds and beasts. Although some of them fall into bathos or self-pity, this one carries the amusing sense of someone determined, however futile or misguided the task may be, to put a smile on his neighbor's face.

As may be seen from this example and figure 29, Issa's sketches are valued for the extremity of their abbreviation. In keeping with the idea of haiku as a simplification of certain kinds of experience, only the bare essentials remain. Issa's approach is similar to that of Sengai (see fig. 24).

Fig. 29. Issa. *Swallow* [*Tsubame jigasan*]. Hanging scroll, 29.9 cm. by 44.8 cm. Ink monochrome on paper. Text:

   Again to no avail,   Mata muda-ni
   The bird opens up its mouth— kuchi aku tori-no
   Only a stepchild.   mama-ko kana.
    [Signed, on right] *Swallow also by Issa* [written seal, lower left]

Whereas the pigeon in figure 28 is made up mostly of dots and a few curved lines, the swallow's main form comes from six sharp straight lines, several curves, and two auxiliary lines for a beak, imparting sleekness rather than fluffiness.

As a form of poetry, the haiku is open-ended and subject to a variety of interpretations, a quality that is necessary for successful linking in chain poems. For example, Issa's swallow may be taken as singular, as done here and in other commentaries, or as plural, in the sense of an abandoned nest. The flying bird in the painting may represent the parent who left its nest, or possibly the young bird that has somehow grown up without a mother, a situation that Issa himself experienced.

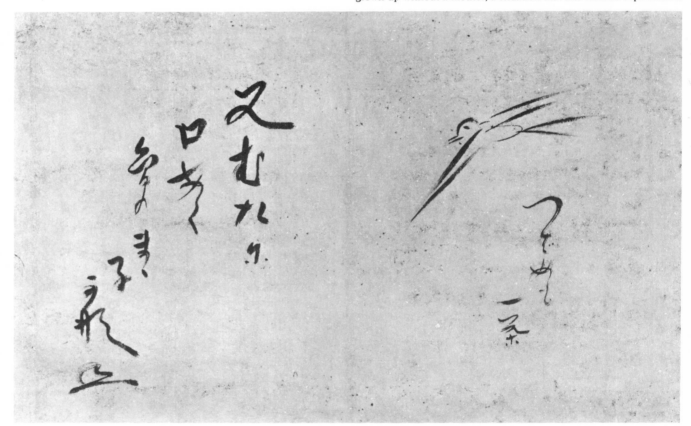

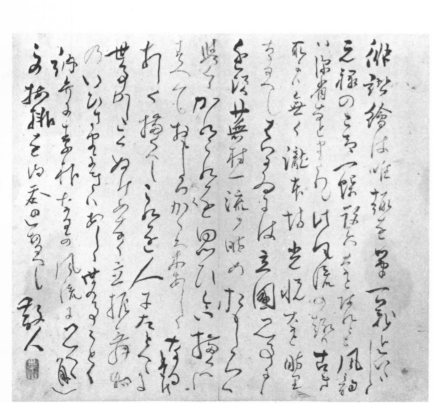

Fig. 30. Watanabe Kazan. *Absorption in Pleasure* [*Yūgi-zammai gasan*]. Album, seventeen leaves, 28.9 cm. by 32.2 cm. each. Illustrated here is leaf 17b. Ink on paper. (See also pls. 30–32 for other leaves.) Text:

In haikai painting the idea is the most important element. Itchō and Kyoriku are good examples from the Genroku era. The atmosphere of their art conveys introspection. The idea of such an art is not ancient. It probably began with people such as Takimoto-bō Kōetsu. Ryūho applied it admirably to haikai. More recently, Buson and his followers have produced excellent examples. The essence of this art is just to sketch, to represent everything in a catchy way, and to draw as roughly as possible. If one were to compare this to people, someone who is wise, prudent, and eloquent in practical affairs would be bad. Someone who is awkward in practical affairs and untutored would be regarded as artistic. This combination should be kept in mind.
   [Signed] *The Hermit* [seal] *Kazan*

Kazan's brief text represents the earliest known definition and survey of the genre. It makes the point, ironically, that in haiku painting worse seems better, idea excels technique, and sloppiness is preferable to neatness. In spite of his satirical tone, however, Kazan was obviously attracted to haiku painting and apparently regarded it with respect. Of the people mentioned in his text, Itchō (1652–1725) illustrated Bashō's verse given in figure 6, and Kyoriku is represented in figure 7. Kōetsu refers to Hon'ami Kōetsu (1558–1637), a master craftsman and painter of the Momoyama and early Tokugawa period, who pioneered what later became known as the Rimpa style. For Ryūho, see plate 1. Buson's work is presented in plates 9–21 and figures 14–20. The Genroku era (1688–1704) refers to a period known for its flourishing popular culture, the first of several such high points during the Tokugawa period (1600–1868).

HAIKU PAINTING

HAIKU POETRY: BASIC PRINCIPLES

Haiku, a kind of poetry that was conceived and grew to maturity in Japan, is more widely practiced today than ever before, not only in the country of its origin but in Africa, Asia, Europe, North and South America. Many people are discovering the pleasures and rewards of reading and writing haiku and of exploring its various branches. Indeed, haiku is often taught in the schools as a way of developing the power to organize words in the form of poetry.

In basic form, haiku traditionally and typically has seventeen syllables in three uneven, unrhymed clusters of five, seven, and five syllables. It combines some aspect of nature or human life, an element of one of the four seasons of the year, and something that relates or represents human feeling, experience, or observation. An example of one written originally in German and translated into English may help to show how this kind of poetry works:

> *Smoke from the chimney.*
> *Glimmering rays of starlight*
> *tangled in the snow.*
> (Gunther Kling)*

Smoke from the chimney in winter tells that people live and work, sometimes together, sometimes alone, in a complex and changing universe. A break in the sense between the first and second lines signifies how one image placed against another may create surprising effects. In Japanese this technique is enhanced by the use of a part of speech known as a "cutting word" (*kireji*), which serves to interrupt the normal flow of language. Also, haiku by nature of its brevity tends to compress human experience.

This classical Japanese verse conveys the idea of a grand sight in nature:

> *Wild and stormy sea—*   Ara-umi-ya
> *And bridging it to Sado,*   Sado-ni yokotō
> *The Milky Way.*   Ama-no-gawa.
> (Bashō)

The vastness of the water, life or exile on a lonely island far away (Sado), and the countless stars in the galaxy—these three elements have been brought together in an autumn setting (the seasonal element) to create a great triangle of heaven, earth, and man. A high degree of abstraction occurs in the context of a specific place with vivid imagery.

Another Japanese haiku focuses on a tiny event in nature, easily overlooked:

---

*Adapted from the German by Ann Atwood; in *Modern Haiku*, 13, no. 3 (1982): 8.

> *Fallen peonies—*   Botan chitte
> *Scattered on one another,*   uchi-kasanarinu
> *Two or three petals.*   ni-sam-pen.
> (Buson)

The peony is a season word for summer. A general observation about the passing of a certain kind of beauty is matched with detailed scrutiny of a particular scene and an instant in time.

Deeply personal sorrow and sadness often find expression in Japanese haiku:

> *A dewdrop falling—*   Tsuyu-no yo-no
> *Of this sordid world it wants*   tsuyu-no yo nagara
> *No more part at all.*   sarinagara.
> (Issa)

The dewdrop, standing for summer and also for the poet's infant daughter, who had recently died, may refer by extension to any profoundly felt loss, great or small.

All of the above verses suggest the ability of haiku to embody the pleasure of representation, a natural need of all people, and to simplify human experience, often to the point of caricature, or as if in analogy to the abstract movement of certain kinds of dance, especially that of the Japanese Noh.

As a new type of international poetry, haiku is taught and written all over the world. Students in school and people in private groups take part in this subtle form of literary art, where inner feeling matters more than surface meaning and in which throbbing silences and fertile pauses generate poetic effects. Thousands of haiku books and magazines appear each year. Lively discussion and debate about the art continues to rage.

HAIKU POETRY: DIMENSIONS OF THE ART

Yet the world of haiku goes beyond the short poem, which nowadays assumes a variety of forms and may often be exceedingly free in style. Besides the brief haiku itself, there are broader dimensions to the art, which help explain the complex delight that rewards reader and poet alike. First of all, there is a communal branch of haiku poetry, characterized by a kind of chain poem. Sometimes the Japanese term *haikai* (literally "witty amusement"), a word that is older than the expression "haiku" and suggests light and amusing play with words, is used to refer to the product of a group of like-minded people coming together to compose poetry in linked units. Formerly the nucleus of haiku practice, this kind of poetry was also known as *renga*, or "linked verse." It developed much earlier than haiku, which stresses individual and private composition of verse, and it usually involved combining a cluster of five-seven-five syllables with one of seven-

seven syllables, which together make up thirty-one syllables—the basic form of the classical verse known as *waka* or *tanka*, from which haiku ultimately emerged. This basic unit might then be repeated and combined into chains of thirty-six, fifty, one hundred, one thousand, or even ten thousand units. Complicated rules governed composition of chain poems. After a decline, the practice of chain poems, or linked verse, has been coming back, and poets in the Western world are experimenting with its possibilities.

Prose poems in the style and spirit of haiku also began to be written and collected in anthologies as the haiku movement gained momentum. Often these were composed for special occasions, such as when a poet enjoyed a friend or patron's hospitality and repaid him with a literary or artistic composition. Buson's *Chrysanthemum* and *Song of Uji* (figs. 17, 20) are obvious examples. At other times the prose poem was used as a vehicle that allowed the poet to explore the limits of his creative ability. Prose poems in the haiku manner are known in Japanese as *haibun*, literally "light compositions." Captions and texts for paintings were frequently in this form (e.g., pls. 3, 10; fig. 18). Likewise, travel literature, a kind of poetic diary known as *kikōbun*, or "records of travel," also came to be written in haiku style. Writing of this nature includes some of the most famous works in Japanese literature. One of these works, *The Narrow Road to a Far Province* (*Oku-no hosomichi*) by Bashō, the best-known Japanese haiku poet, is among the most widely read and admired texts in Japanese literature (e.g., pls. 17–19).

Another development of the haiku movement was the emergence of criticism and discussion of the theory, practice, and aesthetics of haiku, which had their origin in similar writings about earlier Japanese poetry. In Japanese this branch of haiku is called *hairon*, meaning "essays on haiku." Kazan's text in figure 30 is related to this tradition.

THE VISUAL ASPECT OF HAIKU

Fresh and vivid though the lyrical poetry of haiku may be, human language has its limitations as a symbolic mode of communication. Poets in Japan quickly began to explore other forms of communicative energy, such as image, theater, and dance. Composite forms of art such as Noh developed. One of these, combining word and picture, led in time to the kind of painting now known as *haiga*, or "haiku painting," forming yet another branch of the literary art or craft of haiku poetry. The ideals of haiku as a way of life, which combined aesthetic, moral, and religious experience, thus became integrated with calligraphy and painting, lending visual dimension to the art. Given the highly developed sense of visual beauty from early times on in Japan, it was perhaps natural that an allusive, highly suggestive, and often imagistic literary art such as haiku should generate a visual complement. It is likewise no wonder that the masterpieces

of haiku painting are treated as valuable art treasures, that some of them have even been designated as important cultural properties by the Japanese government.

As for the formal characteristics of haiku painting, virtually all examples now so regarded are characterized by restraint in pigmentation, free and flowing line work, and elimination of unnecessary detail. There is often a light or frivolous touch suggestive of irony or amusement, even when the subject of the painting is serious. Although the example is marginal in terms of haiku poetry, Taiga's *Hare* (pl. 22) represents an especially high degree of frivolity. To every rule there must be exceptions, and Hōitsu's *Triptych of Dolls* (pl. 28) stands as an example of haiku painting that employs the full range of traditional pigments and the formality of the decorative style known as Rimpa.

This book is mostly about the visual side of haiku, especially about how word and picture may combine in a hybrid form that goes beyond the limits of either language or pictorial image. The product of this combination, haiku painting, is based on principles of abstraction in which only a limited number of possible features are delineated, thereby revealing unsuspected resemblances and similarities.

DEVELOPMENT AND CHARACTERISTICS OF HAIKU PAINTING

The examples illustrated here, of which many are discussed for the first time in English, represent the period of formation and maturity of this composite art, roughly from the seventeenth to the middle of the nineteenth century. Since the middle of the nineteenth century the art has continued to grow in a number of directions. This aspect deserves separate treatment, however. The haiku paintings illustrated in this book should serve to demonstrate to all people how the visual and literary imagination are intimately related to a pair of the most primitive and universal of human activities—"babble" and "doodle." Who has not on occasion sketched or drawn pictures in his or her notebook in moments of abstraction?

As a wedding of word and image similar to that seen nowadays in cartoons, comic strips, posters, and other emblematic forms, haiku painting emerged at almost the same time as the poetry itself. These twin arts developed hand in hand. At first the visual aspect that shared the space with the calligraphic text on items such as horizontal scrolls (*makimono*), hanging scrolls (*kakejiku*), albums (*gajō*), or fans (*semmen*) was rendered more or less in the accepted styles and in the manner of the orthodox schools of the day. The earliest items now treated as haiku paintings are rendered either in the style of native Japanese painting, known as Yamato-e, the roots of which extend back at least to the tenth or eleventh century, or in the eclectic style practiced by the Kanō school, which emerged in the sixteenth century toward the end of the middle ages.

As a case in point, the simple line and abbreviated treatment of the human figure in Ryūho's representation of Lady Murasaki (pl. 1), the eleventh-century authoress of the *Tale of Genji* (*Genji monogatari*), draws on antecedents at least as far back as the twelfth-century caricatures of frogs and monkeys enjoying the sort of religious activities and casual amusements in which people engaged, as well as the conventional ink drawings of famous poets that developed during the middle ages. Ryūho's art is also related to the aristocratic Tosa school, which may be thought of as a modification of the older mode of Yamato-e, as well as to a newer revival of the decorative impulse that later became known as the Rimpa style.

Ryūho's extreme abbreviation of human features extends the older tradition of the so-called slash for an eye, hook for a nose (*hiki-me kagibana*) of famous scroll paintings in the style of Yamato-e. The device of abbreviation, which it should be noted took inspiration from Chinese models as well as Japanese, emerged as the central concept in haiku painting as well as poetry.

Poet and artist alike endeavored to eliminate every superfluous element and to attain an austere beauty akin to that of abstract art or to the stylized patterns of movement in the dance element (*shimai*) of the Noh drama. This tendency may be related to the religious discipline of Zen and a spiritual emphasis on purity and simplicity associated with the indigenous religion of Shinto. Indeed, the very essence of Japanese design may be found in the tendency to abbreviate and reduce formal elements to the utmost degree. Issa's haiku paintings, for instance (figs. 28, 29), stand as the ultimate in abbreviation. The same tendency is also described in Kazan's pioneering definition of haiku painting (fig. 30).

A CROSS SECTION OF STYLES AND SCHOOLS

There was no separate school of haiku painting in Japan until the twentieth century. Awareness of this art as a genre of its own has been a gradual process, and only during the past decade or two have scholars paid close attention to the matter of definitions and scope. Except for the general consideration of abbreviation and simplification, probably the sole defining characteristic of haiku painting was that it combined the pictorial feature with a calligraphic text, typically, though by no means exclusively, one associated with the haiku movement. Accordingly, most of the examples represented here are by artists who had some connection, however slight or tenuous, with the art of haiku poetry.

Thus haiku painting of the seventeenth to the middle of the nineteenth century presents a cross section of the various styles and schools that flourished during this time. Besides the influences of the Yamato-e, Tosa, and Rimpa styles, which have already been noted, there was a powerful impulse from the Kanō school, the dominant style in the seventeenth century owing largely to the patronage of the shogun and the powerful warrior clans. Almost all the examples of Bashō's paintings illustrated here reveal indebtedness to Kanō conventions. In brushwork, composition, and use of pigment, they follow the Kanō tradition of masters who admired the firmness and stiffness derived from such medieval predecessors as Sesshū (1420–1506), albeit with various modifications.

Of all the paintings presented here, that most obviously painted in the Kanō style is *Prose Poem on Stopping in the Rain and Autumn Crow Verse* (pl. 3), which is now thought most likely to be a joint work by Bashō and an unidentified Kanō master. It may be treated as a haiku painting mainly by virtue of the verse and prose poem that Bashō inscribed. To a greater or lesser degree all the examples by Bashō, as well as those of his collaborators and immediate disciples, are of Kanō derivation.

Among Bashō's paintings, the *Solitary Traveler in Winter Shower* (pl. 7) is probably closest to the medieval prototypes of the Kanō school. The treatment of the human figure, the handling of elements of the natural landscape, and the choice of subject are reminiscent of ink monochromes in the monastic tradition of Zen. What is new is a sense of irony and lightness that can also be found in Bashō's poetry during the last years of his life.

Similarly, haiku paintings by Bashō's disciples and followers in the late seventeenth and early eighteenth century also belong to the Kanō tradition. For example, Kyoriku's *Sparrows* (fig. 7), Sampū's *Chrysanthemum* (fig. 8), Shikō's *Figures in a Round Window* (fig. 9), and the illustration for Chiyo-ni's verse, *A Morning Glory*, by Yata Shijoken (fig. 13), all evince features of the Kanō school, which kept a distinctive identity until late in the nineteenth century. The school furnished an academic standard during most of the Tokugawa period, and certified teachers often provided training for poets who took part in haiku circles, where visual expression was valued along with verbal skill.

THE RISE OF THE INDEPENDENT SCHOOLS

There were a number of painters, however, in such cities as Kyoto, Osaka, and Edo, who worked independently of the Kanō and other schools. Ryūho, whose work has been briefly discussed and who Kazan singled out as a pioneer of haiku painting (pls. 30–32; fig. 30), was one such person. Another was Ichū, whose technique in *Oto-Goze* (pl. 2), like the work of Ryūho, lies close to the tradition of depicting everyday life that later became known as *ukiyo-e*, or "pictures of the floating world."

Although Buson is not usually thought of in such terms, some of his figures also show similarity to those of *ukiyo-e* painters (see, for instance, pls. 13, 21). Paintings such as Hakuen's *Retiring from the Stage* (pl. 27) likewise have features in common with the *ukiyo-e* paintings and prints of famous actors. Hakuen, however, shuns

the conventional front view of the actor, showing instead the side and rear.

With Buson and his disciple, Gekkei, as all commentators on haiku painting agree, the combination of text and image in the spirit of haiku reached a maturity and felicity hard to surpass. Imaginative in word and picture alike, their works provide a sense of pleasure that is the result of combining suggestions of everyday life with elevated poetic or artistic expression.

NANGA AND ITS INFLUENCE

Aside from his stature as a haiku poet, second only to Bashō, Buson is also remembered along with Ike Taiga (1723–76) for bringing to maturation the style of painting known as Nanga, literally "Southern School" (also known as *bunjin-ga*, or the "literary-men's style"), which had originally been imported from China. In the work of the pioneer Nanga painter Hyakusen (fig. 10), as well as in many of Buson's haiku paintings, Chinese influences have become so thoroughly digested and naturalized that only with fine analysis may they be distinguished. Themes often employed in landscape paintings in the new Chinese style—that is, rocks, plum blossoms, bamboos—are seen in *Rocks Scattered Here and There* (pl. 11), the blossoming plums in the scene from *Records of a Weather-Exposed Skeleton* (pl. 16), and *Young Bamboos* (pl. 20), all by Buson. The handling of these themes, in terms of brushwork, composition, and pigmentation, reflects the literary-men's style that Buson and Taiga practiced, and that by the early nineteenth century surpassed the Kanō school in creative energy and even in prestige.

To be sure, Taiga is never discussed as a haiku poet. Still, he and Buson collaborated to produce an album of illustrations and calligraphy for a series of Chinese poems, the *Ten Pleasures and Ten Conveniences* (*Jūben jūgi-jō*), now classified as a national treasure. Other works ascribed to both of them include a haiku painting by Taiga to go with one of Buson's most famous verses, "The sea in the spring— / All day long it rises and falls, / Just rises and falls" (*Haru-no umi / hinemosu notari / notari kana*). Taiga's *Hare* (pl. 22) serves partly to contrast with Buson's *Mr. Hare on a Moonlit Night* (pl. 10) and partly to show how an established Nanga artist also combined text and image in a light and witty way.

Buson's disciple Gekkei, widely known by the name of Goshun and as the founder of the Shijō school of painting, rivaled his teacher's skill in creating humorous and imaginative drawings characteristic of the spirit of haiku. He lacked Buson's literary and poetic talent, however, and consequently many of his haiku paintings feature inscriptions or verses by other people, especially Buson. His forlorn-looking deer (pl. 23) reflects the literary style and is also typical of his tendency to illustrate texts by others. His *Tiger and Hare*

(pl. 26), however, is an exception. The verse is his own, and the hare deserves comparison with the representations Buson and Taiga mentioned above. His *Scarecrow* (fig. 25) is another such exception.

The haiku poets and painters that followed Buson, Taiga, and Gekkei in the late eighteenth and early nineteenth centuries continued the tendency to stand outside clearly defined schools and techniques. The world of Japanese art became increasingly rich and complex. Besides paintings by haiku masters, such as Ōemaru (figs. 21, 22), Seibi (fig. 23), Sobaku (fig. 26), and Issa (figs. 28, 29), there were also people either marginally connected with the haiku movement, such as Hakuen (pl. 27) and Hōitsu (pls. 28, 29; fig. 27), or with practically no connection at all—Sengai (fig. 24), Tani Bunchō (pl. 29), and Watanabe Kazan (pls. 30–32; fig. 30). Such a development reflects not only the growing richness and variety of Japanese art but also the pervasiveness and popularity of the haiku movement, as well as the spread of culture and literacy to virtually the farthest reaches of the countryside.

HAIKU POETRY AND PAINTING IN TOKUGAWA POPULAR CULTURE

Between 1600 and 1868 (the Tokugawa period), popular culture flourished in Japan as rarely before in the history of the world. With an era of peace and a policy that encouraged art and education, the level of material civilization rose throughout Japan. People of all classes had unprecedented opportunities to enjoy leisurely activity (on however small a scale when compared with the situation today) as well as to pursue the spiritual life. Many aspects of Tokugawa popular culture foreshadowed modern social developments in Japan and the West. It was in such a context that the haiku movement developed.

From early times poetic activity had been carried on in a communal setting. Cliques and circles of *waka* poets during the Heian period and the early middle ages, from the ninth to the thirteenth century, gave way to groups of linked verse poets in the fourteenth and fifteenth centuries. Gradually, these expanded, and the practice of light linked verse (*haikai-no renga*) became part of the activities of these literary salons. Oftentimes dinner parties and study sessions included lectures on the *Tale of Genji* (see pls. 1, 2) as well as poetry composition in accord with the complex rules that came to govern linked verse.

The ardor and zeal with which people participated in such poetry circles, not only during the middle ages but in the Tokugawa period as well, may be imagined from the saying that the only people roaming the streets late at night were robbers and linked verse poets, the latter presumably on their way home from a satisfying meal, a joyful poetry party, or perhaps a stimulating lecture or discussion. Typically, members of the group would take turns being host on such occa-

sions. When one's own personal residence was not fit for such a meeting, public restaurants, temples, and shrines might serve instead. Bashō and Buson, it should be noted, were each the recognized master of a poetry circle.

One of the grandest poetry parties was held during cherry-blossom time in 1783, ninety years after Bashō's death, in honor of the forthcoming centennial of the event. Buson with his group in Kyoto, and Kyōtai (cf. pl. 23, discussion) with his in Nagoya, cooperated in the preparations. About forty days before the meeting took place, Buson was already writing to friends and patrons who lived outside the city. He explained that Kyōtai was the host and that sessions would be held for seven days, first at a temple near Lake Biwa, then at another one on Maruyama hill in Kyoto, and finally at a clubhouse called the Bashō Hut in the northeastern part of Kyoto, which Buson and his friends had built several years before. "It will be the greatest poetry event of our age," Buson wrote. "By all means come to Kyoto. The flowers in the imperial city will be at their very best." He explained that there would be no strict rules for chain poems, and that poets would be coming from everywhere. Kyōtai was looking after all the expenses.

As local arrangements went on, Kyōtai, who had spent most of the previous year gathering memorabilia and drumming up interest, arrived in Kyoto with his companions. The poetry party began with Buson, Kyōtai, and their friends making a trip from Saga to Lake Biwa, and then back to Kyoto. This was done in emulation of Bashō's travels back and forth from Lake Biwa to Saga (the area described in pl. 16 and fig. 2) during the last year of his life, when he stayed with one disciple or another, composing verses about such things as the clear waterfalls, the bamboos, the clouds, the mountains.

For the second stage of the poetry party everyone went to the Sōrinji temple on Maruyama hill above the Gion district in Kyoto, the most famous spot in the city for cherry blossoms. Bashō himself had once stayed there, and his disciple Shikō (see fig. 9) had raised a memorial stone engraved with one of Bashō's verses. In earlier times Saigyō (mentioned in pl. 3) had once lived there, and so had Ton'a (1289–1372), a monk and linked verse poet. In honor of the occasion and the poetic associations of the spot, everyone wore somber gray and black ceremonial dress marked with the crest of his house. Thus attired, the poets composed a linked poem, for which a verse by Bashō was chosen as the initial unit: "Cherry-blossom time— / The crane stays for seven days / Around the mountain" (*Hana sakite / nanuka tsuru miru / fumoto kana*). To these were added seventeen additional links to make half of a "poetic immortal" (*kasen*), as the thirty-six link chain poems had come to be called.

Kyōtai's second link was, "Where the water flows, / Spring bursts out in full beauty" (*Mizu yuku-kata-ni / haru-ya mitsuran*). Then

Buson added a third link, "Swirl us back again / To the ninth year of Yung ho, / And the Chinese cloaks" (*Hirugaese / Eiwa ku-nen-no / Kara-goromo*). Each successive link thereafter was by another poet.

The third stage of the gathering of 1783 took place at the Bashō Hut, where another linked poem was composed with the initial verse by Bashō. Twenty-nine poets each added a link, making thirty in all. After the scheduled activities were over, one of Buson's fellow poets treated everyone to a lavish dinner that lasted far into the night. Then he ordered palanquins, and each of the guests was escorted home in a manner fit for a lord. The greatest poetry meeting of the age was over—the memory of a lifetime for all who attended.

This lengthy description should give some idea of how haiku poetry functioned in a communal setting within the context of the society of Tokugawa Japan. Among the participants were people of both samurai and commoner origin—small business people, prosperous farmers, physicians, and artisans, as well as members of specific warrior clans, thus presenting a cross section of Tokugawa life. Besides activities such as these, there were also the publication of poetry anthologies, the issuing of single-sheet prints (*surimono*) to be purchased by subscription, and the organization of various group trips to famous places near and far. By the end of the Tokugawa period, regular monthly haiku meetings (*tsukinami-kai*), for which topics were set in advance, were scheduled in the principal cities. Gradually, the practice of linked verse gave way to the composition of independent opening verses (*hokku*) for their own sake. Toward the end of the nineteenth century this became standardized, and a new independent short form of poetry, the haiku, came to be distinguished from the group activities of *haikai*.

All the while, the twin arts of painting and calligraphy were never far away from haiku poetry circles. Since early days in Japan word and image formed an intrinsic unit. This was especially true of the best examples of haiku painting. Artists and poets achieved an imaginative and integrated product that began with a text but went beyond it, because the resultant haiku painting embodied visual qualities that were not possible to express in words. At times haiku painting approached moral and social instruction, not by means of overt pedagogy or oppressive didacticism, but rather through implication and suggestion. As with the best products of the Japanese aesthetic temperament, haiku painting communicates states of feeling. By means of skillful creation of mood and emotion it does its work of persuasion. Japanese literature without illustrations is like bread without butter, cake without frosting, or strawberries without cream. You can enjoy the one dish by itself, but when the other complements it, the taste is better.

JUN 25 '84 C

H53990

OVERSIZE
ND2462   Zolbrod, Leon M. $18.95
Z6   Haiku painting.

oversize

Please Do Not Remove Card From Pocket
_____
YOUR LIBRARY CARD
may be used at all library agencies. You
are, of course, responsible for all materials
checked out on it. As a courtesy to others
please return materials promptly. A service
charge is assessed for overdue materials.
_____
The SAINT PAUL PUBLIC LIBRARY

DEMCO